THE WORLD'S CLASSICS
COUSIN BETTE

HONORÉ BALZAC was born in 1799 at Tours, the son of a civil servant. Put out to nurse and sent later to boarding school, he had, except between the ages of 4 and 8, little contact with home. In 1814 the family moved to Paris, where Honoré continued his boarding-school education for two years, and then studied law at the Sorbonne. From 1816 to 1819 he worked in a lawyer's office, but having completed his legal training he knew he wanted to be a writer. While his family gave meagre financial support he wrote a play, *Cromwell*, but it was a complete failure. He also collaborated with other writers to produce popular novels. During the 1820s he dabbled in journalism, and tried to make money in printing and publishing ventures, whose lack of success laid the foundation for debts that plagued him for the rest of his life.

In 1829 Balzac published his first novel under his own name, *Le Dernier Chouan* (later *Les Chouans*), and *La Physiologie du mariage*. In 1830 came a collection of six stories called *Scènes de la vie privée*. Self-styled 'de Balzac', he became fashionable in the literary and social world of Paris, and over the next twenty years, as well as plays and articles, wrote more than ninety novels and stories. In 1842 many of these were published in seventeen volumes as *La Comédie humaine*. Important works were still to come, but ill-health interfered with his creativity and marred the last years of his life.

In 1832, in his extensive fan-mail, Balzac received a letter from the Polish Countess Hanska, whose elderly husband owned a vast estate in the Ukraine. The next year he met Madame Hanska in Switzerland, and in 1835 the couple agreed to marry after Count Hanski's death. For seventeen years, with intermissions, they conducted a voluminous correspondence, until their marriage finally took place in March 1850. Balzac died three months later in Paris.

DAVID BELLOS is Professor of French Studies at the University of Manchester. His biography of Georges Perec will be published in 1992.

SYLVIA RAPHAEL has taught French language and literature at the universities of Glasgow and London, specializing in nineteenth-century literature. Her translations include a selection of Balzac's short stories as well as a translation of *Eugénie Grandet* in the World's Classics series.

THE WORLD'S CLASSICS

HONORÉ DE BALZAC

Cousin Bette

Translated by
SYLVIA RAPHAEL

With an introduction by
DAVID BELLOS

Oxford   New York
OXFORD UNIVERSITY PRESS
1992

Oxford University Press, Walton Street, Oxford OX2 6DP
Oxford New York Toronto
Delhi Bombay Calcutta Madras Karachi
Petaling Jaya Singapore Hong Kong Tokyo
Nairobi Dar es Salaam Cape Town
Melbourne Auckland
and associated companies in
Berlin Ibadan

Oxford is a trade mark of Oxford University Press

Translation and notes material © Sylvia Raphael 1992
Introduction and Appendix © David Bellos 1992
First published as a World's Classics paperback 1992

British Library Cataloguing in Publication Data
Data available
ISBN 0-19-282606-9

Library of Congress Cataloging in Publication Data
Balzac, Honoré de, 1799-1850.
[Cousine Bette. English]
Cousin Bette / Honoré de Balzac : translated by Sylvia Raphael.
p.   cm.—(The World's classics)
Translation of: La cousine Bette.
Includes bibliographical references.
I. Raphael, Sylvia.   II. Title.   III. Series.
PQ2165.C5E5   1992   843'.7—dc20   91-24417
ISBN 0-19-282606-9

Typeset by Cambridge Composing (UK) Ltd
Printed in Great Britain by
BPCC Hazells Ltd.
Aylesbury, Bucks

CONTENTS

Introduction   vii
Note on the Text   xxi
Select Bibliography   xxii
A Chronology of Honoré de Balzac   xxiii

COUSIN BETTE   I

Appendix   463
Explanatory Notes   466

INTRODUCTION

Cousin Bette tells the story of the fall of the house of Hulot, plotted and precipitated by Lisbeth Fischer, a poor relative, the 'cousin Bette' of the novel's title. The Hulot family owes its standing in the fictional society of Balzac's novel not to aristocratic ancestry but to the careers of two brothers. In the reign of Napoleon I, between 1805 and 1815, Hector Hulot had risen to a senior post in the military administration of Alsace, and his brother had fought with distinction in Napoleon's armies. The two survive the fall of France but are under-employed for fifteen years; they can only re-establish themselves fully after the July Revolution of 1830. The colonization of Algeria provides them with the opportunity to accumulate wealth to add to the prestige with which the Napoleonic past now endows them. But there is a worm in the apple. As he grows into middle age, Hector Hulot becomes increasingly obsessed with sexual conquest. By playing on that passion, Lisbeth, called Bette like a child or a servant, a poor and powerless spinster, a mere hanger-on in the outwardly splendid Hulot household, brings the family almost to its ruin. *Cousin Bette* is both a vast fresco of Parisian life in the first half of the nineteenth century, and a sharply-focused study of two contradictory human impulses: sexual desire, and the desire for destruction. Sigmund Freud, in his later works, presented *eros*, the drive towards life, and sex, and *thanatos*, the drive towards death, and destruction, as the two sides of the same coin. Almost a century earlier, Balzac had imagined them as two members of the same family.

Cousin Bette was written and published between July and December 1846. Honoré de Balzac, aged 47, was in declining health and aware that he was growing old. He wrote nothing of substance after *Cousin Bette*, except to complete its twin novel, *Cousin Pons*, which he had begun first, and from which *Cousin Bette* had effectively sprung. In 1848 he left Paris for Wierzchowna, in the Ukraine, to live with Madame Hanska, whom he married in March 1850. He then returned to Paris with his wife, fell ill during the journey, took to his bed on arrival, and died on 19 August following. *Cousin Bette* and *Cousin Pons* had been his last great novels.

Balzac was born in 1799, and began writing commercial fiction in the 1820s as 'Horace de Saint-Aubain', 'Lord R'Hoone', and other invented or shared aliases, with little success. For a brief period he went into business as a publisher, printer, and type-founder, and incurred the substantial debts (the largest of them to his mother) which were to burden him for the rest of his life. The first of his works to appear under the name Honoré Balzac dates from 1828. Shortly after the liberal revolution of July 1830, which brought the 'citizen king' Louis-Philippe to the throne, Balzac published *The Wild Ass's Skin* (*La Peau de chagrin*), a romantic and purportedly 'philosophical' novel which brought considerable notoriety to the name Honoré de Balzac, the name he would retain for the remainder of his life and work. For the following fifteen years Balzac wrote at a tremendous rate, working as much as sixteen hours a day, fuelling his imagination with coffee made from unroasted beans. From the start of his new career, he sought to connect his fictions to each other within larger structures. *The Last Chouan* was announced in 1828 as the first chapter in what would be a 'picturesque history of France'—to rival Walter Scott's *Waverley* novels, seen in France as a 'picturesque' history of Scotland. Balzac's first collection of short stories about marriage in the middle classes was entitled *Scenes of Private Life* (1830), which prompted him to group subsequent works into 'Scenes of Provincial Life', then 'Scenes of Parisian Life'. In 1833 he undertook an eight-volume series entitled *Études de mœurs* ('Studies of Manners'), bringing under one roof, so to speak, many previously published 'scenes' together with new novels and stories, such as *Eugénie Grandet*, to balance the different sections. In 1835 he hit upon the idea of an overarching structure for all he had written and still had to write, and he entitled it *The Human Comedy*, nodding respectfully, if not modestly, towards Dante's *Divine Comedy*. His individual works would be henceforth only chapters in this vast enterprise, the description of an entire society considered in its actual practice (in the section entitled, once again, 'Studies of Manners'), in its causes (in the section entitled 'Philosophical Studies'), and in its underlying principles (in the section entitled 'Analytical Studies'). In fact, Balzac wrote little of the latter two sections: the bulk of *The Human Comedy* consists of 'Studies of Manners', divided into 'Scenes of Private Life', 'Scenes of Parisian Life', 'Scenes of Provincial Life', 'Scenes of Country Life', 'Scenes of Political Life', and 'Scenes of Military Life'. Balzac filled in the slots created by his structure in a manner that looks somewhat haphazard; and the structure itself underwent many amendments over the years. From 1835 on, however, Balzac used more than section titles and groupings to weld his different subjects and stories together. He adopted what is known as *the device of reappearing characters*: characters who appear perhaps as incidental figures in the plot of one novel, and as the protagonists of a prior or subsequent fiction. Balzac's 'invention' arose in the early stages of writing *Père Goriot*, and he was so taken with its potential for saturating an imaginary world constructed in the image of the real one that he rushed round to see his sister, Laure Surville, to tell her that he was 'in the process of becoming a genius'. Although many later authors have sought to link series of novels through 'sequential' characters and casts, none has ever rivalled the inexhaustible complexity of Balzac's fictional universe, which alone required and justified the invention of the reappearing characters.

The Human Comedy contains more than two thousand named characters, of whom about five hundred appear in several different novels; of those five hundred, several dozen major and minor characters reappear in over a score of stories and novels. Balzac's reader is therefore always more or less aware of a great hinterland of fiction lying behind or around the story being read. The result is a magical paradox. Balzac's world is potentially entirely knowable; it is in principle a grid completely filled in. But because characters and plots are not like crossword puzzles, every 'solution' provided by a reappearance of the same character raises more questions than it solves, and the gaps in Balzac's world—in the reader's experience of it—grow in geometrical proportion to the number of connections made. The paradox is that a device designed to give solidity to a vast panorama of social life actually gives it what is perhaps its most life-like feature—inexhaustible fragmentariness. Balzac's world opens on to infinity through the central device that first appeared as a means of closing it off.

Balzac's novels began to appear in a sixteen-volume work entitled *The Human Comedy* in 1842, and over the following four years the writer laboured to fill in the gaps by writing more novels and by expanding, amending, and correcting the already written works to make them fit better into the pyramid. By 1846, volume sixteen was done, and in the press, and Balzac's great work was in principle complete. The Hercules of the novel might well have expected to be in a position to rest on well-earned laurels at that point in his middle age. However, he had not earned the respect that he knew was due to him, and, in the years during which the volumes of *The Human Comedy* had appeared, his name had been overshadowed by another: Eugène Sue, the author of unprecedentedly popular serial novels published in the daily press.

The publication of new fiction by instalments in daily and weekly newspapers was a relatively recent innovation. In Britain Dickens's *Pickwick Papers* and in France Balzac's *The Old Maid* had both appeared in 1836 as the first serials in their respective countries. However, Balzac's procedure was to write books in the first place and to cut them up into episodes subsequently. It was not until the early 1840s that French fiction was first composed in instalments, and the first of these truly 'serial' novels, Sue's *Mysteries of Paris*, brought its author more substantial rewards than the whole of *The Human Comedy* had yet brought Balzac. Sue pandered to his large and by definition uncultivated readership with great technical skill. Each episode of his serial ends on a moment of narrative suspense; each episode contains an appeal to readers' sentimentality, and also to their curiosity; and many episodes echo the contents of Sue's post-bag of readers' letters, giving voice, in particular, to pleas for greater social equity and to what the monarchist Balzac regarded as socialist propaganda. Sue's second serial, *The Wandering Jew* (1844–5), repeated the formula, and reaped similar rewards.

'The present situation requires me to write two or three masterful works which will topple the false gods of this bastard literature, and which must demonstrate that I am a younger, fresher, and greater writer than ever before!', Balzac wrote to Madame Hanska on 15 June 1846. Balzac met the challenge that Sue had set him, that he had set himself. From the heroic resolve expressed to Madame Hanska came two novels, *Cousin Pons* and *Cousin Bette*, collectively entitled *Poor Relations*, which were first published in serial form in a daily newspaper and then added to *The Human Comedy* in a supplementary seventeenth volume in 1847. They are not so much additions to the pre-existing *Human Comedy* as entire 'human comedies' of their own, using some familiar and some quite new techniques to give expression to a vision of the social and moral order that is distinctly blacker than that of Balzac's earlier work.

When Balzac conceived the last two novels of his career, he was in a strange emotional position. He had been engaged for thirteen years in a mostly (but not exclusively) epistolary romance with a wealthy Polish noblewoman living in the Russian part of Ukraine. His letters to Madame Hanska constitute a running commentary on his life and works throughout the 1830s and 1840s, and, if they are to be believed absolutely, in 1846 Balzac was deeply in love with his eastern muse and intent upon marrying her. At the same time he was living in Paris with Louise Breugniot, who kept house for him. The servant-mistress became increasingly jealous of Balzac's devotion to his distant love, stole a set of her letters to him, and threatened to blackmail the pair of them. Balzac was forced to inform Madame Hanska of the threat; the crisis was resolved when he bought the letters back from Louise, and then burned them. In his letters to Madame Hanska Balzac describes Louise as a hideous creature, but it seems, from other sources, that she was an intelligent and charming person. Balzac's emotions in this affair are unclear: was he truly fond of Louise, but intent on marrying Madame Hanska for her status and wealth? Was the theft of the letters a put-up job? Or was Balzac exactly what he said he was: the manipulated victim of a vile woman intent on bringing him down? *Cousin Bette* is not a directly autobiographical novel, and the character of Lisbeth Fischer is the product of Balzac's imagination. That imagination was certainly fed by Balzac's personal experiences—and by his own feelings about his mother, without a doubt—but it would be unwise to jump to the conclusion that in Lisbeth Fischer Balzac has only portrayed his own image of the woman he was living with.

Balzac began *Cousin Pons* in the summer of 1846. It is the story of a poor relation hounded to his grave by relatives far richer than he who covet his one treasure, a collection of works of art. But when he was still only drafting the first sketch of *Cousin Pons*, Balzac hit upon the idea of that novel's 'twin', the story of a female 'poor relation' who would be not the victim but the perpetrator of a campaign of persecution. Balzac's imagination frequently worked by the creation of opposite or complementary pairs: *Cousin Bette* arose as an opposite, and it is itself structured almost entirely by opposing and complementary doublets.

Both of the *Poor Relations* were written to beat Eugène Sue at his own game, and both were therefore designed for serial publication. *Bette* began to appear in the daily *Le*

Constitutionnel on 8 October 1846; Balzac had fourteen days' copy in hand. He went to Germany from 9 to 17 October, and on his return he soon found he had the printers breathing down his neck. He was obliged to write chapters that were set in type immediately and published the following day. He made superhuman efforts to race ahead of the newspaper, writing and correcting up to eight sheets of 'copy' per day, living and sleeping on a camp-bed at the printing works. He still found time to scribble letters to Madame Hanska, and never ceased to calculate how many days' work remained on *Cousin Bette*—but his calculations undershot, not because he worked too slowly for his own ambitions, but because the subject kept on growing. On 3 November he reported: 'There are some tremendous scenes in it, believe me! I didn't know what I was doing, but now I do.' Four days later: 'It's one of the finest of my finest works.' And a few days after that: 'I am out on my own, more brilliant, more youthful, more fertile than ever I was before.' It took another three weeks before the manuscript was complete, and in its entirety *Cousin Bette* fully justifies Balzac's trumpet-blasts in advance. It is a triumph over the nightmarish conditions of its composition; it is a triumph for Balzac in competition with his contemporaries; but most of all, *Cousin Bette* is one of the great triumphs of the novel form.

There really is nothing like *Cousin Bette* in English literature. Tolstoy is perhaps the only other writer who rivals Balzac's ability to portray a whole society and its momentum; and Dostoevsky's great novels of good and evil are constantly reminiscent of the technique, the intensity, and the world-view of Balzac, and especially of *Cousin Bette*. Like Dostoevsky in *The Idiot*, Balzac wished to portray good in a contemporary and real setting. In *Cousin Bette*, the vehicle of that portrayal is Hector Hulot's wife Adeline, Bette's cousin and childhood companion. Adeline is beautiful, with a nobility that comes from her soul, not from her ancestry. She is intelligent, but not an educated intellectual. She is faithful to her husband, and intensely loyal to him, despite the liberties he takes with his marriage vows; and she is motivated in all her actions by Christian faith. For those reasons she is also, for many readers, a failure as a fictional character: flat, in E. M. Forster's terms, or boring, to put it less politely, as some of Balzac's contemporary critics did. To the modern reader she may seem unbelievably spineless; to the feminist reader (or even just to women readers generally), she may seem repellently acquiescent in the asymmetric social, financial, and sexual rights of nineteenth-century males. But Balzac the novelist is actually more subtle, and more cynical, than Balzac the propagandist of conservative values. The novel opens with the attempted seduction of Adeline by Crevel, Hulot's comic rival and comrade-in-skirts; the plot reaches its climax when Adeline, in order to save her own uncle from a disgrace of which her profligate husband Hector is the real culprit, offers herself to Crevel for 200,000 francs. It is a terrible moment. Adeline is doing what offends her sensibilities to the utmost out of love, and out of a Christian doctrine of self-sacrifice. She fails, having miscalculated her timing and her price. In *Cousin Bette*, as in life, the professionals do it better. Adeline is emotionally ruined, and her humiliation leaves her with a disfiguring facial twitch, a parody of the stigmata of the cross. Balzac shows the goodness of a good person; he takes it, as he takes everything in this sombre novel, to a fantastical, but plausible extreme; and in its extremity, Adeline's goodness becomes its opposite—naïveté, foolishness, self-delusion, clumsiness, and plain bad behaviour. Readers who object to Adeline are not necessarily critics of Balzac; Adeline's cruellest critic is the author himself.

Balzac plays similar tricks of moral perspective with Bette, the incarnation of negativity. She has taken under her wing a fey Polish émigré, Wenceslas Steinbock, whom she nurtures, more as mother than mistress. Steinbock is an artist; without Bette's strict protection he would have dissipated his energies on ordinary life—on women, and vanity, and social climbing. Balzac takes a very special view of energy. In his mind, it is almost a physical substance, which individuals possess in finite quantity. To achieve any worthwhile result, energy must be concentrated on a single target, and it is to Bette alone that Steinbock owes that lesson, and its strict imposition. Steinbock's first significant work is a bronze statuette of Samson tearing a lion to death—a mythological representation of the male strength which Bette has given him. The young man then gives it as a love-offering to Hector Hulot's daughter, Hortense, and commits an unpardonable crime. From Bette's point of view, Steinbock's gift is less a betrayal than a theft, for it removes from her with quite transparent symbolism the only thing that was truly hers: not her feminine self (for she is the least feminine of women), but the virile power she can muster by force of concentration. Bette's campaign of revenge on the Hulot household is not arbitrary, nor is it merely an expression of jealousy. In her unappealing person Balzac concentrates all the revenge of the dispossessed, and all their energy. The propagandist in Balzac would like Bette to be all evil; the novelist in him makes the issue infinitely more complex.

Behind the material, emotional, and sexual transactions of recognizably middle-class members of Parisian society in the 1840s Balzac sketches in reminiscences of older stories, which lend *Cousin Bette* some of its strange power. Balzac hesitated over displaying the use he makes of the parable of the Prodigal Son (in some editions, *Cousin Bette* begins with a sub-title, 'Part One: The Prodigal Father', and in others, such as the one used for this translation, 'The Return of the Prodigal Father' is used as a chapter-title). In Luke 15, the Prodigal Son's return is greeted with forgiveness and joy: 'It was meet that we should make merry, and be glad; for this thy brother was dead, and is alive again; and was lost, and is found'. In Balzac's story, the prodigal father Hector Hulot has 'wasted his substance with riotous living'; and forgiveness is extended to him by his wife Adeline. She accepts the return of Hector three times: in 1838, when he is thrown out by the courtesan Josépha; in 1841, when he is forced to abandon his altogether more rapacious mistress Valérie Marneffe and to resign from the War Ministry; and again in 1845, when he is found living in squalor under the name of *Père Vyder* (an anagram of d'Ervy). We do not know what happens after the celebration of the return of the Prodigal Son in the biblical parable; but in Balzac's modern inversion of it, forgiveness has lost its purchase. Hector simply goes on, his sexual monomania unabated, and in the end he causes the death of the person who forgave him three times, perhaps three times too often. When Adeline overhears him, at the age of 75, offering to make the kitchen-maid the second Baroness Hulot, she dies of shock. It is not just her heart that is finally broken, but her Christian beliefs also. Balzac reverses the shape of the parable and therefore its meaning. The biblical myths that hover over the world of *Cousin Bette* make it clear that it is a world bereft of goodness.

The principal comic character in the novel, Crevel, declares that the France of the 1840s has 'returned to biblical times'—that is to say, to the times of Exodus 32, when the Hebrews worshipped the Golden Calf. France now worships the five-franc coin above King and constitution, he claims, and his words are borne out by the novel's action. In the end Adeline, the emblem of moral virtue, offers to sell herself to him for a pot of gold.

The myths of the Prodigal Son and the Golden Calf are used in *Cousin Bette* to give the gravity of biblical prophecy to Balzac's moral pessimism, and thereby to constitute his political reply to Eugène Sue. However, the myth-figure which lies at the centre of this novel is that of Napoleon Bonaparte, 'the little corporal who came to rule the world', protected in battle (according to popular legend) by a pact with God. Hector Hulot is a man of common stock who rose to eminence in the military administration of Alsace under the reign of Napoleon, who ennobled him for his services. Hulot's early career conforms to an important element in the myth of the Napoleonic golden age, that of the 'career open to talent'. He meets and marries Adeline, and raises her from 'her village

mud' to the splendid heights of the Imperial court, explic-
itly likened to paradise. Their marriage ('like an Assumption') is productive and successful, as is Hulot's career
until Napoleon's defeat at Waterloo in 1815. When the
novel opens in 1838, the Napoleonic era is a memory of
past happiness, of a time of social, conjugal, and professional integration. Hulot's sexual extravagances begin only
after the fall of the Empire: they are the signs of a fallen
world.

From his first presentation, Hulot harks back to the
Napoleonic past. He wears a blue jacket with gold buttons
and a black cravat, and his deportment and self-possessed
stride make him an obvious 'Empire man', just as a table
might be an obvious piece of Empire furniture. Other
characters provide contextual props for this historical and
mythical identification: Josépha sees Adeline as Hector's
Empress Josephine, and Marneffe, the repugnant husband
of Hulot's mistress Valérie, remarks pointedly that 'Empire
men' suffer the delusion that they are immortal. When
Hulot is summoned by the Minister of War for a disciplin-
ary interview, he falls into his own trap: 'But, Prince, the
Imperial Guard is immortal!'

Hulot is not a latter-day Napoleon, but an affectionate
and cruel portrayal of the Napoleonic *myth* still present in
French society in the 1840s. In Balzac's approach to it, the
myth still has the beauty of a ruined monument, like the
Roman ruin that Hulot has begun to resemble as the senile
hair sprouting from his nostrils and on his fingers resem-
bles the moss on long-abandoned but 'almost eternal' stone
walls. It is not by narrative accident that Hulot is the only
character of his generation to live on beyond the novel's
conclusion. The apparent immortality of the rake is the
characteristic which links him most closely to the Napoleonic myth, which included, in popular imaginations, the
belief that the Emperor was still alive and would return to
save France again one day. But Hulot's life-story also
demonstrates the degradation of an ideal into vice and
venality. Twenty years after, the fabled comradeship of the
old guard has become no more than a squalid old-boy

network, with no more nobility than a bunch of crooks. It breaks the heart of the real old soldier, Hulot's brother, the Maréchal.

Balzac' achievement is to have given us a double vision. He makes us believe in the past as a projection of our present myths (the myth of the golden age in general, of the glory of the Napoleonic era in particular), whilst also convincing us that the novel's present is a shabby simulacrum of the mythical past. With *Cousin Bette*, Balzac finally makes fiction the meeting point of history and myth, inventing and almost exhausting the potential of what Fredric Jameson has called 'allegorical realism'.

Cousin Bette does not begin (as *Père Goriot* does) with a guided tour of a town, a quarter, a building, and its rooms before introducing characters and action: it jumps almost immediately into dialogue; the dramatic construction is maintained throughout; and for that reason *Cousin Bette* seems to mark the point beyond which the novel must give way to theatre or to grand opera. In the original or in translation, each character in the cast of *Cousin Bette* speaks with a different, marked voice—from the pidgin-French of the German banker to the pompous vulgarity of the well-to-do shopkeeper, from the meek elegance of Adeline to the sulphurous directness of Bette Fischer herself. The old soldiers use old soldiers' set phrases, the courtesans use the authentic slang of their trade, and the working classes, who make their piteous appearance in the closing stages of Hulot's downfall, speak with only slightly modified working-class vocabulary and syntax. *Cousin Bette* is a pageant of characters created by varieties of speech, and the comical, dramatic effect of that technique makes it Balzac's most Dickensian novel by far.

It is also, by design, melodramatic to a degree. Balzac's conscious aim was to appeal to the readers who had lapped up Sue's pot-boiling serials, so as to lead them to a proper understanding of the great issues of good and evil, and to convince them of the need for absolute monarchy and the reimposition of the Catholic religion. Baron Montès de

Montéjanos, the sleek-haired, jealous Brazilian lover with his phial of curare, comes straight out of popular theatre, as do the stereotypes of many of the novel's major characters—the long-suffering wife, the evil hag, the *femme fatale*, the bourgeois buffoon, the tart with the heart of gold, and her protector, the aristocrat of unlimited wealth. Balzac's drama takes its elements from a kind of popular entertainment not so far removed from the soap operas of today; but it takes them much further. Whilst every detail of the plot remains meticulously plausible, and every date correctly inscribed into a real history of France, every character is heightened, overlit, rendered more intense, more fantastical, more extreme, and infinitely more ambiguous than nineteenth-century melodrama or contemporary soap opera could ever permit.

Despite Balzac's intentions, *Cousin Bette* is not a moral tract, and it raises questions that are far more interesting than the answers it seeks to give in occasional 'nuggets' of inserted propaganda. Is the 'rule of money' inherently incompatible with the rule of morality? Balzac shows the older generation (Bette, Hulot, Crevel, and Adeline) morally destroyed by the market economy of the 1830s and 1840s, and has his spokesman Bianchon declare that the 'deep-seated evil' comes directly 'from the lack of religion and the pervasion of finance'. But things are not so clear to the reader of Balzac's work. Hulot's son Victorin, who has grown up not in the France of Napoleon but in the France of Louis-Philippe, re-establishes the fortunes of a family his father has ruined by skilful and honest use of the new rules of life's game. Balzac's novel ends not with a cataclysm or a hecatomb, but with the transfer of authority from a discredited generation to a new and passably competent and honest one. Sober realism gets the better of Balzac's melodramtic intentions.

Bette's campaign of destruction does not really succeed. She may be characterized as an erupting volcano, a hissing snake, and just short of the devil incarnate, but her plotting still requires the concomitant help of unplanned historical circumstances in order to bring Hulot to ruin. Bette dies before the novel's end; Valérie Marneffe and Crevel die in horrible agonies for their sins, very like the protagonists of *Dangerous Liaisons*: Adeline dies, despite and also because of her virtue. Hulot alone, the ineradicably irresponsible skirt-chaser, the cause of infinite woe to his family and to his old comrades, lives on beyond them. Humiliated professionally and socially, he survives like some Protean figure of desire, taking on pseudonyms (all of them anagrams of his real name), attaching himself to one then another teenage mistress in ever more squalid corners of the city, reduced to nothing but his desire, and thus magnified into Desire itself. Hulot is certainly repulsive as a human being, but there is something magnificent about his unwavering devotion to a single passion: sexual passion untarnished and undeterred by sentiment, by social life, by anything outside of itself—not even by the ugliness of an overweight scullery maid. Good and evil simply dissolve, at the conclusion of *Cousin Bette*, in the face of the force of life itself.

Hulot is not really like any of Balzac's other 'monomaniac' characters—Grandet the passionate miser, Goriot the absolute father, Bridau the painter, Claes the alchemist, David Séchard the inventor, and so on—for by the end of the novel it has to be understood that Hulot's sexual obsession is abstract, infinite, quite useless, and fundamentally asocial. It is the opposite of the negative passion of his defeated enemy, Lisbeth Fischer, but in its extremity more like it than it is like any of the lesser social passions of the other characters on stage. Is it *eros* or *thanatos* which constitutes the driving force behind the action of the novel? Is it love or hatred which structures Balzac's vision of the world in his last recreation of it? If the answer had been clear to the author, he would probably have written a far less probing work than this one which, in its rich ambiguity, allows every reader to explore his or her own imagination of what life is really like.

David Bellos

NOTE ON THE TEXT

La Cousine Bette was first published as a serial in *Le Constitutionnel* in 1846. In 1847 it was published as a book by Chlendowski and in 1848 it was published as Volume XVII of the *Comédie humaine* (the Furne edition), the last to appear in Balzac's lifetime. This is the text that is translated here, but the chapter and paragraph divisions of the Chlendowski edition, which were suppressed in the Furne edition to save space, are reintroduced for the convenience of the reader.

SELECT BIBLIOGRAPHY

BIOGRAPHY

André Maurois, *Prometheus: The Life of Balzac* (London, 1965).

H. J. Hunt, *Honoré de Balzac: A Biography* (London, 1957; reprinted and updated, New York, 1969).

GENERAL STUDIES

P. Bertaut, *Balzac and the Human Comedy* (New York, 1963).

H. J. Hunt, *Balzac's 'Comédie humaine'* (London, 1964).

E. J. Oliver, *Honoré de Balzac* (London, 1965).

F. W. J. Hemmings, *Balzac: An Interpretation of 'La Comédie humaine'* (New York, 1967).

F. Marceau, *Balzac and his World* (London, 1967).

V. S. Pritchett, *Balzac* (London, 1973).

D. Festa-McCormick, *Honoré de Balzac* (Boston, 1979).

ON 'COUSIN BETTE'

F. Jameson, '*La Cousine Bette* and Allegorical Realism', *PMLA* (Jan. 1971).

C. Prendergast, *Balzac, Fiction and Melodrama* (London, 1978).

D. Bellos, *Balzac: La Cousine Bette* (London, 1980).

A CHRONOLOGY OF
HONORÉ DE BALZAC

1799   Born at Tours, the son of Bernard-François Balzac and his wife Anne-Charlotte-Laure Sallambier. Put out to nurse till age of 4.

1804   Sent as a boarder to the Pension Le Guay, Tours.

1807–13   A boarder at the Oratorian college in Vendôme.

1814   Restoration of the Bourbon monarchy in France with the accession of Louis XVIII. The Balzac family moves to Paris, where Honoré continues his education.

1815   Flight of Louis XVIII on Napoleon's escape from Elba, but second Restoration of the Bourbons after Napoleon's defeat at Waterloo.

1816   Honoré becomes a law student and works in a lawyer's office.

1819   Becomes a Bachelor of Law. The family moves to Villeparisis on the retirement of Bernard-François. Honoré stays in Paris, living frugally at the Rue Lesdiguières, in an effort to start a career as a writer. He writes a tragedy, *Cromwell*, which is a failure.

1820–5   Writes various novels, some in collaboration, none of which he signs with his own name.

1822   Beginning of his liaison with 45-year-old Laure de Berny, who remains devoted to him till her death in 1836.

1825–8   Tries to make money by printing and publishing ventures, which fail and saddle him with debt.

1829   Publication of *Le Dernier Chouan*, the first novel he signs with his own name and the first of those to be incorporated in *La Comédie humaine*. Publication of the *Physiologie du mariage*.

1830   Publication of *Scènes de la vie privée*. Revolution in France resulting in the abdication of Charles X and the accession of Louis-Philippe.

1831   Works hard as a writer and adopts a luxurious, society
            life-style which increases his debts. Publication of *La
            Peau de chagrin* and some of the *Contes philosophiques*.

1832   Beginning of correspondence with Madame Hanska.
            Publication of more 'Scènes de la vie privée' and of
            Louis Lambert. Adds 'de' to his name and becomes
            'de Balzac'.

1833   Meets Madame Hanska for the first time in Neuchâtel,
            Switzerland, and then in Geneva. Signs a contract for
            Études de mœurs au XIXe siècle, which appears in
            twelve volumes between 1833 and 1837, and is divided
            into 'Scènes de la vie privée', 'Scènes de la vie de
            province', and 'Scènes de la vie parisienne'. Publica-
            tion of *Le Médecin de campagne* and the first 'Scènes
            de la vie de province', which included *Eugénie
            Grandet*.

1834   Publication of *La Recherche de l'absolu* and the first
            'Scènes de la vie parisienne'.

1834–5   Publication of *Le Père Goriot*.

1835   Publication of collected *Études philosophiques*
            (1835–40). Meets Madame Hanska in Vienna, the last
            time for eight years.

1836   Publication of *Le Lys dans la vallée* and other works.
            Starts a journal, *La Chronique de Paris*, which ends
            in failure.

1837   Journey to Italy. Publication of *La Vieille Fille*, the
            first part of *Illusions perdues*, and César Birotteau.

1838   Publication of *La Femme supérieure* (*Les Employés*)
            and *La Torpille*, which becomes the first part of
            Splendeurs et misères des courtisanes.

1839   Becomes president of the Société des Gens de Lettres.
            Publication of six more works, including *Le Cabinet
            des antiques* and *Béatrix*.

1840   Publication of more works, including *Pierrette*.

1841   Makes an agreement with his publisher, Furne, and
            booksellers for the publication of *La Comédie
            humaine*. Publication of more works, including *Le
            Curé de village*.

1842   Publication of *La Comédie humaine*, with its import-
            ant introduction, in seventeen volumes (1842–8); one
            posthumous volume is published in 1855. Publication
            of other works, including *Mémoires de deux jeunes
            mariées*, *Ursule Mirouet*, and *La Rabouilleuse*.

1843   More publications, including *La Muse du départe-
            ment*, and the completion in three parts of *Illusions
            perdues*. Visits Madame Hanska (widowed since 1841)
            at St Petersburg.

1844   Publication of *Modeste Mignon*, of the beginning of
            Les Paysans, of the second part of *Béatrix*, and of the
            second part of *Splendeurs et misères des courtisanes*.

1845   Travels in Europe with Madame Hanska and her
            daughter and future son-in-law.

1846   Stays in Rome and travels in Switzerland and Ger-
            many with Madame Hanska. A witness at the mar-
            riage of her daughter. Birth to Madame Hanska of a
            still-born child, who was to have been called Victor-
            Honoré. Publication of *La Cousine Bette* and of the
            third part of *Splendeurs et misères des courtisanes*.

1847   Madame Hanska stays in Paris from February till
            May. Publication of *Le Cousin Pons* and of the last
            part of *Splendeurs et misères des courtisanes*.

1848   Revolution in France resulting in the abdication of
            Louis-Philippe and the establishment of the Second
            Republic. Balzac goes to the Ukraine to stay with
            Madame Hanska and remains there till the spring of
            1850.

1849   His health deteriorates seriously.

1850   Marriage of Balzac and Madame Hanska on 14 March.
            He returns with her to Paris on 20 May and dies on
            18 August.

1869–76   Definitive edition of the *Œuvres complètes* in twenty-
            four volumes, published by Michel-Lévy and then by
            Calmann-Lévy.

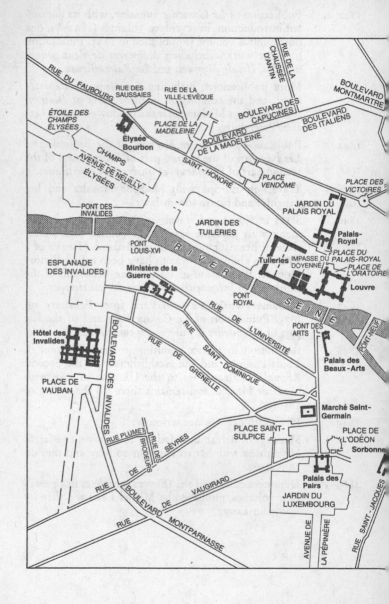

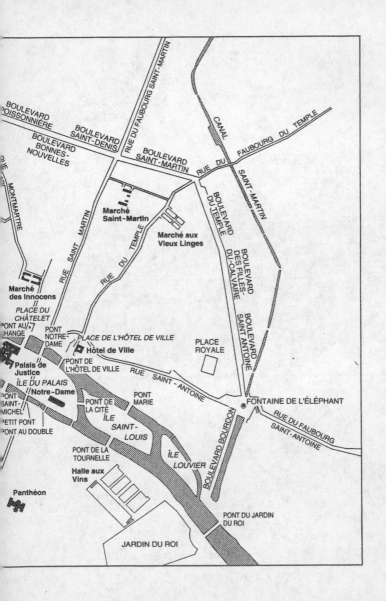

COUSIN BETTE

To Don Michele Angelo Cajetani, Prince of Téano*

IT is not to the Roman prince, nor to the heir of the illustrious house of Cajetani, which has given popes to Christendom, that I dedicate this small fragment of a long story; it is to the learned commentator of Dante.

You have revealed to me the marvellous framework of ideas on which the greatest Italian poet constructed his work, the only modern poem that can rival Homer's. Until I had heard your voice, *The Divine Comedy* seemed to me an immense enigma to which no one had found a solution, the commentators least of all. To understand Dante like this is to be great in the way he is; but you are acquainted with every kind of greatness.

A French scholar would make a reputation for himself and would be awarded a professorial chair and many decorations for publishing in a pedantic volume the improvised talk with which you delighted us on one of the evenings when we were recuperating from sightseeing in Rome. Perhaps you do not know that most of our professors live on Germany, England, the Orient, or the North like insects on a tree, and like the insect they become an integral part of it, taking their worth from their subject. As it happens, Italy has not yet been publicly exploited by the holder of a professorial chair. I shall never be given credit for my discretion in literary matters. By picking your brains I could have become a learned man, as important as the three Schlegels,* but I am going to remain simply a doctor of social medicine, the surgeon of incurable ills; if only to show my gratitude to my cicerone and to add your distinguished name to those of Porcia, San Severino, Pareto, di Negro, and Belgiojoso,* who in *The Human Comedy* represent the close and uninterrupted alliance of Italy and France. As long ago as the sixteenth century, Bandello, the bishop who was the author of some very amusing tales, confirmed that alliance in the same way in a magnificent collection of stories; these are the source of several of Shakespeare's plays, sometimes even complete parts being taken directly *from the text*.

The two sketches which I dedicate to you show the two eternal aspects of the same phenomenon. *Homo duplex*,* said our great Buffon;* why not add *res duplex*?* Everything is two-sided, even virtue. Thus Molière always presents both sides of every human problem. Following him, Diderot* one day wrote *This is not fiction*, perhaps his masterpiece. In it he presents the sublime figure of Mademoiselle de Lachaux abandoned by Gardanne as a pendant to that of a perfect lover whose death was brought about by his mistress. My two stories are therefore placed together as a pair, like two twins of different sexes. It is a literary whim which one can placate for once, particularly in a work that tries to represent all the forms in which thought can be clothed. Most human disputes arise from the fact that there are both learned and ignorant men so constituted that they never see more than one side of a phenomenon or an idea. Each man claims that the aspect he has seen is the only really valid one. So holy writ has made this prophetic statement: *God will deliver the world to debate*. I declare that this one line from scripture ought to oblige the Holy See to give you two-chamber government so as to comply with that judgement, to which Louis XVIII's ordinance* of 1814 provided a commentary.

May your wit and the poetry within you protect these two episodes of *Poor Relations** by your affectionate servant,

De Balzac
Paris, August–September 1846

1. *Where will love find a niche?*

Towards the middle of July in the year 1838, a vehicle of the kind known as a *milord*,* which had recently appeared on the Paris streets, was going along the Rue de l'Université. In it was a portly man of middle height, wearing the uniform of a captain of the National Guard.*

Amongst Parisians, who are reputed to be so intelligent, there are some who think they look infinitely better in uniform than in their ordinary clothes and who assume that women's tastes are so depraved that they will be favourably impressed by the sight of a bearskin cap and military accoutrements.

The Captain, who belonged to the second company, had a self-satisfied expression which cast a glow over his ruddy complexion and his rather chubby face. One could see from the halo that wealth sets upon the brows of retired shopkeepers that he was an elected member of the Paris administration, a former deputy mayor of his district at the very least. So you may be sure that the ribbon of the Legion of Honour* was not missing from his chest, which bulged out swaggeringly in the Prussian manner. Proudly ensconced in a corner of the milord, this member of the Legion of Honour let his glance wander over the passers-by, who, in Paris, thus become the recipients of pleasant smiles intended for the bright eyes of absent beauties.

The milord stopped in the part of the street between the Rue de Bellechasse and the Rue de Bourgogne, at the door of a large house recently built on a section of the courtyard of an old mansion standing in its own garden. The mansion had been preserved and remained in its original form at the bottom of the courtyard, now reduced to half its size.

Merely from the way the Captain accepted the help of the driver in getting down from the milord, you would have known that he was in his fifties. There are movements which are obviously ponderous and thus as revealing as a birth-certificate. The Captain put his yellow glove back on his right hand and, without a word to the porter, made his way to the ground floor of the mansion with an air which proclaimed, 'She is mine!' Paris porters have a knowing eye. They do not stop men who wear a decoration, are dressed in a blue uniform, and have a heavy gait. In short, they recognize the rich.

This ground floor was wholly occupied by Monsieur le Baron Hulot d'Ervy, Commissary-in-Chief under the Republic, former Intendant-General of the army, and at that time head of one of the most important departments of the War Ministry, Councillor of State, Grand Officer of the Legion of Honour, etc., etc.

Baron Hulot had called himself d'Ervy, the name of his birthplace, so as to be distinguished from his brother, the famous General Hulot, Colonel of the Grenadiers of the Imperial Guard, who had been made Count de Forzheim by the Emperor after the 1809 campaign.*

The older brother, the Count, given the responsibility of looking after his younger brother, had, with paternal prudence, placed him in the army administration. There, thanks to the services rendered by both brothers, the Baron had deserved and gained Napoleon's favour. From 1807, Baron Hulot was Intendant-General of the armies in Spain.*

After ringing the bell, the citizen Captain made strenuous efforts to straighten his jacket, which, owing to the dimensions of his pear-shaped corporation, had rucked up both in front and behind. Admitted as soon as a liveried footman had caught sight of him, this important and imposing man followed the servant, who, as he opened the drawing-room door, announced, 'Monsieur Crevel!'

On hearing this name, admirably suited to the figure of its owner, a tall, fair, very well-preserved woman jumped up as if she had received an electric shock.

'Hortense, my love, go into the garden with Cousin Bette,' she said quickly to her daughter, who was doing her embroidery nearby.

After dropping a graceful curtsey to the Captain, Mademoiselle Hortense Hulot went out by a french window, together with a dried-up old maid, who looked older than the Baroness although she was five years younger.

'It's about your marriage,' whispered Cousin Bette to her young cousin Hortense, not appearing to be offended by the way in which the Baroness dismissed them as if she hardly counted at all.

The cousin's dress would, if necessary, have explained this lack of ceremony.

The old maid wore a wine-coloured dress of merino wool, whose cut and trimmings were of the style in fashion at the time of the Restoration,* an embroidered collar worth about three francs, and a stitched straw hat with blue satin bows edged with straw, like those worn by old-clothes women at the market. On seeing her kid-leather shoes, whose style indicated the lowest class of shoemaker, a stranger would have hesitated to greet Cousin Bette as a relative of the family, for she looked exactly like a daily sewing-woman. Nevertheless, before leaving the room, the old maid gave Monsieur Crevel a little friendly nod, to which that dignitary replied with a sign of mutual understanding.

'You will come tomorrow, won't you, Mademoiselle Fischer?' he said.

'You won't be having company?' asked Cousin Bette.

'My children and you, that's all,' replied the visitor.

'Very well,' she replied, 'then you can count on me.'

'I am at your service, Madame,' said the captain of the citizen militia, bowing again to Baroness Hulot.

And he gave Madame Hulot a look like the one Tartuffe* casts at Elmire when a provincial actor at Poitiers or Coutances* thinks he should make the character's intentions clear.

'If you will follow me this way, Monsieur, we shall be much more comfortable for discussing business than in the drawing-room,' said Madame Hulot, indicating an adjoining room, which, in the arrangement of the flat, was used as a card-room.

Only a thin partition divided this room from the bou-

doir, whose window looked on to the garden, and Madame
Hulot left Monsieur Crevel alone for a moment, for she
thought it necessary to close the boudoir door and window
so that no one could go in there and listen. She even took
the precaution of also shutting the drawing-room french
window, smiling as she did so at her daughter and cousin,
whom she saw settled in an old summerhouse at the bottom
of the garden. She returned to the card-room, leaving the
door open so that she could hear the drawing-room door
being opened if anyone should come in. As she came and
went, the Baroness, being unobserved, revealed all her
thoughts in the expression of her face, and anyone seeing
her would have been almost shocked by her agitation. But
as she returned from the main drawing-room door to the
card-room, her face assumed that veil of impenetrable
reserve which all women, even the most open, seem to
have at their command.

During these preparations, which were singular, to say
the least, the National Guardsman examined the furniture
of the room where he found himself. As he looked at the
silk curtains which had been red but were now faded violet
by the sun and worn threadbare at the folds by long use, at
a carpet whose colours had vanished, at chairs which had
lost their gilt and whose stained silk covers were worn out
in strips, expressions of disdain, satisfaction, and hope
followed each other in turn on his dull, parvenu shopkeeper's face. He was looking at himself in the mirror
above an old Empire clock,* passing himself in review, as
it were, when the rustle of her silk dress indicated the
Baroness's return. And he immediately adopted a pose.

Having installed herself on a little couch, which
undoubtedly must have been a very fine one about 1809,
the Baroness motioned Crevel to an easy chair, with arms
ending in bronze sphinx heads from which the paint was
flaking off, so that parts of the wood were visible. She
signed to him to sit down.

'The precautions you are taking, Madame, would be a
charming omen for a . . .'

'A lover,' she said, interrupting the National Guardsman.

'That's a weak word,' he said, placing his right hand on his heart and rolling his eyes in a way which nearly always makes a woman laugh when she sees them assume such an expression in cold blood. 'Lover! Lover! say rather a man bewitched.'

2. *From father-in-law to mother-in-law*

'Listen Monsieur Crevel,' continued the Baroness, whose mood was too serious to permit of laughter. 'You are 50 years old. That's ten years less than Monsieur Hulot, I know. But, at my age, a woman's folly has to be justified by good looks, or youth, or fame, or ability, or some of the brilliance that dazzles us to such an extent that we forget everything, even our age. You may have an income of fifty thousand livres, but your age outweighs your fortune. So, of everything that a woman requires, you possess nothing at all.'

'And love?' said the National Guardsman, rising and going towards her. 'A love which . . .'

'No, Monsieur, obstinacy!' said the Baroness, interrupting him so as to put an end to this absurd situation.

'Yes, obstinacy and love,' he went on, 'but also something better, rights . . .'

'Rights?' exclaimed Madame Hulot, who was sublime in her scorn, defiance, and indignation. 'But', she continued in the same tone, 'this is a futile discussion and I didn't ask you to come here to talk about a subject which has made me forbid you the house in spite of the connection between our two families.'

'I thought you had . . .'

'Again!' she went on. 'Don't you see, Monsieur, from the free and unconcerned way I speak of lovers and love, of everything that is most improper for a woman, that I am absolutley sure of remaining virtuous? I am not afraid of anything, not even of arousing suspicion by being closeted alone with you. Is that the way a weak woman would behave? You know quite well why I asked you to come.'

'No, Madame,' replied Crevel, assuming a cold manner.

He pursed his lips and took up his pose again.

'Well, I'll be brief, so as to cut short our mutual ordeal,' said the Baroness, looking at Crevel.

Crevel made an ironic bow, in which a fellow tradesman would have recognized the airs and graces of a former commercial traveller.

'Our son has married your daughter . . .'

'And if that were to be done again! . . .' said Crevel.

'The marriage would not take place,' replied the Baroness quickly. 'I don't doubt it. Yet you've nothing to complain of. My son is not only one of the leading lawyers in Paris, but he's also been a deputy for a year now and his début at the Chamber* has been outstanding enough to lead one to suppose that before long he will be a minister. Victorin has twice been appointed government spokesman for important bills, and if he wanted to he could become a public prosecutor in the Court of Appeal today. So if you are implying that you have a son-in-law with no money . . .'

'A son-in-law whom I have to support,' continued Crevel, 'and that seems worse to me, Madame. Of the five hundred thousand francs which were my daughter's dowry, two hundred have gone, goodness knows where! . . . to pay the debts of Monsieur, your son, to furnish his house in outlandish style, a house costing five hundred thousand francs but bringing in barely fifteen hundred since he occupies the greater part of it, and on which he owes two hundred and sixty thousand francs. . . . The rent he gets barely covers the interest on the debt. This year I am giving my daughter about twenty thousand francs so that she can make ends meet. And my son-in-law, who they said was earning thirty thousand francs at the law-courts, is going to desert the law courts for the Chamber of Deputies . . .'

'This, Monsieur Crevel, is still not the main purpose of our meeting and takes us off the point. But to finish with that matter, if my son becomes a government minister and has you appointed an Officer of the Legion of Honour and a councillor of the Paris prefecture,* for a former perfumer you have no cause for complaint! . . .'

'Ah, there we are, Madame. I am a grocer, a shopkeeper, a former dealer in almond paste, Portuguese water, and cephalic oil. I ought to think myself very honoured to have married my only daughter to the son of Monsieur le Baron Hulot d'Ervy. My daughter will be a baroness. It's like the days of the Regency,* of Louis XV, of the eighteenth century. That's all very fine. . . . I love Célestine as one loves an only daughter. I have accepted all the difficulties of being a widower in Paris (and in the prime of life, Madame!). But let me tell you that in spite of my excessive love for my daughter, I won't cut into my fortune for your son, whose expenses are not clear to me, to me, a former tradesman . . .'

'Monsieur, at this very moment, Monsieur Popinot, a former chemist of the Rue des Lombards, is Minister of Trade.'

'A friend of mine, Madame! . . .' said the retired perfumer. 'For I, Célestin Crevel, formerly old César Birotteau's* head salesman, I bought the business of said Birotteau, Popinot's father-in-law, Popinot being then a junior salesman in the establishment. And it is he who reminds me of that, for he's not proud (to do him justice) with people in a good position who have an income of sixty thousand francs.'

'Well, Monsieur, so the ideas that you call Regency are no longer appropriate in an age when men are accepted for their personal qualities. And that's what you've done in marrying your daughter to my son . . .'

'You don't know how this marriage was arranged,' exclaimed Crevel. 'Oh, this accursed bachelor life! But for my dissipations, my Célestine would today be Viscountess Popinot!'

'But let us not recriminate about what has been done,' continued the Baroness firmly. 'Let us talk of the cause for complaint which your strange behaviour has given me. My daughter, Hortense, could have married. The marriage depended entirely on you. I thought you had generous feelings. I thought you would have been fair to a woman who kept in her heart no image but her husband's, that you would have realized that she could not receive a man who might compromise her, and that you would have done your best, out of respect for the family to which you allied yourself, to promote Hortense's marriage to Councillor Lebas. . . . And you, Monsieur, you caused this marriage to fall through . . .'

'Madame,' replied the former perfumer, 'I behaved as an honest man. I was asked if Mademoiselle Hortense's dowry of two hundred thousand livres would be paid. These were the words of my reply: "I wouldn't vouch for it. My son-in-law, to whom the Hulot family agreed to give that amount as a dowry, had debts, and I think that if Monsieur Hulot d'Ervy were to die tomorrow, his widow would be penniless." That's what I said, dear lady.'

'Would you have spoken like that, Monsieur, if for your sake I had failed in my duty?' asked Madame Hulot, looking steadily at Crevel.

'I would not have had the right to, dear Adeline,' exclaimed the strange lover, interrupting the Baroness, 'for you would have found the dowry in my wallet.'

And backing up his words with action, the portly Crevel went down on one knee and kissed Madame Hulot's hand, mistaking her speechless horror at these words for hesitation.

'To buy my daughter's happiness at the price of . . . Oh, get up, Monsieur, or I shall ring.'

The former perfumer got up with great difficulty. This infuriated him so much that he took up his pose again. Nearly all men assume a posture which they think will show off the advantages with which nature has endowed them. With Crevel, this attitude consisted of crossing his arms like Napoleon, turning his head three-quarters round, and looking towards the horizon as the painter made Napoleon do in his portrait.

'To remain faithful to a libert . . .' he said with well-simulated rage.

'To a husband, Monsieur, who is worthy of it,' replied Madame Hulot, interrupting Crevel so as not to let him utter a word that she did not want to hear.

'Look, Madame, you wrote asking me to come. You want to know the reasons for my behaviour. You exasperate me with your imperial airs, with your scorn, and your . . . contempt! Anyone would think I was a nigger. I repeat, believe me, I have the right to . . . to court you . . . for . . . But, no, I love you enough to keep silent . . .'

'Speak, Monsieur. In a few days I shall be 48. I'm not a silly prude. I can listen to anything.'

'Well, will you give me your word as a virtuous woman (for, unfortunately for me, you are a virtuous woman) never to mention my name, never to reveal that I told you the secret?'

'If that is the condition of the revelation, I swear not to tell anyone, not even my husband, where I learned of the enormities that you are going to confide in me.'

'That I can well believe, for it concerns only you and him.'

Madame Hulot turned pale.

'Oh, if you still love Hulot, you are going to suffer! Would you like me to say nothing?'

'Speak, Monsieur, for, according to you, it's a question of justifying in my eyes the strange declarations you have made to me and your persistence in tormenting a woman of my age, who would like to see her daughter married and then . . . die in peace!'

'You see, you are unhappy.'

'I, Monsieur?'

'Yes, beautiful and noble creature!' exclaimed Crevel. 'You have suffered only too much.'

'Monsieur, say no more and go! Or speak to me as you should.'

'Do you know, Madame, how Master Hulot and I became acquainted? . . . Through our mistresses, Madame.'

'Oh, Monsieur . . .'

'Through our mistresses, Madame,' repeated Crevel melo-
dramatically, uncrossing his arms to make a gesture with his
right hand.

'Well, what of it, Monsieur?' said the Baroness calmly,
to Crevel's great amazement.

Petty-minded seducers never understand noble hearts.

3. *Josépha*

'I'd been a widower for five years,' continued Crevel,
speaking like a man who is going to tell a story, 'and in the
interests of my daughter, whom I idolize, I didn't want to
marry again; and I also didn't want to have liaisons in my
own house, although at the time I had a very pretty cashier.
So I furnished a set of rooms, as they say, for a little
working-girl of 15. She was marvellously beautiful and I
confess I fell head over heels in love with her. I therefore
asked my own aunt, my mother's sister, whom I brought
to Paris from my native countryside, to live with the
charming creature and to keep an eye on her so that she
should remain as virtuous as possible in this—how shall I
put it?—compromising—no, irregular situation. The girl,
who had an obvious talent for music, was given teachers
and received some education. (She had to be kept occupied!) Besides, I wanted to be, at one and the same time,
her father, her benefactor, and, not to mince matters, her
lover; to kill two birds with one stone, to do a good deed
and have a nice mistress. I had five years of happiness. The
child had one of those voices that make a theatre's fortune,
and the only way I can describe her is to say that she is a
Duprez* in petticoats. She cost me two thousand francs a
year, just to develop her talent as a singer. She made me
crazy about music, and I had a box for her and for my
daughter at the Italian Opera. I used to go there with them
alternately, one day with Célestine and one day with
Josépha.'

'What, the famous singer?'

'Yes, Madame, that celebrated Josépha owes me everything. . . . Finally, in 1834, when the girl was 20, I thought I had bound her to me for life. And so I became very indulgent to her and, wanting to allow her some amusements, I let her meet a pretty little actress, Jenny Cadine, whose fortunes were rather like her own. This actress also owed everything to one protector, who had brought her up with the utmost care. That protector was Baron Hulot . . .'

'I know, Monsieur,' said the Baroness calmly, with no sign of emotion.

'Oh! Indeed! exclaimed Crevel, more and more taken aback. 'Well, but did you know that your monster of a husband was *protecting* Jenny when she was 13?'

'Well, Monsieur, and what of it?' said the Baroness.

'As Jenny Cadine was 20,' continued the former tradesman, 'the same age as Josépha when they got to know each other, the Baron, since 1826, had been playing the part that Louis XV played to Mademoiselle de Romans,* and you were twelve years younger then.'

'Monsieur, I had my reasons for leaving Monsieur Hulot free.'

'No doubt that lie will suffice to wipe out all the sins you have committed, Madame, and will open the gates of Paradise for you,' replied Crevel with a knowing look that made Madame Hulot blush. 'Tell that to others, sublime, adored woman, but not to Père Crevel. For you must know that I have dined too often in a foursome with your scoundrel of a husband not to be fully aware of your worth. Sometimes, in his cups, he would reproach himself as he dwelt upon your perfections. Oh, I know you well; you are an angel. A libertine might hesitate between a girl of 20 and you. *I* do not.'

'Monsieur!'

'All right, I'll say no more. But I can tell you, noble, saintly woman, that husbands, when they are drunk, tell many tales of their wives to their mistresses, who split their sides laughing at them.'

Tears of shame, that trickled down from under Madame

Hulot's beautiful eyelashes, made the National Guardsman stop short and he no longer thought of taking up his pose.

'I continue my tale,' he said. 'The Baron and I became friends through our rascally little mistresses. The Baron, like all depraved characters, is very agreeably and thoroughly good-natured. Oh, I liked him a lot, the old scoundrel! He was up to all sorts of tricks ... but that's enough of these reminiscences. ... We became like two brothers. The rogue, quite in the Regency style, did his best to corrupt me, to preach Saint-Simonism* to me with regard to women, to give me aristocratic, military ideas. But, you see, I loved my little mistress so much that I would have married her, if I hadn't been afraid of having children. Between two old papas, friends as ... as we were, how do you suppose that we could have failed to think of arranging a marriage between our children? Three months after his son's marriage to my Célestine, Hulot (I don't know how I can bring myself to utter his name, the villain! for he deceived both of us, Madame!), well, the villain stole my little Josépha from me. The scoundrel knew that he had been supplanted by a young Councillor of State and by an artist (enough to be going on with!) in the heart of Jenny Cadine, whose success was becoming more and more stunning. And so he robbed me of my poor little mistress, a darling of a girl. But you must certainly have seen her at the Italian Opera, where he used his influence to get her engaged.

'Your husband isn't as well-organized as I am. I am as orderly as a sheet of music-paper. His finances had already been well eaten into by Jenny Cadine, who cost him nearly thirty thousand francs a year. Well, you must know, he's ruining himself completely for Josépha. Josépha, Madame, is a Jewess; her name is Mirah—an anagram of Hiram—an Israelite device to enable her to be recognized, for she was abandoned as a child in Germany. I've made some inquiries, which prove that she's the natural daughter of a rich Jewish banker. Thanks to the theatre and, above all, to the lessons of Jenny Cadine, Madame Schontz, Malaga, and Carabine* about how to treat old men, my little girl, whom

I had been keeping on a path of economy and virtue, developed the first Hebrews' instinct for gold and jewels, for the Golden Calf.* The famous singer, who has become eaten up with greed, wants to be rich, very rich. So she doesn't squander any of the money that is squandered on her. She tried her hand on Master Hulot, and plucked him clean. Oh, plucked him, skinned him, rather! The poor fellow, after competing against one of the Kellers* and the Marquis d'Esgrignon,* both of them crazy about Josépha, not to mention her unknown adorers, is going to be robbed of her by that mightily rich duke who patronizes the arts. What's his name? . . . a dwarf-like man, oh yes, the Duc d'Hérouville.* That great lord has the presumption to want Josépha all to himself. All the courtesan world is talking about it, but the Baron knows nothing about it. For in the thirteenth district* it is the same as in all the others. The lover, like the husband, is the last to know. Now, do you understand my right? Your husband, lovely lady, has deprived me of my happiness, of the only joy I've had since I was widowed. Oh, if I hadn't had the bad luck to meet that old dandy, I would still have Josépha. For, you see, *I* would never have let her go on the stage. She would have remained unknown, virtuous, and all mine. Oh, if you had seen her eight years ago, slim and trim, with her golden Andalusian complexion, as they say, her black hair shining like satin, her eyes flashing beneath long brown lashes, her gestures elegant as a duchess's, all this together with the modesty of poverty and the innocent grace and pretty ways of a wild deer. Thanks to Master Hulot, those charms, that purity, have all become a snare for wolves, a trap for hundred-sou pieces. The girl is the queen of the tarts, as they say. Finally, she pulls wool over your eyes, nowadays, she who used to know nothing about anything, not even that expression.'

At this, the former perfumer wiped his eyes, where a few tears had gathered. The sincerity of his grief touched Madame Hulot, who emerged from the daydream into which she had fallen.

4. *The perfumer's sudden access of pity*

'Well, Madame, will I find such a treasure again at the age of 52? At that age, love costs thirty thousand francs a year. I have learned the figure through your husband, and, for my part, I am too fond of Célestine to ruin her. When I saw you at the first evening party you gave for us, I didn't understand how that scoundrel Hulot could keep a Jenny Cadine. You had the bearing of an empress. You are not yet 30, Madame,' he continued. 'You look young to me, you are beautiful. On my word of honour, I was touched to the core that day. I said to myself, "If I didn't have my Josépha, since Père Hulot neglects his wife, she would fit me like a glove." (Oh, excuse me! That's an expression from my former trade. The perfumer reappears from time to time. That's what prevents me from aspiring to be a deputy.) So when I was deceived by the Baron in such an underhand way (for between old rascals like us, our friends' mistresses should be sacred), I swore to myself that I would take his wife. It's only fair. The Baron could say nothing and we would have nothing to fear. You showed me the door like a mangy dog the first time I mentioned the state of my heart to you. That redoubled my love, my obstinacy, if you like, and you will be mine.'

'And how will that come about?'

'I don't know, but it will. You see, Madame, a silly old perfumer (retired!) who has only one idea in his head is stronger than a clever man who has thousands. I am crazy about you and you are my revenge! It's as if I were in love twice over. I'm speaking to you frankly, as a man who has made up his mind. Just as you tell me, "I won't be yours", I am talking to you quite dispassionately. In short, as the saying goes, I am putting my cards on the table. Yes, you will be mine at the right moment. Oh, if you were 50, you would still be my mistress! And it will happen, for I, for my part, expect every assistance from your husband.'

Madame Hulot cast such a staring look of terror at the

scheming tradesman that he thought she had gone mad and he stopped short.

'You asked for it. You have covered me with your contempt. You have defied me. And so I've spoken out!' he said, feeling the need to justify the brutality of his last words.

'Oh, my daughter, my daughter!' moaned the Baroness faintly.

'Oh, nothing matters to me any more!' Crevel continued. 'The day Josépha was taken from me, I was like a tigress whose young have been removed. In short, I was in the state I see you in now. Your daughter! For me, she's the means of obtaining you. Yes, I blocked your daughter's marriage . . . and you won't be able to arrange a marriage for her at all without my help! However beautiful Mademoiselle Hortense may be, she must have a dowry.'

'Alas! Yes,' said the Baroness, wiping her eyes.

'Well, try asking the Baron for ten thousand francs,' Crevel went on, taking up his pose again.

He waited a moment, like an actor who pauses after making his point.

'If he had them, he would give them to Josépha's successor,' he said, pitching his voice on a higher note. 'Does anyone stop on the path he is following? First of all, he's too fond of women. (There's a happy mean in everything, as our King* said.) And then, his vanity is involved. He's a fine figure of a man. He'll ruin you all for the sake of his pleasure. In any case you're half-way to the poorhouse already. Look, since I first set foot in your house, you haven't been able to renew your drawing-room furniture. The word "hard-up" belches out from every rent in those hangings. What prospective son-in-law will leave the house without being appalled at the ill-disguised evidence of the most horrible kind of poverty, that of good families? I've been a shopkeeper. I know what I'm talking about. There's nothing like the eye of a Paris tradesman for distinguishing between real and apparent wealth. You're penniless,' he said in a low voice. 'That's obvious in everything, even in your servant's livery. Would you like me to reveal frightful mysteries which are concealed from you?'

'Monsieur,' said Madame Hulot, who was soaking her handkerchief with tears, 'enough, enough!'

'Well, my son-in-law gives his father money, and that's what I was trying to tell you when I talked about your son's expenditure at the beginning of our conversation. But I watch over my daughter's interests; set your mind at ease.'

'Oh, to see my daughter married and then to die!' said the unhappy woman, beside herself.

'Well, this is the way to do it,' continued Crevel.

Madame Hulot gave Crevel a hopeful look, which changed her expression so quickly that this one movement ought to have softened his heart and made him give up his absurd scheme.

5. *The way to arrange a marriage for a beautiful girl with no money*

'You will be beautiful for another ten years,' Crevel continued, maintaining his pose. 'Be kind to me and Mademoiselle Hortense's marriage is assured. As I told you, Hulot has given me the right to propose the deal—to put it bluntly—and he won't be annoyed. For the last three years I have invested my capital well, for my escapades have been limited. I have made three hundred thousand francs over and above my fortune, and they are at your disposal.'

'Go, go and never show your face to me again!' said Madame Hulot. 'If I hadn't had to know the secret of your treacherous behaviour with regard to Hortense's proposed marriage . . . Yes, treacherous,' she repeated, in response to a gesture by Crevel. 'How can you make a poor girl, a beautiful innocent creature, bear the brunt of such hostility? . . . If I hadn't had to know that secret which was gnawing at my maternal heart, you would never have spoken to me again, you would never have set foot in my house again. Thirty-two years of honour, of wifely loyalty, will not be wiped out by the attacks of Monsieur Crevel.'

'Former perfumer, César Birotteau's successor at *La Reine des Roses*,* Rue Saint-Honoré,' said Crevel, mockingly, 'former deputy mayor, captain in the National Guard, Chevalier of the Legion of Honour, just like my predecessor.'

'Monsieur,' the Baroness continued, 'after twenty years of fidelity, Monsieur Hulot may have tired of his wife; that concerns no one but me. But you see, Monsieur, that he has been very secretive about his infidelities, for I didn't know that he had succeeded you in the heart of Mademoiselle Josépha.'

'Oh,' exclaimed Crevel, 'at a price, Madame! That songbird has cost him more than a hundred thousand francs in the last two years. And you haven't seen the last of it yet.'

'No more of this, Monsieur Crevel. I won't, for your sake, give up the happiness a mother feels in being able to kiss her children without feeling remorse in her heart, in knowing she is respected and loved by her family, and I shall give up my soul to God without a blemish.'

'*Amen!*' said Crevel, with that expression of diabolical bitterness which spreads over the faces of pretentious people when they are thwarted a second time in their enterprises. 'You don't know the final stage of poverty, the shame, the dishonour. I've tried to enlighten you. I wanted to save you and your daughter. Well, you'll spell out the modern parable of the *prodigal father* to the very last letter. I'm touched by your tears and your pride, for it's frightful to see a woman one loves crying,' said Crevel, sitting down. 'All I can promise you, dear Adeline, is to do nothing against you or your husband. But don't come to me for information. That's all!'

'Oh, what shall I do?' cried Madame Hulot.

Up till then the Baroness had courageously endured the triple torture which this explanation had inflicted on her feelings, for she suffered as a woman, as a mother, and as a wife. Indeed, as long as her son's father-in-law was arrogant and aggressive, she found strength in standing up to the shopkeeper's brutality. But the good nature which he showed in the midst of his exasperation as a rejected lover, as a humiliated, fine National Guardsman, relaxed her overwrought nerves; she wrung her hands, burst into tears, and was so benumbed and prostrated that she let Crevel, on his knees, kiss her hands.

'Good God, what will become of us?' she continued, wiping her eyes. 'Can a mother look on in cold blood while her daughter fades away before her eyes? What will be the fate of such a magnificent young woman, as strong in the virtuous life she has lived at her mother's side as in her richly endowed nature? Some days, she walks in the garden, sad without knowing why, and I find her with tears in her eyes.'

'She's 21,' said Crevel.

'Shall I have to put her in a convent?'asked the Baroness. 'For in such crises, religion is often powerless against nature and girls who have had a very religious upbringing lose their heads. But do get up, Monsieur. Don't you see that now everything is at an end between us, that you fill me with horror, that you have destroyed a mother's last hope?'

'And if I were to revive it?' he said.

Madame Hulot looked at Crevel with a frenzied expression which touched him, but he drove pity back into his heart, because of the phrase, *'you fill me with horror!'* Virtue is always a little too absolute; it is unaware of the shades and compromises which people use to manœuvre themseves out of a false position.

'These days, you can't marry off a girl as beautiful as Mademoiselle Hortense without a dowry,' continued Crevel, resuming his stiff manner. 'Your daughter is one of those beauties who frighten off husbands. She's like a thoroughbred horse which requires too much expensive care to have many buyers. You can't go on foot with a woman like that on your arm. Everyone will look at you, will follow you, will covet your wife. This success alarms many men, who don't want to have lovers to kill. For, after all, you never kill more than one. In your situation, you can only get your daughter married in three ways: through my help, which you don't want—that's one; by finding a very rich, childless, old man of 60 who would like to have children—that's difficult but it can be done. There are so many old men who take girls like Josépha and Jenny Cadine; why shouldn't you find one who'd commit the same folly legitimately?—If I didn't have my Célestine and our two grandchildren, I'd marry Hortense myself. That's the second way. The last way is the easiest.'

Madame Hulot raised her head and looked anxiously at the former perfumer.

'Paris is a town where all the energetic fellows who sprout like young trees everywhere on French soil come together; and it harbours a swarm of talented men without hearth or home, but with courage capable of anything, even of making their fortunes. Well, those lads—(your servant was one of them in his day, and he knows what he's talking about! What did du Tillet or Popinot have, twenty years ago? They were both floundering around in Papa Birotteau's shop with no other capital than the desire to get on, which, in my view, is worth any amount of money! You can eat up your capital, but you don't eat up your moral fibre! What did *I* have? The desire to get on, and a stout heart. Today, du Tillet is equal to the highest in the land. Little Popinot, the richest chemist in the Rue des Lombards, became a deputy and now he's a minister.) Well, one of those *condottieri*, as they say, of the business world, of the pen, or the paintbrush is, in Paris, the only being capable of marrying a beautiful girl who is penniless, for they are game enough for anything. Monsieur Popinot married Mademoiselle Birotteau without expecting a farthing of a dowry. Those men are crazy! They believe in love, as they believe in their fortune and their own powers. Look for some energetic fellow who will fall in love with your daughter and marry her without caring about the wedding present. You must admit that, for an enemy, I don't lack generosity, for this advice is against my own interest.'

'Oh, Monsieur Crevel, if you want to be my friend, abandon your ridiculous notions!'

'Ridiculous, Madame? Don't denigrate yourself in that way. Take a look at yourself. I love you and you will come to me. One day, I want to say to Hulot, "You took Josépha from me, I have taken your wife." It's the old law of retaliation. And I shall work towards the fulfilment of my plan unless you become excessively ugly. I shall succeed, and I'll tell you why,' he said, taking up his pose and looking at Madame Hulot.

6. *The Captain loses the battle*

'You won't meet an old man, or a young man in love,' he continued after a pause, 'because you love your daughter too much to subject her to the stratagems of an old rake, and because you, Baroness Hulot, sister of the old Lieuten-ant-General who commanded the old grenadiers of the Imperial Guard, will not bring yourself to accept the man of energy whatever his origins. For he might be an ordinary workman, just as someone who is a millionaire today was an ordinary mechanic, overseer, or foreman ten years ago. And then, seeing your daughter, with the impulses of a 20-year-old, perhaps about to dishonour you, you will say to yourself, "Better that I should be the one to dishonour myself, and if Monsieur Crevel will keep my secret, I'll earn my daughter's dowry, two hundred thousand francs, for ten years of attachment to that former glove-merchant, Père Crevel!" I'm irritating you, and what I'm saying is profoundly immoral, isn't it? But if you were consumed by an irresistible passion, you would reason in the way women in love do, so as to justify yielding to me. Well, Hortense's interests will put these capitulations of con-science in your heart.'

'Hortense still has an uncle.'

'Who? Père Fischer? He's winding up his business, and that's the Baron's fault too, for he takes his rake-off from all the cash-boxes that are within his reach.'

'Count Hulot . . .'

'Oh, Madame, your husband has already run through the old Lieutenant-General's economies. He's furnished his singer's house with them. Come, are you going to let me go with no hope?'

'Goodbye, Monsieur. It is easy to recover from a passion for a woman of my age, and you will come to have Christian thoughts. God protects the unfortunate.'

The Baroness got up to compel the Captain to withdraw and she made him go back into the drawing-room.

'Should the beautiful Madame Hulot be living amidst such tattered furnishings?' he said.

And he pointed to an old lamp, a chandelier that had lost its gilt, the threadbare carpet, in short to all the ragged remnants of opulence which turned the big white, red, and gold drawing-room into a corpse of the festivities of the Empire.

'Virtue sheds its lustre on all that. I have no desire to owe magnificent furnishings to the beauty which you say I have, by turning it into a snare for wolves, *a trap for hundred-sou pieces*!'

The captain bit his lip as he recognized the terms he had used to denounce Josépha's greed.

'And for whose sake are you so determined?' he asked.

By now the Baroness had conducted the former perfumer as far as the door.

'For a libertine!' he added, pursing his lips with all the contempt of a virtuous millionaire.

'If you were right, Monsieur, there would be some merit in my faithfulness, that's all.'

She left the Captain with a farewell nod of the kind one makes to get rid of a tiresome visitor, and turned round too smartly to see him assume his pose for the last time.

She went to re-open the doors she had closed and could not see Crevel's threatening farewell gesture. She walked with a proud, noble bearing like a martyr going to the Coliseum. Nevertheless, her strength was exhausted, for she collapsed onto the sofa of her blue boudoir like a woman about to faint, and her eyes remained fixed on the

ruined summerhouse where her daughter was chatting with
Cousin Bette.

From the first days of her marriage until now, the
Baroness had loved her husband as Josephine, finally, had
come to love Napoleon, with an admiring, maternal, but
submissive love. Though she had been unaware of the
details which Crevel had just given her, she nevertheless
knew very well that, for twenty years, Hulot had been
unfaithful to her. But she had drawn a leaden veil over her
eyes; she had wept in silence and had never let fall a word
of reproach. In return for this angelic sweetness of temper,
she had earned her husband's veneration and was surrounded by an almost divine cult.

A woman's affection for her husband, the respect with
which she surrounds him, are contagious in her family.
Hortense thought her father was a perfect model of conjugal love. As for Hulot's son, brought up as he was to
admire the Baron, whom everyone saw as one of the giants
who had helped Napoleon, he knew he owed his position
to his father's name, position, and reputation. Besides, the
influence of childhood impressions lasts a long time and he
was still afraid of his father. So even if he had suspected
the misdemeanours revealed by Crevel, he would have
respected his father too much to complain, and he would
have excused them with reasons stemming from a man's
way of looking at these things.

The extraordinary devotion of this noble, beautiful
woman must now be explained, and here, in a few words,
is the story of her life.

7. *A woman's fine life-story*

From a village on the most distant frontier of Lorraine, at
the foot of the Vosges, three brothers called Fischer,
conscripted by the Republic,* set off to join the so-called
Army of the Rhine.

In 1799 the second of the brothers, André, a widower
and Madame Hulot's father, left his daughter in the care of

his older brother, Pierre Fischer, who, unfit for service because of a wound he had received in 1797, was engaged in some small-scale enterprises for Military Transport, an employment which he owed to the protection of Hulot d'Ervy, the officer in charge. Not unnaturally, it happened that Hulot, who came to Strasbourg, saw the Fischer family. At that time Adeline's father and his younger brother were contractors for the supply of forage in Alsace.

Adeline, then 16 years old, could be compared to the famous Madame du Barry* who, like her, was a daughter of Lorraine.

She was one of those perfect, dazzling beauties, one of those women like Madame Tallien* whom Nature fashions with particular care, giving them her most precious gifts, distinction, nobility, grace, refinement, elegance, an incomparable physique, and a complexion with colouring devised in the unknown studio where chance is at work.

These beautiful women all resemble each other. Bianca Capella, whose portrait is one of Bronzino's* masterpieces; Jean Goujon's* Venus, whose original was the famous Diane de Poitiers;* Signora Olympia,* whose portrait is in the Doria gallery; and Ninon,* Madame du Barry, Madame Tallien, Mademoiselle George,* Madame Récamier;* all these women, who remained beautiful in spite of their years, their passions, or their dissipated lives, are strikingly similar in their figures, their build, and their type of beauty, so that one is led to think that in the ocean of generation there is an aphrodisian current from which all these Venuses emerge, daughters of the same salty waters!

Adeline Fischer, one of the most beautiful of that divine race, had the sublime characteristics, the willowy figure, the seductive fabric of those women born to be queens. The fair hair that our mother Eve received from God's hand, the bearing of an empress, an aristocratic air, a majestically contoured profile, and the modesty of a village girl made men stop and look at her as she passed by; they were charmed as art-lovers are before a Raphael. So, when he saw Adeline Fischer, the officer in charge of transport made her his wife as soon as the law allowed, to the great astonishment of the Fischers, who had all been brought up in awe of their superiors.

The oldest brother, a soldier of 1792 badly wounded at the attack on Wissembourg, adored Napoleon and everything connected with the *Grande Armée*.

André and Johann spoke with respect of Hulot, the chief transport officer. He was a protégé of the Emperor and moreover they owed their position to him, for Hulot d'Ervy, finding them to be intelligent and honest, had pulled them out of the army forage wagons and put them at the head of an emergency supply department. The brothers had rendered good service during the 1804 campaign. At the peace, Hulot had obtained for them the forage contract in Alsace, not knowing that, later, he would be sent to Strasbourg to prepare the 1806 campaign.

For the young peasant girl, this marriage was like an Assumption. The beautiful Adeline went directly from her village mud to the paradise of the Imperial Court.

In fact it was at that time that the chief transport officer, one of the most active and upright workers in his corps, was made a baron, summoned to attend the Emperor, and attached to the Imperial Guard. Out of love for her husband, with whom she was quite besotted, the beautiful village girl had the courage to educate herself.

The chief transport officer was, moreover, as a man the counterpart of Adeline as a woman. He was one of the élite body of handsome men. Tall, well-built, fair, with blue eyes irresistible in their sparkle, animation, and variety of expression, and an elegant figure, he was outstanding amongst men like d'Orsay, Forbin, and Ouvrard,* in short, among the ranks of the Empire beaux. Although he was a man of many feminine conquests and imbued with the ideas of the Directory* about women, his philandering activities were interrupted for quite some time by his attachment to his wife.

For Adeline, therefore, the Baron was, from the start, a kind of god who could do no wrong. She owed everything to him: fortune—she had a carriage, a town house, and all the luxury of the time; happiness—she was openly loved;

a title—she was a baroness; celebrity—in Paris she was called the beautiful Madame Hulot; and finally, she had the honour of refusing the advances of the Emperor, who gave her a diamond necklace and continued to single her out, for, from time to time, he would ask, 'And is the lovely Madame Hulot still so virtuous?' in the tone of a man prepared to avenge himself on anyone who might have triumphed where he had failed.

It is not, therefore, very difficult to appreciate the reasons for the fanaticism that mingled with love in Madame Hulot's simple, innocent, and pure soul. Having told herself that her husband could do her no wrong, she turned herself, in her inmost heart, into the humble, blind, devoted servant of the man who had made her life.

It must be said, however, that she was gifted with great good sense, the good sense of ordinary people, which gave her education a firm foundation. In society she spoke little, talked no ill of anyone, and did not try to shine. She thought carefully about everything, listened and modelled herself on the most virtuous and well-born women.

In 1815 Hulot followed the same line of conduct as the Prince de Wissembourg, one of his closest friends, and was one of the organizers of the improvised army whose defeat concluded the Napoleonic saga at Waterloo.

In 1816 the Baron became one of the pet aversions of the Feltre ministry* and was not reappointed to the Quartermaster General's department till 1823, when he was needed for the Spanish war.* In 1830* he reappeared in the administration as a minister's aide, following Louis-Philippe's policy of conscripting, as it were, old Napoleonic supporters.

Since the accession to the throne of the younger branch,* of which he was an active supporter, he had remained an indispensable head of department at the War Ministry. He had also obtained his marshal's baton, and the King could do no more for him unless it were to make him a minister or a peer of France.

Having little to do between 1818 and 1823, Baron Hulot had been engaged on active service with women. Madame

Hulot dated her Hector's first infidelities back to the grand *finale* of the Empire, and so for twelve years the Baroness had played the role of *prima donna assoluta** without a rival. She still enjoyed the old, deep-seated affection which husbands feel for their wives when they have become resigned to the role of gentle, virtuous companions. She knew that no rival would last for two hours against a word of reproach from her, but she closed her eyes, shut her ears, and did not want to know of her husband's behaviour away from home. In short, she treated her Hector as a mother treats a spoilt child.

Three years before the conversation that had just taken place, Hortense had recognized her father in a front stalls box at the *Variétés* with Jenny Cadine, and she had exclaimed, 'There's Papa.' 'You're mistaken, my love, he's with the Marshal,' the Baroness had replied. She had certainly seen Jenny Cadine, but instead of feeling a pang in the heart on seeing how pretty the girl was, Adeline had said to herself, 'That rascally Hector must be very happy.'

Nevertheless, she suffered; she gave way in secret to frightful attacks of rage. But whenever she saw her Hector again, she would always recall her twelve years of undiluted happiness and lose the power to utter a single complaint.

She would have liked the Baron to confide in her, but out of respect for him she had never dared hint that she knew of his goings-on. This excessive delicacy is only to be found amongst those beautiful daughters of the people who know how to receive blows without returning any. The blood of the first martyrs flows in their veins. Well-born girls, being their husbands' equals, feel the need to torment them and to mark their acts of tolerance with biting words, as one marks up the score at billiards, in a diabolical spirit of vengeance and to assure themselves either of their own superiority or of a right of revenge.

8. *Hortense*

The Baroness had a fervent admirer in her brother-in-law, Lieutenant-General Hulot, the venerable commander of the Infantry Grenadiers of the Imperial Guard, who was to be awarded a marshal's baton in his declining years. The old man, who from 1830 to 1834 had commanded the military region that included the Brittany departments, the scene of his exploits in 1799 and 1800,* had settled in Paris, near his brother, for whom he still had a fatherly affection.

His old soldier's heart was strongly drawn to his sister-in-law's. He admired her as the most noble and saintly of her sex. He had not married, because he wanted to find a second Adeline, whom he had sought in vain throughout twenty countries and in twenty campaigns. So as not to fall from grace in the heart of this irreproachable, blameless old republican, of whom Napoleon used to say, 'That good old Hulot is the most stubborn of republicans, but he will never betray me', Adeline would have endured sufferings far more acute than those she had just experienced. But the old man, at the age of 72, his health broken by thirty campaigns, wounded for the twenty-seventh time at Waterloo, gave Adeline admiration but not protection. The poor Count, among other infirmities, could hear only with the help of an ear-trumpet!

As long as Baron Hulot d'Ervy was a handsome man, his love affairs did not affect his fortune, but at the age of 50 he had to pay attention to his appearance. Love in old men of that age becomes a vice; absurd vanities are mingled with it. So, about this time, Adeline noticed that her husband had become extremely fussy about his grooming, dyeing his hair and whiskers and wearing belts and corsets. He was determined to stay handsome at any price.

He carried this cult of his person, a fault that he used to make fun of, to the minutest details. Adeline became aware that the Pactolus* which flowed to the houses of the Baron's mistresses had its source in her own home. During the last eight years a considerable fortune had been squandered, and so completely that, at the time of young Hulot's marriage, the Baron was forced to admit to his wife that his salary was their whole fortune.

'Where will that lead us?' asked Adeline.

'Set your mind at ease,' replied the Councillor of State. 'I'll turn my salary over to you, and I'll provide for Hortense's marriage settlement and our future by going into business.'

Madame Hulot's profound faith in the power and great merit of her husband, in his abilities and character, had calmed her momentary anxiety.

Now the nature of the Baroness's reflections and her tears after Crevel's departure can be readily imagined.

For two years the poor woman had known that she was at the bottom of an abyss, but she thought she was there alone. She had not known how her son's marriage had been arranged, she had not known about Hector's liaison with the greedy Josépha, and she had hoped that no one in the world knew of her sorrows. But if Crevel spoke so lightly of the Baron's dissipations, Hector would lose the high esteem in which he was held. From the vulgar talk of the annoyed ex-perfumer she could form an idea of the hateful scheming to which the young lawyer owed his marriage. Two fallen women had been the priestesses of that union which had been mooted at some orgy in the midst of the degrading liberties taken by two tipsy old men!

'So he's forgetting Hortense,' she thought, 'yet he sees her every day. Will he then try to find a husband for her amongst those good-for-nothings?'

At that moment, Adeline was dominated more by maternal than by conjugal feelings, for she could see Hortense with her cousin Bette, laughing with the unrestrained laughter of heedless youth, and she knew that this nervous laughter was a symptom no less alarming than the tearful reverie of a solitary walk in the garden.

Hortense resembled her mother, but she had golden hair, naturally wavy and remarkably thick. Her complexion was like mother-of-pearl. She was obviously the child of a true marriage, of a pure and noble love at its height. Her lively, mobile face, her laughing expression, her youthful animation, her fresh vitality, her abundant good health all seemed to vibrate and to radiate electric waves around her. Hortense attracted all eyes.

When her deep-blue eyes, with their pure, innocent look, fell on a passer-by, he would feel an involuntary thrill. And not one of the freckles, which are the price these golden blonds often have to pay for their milk-white skins, marred her complexion.

Tall, rounded but not too plump, with a slender figure and a noble bearing equal to her mother's, she deserved the title of goddess so lavishly used by the authors of antiquity. So no one who saw Hortense in the street could help exclaiming, 'My goodness, what a lovely girl!' She was so absolutely innocent that when she returned home, she would say, 'But Mama, what makes them all say, "What a lovely girl!" when you're with me? Aren't you more beautiful than me?'

And indeed, though she was over 47, the Baroness might be preferred to her daughter by lovers of sunsets. For, as women say, she had not yet lost any of her advantages—a rare phenomenon, particularly in Paris, where Ninon* was notorious in this respect, so much did she outshine the plainer women in the seventeenth century.

From thinking of her daughter, the Baroness's mind returned to the father. She saw him falling gradually, from day to day, into the dregs of society, and perhaps dismissed one day from the ministry.

The idea of her idol's downfall, together with a vague picture of the misfortunes prophesied by Crevel, was so painful to the poor woman that she lost consciousness, like someone in a trance.

9. *Character sketch of an old maid*

Cousin Bette, with whom Hortense was chatting, looked from time to time to see when they could go back to the drawing-room, but her young cousin was teasing her so much with her questions just as the Baroness re-opened the french window, that Bette did not notice her doing so.

Though Lisbeth Fischer was five years younger than Madame Hulot, she was the daughter of the eldest of the Fischer brothers. She was far from being beautiful like her cousin, and so she had been extremely jealous of Adeline. Jealousy was the fundamental feature of her character, full of *eccentricities*, a word invented by the English to indicate the follies not of ordinary but of great families.

A peasant woman from the Vosges in the full meaning of those words, thin, dark, with shiny black hair, thick eyebrows joined by a tuft of hair, long, strong arms, large feet, one or two warts on her long, monkey-like face—that, in brief, is a portrait of this spinster.

The family, who lived as one household, had sacrificed the plain girl to the pretty one, the sharp fruit to the brilliant flower. Lisbeth worked in the fields while her cousin was spoiled; and so it happened that one day, finding Adeline alone, the ugly girl tried to pull off the beauty's nose, a real Grecian nose, of the kind old ladies admire.

Although she was smacked for this misdeed, she continued none the less to tear the favourite's dresses and to spoil her collars.

At the time of her cousin's remarkable marriage, Lisbeth bowed to fate, as Napoleon's brothers and sisters bowed before the splendour of the throne and the power of commanding authority. When the almost too kind and sweet-natured Adeline was in Paris, she remembered Lisbeth and sent for her about 1809, with the intention of rescuing her from poverty and arranging a marriage for her.

As it was impossible to arrange a marriage immediately for this dark-eyed girl with coal-black eyebrows, who could neither read nor write, the Baron began by giving her a trade. He apprenticed Lisbeth to the embroiderers to the Imperial court, the famous Pons brothers.

The cousin, called Bette for short, having become an embroiderer in silver and gold, was energetic, as mountain people are, and had the courage to learn to read and write and do arithmetic; her cousin the Baron had convinced her that these skills were necessary if she wanted to run her own embroidery business. She was determined to make her fortune. In two years she was completely transformed. By 1811, the peasant girl had become a rather pleasing, skilful, and intelligent forewoman.

What was called the silver and gold embroidery trade included epaulettes, sword-tassels, and shoulder-knots, in short the countless brilliant decorations which glittered on the rich uniforms of the French army and on civilian formal dress.

The Emperor, with an Italian love of official garb, had gold and silver embroidered on the seams of the uniforms of everyone in his service, and his Empire contained a hundred and thirty-three departments. The supply of these trimmings, usually to wealthy and well-established tailors, or directly to high officials, was a reliable trade.

Just when Cousin Bette, the most skilful worker in the Pons establishment, where she was in charge of the workroom, might have set up on her own, the Empire collapsed. The olive-branch proffered by the Bourbons alarmed Lisbeth. She was afraid of a decline in her trade, which would now have a market of only eighty-six departments instead of a hundred and thirty-three, without taking account of the huge reduction in the size of the army.

Becoming alarmed at the various risks of the trade, she refused the offers of help from the Baron, who thought her mad. She justified her opinion by quarrelling with Monsieur Rivet, the purchaser of the firm of Pons, with whom the Baron had wanted to set her up in partnership, and reverted to being an ordinary worker.

By that time, the Fischer family had relapsed into the precarious situation from which Baron Hulot had rescued it.

Ruined by the disaster at Fontainebleau,* the three Fischer brothers, in desperation, served in the volunteer units of 1815.* The oldest, Lisbeth's father, was killed.

Adeline's father, condemned to death by court-martial, fled to Germany and died at Trier in 1820.

The youngest, Johann, came to Paris to beg for help from the queen of the family, who, they said, ate from silver and gold dishes and never appeared at receptions without wearing in her hair and round her neck diamonds as large as hazelnuts, that the Emperor had given her. Johann Fischer, then 43 years old, was given a sum of ten thousand francs by Baron Hulot to set up a little forage business in Versailles; this was obtained from the War Ministry through the secret influence of friends whom the former Head of Department still had there.

These family misfortunes, Baron Hulot's fall from office, a conviction of being of little importance in the immense turmoil of men, private interests, and public affairs which makes Paris both an inferno and a paradise, were too much for Bette.

Having become fully aware of her cousin's various kinds of superiority, Bette then gave up all idea of rivalry and comparison with Adeline. But envy remained hidden in the depths of her heart, like the germ of a disease which can break out and ravage a town if one opens the fatal bale of wool in which it is enclosed.

From time to time, however, she would say to herself, 'Adeline and I are of the same blood; our fathers were brothers; she lives in a grand house but I live in an attic.' Yet every year, on her birthday and on New Year's Day, Lisbeth would receive presents from the Baroness and the Baron. The Baron, who was very good to her, paid for her winter supply of wood. Old General Hulot had her to dinner once a week and her place was always set at her cousin's table. They made fun of her but they never blushed for her. In fact they had obtained independence for her in Paris, where she lived in her own way.

Bette, in fact, dreaded any kind of tie. If her cousin invited her to live with her, Bette would be aware of the yoke of domestic life. Many times the Baron had solved the problem of finding her a husband, but although attracted at first, she would soon refuse, afraid of being reproached for her lack of education, her ignorance, or her poverty. And if the Baroness suggested that she should live with their uncle and keep house for him, instead of his having a housekeeper who must cost a lot, she would reply that she was still less likely to marry in that situation.

Cousin Bette's ideas had the unusual quality that can be seen in very late developers and in savages, who think a lot and say little. Her peasant intelligence had, moreover, acquired a touch of caustic Parisian wit through her conversations in the workshop and her association with the workers, both men and women. This young woman, whose character was very much like the Corsicans', with no outlet for the instincts of a strong nature, would have loved to look after a man of weak character. But life in the capital had superficially changed her. The Parisian polish turned to rust on that strongly tempered spirit. Like all those dedicated to genuine celibacy, she was gifted with an insight that had become penetrating, and as she expressed her thoughts with a sharp wit, she would have appeared formidable in any other situation. With a malicious nature, she would have disrupted the most united family.

In the early days, when she nursed hopes that she confided to no one, she decided to wear corsets and follow the fashion, and so she had a moment of splendour when the Baron thought her marriageable. Lisbeth was, at that time, the piquant brunette of the old French romances. Her piercing look, her olive complexion, her slender figure, might have tempted a major on half-pay. But she was content with her own admiration, she would say, laughing.

In the end, however, she found her life a happy one after pruning it of all material cares, for she used to dine in town every day having worked from sunrise, and so she had to provide only for her lunches and her rent. She was also given clothes and many useful items of food, such as sugar, coffee, wine, and so on.

In 1837, after twenty-seven years of life half paid for by the Hulot family and her uncle Fischer, Cousin Bette, resigned to being a nobody, let herself be treated without ceremony. She herself refused to come to large dinner-parties, preferring the intimate family meals where her worth could be appreciated and she could avoid blows to her pride. Everywhere, at General Hulot's, at the young Hulots', at the home of Rivet (Pons's successor, with whom she had become reconciled and who made her very welcome), at the Baroness's, she was like one of the family.

Moreover, she knew how to conciliate the servants everywhere, by giving them little tips from time to time and always chatting with them for a few moments before going in to the drawing-room. This familiarity, by which she put herself frankly on the servants' level, won her the underlings' goodwill, something essential for parasites.

'She's a good, decent girl,' was what everyone said of her.

Her willingness to oblige, unlimited when it was not asked for, as well as her assumed good-nature, were, moreover, necessities of her position.

Seeing herself at everyone's mercy, she had come at last to understand life. As she wanted to please everyone, she would laugh with the young people, who liked her because she flattered them in a kind of ingratiating way which always took them in. She understood and championed their wishes; she became their go-between and seemed to them a good confidant, for she had not the right to scold them. Her absolute discretion earned her the confidence of people of mature years, for, like Ninon,* she had some masculine qualities.

Usually, confidences are made to those below us rather than to those above us. We employ our inferiors far more than our superiors in secret affairs, and so they become the accomplices of our inmost thoughts; they are present at our deliberations. Richelieu,* for instance, looked on himself as having reached the top when he had the right to be present at Council meetings.

The poor young woman was so dependent on everyone that she seemed condemned to absolute silence. The cousin called herself the family confessional. Only the Baroness, because of the ill-treatment she had received in childhood from her stronger though younger cousin, retained a certain mistrust. And then, out of shame, she would have confided her domestic sorrows only to God.

Perhaps here attention should be drawn to the fact that the Baroness's house had retained all its splendour in the eyes of Cousin Bette, who, unlike the parvenu trader in perfumery, did not notice the poverty displayed by the worm-eaten armchairs, the faded hangings, and the tattered silk. It is with our furniture as with ourselves. By looking ourselves over every day, we finally, like the Baron, think that we have not changed much, that we are young, when others see our hair becoming tufted like a chinchilla's, circumflex accents on our foreheads, and huge pumpkins on our stomachs. So for Cousin Bette, these rooms, still illuminated by the fireworks of the Imperial victories, were still resplendent.

With time, Cousin Bette had contracted some rather eccentric old maid's habits.

Thus, for instance, instead of following fashion, she wanted fashion to be adapted to her ways and fit in with her wishes, which were always out of date. If the Baroness gave her a pretty new hat, or a dress cut in the style of the day, Cousin Bette immediately took it home and altered it according to her own ideas and spoilt it, turning it into a garment in the style of the Empire period and of the clothes she used to wear in Lorraine. The thirty-franc hat became a limp rag and the dress was wrecked.

In this respect Bette was mulishly obstinate. She wanted to please no one but herself and thought she was charming dressed as she was. In fact, this style of dress, appropriate in that it turned her into an old maid from head to foot, made her so ridiculous that, with the best will in the world, no one could receive her at formal parties.

The stubborn, capricious, independent spirit and the inexplicable unsociability of this young woman, for whom the Baron had four times found a suitable match (a civil servant, a major, a provision merchant, and a retired captain), and who had refused an embroiderer (later to become rich), earned her the nickname of 'Nanny-Goat' which the Baron laughingly gave her. But this name corresponded only to her superficial eccentricities, to those different traits that we all display to each other in social life. A close observation of the young woman would have discerned the fierce side of the peasantry; she was still the child who wanted to pull off her cousin's nose, who, if she had not become more reasonable, would perhaps have killed her in a paroxysm of jealousy. Only her knowledge of the law and of the world enabled her to control that natural quickness of temper with which country people, like savages, pass from feeling to action.

And that, perhaps, is the whole difference between natural man and civilized man. The savage has feeling only, the civilized man has feelings and ideas. Moreover, the savage's brain receives, as it were, few impressions. He is then entirely at the mercy of the feeling that pervades him, while in the civilized man ideas descend into the heart, which they transform. The civilized man has a thousand interests, several feelings, while the savage accepts only one idea at a time. That is the cause of the momentary advantage of a child over his parents, an advantage which is no longer there once his desire is satisfied. In man in a state of nature, however, the cause persists.

Cousin Bette, the primitive woman from Lorraine, a little inclined to treachery, belonged to that class of characters which are more common among the masses than you might think, and may explain their behaviour during revolutions.

At the time when this story begins, if Cousin Bette had been willing to be fashionably dressed, if, like Parisian women, she had become used to wearing every new style, she would have been presentable and acceptable, but she remained as stiff as a poker. Now an unattractive woman counts for nothing in Paris. So the black hair, the beautiful stern eyes, the firm outlines of the face, the tough Calabrian-like* complexion, which made Cousin Bette a Giotto*-like figure, and which a true Parisian woman would have turned to her advantage, above all her strange dress, made her look so odd that sometimes she resembled those monkeys, dressed up as women, that the little Savoyard chimney-sweeps carry about.

As she was well known in the households united by family ties which she frequented, as she restricted her social activities to this circle, and as she liked being in her own home, her eccentricities no longer surprised anyone, and, out of doors, they disappeared in the crowded activity of the Paris streets, where people only look at pretty women.

10. *Bette's admirer*

Hortense's laughter at this moment was occasioned by a victory she had won over Cousin Bette's obstinacy. She had just surprised her into making a confession she had been trying to obtain for three years.

However secretive an old maid may be, one feeling will always break her resolution to say nothing, namely vanity.

For three years Hortense, who had become excessively curious about a certain subject, had been bombarding her cousin with questions, asked, however, in complete innocence. She wanted to know why her cousin had never married.

Hortense, who knew the story of the five rejected suitors, had constructed her own little romance; she thought Cousin Bette had a secret passion, with the consequence that there was a duel of bantering remarks.

Hortense would say, 'We unmarried girls', in talking of herself and her cousin. On several occasions Bette had replied jokingly, 'How do you know that I haven't an admirer?' Cousin Bette's admirer, real or imaginary, then became a subject of friendly teasing.

Finally, after two years of this petty warfare, the last

time Cousin Bette had come, Hortense's first word had been,

'How's your admirer?'

'Not so bad,' she had replied. 'Poor young man. He's not too well.'

'Oh, is he delicate?' the Baroness had asked with a laugh.

'Well, he is really. He's fair ... a coal-black girl like me can love only a moon-coloured blond.'

'But what sort of man is he? What does he do?' asked Hortense. 'Is he a prince?'

'Prince of the tool, as I am queen of the bobbin. Can a poor girl like me be loved by a property-owner with a house of his own and investments in State funds, or by a duke and peer, or by some Prince Charming out of your fairy-tales?'

'Oh, I'd love to see him,' Hortense had exclaimed with a smile.

'To know what sort of a man it is who can fall in love with an old nanny-goat?' Cousin Bette had replied.

'He must be an awful old clerk with a goatee beard,' Hortense had said, looking at her mother.

'Well, that's where you're wrong, Mademoiselle.'

'Oh, then you really have an admirer?' Hortense had asked triumphantly.

'As surely as you have not!' her cousin had replied in an offended tone.

'Well, if you have an admirer, Bette, why don't you marry him?' the Baroness had said, exchanging a glance with her daughter. 'For three years now he has been talked about. You have had time to get to know him, and if he has remained faithful to you, you ought not to prolong a situation which is burdensome to him. Besides, it's a matter of conscience and then, if he's young, it's time to acquire a prop for your old age.'

Cousin Bette had looked hard at the Baroness and, seeing that she was laughing, she had replied:

'It would be to marry hunger and thirst. He is a working man, I am a working woman. If we had children, they

would be working men and women. No, no, we love each
other in spirit. It's less expensive.'

'Why do you conceal him?' Hortense had asked.

'He wears a short jacket,' the old maid had replied,
laughing.

'Do you love him?' the Baroness had enquired.

'Oh, I do indeed. I love him for himself, the cherub. I
have held him in my heart for four years.'

'Well, if you love him for himself,' the Baroness had
replied seriously, 'and if he exists, you are doing him a
great wrong. You don't know what it is to love.'

'We all know that trade from birth,' said her cousin.

'No, there are women who love but who remain selfish,
and you're one of them.'

The cousin had bent her head, and her look would have
made anyone who had seen it shudder, but she had looked
at her bobbin.

'If you were to introduce your love-smitten suitor to us,
Hector might be able to find him a position and enable
him to make his fortune.'

'That's impossible,' Cousin Bette had said.

'But why?'

'He's a sort of Pole, a refugee.'

'A conspirator,' Hortense had cried. 'You *are* lucky!
Has he had adventures?'

'Well, he fought for Poland. He was a teacher in the
school whose pupils began the revolt, and as it was the
Grand-Duke Constantine* who appointed him, he cannot
hope for a pardon.'

'Teacher of what?'

'Art.'

'And he came to Paris after the defeat?'*

'In 1833 he crossed Germany on foot.'

'Poor young man. And how old is he?'

'He was barely 24 at the time of the insurrection. Now
he's 29.'

'Fifteen years less than you,' the Baroness had said.

'What does he live on?' Hortense had asked.

'On his talent.'

'Oh, does he give lessons?'

'No,' Cousin Bette had replied, 'he receives them, and hard ones at that!'

'And his first name, is it a nice one?'

'Wenceslas!'

'What imaginations old maids have!' the Baroness had cried. 'From the way you talk, anyone would believe you, Lisbeth.'

'Don't you see, Mama, that since he is a Pole, well used to the knout, Bette reminds him of that little luxury of his native land?'

All three had begun to laugh and Hortense had sung, *Wenceslas, idol of my heart*, instead of *Ô Matilda.**

For a few moments there had been a kind of armistice.

'These little girls, they think that only they can be loved,' Cousin Bette had said, looking at Hortense when she had come back beside her.

'Well, prove to me that Wenceslas isn't an invention, and I'll give you my yellow cashmere shawl.'

'But he's a count.'

'All Poles are counts.'

'But he's not a Pole, he's from Li . . . va . . . Lith . . .'

'Lithuania?'

'No.'

'Livonia?'*

'That's it.'

'But what's his name?'

'First, I'd like to know if you can keep a secret.'

'Oh, Cousin, I shall be dumb . . .'

'As a fish?'

'As a fish!'

'By your life in the world to come?'

'By my life in the world to come!'

'No, by your happiness in this world?'

'Yes.'

'Well, his name is Count Wenceslas Steinbock.'

'One of Charles XII's* generals had that name.'

'That was his great-uncle. *His* father settled in Livonia after the King of Sweden's death. But he lost his fortune in the 1812 campaign,* and he died leaving the poor child penniless at the age of 8. Grand-Duke Constantine took him under his wing, because of the name of Steinbock, and placed him in a school.'*

'I don't take back what I said,' Hortense had replied. 'Give me a proof of his existence, and my yellow shawl is yours. Oh, that colour is the best make-up for a dark skin.'

'You will keep my secret?'

'You shall have mine.'

'Well, the next time I come, I shall have the proof.'

'But the proof is your admirer,' Hortense had said.

11. *Conversation between an old maid and a young one*

Ever since she had arrived in Paris, Cousin Bette had been eaten up with admiration for cashmere shawls and had become obsessed with the idea of having the yellow cashmere shawl which the Baron had given his wife in 1808. In accordance with the custom in some families it had passed in 1830 from mother to daughter.

During the last ten years, the shawl had become very worn, but the precious material, still kept in a sandalwood box, seemed, like the Baroness's furniture, still new in the old maid's eyes. She had brought in her bag a present that she intended to give to the Baroness on her birthday, and which, so she thought, would prove the real existence of her strange lover.

The present was a silver seal, composed of three figures back to back, clothed in leaves and holding up the globe. The three figures represented Faith, Hope, and Charity. Their feet were resting on monsters which were tearing each other apart, and between them the symbolic serpent was wriggling. In 1846, after the great advance in the appreciation of the art of Benvenuto Cellini* made by Mademoiselle de Fauveau,* Wagner,* Jeanest,* Froment,* Meurice,* and others, and by wood-carvers like Liénard,* this masterpiece would surprise no one. But at that time, a young girl with a knowledge of jewellery must have been amazed as she handled the seal, after Cousin Bette had shown it to her, saying, 'Now, what do you think of that?'

The figures, in their outlines, their draperies, and their attitudes, were in the style of Raphael: their workmanship was reminiscent of the school of Florentine bronzes created by Donatello,* Brunelleschi,* Ghiberti,* Benvenuto Cellini, Jean de Bologne,* etc. In France, the Renaissance had fashioned no more fantastic monsters than those which symbolized the evil passions. The palms, ferns, reeds, and rushes surrounding the virtues were so effectively and tastefully arranged that they could have driven fellow-craftsmen to despair. A ribbon linked the three heads, and in the gaps between each of the heads, there was a W, a chamois, and the word *fecit*.

'Whose work is that?' asked Hortense.

'My admirer's,' replied Cousin Bette. 'There's ten months' work in it. I earn more by making sword-tassles. He told me that in German Steinbock means *animal of the rocks* or chamois. He plans to sign all his work like that. Oh, I'll get your shawl.'

'And why?'

'Can I buy such a trinket or have one made to order? It's impossible, so it must have been given to me. Who can give such presents? An admirer!'

Hortense, hiding her feelings in a way that would have frightened Lisbeth Fischer if she had noticed, took great care not to show the extent of her admiration; she experienced nevertheless the thrill felt by people who appreciate beauty when they unexpectedly see a flawless, perfect masterpiece.

'Really,' she said, 'it's very nice.'

'Yes, it's nice,' continued the old maid. 'But I prefer an orange cashmere. Well, my dear, my admirer spends his time making this type of work. Since his arrival in Paris he has made three or four little trifles of that kind; so much for four years' study and work! He has served as an apprentice to metal-casters, moulders, and jewellers.—Bah, hundreds and thousands of others have done the same thing. Monsieur tells me that in a few months now he'll be famous and rich.'

'So you do see him?'

'Of course! Do you think he's my invention? I told you the truth as we were joking.'

'And he loves you?' Hortense asked eagerly.

'He adores me,' replied her cousin, looking serious. 'You see, my dear, he has known only pale, insipid women, as they all are in the North. A dark girl, slim and young like me, has warmed his heart. But, *mum's the word*! You promised me.'

'He will have the same fate as the five others,' said the young girl, mockingly, looking at the seal.

'Six, Mademoiselle. I left one behind in Lorraine, who would bring down the moon for me, even now.'

'This one does better,' replied Hortense. 'He brings you the sun.'

'Where can you turn that into hard cash?' asked Cousin Bette. 'You need a lot of land to get the benefit of the sun.'

These bantering remarks, made in quick succession and followed by the sort of nonsense one can imagine, gave rise to the laughter which had intensified the Baroness's anxiety, for it made her compare her daughter's future with the present in which she saw her indulging in all the high spirits of her age.

'But to give you jewels that involve six months' work, must he not be under great obligations to you?' enquired Hortense, in whom this jewel aroused deep reflections.

'Oh, you want to know too much at once,' replied Cousin Bette. 'But listen, I'm going to bring you into a conspiracy.'

'Will I be in it with your admirer?'

Oh, you'd very much like to see him! But you know, an old maid like your Bette, who has been able to retain an admirer for five years, keeps him well hidden. So leave us alone. You see, *I* don't have a cat, or a canary, or a dog, or a parrot. An old nanny-goat like me must have some little thing to love and to fuss over, so I've got a Pole.'

'Has he got a moustache?'

'As long as these,' said Bette, pointing to a shuttle filled with gold threads. She always took her embroidery with her when she was out visiting and worked while waiting for dinner.

'If you go on asking me questions, I shan't tell you anything,' she continued. 'You're only 22 and you're more of a chatterbox than I am at 42, in fact nearly 43.'

'I'm listening. I'll be as silent as a graven image,' said Hortense.

'My admirer has made a bronze group, ten inches high,' continued Bette. 'It represents Samson tearing a lion apart, and he has put it in the ground and made it rusty so that anyone would think now that it's as old as Samson himself. This masterpeice is in the window of one of the antique shops in the Place du Carrousel, near where I live. Perhaps your father, who knows Monsieur Popinot, the Minister of Trade and Agriculture, and the Comte de Rastignac, could talk to them about this group as if it were a beautiful antique he had noticed in passing. It seems that these great personages are keen on that kind of thing rather than on our sword-tassles, and that my admirer's fortune would be made if they were to buy or even to come and look at that miserable piece of metal. The poor lad maintains they would take that silly trifle for an antique and give a lot of money for it. Then, if one of the ministers buys the group, my admirer will go and see him, prove that he made it, and have a triumphant success. Oh, he thinks he's at the height of fame. He's as proud as two new counts, that young man.'

'He's Michelangelo all over again. But though he's in love, he hasn't lost his wits,' said Hortense. 'And how much does he want for it?'

'Fifteen hundred francs. The dealer can't let it go for less, for he has to have a commission.'

'Papa is the King's commissioner at the moment,' said Hortense. 'He sees the two ministers every day at the Chamber. He'll look after the matter for you; I'll see to that. You'll be rich, Madame la Comtesse Steinbock.'

'No, my young man is too lazy. He spends whole weeks messing about with red wax and gets nowhere. Bah! He spends his life at the Louvre, or in the library looking at engravings and sketching them. He's an idler.'

And the two cousins chatted on jokingly.

Hortense laughed as one does when one forces oneself to laugh, for she was overcome by the love that is experienced by all girls, love of the unknown, a vague kind of love which becomes attached to a figure thrown up by chance, just as frost crystals cling to straws driven by the wind on to a window-sill.

For ten months she had fashioned a real person out of Bette's imaginary admirer, since, like her mother, she believed in her cousin's life-long celibacy. And for a week now, this shadowy creature had been Count Wenceslas Steinbock. The dream had a birth-certificate, the vapour had solidified and turned into a young man of 30.

The seal which she held in her hand, a kind of Annunciation in which genius glowed like light, had the power of a talisman. Hortense felt so happy that she began to suspect that Bette's story was true. Her blood was in a ferment and she laughed madly to put her cousin off the scent.

12. *Monsieur le Baron Hector Hulot d'Ervy*

'But I think the drawing-room door is open,' said Cousin Bette. 'Let's go and see if Monsieur Crevel has gone.'

'Mama has been very depressed for the last two days. The marriage they were talking about has presumably been broken off.'

'Oh, it can be re-arranged. The man in question is a councillor of the Royal Court. That much I can tell you. How would you like to be Madame la Présidente? Well, if it depends on Monsieur Crevel, he'll certainly say something about it to me and I'll know tomorrow if there's any hope.'

'Cousin, leave the seal with me,' said Hortense. 'I shan't

show it to anyone. Mama's birthday is not for a month yet. I'll give it back to you in the morning.'

'No, give it back to me. I must get a case for it.'

'But I'll show it to Papa, so that he can speak to the minister with some knowledge of what he's talking about, for men in authority must not compromise themselves,' she said.

'Well, don't show it to your mother, that's all I ask of you, for if she knew I had an admirer she would laugh at me.'

'I promise.'

The two cousins reached the boudoir door just as the Baroness had fainted and Hortense's cry was enough to revive her. Bette went in search of smelling-salts. When she returned, she found the mother and daughter in each other's arms, the mother soothing her daughter's fears and saying to her:

'It's nothing, it's just an attack of nerves. Here's your father,' she added, recognizing the Baron's ring. 'Don't on any account say a word to him about this.'

Adeline got up to meet her husband, intending to take him into the garden until dinner-time; she wanted to talk to him about the broken marriage negotiations, to make him discuss the future, and to try to give him some advice.

Baron Hector appeared, dressed in a style that was both parliamentary and Napoleonic, for it is easy to identify the Imperialists (men attached to the Empire) by their military bearing, their blue coats with gold buttons fastened up to the neck, and their black taffeta cravats. They have, too, an authoritarian gait acquired through the habit of despotic command resulting from the swift march of events in which they were involved.

It must be admitted that there was nothing about the Baron which smacked of an old man. His sight was still so good that he could read without glasses. His handsome, oval face, framed by whiskers (that were, alas, too black), had the mottled complexion which indicates a sanguine temperament, and his figure, controlled by a belt, was still what Brillat-Savarin* calls majestic. A noble, aristocratic manner and great affability disguised the libertine with whom Crevel had had so many jolly parties. He was indeed one of those men whose eyes light up at the sight of a pretty woman and who smile at all the good-looking ones, even those who pass them in the street and whom they will never see again.

'Did you speak, my dear?' asked Adeline, seeing that he looked rather careworn.

'No,' Hector replied, 'but I'm fed up listening to speeches for two hours without getting to a vote. They have battles of words in which the speeches are like cavalry charges that don't scatter the enemy. They have substituted words for deeds; which isn't much to the liking of people who are used to marching, as I told the Marshal when I left him. But it's quite enough to be bored on the ministerial benches. Let's enjoy ourselves here. Hello, old Nanny-Goat, hello, young one!'

He put his arm round his daughter's neck, kissed her, caressed her, sat her upon his knee, and placed her head upon his shoulder so that he could feel her golden hair on his face.

'He's irritated and tired,' Madame Hulot said to herself. 'And now I'll annoy him still more. I'll wait a bit. Are you going to stay in with us this evening?' she asked aloud.

'No, my dears. After dinner I must leave you, and if it weren't the day when Nanny-Goat, my children, and my brother come, you wouldn't have seen me at all.'

The Baroness picked up the newspaper, looked at the theatre announcements, and put down the sheet where she had read that *Robert le Diable** was on at the Opera. Josépha, who had gone from the Italian Opera to the French Opera six months before, was singing the part of Alice. These movements did not escape the notice of the Baron, who looked hard at his wife. Adeline lowered her eyes and went out into the garden; he followed her there.

'Well, what's the matter, Adeline?' he said, putting his arm round her waist and drawing her to him. 'Don't you know that I love you more than . . .'

'More than Jenny Cadine and Josépha?' she replied boldly, interrupting him.

'And who told you that?' asked the Baron, releasing his wife and drawing back a few steps.

'Someone wrote me an anonymous letter, which I burnt, and in it, my dear, I was told that Hortense's marriage fell through because of the financial difficulties we're in. As your wife, dear Hector, I would never have said a word. I knew of your liaison with Jenny Cadine; did I ever complain? But as Hortense's mother I must tell you the truth.'

After a moment's silence, terrible for his wife, whose pounding heart was beating audibly, Hulot unfolded his arms, grasped her in them, pressed her to him, kissed her on the forehead, and said with an emotional outburst of enthusiasm:

'Adeline, you're an angel and I'm a wretch.'

'No, no,' replied the Baroness, quickly putting her hand on his mouth to prevent him talking ill of himself.

'Yes, I haven't a sou at the moment to give to Hortense, and I'm very distressed. But since you open your heart to me in this way, I can pour into it sorrows that are overwhelming me. If your Uncle Fischer is in financial difficulties, it's I who am responsible. He has signed bills of exchange to the value of twenty-five thousand francs for me! And all that for a woman who deceives me, who laughs at me behind my back, who calls me an old *dyed cat*! Oh, it's terrible that it costs more to satisfy a vice than to feed a family. And it's irresistible. . . . I might promise you here and now never to go back to that abominable Jewess, but if she were to write me two lines, I would go, as one went into the firing line under the Emperor.'

'Don't worry, Hector,' said the poor woman in despair, forgetting her daughter at the sight of the tears which filled her husband's eyes. 'Look, I've got my diamonds. It's more important to save my uncle.'

'Your diamonds are worth barely twenty thousand today. That wouldn't be enough for old Fischer. So keep them for Hortense. I'll see the Marshal tomorrow.'

'Poor dear!' exclaimed the Baroness, taking her Hector's hands and kissing them.

That was the whole of her reprimand. Adeline was offering her diamonds, the father was giving them to Hortense. She thought this gesture sublime and she was powerless.

'He's the master; he can take everything here but he's leaving me my diamonds. He's a god.'

Such were the thoughts of this poor woman, who had certainly obtained more by her gentleness than another would have done by an outburst of jealous anger.

The moralist cannot deny that, generally, well-bred, very dissolute people are much more agreeable than the virtuous. Having crimes to compensate for, they seek indulgence in advance by being lenient with their judges' failings and have the reputation of being delightful. Although there are charming people amongst the virtuous, virtue thinks itself fine enough on its own, so that it can dispense with making any special effort. And then the genuinely virtuous (for we must except hypocrites) are nearly always a little unsure of their position. They think they have been cheated in the great market of life and they speak a little sharply, like people who claim to be misunderstood.

Thus the Baron, who reproached himself for ruining his family, displayed all his wit and seductive charm for the benefit of his wife, his children, and his Cousin Bette.

When he saw his son arrive with Célestine Crevel, who was nursing an infant Hulot, he was charming to his daughter-in-law. He showered her with compliments, a diet to which Célestine's vanity was not accustomed, for never was a daughter of the rich more commonplace or more completely undistinguished.

The grandfather picked up the little fellow, kissed him, and declared him to be delightful and lovely. He talked baby-talk to him, prophesied that the chubby youngster would grow taller than himself, slipped in some flattering remarks for his son Hulot, and handed the child back to the plump Norman girl employed to hold him.

So Célestine exchanged a look with the Baroness which

said, 'What a charming man!' Naturally she defended her father-in-law against her own father's attacks.

Having shown himself to be an amiable father-in-law and an indulgent grandfather, the Baron took his son into the garden to make some very sensible comments about the attitude he should adopt in the Chamber with reference to a delicate matter which had arisen that morning. The young lawyer was filled with admiration for the penetration of his father's views, he was touched by his friendly manner and above all by the almost deferential way in which the Baron seemed henceforth to want to treat his son as an equal.

The younger Monsieur Hulot was a typical example of the young men produced by the 1830 Revolution.* His mind was obsessed with politics, but he was reticent about his ambitions, concealing them under an assumed gravity, and very envious of established reputations. He expressed himself in long sentences instead of in those incisive remarks which are the jewels of French conversation. But his manners were good, though he mistook haughtiness for dignity.

Such men are walking coffins containing a Frenchman of former times; the Frenchman stirs from time to time and beats against his English container. But ambition holds him back and he resigns himself to suffocation. The coffin is always draped in black.

'Oh, here's my brother,' said Baron Hulot, going to receive the Count at the drawing-room door.

He greeted the probable successor of the late Marshal Montcornet and, taking him by the arm, led him affectionately and respectfully into the room.

This peer of France, who was excused from attending meetings of the legislature because of his deafness, had a handsome face, made expressionless by age and crowned by grey hair which was still abundant enough to seem flattened by the pressure of his hat. Small, thick-set, but gaunt in his later years, he wore his green old age in a sprightly manner, and since he was still full of energy which had no active outlet, he divided his time between reading and walking. His gentle ways were reflected in his pale face, in his bearing, and in the sincerity and good sense of his opinions. He never talked of war or military campaigns. He knew that he was too great to need assumed airs of greatness.

In drawing-rooms he limited his activity to an unremitting attention to the wishes of the ladies.

'You are all very merry,' he said, noticing the animation which the Baron had aroused in the little family gathering. 'Though Hortense isn't married yet,' he added, noticing traces of melancholy on his sister-in-law's face.

'That will come soon enough,' Bette shouted in his ear, at the top of her voice.

'That's just what *you* think, for you're a bad seed that refused to flower!' he replied, laughing.

The hero of Forzheim* was quite fond of Cousin Bette, for they had some things in common.

Without education, a man of the people, he owed his military fortune to his courage alone and his common sense took the place of quickness of wit. Completely honourable, with clean hands, he was ending his fine life happily, in the midst of his family, the centre of all his affections, and with no suspicion of his brother's still undisclosed misdemeanours.

No one enjoyed more than he did the pleasing sight of these gatherings, where no disagreement ever arose and where brothers and sisters reciprocated each other's affection, for Célestine had been accepted immediately as one of the family. The good Count Hulot even asked from time to time why Père Crevel did not come.

'My father's in the country,' Célestine would shout to him. This time he was told Père Crevel was out of town.

The gathering of her family, united by such genuine affection, made Madame Hulot think: 'This is the most secure kind of happiness, and who could take it away from us?'

When he saw his favourite, Adeline, the object of the Baron's attentions, the General teased him about it so much that the Baron, afraid of being thought ridiculous, transferred his compliments to his daughter-in-law. At these family dinner-parties she was always the object of his flattery and attention, for he hoped that, through her, he would bring Père Crevel round and make him abandon all his resentment.

Anyone looking at this domestic scene would have found it hard to believe that the father was in dire straits, the mother in despair, the son eaten up with anxiety about his father's future, and the daughter in the course of stealing an admirer from her cousin.

13. *The Louvre*

At seven o'clock the Baron, seeing his brother, his son, the Baroness, and Hortense all engaged in playing whist, left to go and applaud his mistress at the Opera. He took with him Cousin Bette, who lived in the Rue du Doyenné and always made the loneliness of that deserted neighbourhood a pretext for leaving after dinner.

Parisians will all admit that the old maid's caution was perfectly reasonable.

The existence of the block of houses alongside the old Louvre is one of those manifestations against common sense which the French love to make so that Europe should be reassured about the amount of intelligence bestowed on them and fear them no longer. Perhaps, without realizing it, we have hit here upon some political idea.

It will certainly not be irrelevant to describe this corner of present-day Paris. In the future it would be impossible to imagine it, and our nephews, who no doubt will see the completed Louvre, would refuse to believe that such a horror endured for thirty-six years, in the heart of Paris, opposite the palace where three dynasties, during the last thirty-six years, received the élite of France and Europe.

Anyone who comes to Paris, even for only a few days, notices, between the wicket-gate that leads to the Pont du Carrousel and the Rue du Musée, ten or so houses with decaying façades. Their disheartened owners carry out no repairs and they are the remains of an old quarter which has been in process of demolition since the day Napoleon decided to complete the Louvre. The Rue and the Impasse du Doyenné are the only streets in this dark, deserted block whose inhabitants are probably ghosts, for you never see anyone there. The pavement, much lower than the roadway of the Rue du Musée, is on the same level as that of the Rue Froidmanteau. Half-buried already by the raising of the square, these houses are permanently in the shadow of the tall galleries of the Louvre, which on that side are blackened by the north wind. The darkness, the silence, the icy blast, the low-lying cave-like site, all combine to make these houses seem like crypts, living tombs.

When one drives in a cab past this lifeless remnant of a district and looks down the narrow Rue du Doyenné, one's soul is chilled, one wonders who can live there, what must happen there after dark, when the lane becomes a haunt of criminals and when the vices of Paris, wrapped in the cloak of night, indulge themselves to the full.

The problems of the area, already alarming enough, become appalling when one sees that these so-called houses are bounded by a marsh on the Rue de Richelieu side, by a sea of heaped-up paving-stones on the Tuileries side, by little gardens and evil-looking hovels on the side opposite the galleries, and by expanses of hewn stone and demolitions on the side facing the old Louvre.

Henri III and his favourites,* looking for their breeches, Marguerite's lovers,* looking for their heads, must dance sarabands by moonlight in these deserted spots which are overlooked by the vault of a chapel, still standing, as if to prove that the Catholic religion, so deeply rooted in France, survives everything.

For nearly forty years now the Louvre has been shrieking through every gash in its ripped-up walls: 'Root out these warts from my face!' The authorities have no doubt recognized the utility of this cut-throats' den and the necessity of symbolizing, in the heart of Paris, the intimate alliance of poverty and luxury characteristic of the queen of capitals. So these cold ruins, in whose heart the legitimist newspaper* contracted the disease from which it is dying, the squalid hovels in the Rue du Musée, the boarded-over area ringed with stall-holders, may have a longer and more prosperous life than three dynasties.

Since 1823, the low rent of rooms in the houses destined for demolition had led Cousin Bette to establish herself there, in spite of the requirement, imposed on her by the state of the district, of being home before nightfall. This necessity, however, was in accord with the villager's habit, which she had retained, of going to bed and getting up with the sun, which enables country people to make considerable savings in heating and lighting. She lived, then, in one of the houses which, thanks to the demolition of the famous mansion formerly occupied by Cambacérès,* now had a view of the square.

14. *In which one can see that pretty women cross the libertine's path, just as dupes put themselves in the way of scoundrels*

Just as Baron Hulot had seen his wife's cousin to the door of her house and said, 'Goodbye, Cousin,' a small, slim, pretty, very smartly dressed young woman, exuding an expensive perfume, passed between the carriage and the door, to enter the same house.

Without any kind of premeditation, this lady exchanged a look with the Baron, simply to see the tenant's cousin. But the libertine experienced the keen impression felt momentarily by all Parisians when they encounter a pretty woman who fulfils what entomologists call their *desiderata*. Slowly and deliberately he put on one of his gloves before getting back into his carriage, so as to give himself an excuse for allowing his eyes to follow the young woman, whose dress was swaying agreeably over something other than those frightful, deceptive, crinoline petticoats.

'There's an attractive little woman whom I should be

very glad to make happy, for she would make me happy,' he said to himself.

When the unknown woman had reached the landing of the staircase which served the main body of the building fronting the street, she looked at the carriage entrance out of the corner of her eye, without actually turning round, and saw the Baron rooted to the spot with admiration and consumed by desire and curiosity. Such an event is like a flower which all Parisian women delight to smell when they find one in their path. Some women who are devoted to their duties, virtuous and pretty, come home quite out of humour if they have not collected their little nosegay in the course of their outing.

The young woman went quickly up the stairs. Soon a window of the second-floor flat was opened and she appeared, but in the company of a gentleman whose bald head and not at all angry look showed that he was her husband.

'How knowing and clever such young women are,' said the Baron to himself. 'That's her way of showing me where she lives. She's a little too quick off the mark, especially for this district. I must be careful.' He looked up when he had got into the milord, and then the husband and wife quickly withdrew, as if the Baron's face had the effect on them of the mythological Medusa's head.*

'They seem to know me,' thought the Baron. 'In that case, everything would be explained.'

In fact, when the carriage had gone back up the Rue du Musée, he leaned out to have another look at the unknown lady and found that she had returned to the window. Ashamed at being caught gazing at the hood which sheltered her admirer, the young woman retreated hastily.

'I'll find out from Nanny-Goat who she is,' the Baron said to himself.

The sight of the Councillor of State had produced a deep impression on the couple, as we shall see.

'But it's Baron Hulot. My office is in his department!' exclaimed the husband as he left the balcony.

'Well, Marneffe, the old maid on the third floor at the

end of the courtyard, who lives with that young man, must
be his cousin! Isn't it odd that we should find that out only
today, and by chance?'

'Mademoiselle Fischer live with a young man!' repeated
the clerk. 'That's porter's gossip. We mustn't speak so
lightly of the cousin of a Councillor of State who's the big
boss at the ministry. Anyway, come and have dinner. I've
been waiting for you since four o'clock.'

15. *The Marneffe household*

Madame Marneffe, a very pretty woman, was the natural
daughter of the Comte de Montcornet, one of Napoleon's
most famous lieutenants. A dowry of twenty thousand
francs enabled her to marry a minor official at the War
Ministry. Through the influence of the distinguished Lieutenant-General, a Marshal of France for the last six months
of his life, this pen-pusher had reached the unhoped-for
position of head-clerk in his office. But when he was on
the point of being made assistant-manager, the Marshal's
death had dashed the hopes of Marneffe and his wife to the
ground.

Master Marneffe's scanty means (Mademoiselle Valérie
Fortin's dowry had already vanished, partly in payment of
the clerk's debts, partly in the purchases a bachelor needs
to make when setting up house, but above all in the
demands made on it by a pretty woman accustomed in her
mother's home to luxuries she did not want to give up) had
obliged the couple to be economical in their rent. The
situation of the Rue du Doyenné, not far from the War
Ministry and the centre of Paris, appealed to Monsieur and
Madame Marneffe, who for about four years had been
living in the same house as Mademoiselle Fischer.

Master Jean-Paul-Stanislas Marneffe was the kind of
petty official who withstands the dulling of his faculties
thanks to the sort of power bestowed by depravity. This
thin little man, with wispy hair and beard, an unhealthy,
pale face that was more weary than lined, bespectacled eyes

with slightly reddened lids, of shabby appearance and even shabbier bearing, was the embodiment of the type that everyone imagines to be that of a man brought before the assize court for indecent behaviour.

The flat occupied by the couple, typical of many Parisian couples, gave the deceptive appearance of pseudo-luxury that is prevalent in many homes.

In the drawing-room, the furniture was upholstered in shabby cotton velvet, the plaster statuettes imitated Florentine bronzes, the chandelier, badly carved and merely painted over, had moulded glass sconces, and the cheapness of the carpet was explained after some time by the amount of cotton introduced by the manufacturer which had become visible to the naked eye. All these things, as well as the curtains which would have told you that the splendour of woollen damask does not last three years, proclaimed poverty like a poor man in rags at a church door.

The dining-room, badly cleaned by a single maid, had the nauseous appearance of a provincial hotel dining-room; everything in it was filthy and ill-cared for.

Monsieur Marneffe's room, rather like a student's, equipped with his bachelor bed and furniture, was faded and worn like himself and cleaned once a week. This horrible room, where everything was left lying about, where old socks were hanging on horsehair chairs whose floral patterns were outlined by the dust, clearly proclaimed a man who cared nothing for his home and who was always out and about, in gaming rooms, in cafés, or elsewhere.

Madame's room was an exception to the degrading slovenliness which dishonoured the public rooms, whose curtains were all yellow with smoke and dust, and where the child, evidently abandoned to his own devices, left his toys lying about everywhere.

Valérie's bedroom and dressing-room were in the wing of the house linking, on only one side, the section facing the street to the main building, which backed on to the courtyard of the neighbouring property. These rooms, with their elegant chintz hangings, rosewood furniture, and a carpet, proclaimed the pretty woman and, to be frank, almost the kept woman. On the velvet-covered mantelpiece stood a clock of the style fashionable at the time. There was a little cabinet quite well filled with trinkets and Chinese porcelain flower-baskets on expensive stands. The bed, the dressing-table, the wardrobe with a long mirror, the small settee, the obligatory knick-knacks, were in accordance with the styles and fancies of the day.

Although it was third-rate as far as richness and elegance were concerned, and everything was three years old, a dandy would have found nothing to object to, unless it was that this luxury had a middle-class stamp. Art, and the distinction which stems from the things that taste knows how to select, were totally lacking here. A doctor of social science would have detected the existence of a lover by some of those useless pieces of expensive jewellery which can come only from that demi-god who is ever-present though ever-absent in a married woman's establishment.

The dinner set before the husband, wife, and child, the dinner which had been delayed since four o'clock, would have revealed the financial crisis that this family was experiencing, for the table is the most reliable thermometer of wealth in Parisian households.

A soup made of herbs and bean-stock, a piece of veal with potatoes, swimming in brownish water which did for gravy, a dish of beans, and cherries of inferior quality, all served and eaten from chipped plates and dishes with miserable, non-resonant nickel cutlery—was that a menu worthy of this pretty woman? The Baron would have wept if he had seen it.

The dingy decanters could not hide the awful colour of the wine bought by the litre from the wine-merchant's on the corner. The table-napkins had been in use for a week.

In short, everything revealed a poverty without dignity, the indifference of both husband and wife to the family home.

On seeing them, the most ordinary observer would have said to himself that these two beings had reached that fatal moment when the necessity of living makes them look for some means of tricking their way out of their predicament.

Valérie's first remark to her husband will, in any case, explain the dinner's long delay, due probably to the self-interested devotion of the cook.

'Samanon is willing to take your bills of exchange only at 50 per cent and he requires an assignment of your salary as security.'

Poverty, still secret in the household of the head of the War Ministry and masked by a salary of twenty-four thousand francs, not counting bonuses, had thus reached its last stage with the clerk.

'You've *done* my boss,' said the husband, looking at his wife.

'I think so,' she answered, not at all taken aback by his green-room slang.

'What will become of us?' continued Marneffe. 'The landlord will take our furniture tomorrow. And your father takes it into his head to die without making a will! Upon my word, these Empire fellows think they're all immortal like their Emperor.'

'Poor father,' she said. 'He had no child but me. He was very fond of me. The Countess must have burnt the will. How could he have forgotten me, when, now and again, he used to give us three or four thousand-franc notes at a time?'

'We owe four quarters' rent, fifteen hundred francs. Is our furniture worth that amount? *That is the question!* as Shakespeare said.'

'Well, goodbye, my pet,' said Valérie, who had eaten only a few mouthfuls of veal, from which the servant had extracted the gravy for a gallant soldier returned from Algiers.* 'Desperate ills call for desperate remedies!'

'Valérie, where are you going?' cried Marneffe, barring his wife's way to the door.

'I'm going to see our landlord,' she replied, arranging her curls beneath her pretty hat. '*You* ought to try and get on good terms with that old maid if she really is the Director's cousin.'

16. *The artist's attic*

The ignorance of all the tenants in the same building about their respective social positions is one of the permanent features which are most indicative of the pace of Parisian life. But it is easy to understand that a clerk who goes to his office early every morning, comes home for dinner, and goes out every evening, and a woman addicted to the pleasures of Paris, may know nothing of the life of an old maid living on the third floor at the end of the courtyard of their building, especially when she has the habits of Mademoiselle Fischer.

Lisbeth was the first in the house to go for her milk, bread, and fuel; she spoke to no one and went to bed with the sun. She never received letters or visits and kept herself to herself.

She led an anonymous, insect-like existence, the kind one finds in some houses where, after four years, one learns that there is an old gentleman on the fourth floor who knew Voltaire, Pilastre du Rosier,* Beaujon,* Marcel,* Molé,* Sophie Arnould,* Franklin,* and Robespierre.

What Monsieur and Madame Marneffe had just said about Mademoiselle Fischer, they had learned because the district was so isolated, and also because their financial distress had established a relationship between them and the porters, whose good-will was so essential to them that they had had to cultivate it assiduously. Among the porters the old maid's pride, silence, and reserve had induced that exaggerated respect and formal relationship which indicate the veiled discontent of inferiors. Moreover, the porters thought themselves the equals, in kind, as they say at the Palace, of a tenant whose rent was two hundred and fifty francs.

As Cousin Bette's confidences to her young cousin Hortense were true, everyone will understand that, in some intimate conversation with the Marneffes, the porter had slandered Mademoiselle Fischer, thinking she was simply talking scandalous gossip about her.

When the old maid had taken her candle from the hands of respectable Madame Olivier, the porter, she stepped forward to see if there was a light in the windows of the attic above her flat.

At that hour, in July, it was so dark at the end of the courtyard that the old maid could not go to bed without a light.

'Oh, don't worry, Monsieur Steinbock is at home. He hasn't even been out,' Madame Olivier said knowingly to Mademoiselle Fischer.

The old maid did not answer.

She was still a peasant in that she did not care what was said by people far removed from her; and just as peasants see only their own village, she cared only about the opinion of the little circle in which she lived. So she went firmly upstairs, not to her own flat, but to the attic. And this is why.

At dessert, she had put fruit and sweets in her bag for her admirer, and she came to give them to him, exactly as an old maid brings back a titbit for her dog.

She found the hero of Hortense's dreams working by the rays of a little lamp whose light was increased by passing through a water-filled globe. He was a pale, fair young man, seated at a kind of bench covered with a sculptor's tools, red wax, chisels, rough-hewn pedestals, bronzes copied from models. He was wearing an overall and was holding a little group in modelling wax, at which he was gazing with the attention of a poet at work.

'Look, Wenceslas. See what I have brought you,' she said, placing her handkerchief on a corner of the bench.

Then she took the sweets and fruit carefully out of her basket.

'You're very kind, Mademoiselle,' replied the poor exile sadly.

'That will refresh you, my poor boy. You heat your blood working like this. You weren't made for such a demanding occupation.'

Wenceslas Steinbock looked at the old maid with an expression of amazement.

'Go on, eat,' she replied sharply, 'instead of staring at me like one of your sculptures when you're pleased with it.'

When he received this, as it were, verbal slap, the young man ceased to be amazed, for he then recognized his female mentor whose tenderness continually surprised him, so used was he to being ill-treated. Although Steinbock was 29 years old, like many fair men he appeared five or six years less, and looking at this young man, whose bloom had faded with the fatigue and hardship of exile, beside that wizened, hard face, one would have thought that nature had made a mistake in allocating their sexes. He got up and threw himself into an old Louis XV easy chair covered with yellow Utrecht velvet, as if he wanted to take a rest in it. The old maid then picked up a greengage and offered it gently to her friend.

'Thank you,' he said, taking the fruit.

'Are you tired?' she asked, giving him another.

'I am not tired by work, but tired by life,' he replied.

'What an idea!' she exclaimed, with a certain sharpness. 'Haven't you got a good angel who is watching over you?' she said, giving him the sweets and looking at him with pleasure as he ate them all. 'You see, I thought of you as I was dining with my cousin.'

'I know that, but for you, I would have been dead long ago,' he said, giving Lisbeth a look that was both caressing and plaintive. 'But, my dear lady, artists need distractions.'

'Oh, so that's the trouble!' she exclaimed, interrupting him, putting her hands on her hips and turning to him with flaming eyes. 'You want to go and lose your health in the dissipations of Paris, like so many workers who end up by dying in hospital! No, no, make a fortune for yourself, and when you have a steady income you can amuse yourself, my boy; then you'll have the means to pay for doctors and pleasures, rake that you are.'

On receiving this broadside accompanied by looks which

penetrated his being with a magnetic flame, Wenceslas Steinbock bowed his head.

If the most biting scandalmonger could have seen the beginning of this scene, he would already have realized the falsity of the slanders uttered by the Olivier couple about Mademoiselle Fischer. Everything in the tone, the movements, and the looks of these two people affirmed the purity of their private life. The old maid displayed the tenderness of a rough but genuine maternal feeling. The young man was like a respectful son who submitted to the tyranny of a mother.

This strange alliance seemed to be the result of a powerful will acting constantly on a weak character, upon that instability peculiar to Slavs which, though it endows them with heroic courage on the battlefield, makes their behaviour incredibly inconsistent and gives them a moral flabbiness. The causes for this ought to be studied by physiologists, for physiologists are to politics what entomologists are to agriculture.

'And if I die before I become rich?' Wenceslas asked gloomily.

'Die? . . .' exclaimed the old maid. 'Oh, I shan't let you die. I have life enough for two, and I'll give you an infusion of my blood, if necessary.'

When he heard that frank, impulsive outburst, Steinbock's eyes were suffused with tears.

'Don't be downhearted, my little Wenceslas,' continued Lisbeth, deeply moved. 'Listen, I think my cousin Hortense rather liked your seal. Well, I'll help you to sell your bronze group at a good price, you'll repay your debt to me, you'll do as you like, you'll be free! Come now, cheer up!'

'I shall never be able to repay you, Mademoiselle,' replied the poor exile.

'But why not!' asked the Vosges peasant woman, taking the Livonian's side against herself.

'Because you've not only fed, housed, and cared for me in my poverty, but, what's more, you've given me strength.

You've made me what I am; you've often been hard; you've made me suffer.'

'I?' said the old maid. 'Are you going to start your nonsense again about poetry and the arts, crack your fingers and stretch out your arms, talking about ideal beauty and your crazy Nordic notions? The beautiful is not worth as much as the material, and I am the material! You have ideas in your head? That's all very fine. And I, too, have ideas. . . . What's the use of having ideas if you don't make any use of them? People with ideas are not as far forward then as those with none but who know how to get going. . . . Instead of thinking of your daydreams, you must work. What have you done since I went out?'

'What did your pretty cousin say?'

'Who told you she was pretty?' asked Lisbeth sharply, in a voice like a jealous tiger's.

'Oh, you yourself.'

'That was to see the face you'd make! Do you want to go running after petticoats? You like women; very well, model them; translate your ideas into bronze, for you'll have to do without love affairs for some time, and especially without my cousin, my dear. She's not a fish for your net. That girl needs a man with an income of sixty thousand francs . . . and he's been found. Oh dear, the bed's not made,' she said, looking through to the other room. 'Oh, you poor dear, I forgot about you.'

The energetic spinster immediately took off her cape, hat, and gloves and, like a maid, she quickly made the little trestle-bed where the artist slept. The mixture of sharpness, even harshness, with kindness may explain the power that Lisbeth had acquired over this man whom she had made her own property. Does not life bind us by its alternation of good and bad?

If the Livonian had met Madame Marneffe instead of Lisbeth Fischer, he would have found his protectress always willing to oblige him; this would have led him into some murky, dishonourable path where he would have been lost. He certainly would not have worked; the artist in him would not have developed. So, although he deplored the old maid's fierce greed, his reason told him that her iron rule was better than the idle and precarious existence led by some of his compatriots.

Here is an account of the events that led to the alliance of this energetic woman and that weak man, a kind of reversal of roles which, they say, is not uncommon in Poland.

17. *An exile's story*

In 1833 Mademoiselle Fischer, who sometimes worked at night when she had a lot to do, about one o'clock in the morning smelt carbonic acid and heard the moans of a dying man.

The smell of charcoal and the death-rattle came from an attic above the two rooms of her flat. She assumed that a young man, who had recently come to the house and lived in the attic, was committing suicide.

She went quickly upstairs, forced open the door, pushing against it with her Lorraine peasant's strength, and found the tenant writhing on his trestle-bed in the convulsions of death throes. She put out the brazier.

With the door open, the air streamed in and the exile was saved. Then when Lisbeth had put him to bed like a sick man and he had fallen asleep, she could detect the causes of his suicide in the absolute bareness of the two attic rooms where there were only a rickety table, the trestle-bed, and two chairs.

On the table lay a paper with writing on it, which she read:

'I am Count Wenceslas Steinbock, born in Prelia, in Livonia. Let no one be blamed for my death; the reasons for my suicide lie in these words of Kosciusko; *Finis Poloniae*!*

'The great-nephew of a brave general of Charles XII* did not want to beg. My weak constitution debarred me from military service and yesterday I saw the last of the hundred thalers with which I came from Dresden to Paris. I leave twenty-five francs in the table-drawer to pay the rent I owe the landlord.

'Since I have no relations left, my death is of no interest to anyone. I beg my compatriots not to accuse the French government. I have not made myself known as a refugee; I have asked for nothing; I have not met any of the exiles; no one in Paris knows of my existence.

'I shall die as a Christian. My God forgive the last of the Steinbocks!

WENCESLAS'

Mademoiselle Fischer, deeply touched by the dying man's honesty in paying his rent, opened the drawer and found, in fact, five hundred-sou pieces.

'Poor young man,' she exclaimed, 'and with no one in the world to take an interest in him!'

She went down to her own room, fetched her work, and settled down to sew in the attic as she watched over the Livonian nobleman. You can imagine the exile's astonishment when he woke up to find a woman at his bedside; he thought he was still dreaming. As she sat making gold shoulder-knots for a uniform, the old maid had pledged herself to protect this poor boy whom she had admired as he slept. When the young Count was fully awake, Lisbeth put new heart into him and questioned him to find out what he could do to earn his living.

After Wenceslas had told his story, he added that he owed his situation to his acknowledged vocation for art. He had always wanted to be a sculptor, but the time that had to be devoted to study seemed to him too long for a penniless man, and at the moment he felt much too weak to engage in manual work or to undertake a big piece of sculpture.

These words were all Greek to Lisbeth Fischer. In reply, she told the unhappy exile that Paris offered so many opportunities that any determined man was bound to be able to make a living there. People of courage never failed to survive there if they possessed an adequate stock of patience.

'I am only a poor woman myself, a peasant, and yet I have been able to make myself independent,' she added in conclusion. 'Listen to me. If you are really willing to work seriously, I have some savings and I'll lend you, month by month, the money you need to live on, but to live carefully, and not go on the spree or running after women. You can dine in Paris on twenty-five sous a day, and I'll make your breakfast with mine every morning. Then I'll furnish your room and pay for any apprenticeship you think necessary. You'll give me proper receipts for the money I lay out for you, and when you're rich you'll pay it all back. But if you don't work, I shan't feel myself bound in any way and I shall leave you to your own devices.'

'Ah!' cried the unfortunate young man, who still felt the bitterness of his first contact with death. 'Exiles of all countries quite rightly look towards France as souls in purgatory look to paradise. What a nation it is, in which help and generous hearts are to be found everywhere, even in an attic like this! You will be everything to me, my dear benefactress, and I shall be your slave! Be my beloved,' he said, with one of those demonstrations of affection so characteristic of Poles, and for which they are, on the whole wrongly, accused of servility.

'Oh no, I'm too jealous. I'd make you unhappy. But I'd gladly be a kind of comrade,' replied Lisbeth.

'Oh, if you knew how keenly I longed for any being, even a tyrant, who'd bother about me, when I was struggling in the loneliness of Paris,' continued Wenceslas. 'I even longed for Siberia, where the Emperor* would send me if I went home! . . . Be my providence! . . . I'll work, I'll become better than I am, though I'm not a bad fellow.'

'Will you do everything I tell you to do?' she asked.

'Yes! . . .'

'Well, I adopt you as my child,' she said gaily. 'Here I am with a son risen from the dead. Well, let's begin. I'll go down and do my shopping. Get dressed. Come down and share my breakfast when I knock on the ceiling with my broom handle.'

18. *The adventure of a spider who finds in her web a beautiful fly that is too big for her.*

The next day Mademoiselle Fischer enquired from the manufacturers to whom she took her work about the profession of sculptor. By dint of questioning she managed to find out about the studio of Florent and Chanor, a firm which specialized in casting and engraving rich bronzes and luxurious silverware. She took Steinbock there in the capacity of an apprentice sculptor, a proposition which seemed odd, as they carried out the designs of the most famous artists there but didn't teach sculpture.

Thanks to her persistence and obstinacy, the old maid managed to get a job for her protégé as a designer of ornaments. Steinbock quickly learned to model ornaments and he invented new ones; he had the gift.

Five months after he had finished his apprenticeship as an engraver, he met the famous Stidmann, the principal sculptor of the firm of Florent.

At the end of twenty months, Wenceslas knew more than his master. But in thirty months, the old maid's savings, amassed little by little over sixteen years, had completely gone. Two thousand five hundred francs in gold! A sum that she had been planning to invest in an annuity, and represented by what? By a Pole's bill of exchange. So, to meet the Pole's expenses, Lisbeth was then working as she used to in her youth.

When she saw that she had a piece of paper in her hands instead of gold coins, she lost her head and went to consult Monsieur Rivet, who for fifteen years had been the adviser and friend of his chief and most skilful worker.

When they learned of this adventure, Monsieur and Madame Rivet scolded Lisbeth, said she was crazy, abused all refugees whose schemes to restore their nation endangered the prosperity of trade and peace at any price, and urged the old maid to obtain what in business is called guarantees.

'The only guarantee that that fellow can give you is his liberty,' said Monsieur Rivet finally.

Monsieur Achille Rivet was a judge at the Commercial Court.

'And it's no joke for foreigners,' he continued. 'A Frenchman stays in prison for five years and, after that, comes out, without paying his debts, it's true, for only his conscience can force him to do so and it never troubles him. But a foreigner never gets out of prison. Give me your bill of exchange. You will have it endorsed by my book-keeper. He will have it protested, sue you both, and, after a hearing, will obtain a judgement of imprisonment. When everything is in order, he will sign a defeasance. By doing this, your interest will go on growing and you will always have a loaded pistol at your Pole's head.'

The old maid allowed her affairs to be put in order in this way and told her protégé not to be worried by the legal proceedings, undertaken only to give guarantees to a money-lender who agreed to advance her some money. This subterfuge was due to the inventive genius of the judge of the Commercial Court. The innocent artist, with blind confidence in his benefactress, lit his pipe with the official documents, for, like all men who have sorrows or excessive energy to allay, he was a smoker.

One fine day, Monsieur Rivet showed Mademoiselle Fischer a file of papers and said: 'You have Wenceslas Steinbock bound hand and foot, and so effectively that in twenty-four hours you can put him in Clichy* for the rest of his life.'

On that day, the worthy and honest judge of the Commercial Court experienced the satisfaction which must be aroused by the certainty of having performed a bad good deed. Benevolence has so many different forms in Paris that this strange manifestation of it corresponds to one of its varieties.

Once the Livonian was entangled in the meshes of commercial proceedings, it was a question of getting him to pay, for the eminent tradesman looked on Wenceslas as a swindler. In his eyes, feeling, honour, and poetry were disastrous in business affairs.

In the interests of poor Mademoiselle Fischer, who, as he put it, had been fooled by a Pole, Rivet went to see the rich manufacturers whom Steinbock was leaving. It so happened that Stidmann was in Chanor's office when the embroiderer came to enquire about a man called Steinbock, a Polish refugee. It was this Stidmann who with the help of the remarkable Parisian goldsmiths already mentioned was bringing French art to its present perfection which enables it to rival the Florentine masters and the Renaissance.

'Whom do you mean by "a man called Steinbock"?' exclaimed Stidmann mockingly. 'Would it by any chance be a young Livonian I had as a pupil? You must know, Monsieur, that he is a great artist. They say that I think I'm the devil. Well, this poor fellow doesn't know that *he* can become a god.'

'Oh, good—though you speak in a very offhand way to a man who has the honour to be a judge at the Seine court.'

'Beg pardon, consul!' replied Stidmann, putting the back of his hand to his forehead.

'I'm very pleased to hear what you've just said. So this young man will be able to earn money?'

'To be sure,' said old Chanor, 'but he must work. He'd already have made quite a pile if he'd stayed with us. But there you are! Artists hate to be dependent.'

'They have a sense of their own worth and dignity,' replied Stidmann. 'I don't blame Wenceslas for starting out on his own, for trying to make his name and become a great man. That's his right. And yet it was a great loss to me when he left me.'

'There you are!' cried Rivet. 'Those are the pretensions of young men, just hatched from the university egg. But start by getting an income and look for glory afterwards!'

'You spoil your touch by picking up coin!' replied Stidmann. 'It's glory that makes our fortune.'

'What do you expect?' Chanor said to Rivet. 'You can't tie them . . .'

'They would eat the halter!' replied Stidmann.

'All these gentlemen', said Chanor, looking at Stidmann, 'are as capricious as they are talented. They are wildly extravagant, they have mistresses, they throw money out of the window, and they have no time left for work. They then neglect their orders and we go to workers who are nothing like as good as they are and who get rich. Then they complain of hard times, while, if they had applied themselves, they would have mountains of gold.'

'You remind me, old Père Lumignon,' said Stidmann, 'of that pre-Revolution bookseller who used to say: "If I could keep Montesquieu, Voltaire, and Rousseau very hard-up in my garret and keep their trousers in a cupboard, what good little books they would write for me; I'd make a fortune from them!" If fine works could be manufactured like nails, the street-porters would make them. . . . Give me a thousand francs and stop talking!'

The worthy Rivet returned home, delighted for poor Mademoiselle Fischer; she dined at his house every Monday and he would find her there.

'If you can make him work hard,' he said, 'you will be luckier than you were wise. You will be repaid, interest, expenses, and capital. This Pole has talent. He can earn his living. But lock up his trousers and shoes. Keep him from going to the Chaumière* and the Notre-Dame-de-Lorette quarter.* Keep him on a lead. Without these precautions, your sculptor will be a loafer, and if you knew what artists mean by *loafing*! Terrible things, indeed! I have just heard that they can spend a thousand-franc note in one day.'

This incident had a terrible influence on the domestic life of Wenceslas and Lisbeth.

The benefactress dipped the exile's bread in the absinthe of reproaches when she thought that her savings were endangered, and she often thought them lost. The good mother became a cruel stepmother. She scolded the poor boy. She pestered him, reproached him for not getting on with his work quickly enough and for choosing a difficult profession. She could not believe that red-wax models, little figures, designs for ornaments, or sketches could have any value. Then, sorry for her harshness, she would try to wipe out its effect by services and kind attentions.

After groaning at finding himself dependent on a shrew and dominated by a Vosges peasant, the poor young man was delighted by the caressing ways and maternal solicitude of one who cared only for the physical, the material side of life. He was like a wife who forgives a week's ill-treatment for the sake of the caresses of a brief reconciliation.

Mademoiselle Fischer thus acquired absolute control over Wenceslas' heart and mind.

The love of domination, whose germ had lain dormant in her old maid's heart, developed quickly. She could satisfy her pride and her need for action. Did she not have a human being all to herself, to scold, to guide, to flatter, to make happy, without any fear of a rival? The good and the bad side of her character came into play equally.

If at times she made a martyr of the poor artist, she made up for it by delicate attentions as charming as wild flowers. She enjoyed seeing him lack for nothing. She would have given her life for him; Wenceslas was sure of that. Like all noble hearts, the poor fellow forgot the bad things, the old maid's faults. She had, moreover, told him her life-story as an excuse for her roughness, and so he remembered only her acts of kindness.

One day, exasperated because Wenceslas had gone out to idle his time away instead of working, Mademoiselle Fischer made a scene.

'You belong to me!' she said. 'If you were an honourable man, you would try to pay back what you owe me as soon as possible.'

The nobleman, in whose veins the blood of the Stein-bocks was aroused, turned pale.

'Good heavens!' she said. 'Soon we'll have nothing to live on but the thirty sous that I, a poor woman, earn.'

The two, both poverty-stricken, with tempers aroused by the duel of words, became angry with one another. Then, for the first time, the poor artist reproached his benefactress with having snatched him from death to make him lead the life of a galley-slave, far worse than oblivion, where at least one was at rest, he said. And he spoke of going away.

'Go away!' cried the old maid. 'Ah, Monsieur Rivet was right!'

And she explained clearly to the Pole how in twenty-four hours he could be put in prison for the rest of his days. This was a crushing blow. Steinbock fell into a black depression and absolute silence.

The next night, hearing preparations for suicide, Lisbeth went up to her dependant's room and handed him the file of papers and a formal receipt.

'There, my child, forgive me!' she said, with tears in her eyes. 'Be happy, leave me, I torment you too much. But tell me that sometimes you will think of the poor woman who put you in a position to earn your own living. But there you are. It's because of you that I'm nasty. I might die, and what would become of you without me? That's why I'm so impatient to see you in a position to make things that can be sold. I'm not asking for my money back for myself, not at all. I'm afraid of your idleness that you call reverie, of your ideas which consume so many hours when you gaze at the sky, and I wish you had contracted the habit of working.'

This was said in a tone of voice and with a look, tears, and attitude which touched the noble artist to the core. He took his benefactress in his arms, pressed her to his heart, and kissed her on the forehead.

'Keep these documents,' he said almost cheerfully. 'Why should you send me to Clichy? Am I not imprisoned here by gratitude?'

This incident of their joint private life, which had occurred six months earlier, had made Wenceslas produce three items: the seal that Hortense was keeping, the group which had been sent to the antique dealer, and a magnificent clock which he was in the process of finishing, for he was putting the last screws into the model.

This clock represented the twelve Hours, beautifully portrayed by twelve female figures, leading each other on in a dance so wild and swift that three Cupids, mounted on a pile of flowers and fruit, could only grasp at the Hour of midnight as it passed, its torn cloak remaining in the hands of the boldest Cupid. The group was mounted on a round base beautifully decorated with fantastic animals. The time was indicated in a monstrous mouth opened in a yawn. Each hour was represented by appropriate symbols which were characteristic of the occupations usual at that time.

It is now easy to understand the kind of extraordinary attachment that Mademoiselle Fischer had conceived for her Livonian. She wanted him to be happy, yet she saw him wasting away, pining in his garret. The cause of this dreadful situation is understandable. The woman from Lorraine watched over the child of the North with a mother's tenderness, a wife's jealousy, and a dragon's skill. She thus arranged things so that any folly or dissipation was impossible for him, by always keeping him without money. She would have liked to keep her victim and her companion for herself, well-behaved as he was forced to be, and she did not understand the barbarity of this senseless desire, for she herself had become used to every privation. She loved Steinbock enough not to marry him and too much to give him up to another woman. She could not resign herself to being only his mother but realized the folly of thinking of the other role.

These contradictions, the fierce jealousy, the happiness of having a man quite to herself, all agitated the old maid's heart inordinately. She had been really in love for four years and she cherished the crazy hope of making this inconsequential, aimless life last for ever, though her persistence was bound to cause the ruin of the man she called her child.

The struggle between her instincts and her reason made her unjust and tyrannical. She avenged herself on the young man for the fact that she was neither young, nor rich, nor beautiful. Then, after each act of vengeance, she realized herself that she had done wrong and went to extremes of humility and tenderness. She could only think of making sacrifices to her idol after showing her power by hatchet blows. In fact it was Shakespeare's *The Tempest* in reverse, with Caliban master of Ariel and Prospero.

As for the unfortunate, meditative young man, with his noble thoughts and lazy inclinations, his eyes, like those of caged lions in the zoo, showed the desert that his protectress created in his soul. The forced labour that Lisbeth demanded of him did not satisfy the needs of his heart. His unhappiness was becoming a physical illness and he was dying without being able to ask for or obtain the money for a pleasure he often needed.

On certain days when he felt energetic, when the awareness of his unhappiness increased his exasperation, he looked at Lisbeth as a thirsty traveller, crossing a desert, must look at brackish water.

These bitter fruits of poverty and their cloistered life in Paris were savoured by Lisbeth as pleasures. And so she foresaw with terror that the slightest love-affair would snatch her slave from her. Sometimes she blamed herself for having by her tyranny and her reproaches forced this creative artist to become a great sculptor of little things, for having given him the means of doing without her.

The next day, these three existences, so truly wretched in such different ways, a despairing mother's, the Marneffe couple's, and the poor exile's, were all to be affected by Hortense's naïve passion and by the strange events that were to put an end to the Baron's unfortunate passion for Josépha.

19. *How couples separate in the thirteenth district*

As he was about to go into the Opera, the Councillor of State was struck by the rather gloomy appearance of that temple of art on the Rue Lepeletier, where he saw no gendarmes, no lights, no attendants, no barriers to hold back the crowd. He looked at the poster and saw written in gleaming letters the fateful words:

PERFORMANCE CANCELLED OWING TO INDISPOSITION

He immediately rushed off to Josépha's lodgings in the Rue Chauchet, for, like all the artists attached to the Opera, she lived in the neighbourhood.

'Monsieur, what do you want?' enquired the porter to his great surprise.

'Don't you know me any more?' replied the Baron anxiously.

'On the contrary, Monsieur; it's because I have the honour to recognize Monsieur that I ask him, "Where are you going?"'

A mortal chill seized the Baron.

'What's happened?' he said.

'If Monsieur le Baron were to go up to Mademoiselle Mirah's flat, he would find Mademoiselle Héloïse Brise-tout, Monsieur Bixiou, Monsieur Léon de Lora, Monsieur Lousteau, Monsieur de Vernisset, Monsieur Stidmann, and a number of pretty women reeking of patchouli,* who are having a house-warming party.'

'Then, where is . . .?'

'Mademoiselle Mirah? I'm not sure if I'd be doing the right thing to tell you.'

The Baron slipped two hundred-sou pieces into the porter's hand.

'Well, she's living now in the Rue de la Ville-l'Évêque, in a house they say the Duc d'Hérouville has given her,' whispered the porter.

Having asked for the number of the house, the Baron took a milord and alighted at one of those pretty modern houses with double doors where everything, even the gas lamps at the entrance, proclaims luxury.

The Baron, in his blue coat, with a white cravat, white waistcoat, nankeen trousers, shining boots, and well-starched shirt frill, looked to the porter of this new Eden like a belated guest. His bearing, his gait, everything about him, seemed to justify that opinion.

The porter rang and a footman appeared in the hall.

The footman, new, like the house, admitted the Baron,

who said to him in an imperial tone and with an imperial gesture, 'Send this card in to Mademoiselle Josépha.'

The discarded lover looked mechanically round the room he had been shown into and saw that he was in an ante-room, filled with rare flowers; the furnishings alone must have cost twenty thousand francs. The footman returned to the ante-room and asked Monsieur to wait in the drawing-room till the company left the dining-room and came in for coffee.

Although the Baron had been familiar with the undoubtedly extreme luxury of the Empire, whose products cost fabulous sums even though they did not last long, he was dazzled, dumbfounded, by this drawing-room whose windows looked on to an enchanting garden, one of those gardens manufactured in a month, with soil specially brought in and transplanted flowers, and whose lawns seem to have been produced by special chemical processes.

He admired not only the studied elegance, the gilding, the very expensive carving in the so-called Pompadour* style, the marvellous fabrics which any grocer could have ordered and bought for oceans of gold, but even more, those things that only princes have the discrimination to select, find, pay for, and give away: two pictures by Greuze* and two by Watteau,* two Van Dyck* portraits, two Ruysdaël* landscapes and two by Guaspre,* a Rembrandt* and a Holbein,* a Murillo* and a Titian*, two Teniers* and two Metzus,* a Van Huysum* and an Abraham Mignon,* in short, two hundred thousand francs' worth of superbly framed pictures. The frames were worth nearly as much as the canvases.

'Well, now you understand, old boy?' said Josépha.

She had tiptoed over the Persian carpets through a door that opened without a sound, and come upon her adorer in one of those dazes when the ringing in one's ears is so loud that one can hear only the knell of disaster.

The expression *old boy*, addressed to such an important government servant, depicts admirably the impudence with which these creatures abase even the greatest; it left the Baron rooted to the spot. Josépha, all in white and yellow, was so splendidly arrayed for the festivity that she could still shine, in the midst of this unbridled luxury, like a rare jewel.

'Isn't this lovely?' she went on. 'The Duke spent on it all his profit from selling shares in a company he floated. He's no fool, my little Duke! Only the great lords of the old families can change coal into gold like that. Before dinner, the lawyer brought me the purchase agreement to sign, including the receipt for the payment. What real aristocrats we have here: d'Esgrignon, Rastignac, Maxime, Lenoncourt, Verneuil, Laginski, Rochefide, La Palférine!* And as for bankers, there's Nucingen and du Tillet,* with Antonia, Malaga, Carabine, and Madame Schontz.* They all sympathize with your misfortune. Yes, old fellow, you are invited, but on condition that you drink immediately the equivalent of two bottles of Hungarian, Champagne, and Cape wine to bring you up to their level. We're all too tight here not to put off the Opera. My director is as drunk as a cornet-player. He's at the quacking stage.'

'Oh, Josépha!' exclaimed the Baron.

'How stupid explanations are,' she went on with a smile. 'Look, have you got the six hundred thousand francs that the house and furniture cost? Can you give me a certificate of entitlement to thirty thousand francs a year, which the Duke gave me in a white paper cone of sugared almonds? That was a nice idea!'

'What corruption!' said the Councillor of State, who in that moment of rage would have bartered his wife's diamonds to be in the Duc d'Hérouville's shoes for twenty-four hours.

'It's my profession to be corrupt!' she replied. 'Oh, what a way to take it! Why didn't you think of floating a company? Goodness me, my poor dyed pet, you ought to thank me. I'm leaving you just when you might squander your wife's future, your daughter's dowry, on me. . . . Oh, you're crying. The Empire is dying! I salute the Empire!'

She adopted a tragic pose and recited:

'They call you Hulot! I know you no more!'*

And she returned to the dining-room.

Through the door, as she opened it, came a gleam like a flash of lightning, the thundering roar of the orgy as it reached its climax, and the smells of a first-class banquet.

The singer turned round to look back through the half-open door and, seeing Hulot rooted to the spot as if he had been made of bronze, she took a step forward and came back into the drawing-room.

'Monsieur,' she said, 'I've given the Rue Cauchet rubbish to Bixiou's little Héloïse Brisetout. If you want to pick up your cotton night-cap, your boot-jack, your corset, and your moustache-wax, I have stipulated that they should be returned to you.'

This horrible jeer had the effect of making the Baron leave as Lot must have left Gomorrah, but without looking back like Lot's wife.

20. *One woman lost, one woman found*

Hulot went home, striding along like a madman, talking to himself; he found his family calmly playing the game of whist for two sous stakes that he had seen them begin.

When she saw her husband, poor Adeline thought there must have been some terrible disaster, some disgrace. She gave her cards to Hortense and led Hector into the same little room where, five hours earlier, Crevel had prophesied that she would experience the most shameful miseries of poverty.

'What's the matter?' she asked in alarm.

'Oh, forgive me, but let me tell you about the infamous way I have been treated.'

For ten minutes he poured out his fury.

'But, my dear,' replied his poor wife heroically, 'creatures like that don't know what love is, the pure and devoted love that you deserve. How could you, you who are so shrewd, hope to compete with a millionaire?'

'Dear Adeline,' exclaimed the Baron, taking his wife in his arms and pressing her to his heart.

The Baroness had poured balm on his vanity's bleeding wounds.

'To be sure, if you were to take away the Duc d'Hérouville's fortune, *she* wouldn't hesitate between us,' said the Baron.

'My dear,' Adeline went on, making a final effort, 'if you must have mistresses, why don't you do as Crevel does and take inexpensive women who are in a class that is satisfied with a little for a long time? We'd all benefit. I can appreciate your need, but I can't at all understand your vanity.'

'Oh, what a good and wonderful wife you are!' he exclaimed. 'I'm an old fool. I don't deserve to have an angel like you for my partner in life.'

'I'm quite simply my Napoleon's Josephine,' she replied with a touch of sadness.

'Josephine couldn't hold a candle to you,' he said. 'Come, I'm going to play whist with my brother and children. I must apply myself to my job as a family man, arrange a marriage for Hortense, and bury the libertine.'

These kindly words touched poor Adeline so deeply that she said:

'That creature has very poor taste to prefer anyone at all to my Hector. Oh, I wouldn't give you up for all the gold in the world. How can a woman leave you, when she has the good fortune to be loved by you?'

The look with which the Baron rewarded his wife's fanatical devotion confirmed her opinion that gentleness and submission were a woman's most powerful weapons. In this she was mistaken. Noble feelings carried to extremes produce results similar to those of the greatest vices. Bonaparte became Emperor by firing on the crowd two steps away from the spot where Louis XVI lost his crown and his head because he was not willing to shed the blood of a Monsieur Sauce.*

The next day, Hortense, who had put Wenceslas's seal under her pillow so as not to be separated from it while she slept, was dressed early and sent a servant to ask her father to come to the garden as soon as he got up.

About half past nine, the father, in response to his daughter's request, gave her his arm and they walked together along the quays by the Pont Royal to the Place du Carrousel.

'Look as if we're just taking a stroll, Papa,' Hortense said, as they passed through the gate to cross the immense square.

'Strolling here?' queried her father teasingly.

'We are supposed to be going to the museum, and over there,' she said, pointing to the stalls backing on to the walls of the houses at right angles to the Rue du Doyenné, 'there are antique dealers, pictures . . .'

'Your cousin lives there.'

'I know, but she mustn't see us.'

'But what do you want to do?' asked the Baron, finding himself about thirty steps from the windows of Madame Marneffe, who suddenly came into his mind.

Hortense had led her father to the window of one of the shops at the corner of the block of houses which go along by the galleries of the old Louvre and face the Hôtel de Nantes. She went into the shops and left her father outside gazing at the windows of the pretty little lady who, the previous day, had left her image imprinted on the old beau's heart as if to soothe the wound that he was about to receive, and he could not resist the idea of putting his wife's advice into practice.

'Let's fall back on nice little middle-class women,' he said to himself, recalling Madame Marneffe's adorable charms. 'That little woman will soon make me forget greedy Josépha.'

This is what happened simultaneously inside and outside the shop.

As he studied the windows of his new beloved, the Baron caught sight of her husband, who, brushing his frock-coat with his own hand, was obviously on the look out and seemed to be expecting to see someone in the square.

Afraid of being noticed and then recognized afterwards, the Baron turned his back on the Rue du Doyenné but only three-quarters round, so that he could glance down it from time to time. This movement brought him almost face to face with Madame Marneffe, who, coming from the quays, was turning the corner of the block of houses on her way home.

Valérie seemed rather startled at receiving the Baron's astonished look and she answered it with a prudish glance.

'Pretty woman!' exclaimed the Baron. 'One for whom a man would commit many follies.'

'Oh, Monsieur,' she answered, turning round like a woman who is making a desperate decision. 'You're Monsieur le Baron Hulot, aren't you?'

The Baron, more and more amazed, nodded his assent.

'Well, since chance has twice allowed our eyes to meet and I have the good fortune to arouse your curiosity or to interest you, may I tell you that, instead of committing follies, you ought to do justice. My husband's fate depends on you.'

'What do you mean by that?' asked the Baron gallantly.

'He's employed in your department, in the War Ministry, Monsieur Lebrun's section, Monsieur Coquet's office,' she replied, smiling.

'I feel prepared, Madame . . . Madame?'

'Madame Marneffe.'

'My dear Madame Marneffe, to do injustice for your lovely sake. . . . A cousin of mine lives in your house and I'll go and see her one of these days, as soon as possible. Come and make your request to me there.'

'Forgive me for being so bold, Monsieur le Baron, but you will understand how I dared speak to you in this way when I tell you that I have no one to turn to.'

'Aha!'

'Oh, Monsieur, you misunderstand me,' she said, lowering her eyes.

The Baron felt as if the sun had just gone in.

'I am in despair, but I am a virtuous woman,' she continued. 'Six months ago I lost my only protector, Marshal Montcornet.'

'Oh, you are his daughter?'

'Yes, Monsieur, but he never acknowledged me.'

'So that he could leave you a share of his fortune?'

'He left me nothing, Monsieur, for his will has not been found.'

'Oh, poor little woman! The Marshal died suddenly of apoplexy. But don't lose hope, Madame. We owe something to the daughter of one of the Empire's Chevaliers Bayard.'*

Madame Marneffe dropped a graceful curtsey and was as proud of her success as the Baron was of his.

'Where the devil was she coming from so early?' he wondered as he studied the swaying movement of her dress, to which she gave perhaps an exaggerated gracefulness. 'She looks too tired to be coming back from the baths and her husband is waiting for her. It's inexplicable and provides much food for thought.'

21. *The daughter's romance*

Once Madame Marneffe had gone into the house, the Baron wanted to know what his daughter was doing in the shop. Since he was still looking at Madame Marneffe's windows as he went in, he nearly bumped into a pale young man with sparkling grey eyes, dressed in a black merino summer coat and coarse twill trousers and with yellow leather gaiters over his shoes, who was dashing out of the shop like a madman. The Baron saw the young man run towards Madame Marneffe's house and go in.

As she slipped into the shop, Hortense had immediately noticed the famous group prominently placed in the centre and easily visible from the door.

Even apart from the circumstances in which she had learned of it, the girl would probably have been struck by this masterpiece because of what one can only call the *brio* of great works of art; she, herself, could certainly have posed in Italy for a statue of *Brio*.

Not all works of genius have to the same degree that

brilliant splendour which is apparent to everyone, even the ignorant.

For instance, some of Raphael's paintings, such as the famous *Transfiguration*, the *Madonna of Foligno*, the frescoes of the *Stanze* in the Vatican, do not instantly arouse admiration like the *Violin Player* in the Sciarra gallery, the *Portraits of the Doni* and the *Vision of Ezekiel* in the Pitti gallery, the *Christ carrying the Cross* at the Borghese, or the *Marriage of the Virgin* in the Brera in Milan. The *Saint John the Baptist* of the Tribune, *Saint Luke painting the Virgin* in the Academy at Rome, have not the charm of the *Portrait of Leo X* or the Dresden *Virgin*. Nevertheless, they are all of equal merit. Yet one can go even further. The *Stanze*, the *Transfiguration*, the monochromes, and the three easel pictures in the Vatican are sublime and perfect to the highest degree. But these masterpieces demand from even the most knowledgeable admirer a certain application, a careful study, before they can be completely understood, while the *Violinist*, the *Marriage of the Virgin*, and the *Vision of Ezekiel* enter our hearts spontaneously through the gateway of our two eyes and make a place for themselves there. We enjoy receiving them in this way without any difficulty. It is not the highest art, but it is the most enjoyable.

This fact proves that in the production of works of art there are the same elements of chance as in families, where there are children, fortunate in their gifts, who are born beautiful, without pain to their mothers; the world smiles on them and they are successful in everything they do. In short, there are fruits of genius as there are fruits of love.

This *brio*, an untranslatable Italian word which we are beginning to use, is a characteristic of youthful artistic works. It is the product of the vitality and boundless enthusiasm of young talent, a vitality which returns later at certain happy moments. But then that *brio* no longer comes from the artist's heart. Instead of thrusting it into his works like a volcano emitting flames, he submits to it, he owes it to circumstances, to love, to rivalry, often to hatred, and more often still to the requirements of a reputation to be maintained.

Wenceslas' group was to his future works what the *Marriage of the Virgin* is to Raphael's complete work, the first step of talent, taken with a matchless grace, with the enthusiasm and charming total commitment of childhood, its power concealed under the pink and white flesh whose dimples seem like echoes of the mother's laughter. It is said that Prince Eugène* paid four hundred thousand francs for this picture, which would be worth a million to a country where there are no Raphaels, but no one would give that amount for the most beautiful of the frescoes, though their value as works of art is much greater.

Hortense restrained her admiration as she calculated the amount of her young girl's savings. She assumed an air of casual indifference as she asked the dealer:

'How much is that?'

'Fifteen hundred francs,' replied the dealer, with a glance at a young man sitting on a stool in a corner.

The young man was struck dumb on seeing the living masterpiece created by Baron Hulot.

Hortense, alerted by the dealer's look, then recognized the artist by the flush that came over his face, pale with suffering; in his two grey eyes she saw the gleam of a spark lit by her question. She looked at his face, thin and drawn like that of a monk absorbed in asceticism. She was lost in admiration of the red well-shaped mouth, the small delicate chin, and the silky chestnut hair typical of Slavs.

'If it were twelve hundred francs,' she replied, 'I would tell you to send it me.'

'It's an antique, Mademoiselle,' commented the dealer who, like all his colleagues, thought he had said everything with this *nec plus ultra* of the antique trade.

'Excuse me, Monsieur, it was done this year,' she replied very gently, 'and I have come for the express purpose of asking you, if you agree to the price I have offered, to send us the artist, for we might be able to secure quite important commissions for him.'

'If he is to get the twelve hundred francs, what will I get

out of it? I am a dealer,' said the shopkeeper good-naturedly.

'Oh, that's true,' replied the girl with a scornful look.

'Oh, Mademoiselle, take it! I'll arrange things with the dealer,' exclaimed the Livonian, beside himself.

Fascinated by Hortense's sublime beauty and by her evident love of art, he added:

'I made the group. For ten days now I have been coming three times a day to see if anyone will recognize its worth and make an offer for it. You are the first to admire it. Take it!'

'Come with the dealer, Monsieur, in an hour's time. Here is my father's card,' replied Hortense.

Then, when she saw the dealer go into the back shop to wrap up the group in cloth, she added in a low voice, to the great surprise of the artist, who thought he was dreaming:

'In the interests of your future, Monsieur Wenceslas, don't show this card or mention your purchaser's name to Mademoiselle Fischer, for she's our cousin.'

The words 'our cousin' had a dazzling effect on the artist. He had a glimpse of Paradise at the sight of one of the Eves who had fallen from it.

He had been dreaming of the beautiful cousin Lisbeth had talked about as much as Hortense had been dreaming of her cousin's admirer, and when she came into the shop he had thought, 'Oh, if she could be like that!'

One can imagine the look the two lovers exchanged; it was like a flame, for virtuous lovers have not a shred of hypocrisy.

22. *Let girls have their way*

'Well, what on earth are you doing in there?' the father asked his daughter.

'I have spent my twelve hundred francs' savings. Let's go.'

She took her father's arm again, as he repeated. 'Twelve hundred francs!'

'Thirteen hundred, in fact. But you're going to lend me the difference.'

'And in that shop, what could you spend so much money on?'

'Ah, that's the point,' replied the happy girl. 'If I've found a husband, it won't be dear.'

'A husband, my girl, in that shop?'

'Listen, Papa. Would you forbid me to marry a great artist?'

'No, my child. A great artist, today, is a prince without a title. He has fame and fortune, the two greatest social advantages—after virtue,' he added rather sanctimoniously.

'Naturally,' replied Hortense. 'And what do you think of sculpture?'

'That's a very bad bet,' said Hulot, shaking his head. 'A sculptor needs powerful patrons as well as great talent. It's an art without a market today, when there are no people living in great splendour or with great wealth, no entailed mansions or estates. We can only house small pictures and statues, and so the arts are endangered by small-mindedness.'

'But a great artist who could find a market?' Hortense continued.

'That would solve the problem.'

'And who would be powerfully supported?'

'Better still!'

'And a nobleman?'

'What nonsense!'

'A count?'

'And a sculptor!'

'He has no money!'

'And he is counting on Mademoiselle Hortense Hulot's?' said the Baron ironically, with a searching look into his daughter's eyes.

'This great artist, a count who is a sculptor, has just seen your daughter for the first time in his life and only for five minutes, Monsieur le Baron,' Hortense replied calmly to her father. 'You see, yesterday, dear, kind Papa, while you were at the Chamber, Mama fainted. She blamed the faint on her nerves, but it was the result of some distress about the failure of an arrangement for my marriage, for she told me that to get rid of me . . .'

'She loves you too much to have used an expression . . .'

'. . . that is so unparliamentary,' continued Hortense, laughing. 'No, she didn't use those words, but I know myself that a marriageable daughter who doesn't get married is a very heavy cross for conscientious parents to bear. Well, she thinks that if an enterprising, talented man appeared, who would be satisfied with a dowry of thirty thousand francs, we should all be happy. In short, she thought it advisable to prepare me for the modesty of my future lot and to prevent me from indulging in dreams of too much grandeur. . . . That meant that my marriage has been called off, for there's no dowry.'

'Your mother is a very good, noble, and admirable woman,' replied her father, deeply humiliated, though quite pleased by this confidence.

'She told me yesterday that you were allowing her to sell her diamonds to provide for my marriage. But I'd like her to keep her diamonds and I'd like to find a husband. I think I've found the man, the suitor who answers to Mama's specifications.'

'There! On the Place du Carrousel! In one morning?'

'Oh Papa, *there's more behind this than you think*,'* she replied, teasingly.

'Well, come now, my little girl, tell your good father all about it,' he said coaxingly, hiding his anxiety.

Under promise of absolute secrecy, Hortense gave a brief account of her conversations with Cousin Bette. Then, when they arrived home, she showed her father the famous seal to prove how well-founded her conjectures were.

In his inmost heart the father admired the subtle skill of young girls when they act on instinct, and he appreciated the simplicity of the plan which an ideal love had suggested to an innocent girl in a single night.

'You're going to see the masterpiece I've just bought. They're going to bring it and dear Wenceslas will come with the dealer. The creator of a group like that is bound to make his fortune. But use your influence to get him a commission for a statue, and then rooms at the Institute.'

'How you do run on,' exclaimed her father. 'If you had your own way, you would be married as soon as it was legally possible, in eleven days.'

'Why wait eleven days?' she replied, laughing. 'Oh, I fell in love with him in five minutes, just as you fell in love with Mama at first sight. And he loves me; it's as if we had known each other for two years. Oh yes,' she said, in reply to a gesture of her father's, 'I read ten volumes of love in his eyes. And won't you and Mama accept him as my husband when it's proved to you that he's a genius? Sculpture is the greatest of the arts!' she exclaimed, clapping her hands and jumping up and down. 'Listen, I'll tell you everything.'

'So there's still more to tell?' her father asked, with a smile.

Her completely innocent chatter had quite reassured the Baron.

'A confession of the utmost importance,' she replied. 'I loved him before I knew him, but I've been madly in love with him since I saw him an hour ago!'

'A little too madly,' replied the Baron, delighted by the spectacle of this naïve passion.

'Don't punish me for confiding in you,' she continued. 'It's so wonderful to cry into one's father's heart: "I am in love, I am happy to be in love",' she went on. 'You will soon see my Wenceslas. His brow is suffused with melancholy. The sun of genius shines in his grey eyes. And how distinguished he looks! Is Livonia a beautiful country? What do you think? My cousin Bette marry that young man! She's old enough to be my mother! But it would be murder! How jealous I am of what she must have done for him! I can imagine that she won't be pleased at my marriage.'

'Look, my dear, let's not conceal anything from your mother,' said the Baron.

'I would have to show her the seal and I promised my cousin not to betray her confidence, for she says she's afraid of Mama's laughing at her.'

'You are scrupulous about the seal, but you steal your cousin Bette's admirer.'

'I made a promise about the seal, but I have promised nothing about the man who made it.'

Hortense's plan, of a patriarchal simplicity, fitted in remarkably well with the family's secretly difficult circumstances, and so the Baron, while praising his daughter for confiding in him, told her that from now on she must rely on her parents' discretion.

'You must understand, my child, that it's not for you to make sure that your cousin's admirer is a count, that his papers are in order, and that his behaviour proves him to be trustworthy. As for your cousin, she refused five proposals when she was twenty years younger, so she won't be an obstacle. I'll see to that.'

'Listen, Papa, if you want to see me married, don't speak to my cousin about our young man until the marriage contract is on the point of being signed. I've been asking her about him for the last six months. There's something about her I don't understand.'

'What's that?' asked her father, his curiosity aroused.

'Well, she looks hostile when I go too far about her admirer, even in fun. Make your enquiries, but let me paddle my own canoe. My confidence ought to reassure you.'

'The Lord said, "Suffer little children to come unto me!" You are one of those who come back,' replied the Baron with a touch of irony.

23. *An interview*

After lunch the dealer, the artist, and the group were announced. Her daughter's sudden blush made the Baroness first worried and then watchful, and Hortense's embarrassment, the ardour in her eyes, soon revealed the secret that was poorly concealed in her young heart.

Count Steinbock, dressed all in black, seemed to the Baron a very distinguished young man.

'Would you do a statue in bronze?' he asked, holding the group in his hand.

After admiring it with confidence in his own judgement, he passed the bronze group to his wife, who knew nothing about sculpture.

'Isn't it lovely, Mama?' Hortense whispered to her mother.

'A statue! . . . That, Monsieur le Baron, is less difficult to make than the arrangement of figures in a clock like this one, which Monsieur has been so obliging as to bring here,' the artist replied to the Baron's question.

The dealer was busy placing on the dining-room sideboard the wax model of the twelve Hours that the Cupids were trying to catch.

'Leave that clock with me,' said the Baron, astonished at the beauty of the work. 'I want to show it to the Minister of Home Affairs and the Minister of Trade.'

'Who is this young man you are so interested in?' the Baroness asked her daughter.

'An artist rich enough to exploit this model could get a hundred thousand francs for it,' said the antique dealer, looking knowing and mysterious as he noticed the looks of understanding that passed between the girl and the artist. 'He would need to sell only twenty copies at eight thousand francs, for each copy would cost about five thousand francs to make. But if each copy were numbered and the model destroyed, it would be easy to find twenty art-lovers, pleased to be the only ones to own the work!'

'A hundred thousand francs!' exclaimed Steinbock, looking in turn at the dealer, Hortense, the Baron, and the Baroness.

'Yes, a hundred thousand francs,' repeated the dealer, 'and if I were rich enough, I'd buy it from you myself for twenty thousand francs. For if the model is destroyed, the clock becomes a valuable property. But one of the Princes* would pay thirty or forty thousand francs for this masterpiece to decorate his drawing-room. A clock has never yet been made, by a real artist, which pleases both the ordinary man and the connoisseur, and this one, Monsieur, solves the problem.'

'This is for yourself, Monsieur' said Hortense, giving six gold coins to the dealer, who then left.

'Don't tell anyone in the world about this visit,' the artist said to the dealer, following him to the door. 'If you are asked where we took the group, say it was to the Duc d'Hérouville, the well-known collector who lives in the Rue de Varennes.'

The dealer nodded his assent.

'Your name is . . .?' the Baron asked the artist when he returned.

'Count Steinbock.'

'Have you papers that prove your identity?'

'Yes, Monsieur le Baron. They are in Russian and German but not legally authenticated.'

'Do you feel equal to undertaking a nine-foot statue?'

'Yes, Monsieur.'

'Well, if the people I'm going to consult are pleased with your work, I can get the commission for the statue of Marshal Montcornet for you. They want to erect it at Père-Lachaise, on his grave. The Ministry of War and the former officers of the Imperial Guard are giving quite a large sum so that we should have the right to choose the artist.'

'Oh, Monsieur, that would make my fortune!' said Steinbock, stunned by so much good luck happening all at once.

'Don't worry,' the Baron replied graciously. 'I'm going

to show your group and this model to two ministers, and if they think these two works are wonderful, your fortune's on the right path.'

Hortense squeezed her father's arm so hard that it hurt him.

'Bring me your papers and say nothing of your hopes to anyone, not even to our old cousin Bette.'

'Lisbeth?' exclaimed Madame Hulot, at last appreciating the ends though without understanding the means.

'I can give you proofs of my ability by making a bust of Madame,' added Wenceslas.

Struck by Madame Hulot's beauty, the artist had just been comparing the mother and daughter.

'Come, Monsieur, life can turn out very well for you,' said the Baron, completely won over by Count Steinbock's refined and distinguished appearance. 'You will soon learn that in Paris talent doesn't go unrewarded for long and that all steady work brings its reward.'

Hortense, blushing, handed the young man a pretty Algerian purse containing sixty gold coins. The artist, still with something of a nobleman's pride, responded to Hortense's blush with a flush of shame easy enough to interpret.

'Is this by any chance the first money you've received for your work?' asked the Baroness.

'Yes, Madame, for my artistic work, but not for my labour, for I have been a workman.'

'Well, let's hope that my daughter's money will bring you luck,' replied Madame Hulot.

And don't hesitate to take it,' added the Baron, seeing Wenceslas still holding the purse in his hand and not putting it away. 'We'll get the amount back from some important nobleman, perhaps from a prince who will repay us with interest in order to possess such a fine work.'

'Oh, I value it too much, Papa, to give it up to anyone, even the Prince Royal.'*

'I could make another group for Mademoiselle, prettier than this . . .'

'It wouldn't be this one,' she replied.

And as if ashamed of having said too much, she went into the garden.

'Well, I'll break the mould and the model when I get home,' said Steinbock.

'Come now, bring me your papers and you'll hear from me soon if you live up to my expectations, Monsieur.'

At these words, the artist was obliged to leave. After bowing to Madame Hulot and Hortense, who came in from the garden on purpose to receive his bow, he went for a walk in the Tuileries without the strength or the courage to return to his attic, where his tyrant would bombard him with questions and wrench his secret from him.

Hortense's lover imagined groups and statues by the hundred. He felt strong enough to cut the marble with his own hand, like Canova,* who was also not strong and had nearly died in the attempt. He was transformed by Hortense, who for him became a visible inspiration.

'Now then, what does this mean?' the Baroness asked her daughter.

'Oh, dear Mama, you have just seen our cousin Bette's admirer, who, I hope, is now mine. . . . But close your eyes. Pretend you know nothing about it. Goodness me! Here am I, who wanted to hide it all from you, about to tell you everything.'

'Goodbye, my dears,' said the Baron, kissing his wife and daughter. 'Perhaps I'll go and see Nanny and I'll learn a lot of things about the young man from her.'

'Papa, be careful,' said Hortense.

'Oh, my child, my dear child, the most cunning people on earth are always the innocent!' cried the Baroness when Hortense had finished telling her romantic tale, whose last chapter was that morning's adventure.

True passions have their own instinct. Put a gourmet in front of a dish of fruit, he will unfailingly, without even looking, take the best piece. Similarly, if well-bred girls are allowed to choose their own husbands and if they are in a position to have the man they select, they will rarely make a mistake. Nature is infallible. In this field, nature's work is called love at first sight. In love, first sight is quite simply second sight.

The Baroness's happiness, although concealed by her maternal dignity, was as great as her daughter's, for of the three ways suggested by Crevel of arranging a marriage for Hortense, the best, the one that most pleased her, seemed likely to succeed. In what had happened she saw an answer from Providence to her fervent prayers.

24. *In which chance, which often brings about true romances, makes things go so well that they cannot continue like that for long*

Mademoiselle Fischer's galley-slave, obliged nevertheless to return home, had the idea of hiding the joy of the lover beneath the joy of the artist, happy at his first success.

'Victory! My group has been sold to the Duc d'Hérouville, who is going to give me work,' he said, throwing his twelve hundred francs in gold on to the old maid's table.

As one might imagine, he had concealed Hortense's purse. He kept it close to his heart.

'Well,' replied Lisbeth, 'that's fortunate, for I was killing myself with work. You see, my child, that money comes in very slowly in the profession you've chosen, for this is the first you've received and you've been pegging away now for nearly five years. The amount is barely enough to pay back what you've cost me since I got the IOU which represents my savings. But don't worry, it will all be used for you,' she added, after counting the money. 'There's enough here to do for a year. If you continue like this, in a year you'll be able to pay your debts and have a good sum for yourself.'

On seeing the success of his ruse, Wenceslas embroidered his tale about the Duc d'Hérouville.

'I want to get you fashionably dressed in black and buy you some new shirts, for you must be well dressed when you go to see your patrons,' Bette continued. 'And then you'll need a bigger and more suitable flat than your horrible attic and it will have to be well furnished. How cheerful you are! You're quite changed,' she added, looking closely at Wenceslas.

'But they said my group was a masterpiece.'

'Well, so much the better. Make some more,' replied the unemotional, down-to-earth old maid, who was incapable of understanding the joy of success or of artistic beauty. 'Don't think any more about what is sold. Make something else to sell. You've spent two hundred silver francs, to say nothing of your labour and your time, on that wretched Samson. It will cost you more than two thousand francs to have your clock cast. Now, if you take my advice, you ought to finish those two little boys crowning the little girl with cornflowers. The Parisians will love that. I'll call in on Monsieur Graff, the tailor, before going to Monsieur Crevel's. Go up to your own room and let me get dressed.'

The next day the Baron, who had become infatuated with Madame Marneffe, went to see Cousin Bette. On opening the door, she was quite amazed to find him standing in front of her, for he had never come to visit her before. So the thought occurred to her: 'Could Hortense be after my admirer?' For the previous day, at Monsieur Crevel's, she had learned of the breakdown of the projected marriage to the councillor at the Supreme Court.

'What, Cousin, you here? This is the first time in your life you've come to see me, so it's certainly not for my beautiful eyes.'

'Beautiful! They are indeed,' replied the Baron. 'You have the finest eyes I've ever seen.'

'What have you come for? Really, I'm quite ashamed to receive you in such a hovel.'

The first of the two rooms which constituted Cousin Bette's flat was used as a sitting-room, dining-room, kitchen, and workshop. The furniture was that of a prosperous working-class home: straw-bottomed walnut chairs, a little walnut dining-table, a work-table, coloured prints in dark-stained wooden frames, muslin curtains at the windows, and a big walnut cupboard. The floor was well polished, gleaming with cleanliness, and there was not a speck of dust anywhere. But the prevailing tone was cold, a perfect Terborch* picture in every detail, even down to the grey effect produced by the wallpaper, once a shade of blue but now faded to off-white. As for her bedroom, no one had ever set foot in it.

The Baron took it all in at a glance, saw the stamp of mediocrity on everything, from the cast-iron stove to the kitchen equipment, and he felt a sickening revulsion, saying to himself; 'So, this is virtue!'

'Why have I come?' he replied aloud. 'You are much too astute a woman not to find out in the end, so I'd better tell you,' he went on, sitting down as he opened the pleated muslin curtains a little and looked across the courtyard. 'There's a very pretty woman in this house.'

'Madame Marneffe! Oh, now I see!' she said, understanding the whole situation. 'And what about Josépha?'

'Alas, Cousin, it's all over with Josépha. . . . I was dismissed like a lackey.'

'And you would like . . .?' asked his cousin, looking at the Baron with the dignity of a prude taking offence a quarter of an hour too soon.

'As Madame Marneffe is a very respectable lady, an official's wife, and you can visit her without compromising yourself,' continued the Baron, 'I should like to see you on neighbourly terms with her. Oh, don't worry, she'll have the greatest consideration for the cousin of Monsieur le Directeur.'

Just then, they heard the rustle of a dress on the stairs and the steps of a woman wearing dainty, soft ankle-boots. The sound stopped on the landing. After knocking twice at the door, Madame Marneffe made her appearance.

'Forgive me, Mademoiselle, for bursting in on you like this, but you weren't in when I came to see you yesterday. We are neighbours and if I'd known you were Monsieur le Directeur's cousin, I'd have asked you long ago to use your influence with him. I saw Monsieur le Directeur go in and so I took the liberty of coming, for my husband,

Monsieur le Baron, has told me about a report on the staff which will be presented to the minister tomorrow.'

She looked upset and agitated, but she had quite simply run upstairs.

'You don't need to be a petitioner, lovely lady,' replied the Baron. 'It's for me to ask the favour of seeing you.'

'Well, if Mademoiselle doesn't mind, come now,' said Madame Marneffe.

'Yes, go, Cousin. I'll join you presently,' said Cousin Bette discreetly.

The Parisienne was relying so confidently on Monsieur le Directeur's visit and on his understanding of the situation, that she had not only dressed herself suitably for such an interview but had dressed up her flat too. Since the morning, it had been decorated with flowers bought on credit. Marneffe had helped his wife clean the furniture and polish up even the smallest items, washing, brushing, dusting everything. Valérie wanted to be in fresh, bright surroundings in order to attract Monsieur le Directeur, and to attract him enough to give her the right to be cruel, to hold the prize out of reach like a sweet to a child, using all the resources of modern tactics. She had got the measure of Hulot. Give a Parisienne at bay twenty-four hours, and she would bring down a ministry.

A man of the Empire, accustomed to the style of the Empire, Hulot could know nothing of the ways of modern love, the new scruples, the different modes of conversation invented since 1830, in which the *poor, weak woman* succeeds in being considered the victim of her lover's desires, a kind of sister of charity tending wounds, a self-sacrificing angel.

This *new art of love* uses an enormous number of pious words to do the devil's work. Passion is a martyrdom. Lovers aspire to the ideal, to the infinite, and both parties want to become better through love. All these fine phrases are a pretext for being even more ardent in practice, more frenzied in the final surrender, than in the past. This hypocrisy, characteristic of our age, has debased the art of love. Lovers claim to be two angels but they behave like two devils if they have the chance.

Love did not have time for this kind of self-analysis between two campaigns, and in 1809 it achieved success as quickly as the Empire had done. But under the Restoration, the handsome Hulot, now a ladies' man again, had first consoled some old flames, fallen just then like extinguished stars from the political firmament, and had gone on, as an old man, to let himself be captivated by the Jenny Cadines and the Joséphas.

Madame Marneffe had positioned her guns in the light of her knowledge of the Director's past, which her husband had related to her in detail on the basis of information picked up at the office. As the posturings of modern love might have the charm of novelty for the Baron, Valérie had made her plans and, it must be said, the trial she made of her power that morning answered all her hopes.

Thanks to her sentimental, romantic, simpering manœuvres, Valérie obtained for her husband the post of assistant-manager and the Cross of the Legion of Honour, without promising anything.

This little war was not conducted without dinners at the Rocher de Cancale,* visits to the theatre, and many presents of mantillas, scarves, dresses, and jewels.

As the flat in the Rue du Doyenné was not good enough, the Baron planned to furnish one magnificently in a charming modern house in the Rue Vaneau.

Monsieur Marneffe obtained a fortnight's leave, to be taken in a month's time, in order to settle some business in his native province, and a bonus. He promised himself a little trip to Switzerland to study the fair sex there.

Although Baron Hulot was much occupied with his lady protégée, he did not forget his other protégé, the young man. The Minister of Trade, Count Popinot, loved the arts. He paid two thousand francs for a replica of the Samson group on condition that the mould would be broken so that his own copy and Mademoiselle Hulot's would be the only ones in existence. This group aroused the admiration of a prince, who was shown the model of the clock and ordered it on condition that it was to be unique; he paid thirty thousand francs for it.

The artists consulted, one of whom was Stidmann, gave their opinion that the author of these two works could undertake a statue. Marshal Prince de Wissembourg, Minister of War and President of the committee in charge of the fund for erecting a statue of Marshal Montcornet, at once called a meeting where it was agreed to entrust the work to Steinbock.

Comte de Rastignac, at that time Under-Secretary of State, wanted to have a work of the artist now acclaimed by his rivals and with a growing reputation. He bought from Steinbock the delightful group of two little boys crowning a little girl, and he promised him a studio at the government marble depot, situated, as everyone knows, at Le Gros-Caillou.

This was success, but success as it comes in Paris, that is to say, overwhelming, the kind of success that crushes those whose shoulders and loins are not strong enough to bear it—which, by the way, often happens. The newspapers and journals talked of Count Wenceslas Steinbock, though neither he nor Mademoiselle Fischer had the least idea of it.

Every day, as soon as Mademoiselle Fischer had gone out to dinner, Wenceslas went to the Baroness's house. He spent an hour or two there except on the day when Bette dined with the Hulots.

This state of affairs lasted for some days.

The Baron had had confirmation of Steinbock's rank and status, the Baroness was pleased with his character and manners, Hortense was proud of her approved love and of her suitor's reputation, so they no longer hesitated to speak of the projected marriage. In short, the artist was at the summit of bliss, when an indiscretion committed by Madame Marneffe put everything at risk.

This is how it happened.

25. Marneffe's strategy

Baron Hulot wanted his cousin to become friendly with Madame Marneffe so that he could have a spy in her household, and Lisbeth had already dined with Valérie. For her part, Valérie, wanting to be informed about the Hulot family, was very friendly to the old maid. So Valérie had the idea of inviting Mademoiselle Fischer to the house-warming of the new flat to which she was about to move.

The old maid, happy to find yet another house where she could go for dinner and greatly taken with Madame Marneffe, had become fond of her. Of all the people with whom she was on friendly terms, none had gone to so much trouble for her.

In fact Madame Marneffe, full of attentions for Mademoiselle Fischer was, as it were, in the same relation to her as Cousin Bette was to the Baroness, Monsieur Rivet, Crevel, and, in short, all who invited her to dinner. Above all, the Marneffes had aroused Cousin Bette's pity by letting her see their household's dire poverty, presenting it, as always, in the most favourable light: ungrateful friends whom they had helped, illnesses, a mother, Madame Fortin, from whom they had hidden her lack of means and who had died thinking herself to be still wealthy, thanks to their superhuman sacrifices, and so on.

'Poor souls,' she would say to her cousin Hulot, 'you are quite right to take an interest in them. They well deserve it, for they are so courageous, so good. They can barely live on an assistant-manager's salary of a thousand crowns a year, for they have got into debt since Marshal Montcornet's death. It's barbarous of the Government to expect an official who has a wife and family to live in Paris on a salary of two thousand four hundred francs.'

So a young woman who appeared to be very friendly to her, who told her everything, asked her advice, flattered her, and seemed to want to be guided by her, in a very short time became dearer to the eccentric Cousin Bette than all her relations.

For his part, the Baron, admiring in Madame Marneffe a decorum, a standard of education and manners that neither Jenny Cadine nor Josépha nor any of their friends had displayed, had, in a month, fallen in love with her with an old man's passion, a foolish passion that seemed to him quite sensible.

Indeed, here he found no derision, no orgies, no outrageous extravagance, no depravity, no contempt for the social proprieties, none of that absolute independence which had caused all his misfortunes with the actress and the singer. He was also spared the rapacity of the courtesan, whose thirst is as unquenchable as the desert sand's.

Madame Marneffe, who had become his friend and confidante, made a huge fuss about accepting the least thing from him. 'It's all very well to get promotions, bonuses, anything you can from the government. But don't start by impairing the honour of the woman you claim to love,' Valérie would say. 'Otherwise I won't believe you, and I would like to believe you,' she would add, giving him a sidelong glance, in the manner of Saint Teresa* casting her eyes up to heaven.

Every time he gave her a present, he had to storm a fortress, to violate a conscience.

The poor Baron would use all kinds of tricks to give her a trifling gift—which cost a lot, by the way—congratulating himself on discovering a virtuous woman at last, on finding the realization of his dreams. In this simple household (so he thought) the Baron was as much a god as in his own home.

Monsieur Marneffe seemed to be a thousand miles from thinking that the Jupiter of his Ministry intended to descend on his wife in a shower of gold,* and he behaved with obsequious servility to his august chief.

Madame Marneffe, 23 years old, a virtuous, timorous, middle-class housewife, a flower hidden in the Rue du Doyenné, could know nothing of the depravity and corruption of courtesans, who now filled the Baron with disgust. He had never before known the charms of a resisting virtue, and the timid Valérie enabled him to enjoy them, as the song says, *all along the river*.*

Once matters had reached this stage between Hector and Valérie, no one will be surprised to learn that Hector had told Valérie the secret of Hortense's approaching marriage to the great artist, Steinbock.

Between a lover who has no claims and a woman who does not easily bring herself to become his mistress, verbal and moral battles take place; thoughts are often betrayed in them by words which, like foils in a fencing bout, become as active as swords in a duel. The most prudent of men will then follow the example of Monsieur de Turenne.*

So the Baron had hinted at all the freedom of action that his daughter's marriage would give him, by way of reply to the loving Valérie who had more than once exclaimed:

'I cannot imagine that a woman could break her marriage vows for a man who would not be entirely hers.'

The Baron had already sworn a thousand times that *for the last twenty-five years* everything had been over between Madame Hulot and himself.

'They say she is so beautiful,' Madame Marneffe would reply. 'I want proofs.'

'You shall have them,' said the Baron, happy at this request which meant that Valérie was compromising herself.

'But how? You would have never to leave me,' Valérie had replied.

Hector had then been forced to reveal the plans he was making about the Rue Vaneau to prove to his Valérie that he was thinking of giving her the half of his life which belongs to a legitimate wife, on the assumption that the existence of civilized people is divided equally between night and day. He spoke of leaving his wife without scandal once his daughter was married. The Baroness would then spend all her time with Hortense and the young Hulots. He was sure his wife would comply with his wishes.

'From that time, my little angel, my true life, my real home will be in the Rue Vaneau.'

'My goodness, how you dispose of me!' replied Madame Marneffe. 'And my husband?'

'That decrepit creature!'

'Indeed, compared to you, that's just what he is,' she replied, laughing.

26. *A terrible indiscretion*

After hearing his story, Madame Marneffe had a burning desire to see the young Comte de Steinbock. Perhaps she wanted to obtain a piece of jewellery from him while they still lived under the same roof.

The Baron disliked this curiosity so much that Valérie swore never to look at Wenceslas. But when she had been rewarded for abandoning her whim by a complete little tea-service of old soft-paste Sèvres,* she kept her wish in the depths of her heart, like a note written in a memorandum.

So one day, when Valérie had asked *her* Cousin Bette to come and have coffee with her in her room, she turned the conversation towards Bette's admirer, so as to find out if she could see him without danger.

'My dear,' she said, for they called one another *my dear*, 'why haven't you introduced your admirer to me yet? Do you know that he's become famous in a very short space of time?'

'He! Famous?'

'But he's the talk of the town!'

'Oh, nonsense!' exclaimed Lisbeth.

'He's going to make my father's statue, and I'll be able to help him produce a successful work, for Madame Montcornet can't, as I can, lend him a Sain miniature, a masterpiece painted in 1809, before the Wagram* campaign, and given to my poor mother—in fact a young, handsome Montcornet.'

Sain and Augustin* held sway as the leading miniature painters under the Empire.

'My dear, did you say he was going to make a statue?' asked Lisbeth.

'Nine feet high. Commissioned by the Ministry of War. Really, where have you been that I'm the first to tell you the news? But the Government is going to give Comte de Steinbock a studio and living quarters at the Gros-Caillou at the marble depot. Your Pole will perhaps become the Director there, a post worth two thousand francs a year, a sinecure.'

'How do you know all that, when I don't know a thing about it?' said Lisbeth at last, emerging from her stunned amazement.

'Now, my dear little Cousin Bette,' said Madame Marneffe graciously, 'are you capable of a devoted friendship, proof against anything? Are you willing for us to be like two sisters? Will you swear to have no more secrets from me than I shall have from you? Above all, will you swear that you will never betray me, not to my husband, nor to Monsieur Hulot, and that you will never reveal that it was I who told you . . .?'

Madame Marneffe stopped short in her *picador*'s* onslaught. Cousin Bette frightened her.

The expression on the Lorraine peasant woman's face had become terrible. Her black, searching eyes were glaring like a tiger's. Her face had the look of a Pythoness* as we imagine it. She clenched her teeth to prevent them from chattering and a frightful convulsion made all her limbs tremble. She had inserted her half-closed hand between her bonnet and her hair to clutch it and support her head which had become too heavy; she was on fire! The smoke of the fire that ravaged her seemed to issue from the wrinkles of her face as if through fissures opened up by a volcanic eruption. It was an awesome spectacle.

'Well, why are you stopping?' she said in a hollow voice. 'I shall be for you all that I was for him. Oh, I would have given him my last drop of blood.'

'You loved him then?'

'As if he were my child.'

'Well,' continued Madame Marneffe, breathing more

easily, 'since you love him only in that way, you'll be very pleased, for you want to see him happy, don't you?'

Lisbeth replied with a quick nod, like a madwoman's.

'He's going to marry your little cousin, in a month.'

'Hortense,' cried the old maid, beating her brow and jumping up.

'Oh, so you're really in love with this young man?' asked Madame Marneffe.

'My dear, we are friends for life,' said Mademoiselle Fischer. 'Yes, if you have attachments, they will be sacred to me. Indeed, your vices will become virtues in my eyes, for I shall need them, I shall need your vices!'

'Were you living with him then?' exclaimed Valérie.

'No, I wanted to be his mother.'

'Oh, I don't understand this at all,' Valérie continued, 'for in that case you haven't been duped or deceived, and you ought to be very glad to see him make a good marriage. That sets him on the road to success. In any case, it's all over as far as you're concerned. Our artist goes to Madame Hulot's every day, as soon as you go out to dinner.'

'Adeline,' Lisbeth said to herself, 'oh, Adeline, you shall pay for this. I'll make you uglier than I am!'

'But you're as pale as death!' continued Valérie. 'So there's something the matter? Oh, what a fool I am! The mother and daughter must suspect that you would put obstacles in the way of this love affair, since they are acting behind your back,' she exclaimed. 'But if you weren't living with the young man, my dear, all this is more incomprehensible to me than my husband's heart.'

'Oh, *you* don't know,' continued Lisbeth. 'You've no idea of their underhand tricks. It's the last blow that kills! And how my soul has been wounded! You don't know that ever since I was old enough to feel, I've been sacrificed to Adeline. They smacked me and caressed her. I was dressed like a scullery maid, and she was attired like a lady. I used to dig in the garden and peel the vegetables, and she never lifted a finger except to arrange her finery. She married the Baron; she went to shine at the Emperor's court. But I stayed in my village till 1809, waiting for a suitable match for four years. They took me away from there, but only to make me a working woman and to offer me, as husbands, petty officials and captains who looked like porters. For twenty-six years I've had all their leavings. And now, it's like in the Old Testament; the poor man has one single ewe-lamb that is his joy, and the rich man with whole flocks covets the poor man's lamb and steals it from him, without telling him, without asking him for it. Adeline is robbing me of my happiness! Adeline! Adeline! I'll see you in the mud, fallen lower than I am! Hortense, whom I loved, has deceived me. The Baron . . . No, it's not possible. Come, tell me again what's really true in all this.'

'Calm yourself, my dear.'

'Valérie, my love, I'll be calm,' replied the strange woman, sitting down. 'Only one thing can restore my right mind: give me proof.'

'But your cousin Hortense owns the Samson group. Here is a lithograph of it published in a review. She paid for it with her savings and it is the Baron who, in the interests of his future son-in-law, is giving him a start and getting him all those commissions.'

'Water, water!' begged Lisbeth, after taking a look at the print and reading beneath it: *Group belonging to Mademoiselle Hulot d'Ervy*. 'Water! My head's on fire! I'm going mad!'

Madame Marneffe brought water. The old maid took off her bonnet, let down her black hair, and dipped her head in the basin which her new friend held for her. She bathed her forehead in it several times and checked the incipient inflammation. After this immersion she regained all her self-control.

'Not a word,' she said to Madame Marneffe, as she dried her face, 'not a word of all this. Look, I'm completely calm and it's all forgotten. I'm thinking of quite other things.'

'She'll be in Charenton* tomorrow, that's certain,' Madame Marneffe said to herself, looking at the Lorraine peasant woman.

'What am I to do?' continued Lisbeth. 'You see, my

darling, I must say nothing, bow my head, and go to the grave as water flows to the river. What could I try to do? I'd like to grind the lot of them, Adeline, her daughter, and the Baron, all to dust. But what can a poor relation do against a whole rich family? It would be the story of the earthenware pot against the iron pot.'*

'Yes, you're right,' Valérie replied. 'One must only try to get all the hay one can for oneself from the hayrack. That's life in Paris.'

'I'll soon die, anyway, if I lose that boy. I thought I'd always be a mother to him and I counted on spending all my life with him.'

She had tears in her eyes and she stopped. Such depth of feeling in this woman of fire and brimstone made Madame Marneffe shudder.

'But I have found you,' she said, taking Valérie's hand. 'That's a consolation in this great misfortune. We shall love each other dearly and why should we ever leave each other? I'll never poach on your preserves. No one will ever fall in love with *me*! All the men who were willing to have me were going to marry me because of my cousin's patronage. To have enough energy to scale the heights of Paradise and use it on grubbing for bread, water, rags, and a garret! Ah, that, my dear, is martyrdom! It has drained me.'

She stopped short and darted a black look into Madame Marneffe's blue eyes; it pierced that pretty woman's soul as the blade of a dagger would have transfixed her heart.

'But what's the use of talking about it?' she cried, reproaching herself. 'I've never said so much about it before. But *chickens will come home to roost*,' she added after a pause, quoting a nursery proverb. 'As you wisely say: let's sharpen our teeth and pull as much hay from the hayrack as we can.'

'You're right,' said Madame Marneffe, who was frightened by Bette's outburst and did not remember uttering the maxim. 'I think you have the right idea, my dear. After all, life is not that long; one must get as much as one can out of it and use others for one's own advantage. I've realized that myself, even though I'm so young. I was brought up as a spoiled child. Then my father married out of ambition and almost forgot about me, after idolizing me and bringing me up like a queen's daughter! My poor mother, who lulled me with the loftiest dreams from the cradle, died of grief when she saw me married to a petty official with a salary of twelve hundred francs, a cold-blooded rake at 39, as corrupt as a galleyful of convicts, a man who saw in me only what your suitors saw in you, a means of advancement! Well, in the end, I discovered that this unspeakable man is the best of husbands. Since he prefers the filthy street-corner sluts to me, he leaves me free. If he spends all his salary on himself, he never asks me how I get my income.'

Valérie, in her turn, stopped short, like a woman who feels herself being carried away by the torrent of her confidences, and, struck by the attention with which Lisbeth was listening to her, she thought it essential to make sure of her before revealing her most intimate secrets.

'You see, my dear, how much I trust you!' Madame Marneffe went on, and Lisbeth replied with a completely reassuring gesture.

Oaths are often sworn more solemnly with a look or a nod than they are in a court of law.

27. *Final secrets*

'I have all the outward appearance of virtue,' Madame Marneffe continued, laying her hand on Lisbeth's as if to accept her good faith. 'I'm a married woman and I'm my own mistress; so much so that if Marneffe feels like saying goodbye to me before he goes to the Ministry in the morning, and finds my bedroom door locked, he goes off quite unconcerned. He cares less for his child than I do for one of the marble children playing at the foot of one of the statues of the river gods in the Tuileries. If I don't come home to dinner, he dines very comfortably with the maid, for the maid is devoted to Monsieur. And every evening, after dinner, he goes out and doesn't come home till twelve or one. Unfortunately, for the last year I have had no personal maid, which means that for a year I have been a widow. . . . I have had only one real love, one happiness. . . . He was a rich Brazilian, who went away a year ago, my only lapse! He went to sell his property, to realize all his assets so that he could settle in France. What will he find left of his Valérie? Filthy scum! Bah! That will be his fault, not mine. Why is he so long in coming back? Perhaps he has been shipwrecked too, like my virtue.'

'Goodbye, my dear,' Lisbeth said abruptly. 'We shall never separate. I love and esteem you, and I am at your disposal. My cousin has been badgering me to go and live in the house you're going to have in the Rue Vaneau. I didn't want to go, for I easily guessed the reason for this new act of kindness.'

'Oh, yes, you would have kept an eye on me. I'm well aware of that,' said Madame Marneffe.

'It's certainly the reason for his generosity,' replied Lisbeth. 'In Paris, half the good turns are speculations, just as half the manifestations of ingratitude are acts of vengeance! . . . Poor relations are treated like rats who are given a scrap of bacon. I shall take up the Baron's offer, for this house has become hateful to me. Anyway, we're both smart enough to know how to keep quiet about things that would harm us, and to say what has to be said. So be discreet, and a friendship . . .'

'Through thick and thin!' cried Madame Marneffe joyfully, delighted to have a guarantor of respectability, a confidant, a kind of honest aunt. 'Do you know? The Baron is doing things handsomely at the Rue Vaneau.'

'I well believe it,' replied Lisbeth. 'He's spent up to thirty thousand francs; I can't think where he got them from, for Josépha, the singer, had bled him white. Oh, you've landed on your feet,' she added. 'The Baron would steal for the woman who holds his heart between two smooth, little white hands like yours.'

'Well, my dear,' Madame Marneffe went on with a courtesan's confident generosity, which is really a lack of concern, 'just take anything you like from here, anything you like for your new home . . . the chest, the wardrobe with the mirror, the carpet, the curtains.'

Lisbeth's eyes dilated with inordinate delight. She hardly dared believe in the reality of such a gift.

'You do more for me in one moment than my rich relations have done in thirty years,' she exclaimed. 'They never asked themselves whether I had any furniture! Some weeks ago, on his first visit, the Baron pulled a rich man's face at the sight of my poverty. Well, thank you, my dear. I'll repay you for this. You'll see later how.'

Valérie saw her Cousin Bette out on to the landing, where the two women kissed.

'How she reeks of penny-pinching industry,' the pretty woman said to herself. 'I shan't kiss her often, that cousin of mine. Yet I must be careful; I must humour her. She'll be very useful to me; she'll help me make my fortune.'

Like a true Parisian créole, Madame Marneffe hated having to exert herself. She had the indifference of a cat which runs and pounces only when forced to by necessity. In her eyes, life should be all pleasure and pleasure should be easily obtainable. She loved flowers, provided someone sent them to her. She could not conceive of going to the theatre without a good box at her disposal and a carriage to take her there.

These courtesan's tastes Valérie learned from her mother who had been loaded with presents by General Montcornet during his visits to Paris and who, for twenty years, had seen the world at her feet. An extravagant spendthrift, she had squandered her wealth and consumed it all in that life of luxury whose recipe has been lost since the fall of Napoleon.

The notables of the Empire, in their follies, were as bad as the great noblemen of former times. Under the Restoration, the aristocracy never forgot that they had been defeated and robbed, and so, with a few exceptions, they became economical, prudent, and careful, in a word, middle-class and devoid of grandeur. Since then, 1830* has completed the work of 1793.* In France, from now on, there will be great names but no more great families, unless there are political changes which are difficult to foresee. Everything bears the stamp of the individual. The fortune of the most prudent lasts only for a lifetime. The family has been destroyed.

The powerful grip of poverty which was oppressing Valérie's heart on the day when, as Marneffe put it, she had *done* Hulot, had made that young woman decide to use her beauty as a means of fortune. So, for some days, she had, like her mother, felt the need of a devoted friend, to whom she could confide what must be hidden from a maid and who could take action, come and go, and think on her behalf, in short a tool, ready to accept an unequal share in life.

Just as much as Lisbeth, she had understood the Baron's purpose in wanting her to become friendly with Cousin Bette. With the formidable insight of the Parisian créole who spends her time lying on a sofa, turning the lantern of her observation on all the dark corners of human hearts, feelings, and intrigues, she had hit on the idea of turning the spy into an accomplice.

Her terrible indiscretion was probably premeditated. She had recognized the true character of the fiery spinster, deprived of an outlet for her passionate nature, and she wanted to make an ally of her. This conversation was, then, like the stone a traveller throws into a gully in order to ascertain its depths. And Madame Marneffe had been appalled to find both an Iago and a Richard III* in an old maid who was apparently so weak, so humble, and so inoffensive.

28. *Bette's transformation*

In a moment Cousin Bette had become her true self again. In a moment her untamed Corsican nature, having broken the fragile bonds that restrained it, had regained its threatening stature, like the branch of a tree slipping from the grasp of a child who has bent it down to steal the unripe fruit.

To any observer of society, the abundance and perfection of ideas in virgin natures, and the speed with which they are conceived, will always be a source of amazement.

Virginity, like all abnormalities, has its special richness, its own absorbing grandeur. Life, in a virgin, husbands its forces and takes on an incalculable quality of resistance and endurance. The brain, as a whole, has been enriched by the sum total of its unexpended faculties. When chaste people need their bodies or their minds, when they resort to deed or thought, they find that their muscles are of steel or that their minds have been infused with intuitive wisdom; they have diabolical strength or the black magic of the will.

In this respect, the Virgin Mary, to consider her for a moment just as a symbol, eclipses in her greatness all the Hindu, Egyptian, or Greek types of deity. Virginity, the mother of great things, *magna parens rerum*,* holds the key to higher worlds in her beautiful white hands. In short, this grand and awe-inspiring exception deserves all the honours that the Catholic Church bestows upon her.

In a moment, then, Cousin Bette became the Mohican* whose snares are inescapable, whose deceit is impenetrable, and whose swift decisions are based on the incredible perfection of his sense organs. She was the embodiment of uncompromising hatred and vengeance as they are found in Italy, in Spain, and in the East. These two emotions, which are coupled with friendship and love pushed to extremes, are known only in sun-drenched lands. But above all, Lisbeth was a daughter of Lorraine, that is to say, bent on deceiving.

She did not undertake the last part of her role willingly; she made a strange attempt, as a result of her extreme ignorance. She imagined that prison was what all children imagine it to be. She confused solitary confinement with imprisonment. Solitary confinement is the strictest kind of imprisonment and is the prerogative of criminal justice.

On leaving Madame Marneffe, Lisbeth hurried to Monsieur Rivet's and found him in his office.

'Well, my dear Monsieur Rivet,' she said, after locking the office door, 'you were right. Those Poles—they're utter rotters—quite lawless and unprincipled, the lot of them.'

'Men who want to set Europe on fire,' said the peace-loving Rivet, 'to ruin all trade and businessmen for a country which, they say, is all swamp, full of frightful Jews, not to mention the Cossacks and peasants, varieties of wild beasts wrongly classed with humankind. These Poles misunderstand the present age. We're not barbarians any more. War is no longer an option, my dear lady. It went out with the kings. Our age has seen the triumph of trade, industry, and middle-class good sense, which made Holland what she is. Yes,' he said, warming to his subject, 'we're in a period when nations must obtain everything through the legal development of their liberties, and by the peaceful functioning of constitutional institutions. That's what the Poles don't realize, and I hope ... You were saying, my dear?' he added, interrupting himself and seeing from his employee's expression that high politics were beyond her comprehension.

'Here are the papers,' replied Bette. 'If I don't want to lose my three thousand two hundred and ten francs, that scoundrel must be sent to prison.'

'Ah, I told you so!' exclaimed the oracle of the Saint-Denis quarter.*

The firm of Rivet, successor to Pons brothers, had remained in the Rue des Mauvaises-Paroles, in the former Hôtel de Langeais built by that illustrious family at a time when the great noblemen were grouped around the Louvre.

'Yes, and I've been calling down blessings upon you on my way here,' replied Lisbeth.

'If he can be kept from suspecting anything, he'll be locked up by four in the morning,' said the judge, looking at his calendar to verify the time of sunrise. 'But only the day after tomorrow, for he can't be imprisoned without being notified officially that he is to be arrested by an order authorizing imprisonment for debt. So ...'

'What a stupid law,' said Cousin Bette, 'for the debtor will run away.'

'He certainly has the right to,' replied the judge with a smile. 'So look, this is how . . .'

'For that matter, I'll take the paper,' said Bette, interrupting her adviser. 'I'll give it to him and tell him that I've been compelled to raise money and the money-lender has insisted on this formality. I know my Pole. He won't even unfold the paper. He'll light his pipe with it.'

'Oh, not bad, not bad, Mademoiselle Fischer! Well, don't worry, the affair will be rushed through. But wait a minute! To shut a man up isn't everything. People only indulge in that legal luxury in order to get their money. Who will pay you?'

'The people who give him money.'

'Oh yes, I was forgetting that the Minister of War has commissioned him to make the monument of one of our customers. Yes, the firm supplied many a uniform to General Montcornet. He didn't take long to blacken them with cannon-smoke, that fellow! What a brave man he was! And he paid *on the nail*!'

A marshal of France may have saved the Emperor or his country, but *he paid on the nail* will always be the highest praise a tradesman can bestow upon him.

'Well, I'll see you on Saturday, Monsieur Rivet, and I'll bring you your big flat tassles then. By the way, I'm leaving the Rue du Doyenné and I'm going to live in the Rue Vaneau.'

'You're very wise; I didn't like seeing you in that hole, which, I venture to say, in spite of my aversion to anything that seems to favour the Opposition, disgraces, yes, disgraces the Louvre and the Place du Carrousel. I worship Louis-Philippe. He is my idol. He is the august and perfect representative of the class on which he has founded his dynasty, and I shall never forget what he has done for the trimmings business by re-establishing the National Guard.'

'When I hear you talk like that, I wonder why you're not a deputy,' said Lisbeth.

'They are afraid of my attachment to the royal house,'

replied Rivet. 'My political enemies are the King's. Ah! he's a noble character, a fine family. In short,' he went on, continuing his line of argument, 'he is our ideal, in moral behaviour, in direction of the economy, in everything! But the *completion* of the Louvre is one of the conditions on which we gave him the crown, and the civil list, to which no limit was set, leaves, I agree, the heart of Paris in a deplorable state. . . . It's because I'm a *middle-of-the-road* man that I'd like to see the middle of Paris in a different state. Your district makes me shudder. You'd have been murdered there sooner or later. . . . Well, I see your Monsieur Crevel has been appointed Major of his Legion. I hope we shall be supplying his big epaulettes.'

'I'm going there for dinner today; I'll tell him to go and see you.'

Lisbeth thought she would have the Livonian completely under her control, flattering herself that she was cutting all communication between him and the outside world. Since he would no longer be doing any work, the artist would be like a man hidden in a cellar, where only she would visit him. So she had two days of happiness, for she hoped to inflict mortal blows on the Baroness and her daughter.

To go to Monsieur Crevel's house in the Rue des Saussayes, she went by the Pont du Carrousel, the Quai Voltaire, the Quai d'Orsay, the Rue Bellechasse, the Rue de l'Université, the Pont de la Concorde, and the Avenue Marigny.

This illogical route was mapped out by the logic of the passions which is always extremely hard on the legs. As long as she was going along the quais, Cousin Bette looked at the right bank of the Seine, walking very slowly. Her calculation was correct. She had left Wenceslas dressing; she thought that as soon as she was out of the way, the lover would go to the Baroness's house by the shortest route.

In fact, just as she was going along by the parapet of the Quai Voltaire, mentally obliterating the river and walking in her imagination on the other bank, she recognized the artist as he came through the gate of the Tuileries on his way to the Pont Royal. There she caught up with her faithless friend and was able to follow him without his seeing her, for lovers seldom turn round. She accompanied him as far as Madame Hulot's house and saw him go in like a frequent visitor.

At this final proof, which confirmed Madame Marneffe's confidences, Lisbeth was beside herself.

She arrived at the home of the newly elected Major in the state of nervous vexation which incites people to murder, and she found Père Crevel waiting for his children, Monsieur and Madame Hulot junior, in his drawing-room.

But Célestin Crevel is such a naïve and perfect example of the Parisian parvenu that it is difficult to enter the house of César Birotteau's fortunate successor* without due ceremony. Célestin Crevel is a whole world in himself. And so, more than Rivet, he deserves the honours of the palette, because of his important role in this domestic drama.

29. *The life and opinions of Monsieur Crevel*

Have you ever noticed how, in childhood, or at the start of our social life, we fashion a model for ourselves, often unawares? Thus a bank-clerk, as he enters his manager's drawing-room, dreams of owning one just like it. If he is successful, it will not be the luxury then in fashion that he will install in his house twenty years later, but the out-of-date luxury that charmed him years ago.

We don't know all the follies which stem from such retrospective envy, just as we don't know all those due to the secret rivalries which drive men to imitate the ideal type they have set themselves, to consume their strength in pursuit of a moonbeam.

Crevel was a deputy mayor because his employer had been a deputy mayor. He was a major because he had wanted César Birotteau's epaulettes. Consequently, impressed by the marvels created by the architect Grindot at the moment when fortune had carried his employer to the top of her wheel, Crevel, as he said in his own words, *hadn't thought twice about it* when it came to decorating his own home. With closed eyes and open purse he went to Grindot, by that time a quite forgotten architect.

We cannot tell how long faded glories linger on sustained by such out-of-date admiration.

Grindot had recreated there for the thousandth time his gold and white drawing-room hung with red damask. The rosewood furniture, carved rather crudely as is usual today, had aroused in the provinces a well-deserved pride in Parisian workmanship at the time of the Exhibition of manufactured goods.* The candlesticks, the sconces, the fender, the chandelier, and the clock were all in the rococo style.

The round table, a fixture in the middle of the room, displayed a marble top inlaid with every kind of Italian and antique marble brought from Rome, where they make this kind of mineralogical map, rather like a card of tailor's samples; it regularly aroused the admiration of all Crevel's bourgeois guests.

The portraits of the late Madame Crevel, of Crevel, of his daughter and son-in-law (from the brush of Pierre Grassou,* the popular painter in middle-class society, to whom Crevel owed his ridiculous Byronic pose) were hung in matching couples on the walls. The frames, which had cost a thousand francs each, were in keeping with all this café splendour, that would certainly have made a real artist shrug his shoulders.

Money has never lost the least opportunity of showing how stupid it is. We would have ten Venices in Paris today if our retired businessmen had had the instinctive good taste which distinguishes the Italians. Even in our own day, a Milanese merchant might well leave five hundred thousand francs to the *Duomo* for gilding the colossal Virgin on top of its cupola. In his will, Canova* instructed his brother to build a church costing four million, and the brother added something of his own.

Would a bourgeois of Paris (and, like Rivet, they all have

a love for Paris in their hearts) ever think of building the spires missing from the towers of Notre-Dame?

And yet, consider the sums that have reverted to the state from property left without heirs.

All the improvements of Paris could have been completed for the money spent on absurdities of moulded stucco, gilded plaster, and so-called sculptures by individuals of Crevel's stamp.

Beyond this drawing-room was a magnificent study, furnished with imitation Boule* tables and cabinets.

The bedroom, all hung in chintz, also opened out of the drawing-room. Mahogany in all its glory proliferated in the dining-room, whose panelling was decorated with richly framed views of Switzerland. Père Crevel, who dreamed of going to Switzerland, enjoyed possessing that country in paintings until the time came when he would go and see it in reality.

Crevel, a former deputy mayor, a member of the Legion of Honour and of the national Guard, had, as we see, faithfully reproduced all the grandeurs of his unfortunate predecessor,* even to the furniture. Where, under the Restoration, the one had fallen, the other, completely unnoticed, had risen, not because of any unusual stroke of fortune but by force of circumstances. In revolutions, as in storms at sea, solid worth goes to the bottom, and the waves bring lightweight stuff to the surface. César Birotteau, a royalist, in favour and an object of envy, became the target of the bourgeois opposition, while the triumphant bourgeoisie saw Crevel as its own representative.

His flat, rented at a thousand crowns a year, chock-full of all the commonplace fine things that money can buy, occupied the first floor of an old mansion, standing between a courtyard and a garden. Everything in it was kept like beetles in an entomologist's cabinet, for Crevel lived there very little.

This sumptuous *abode* was the official domicile of the ambitious bourgeois. He kept a cook and a valet there, hiring two extra servants and ordering his party dinners from Chevet* when he entertained political friends, people he wanted to impress, or members of his family.

Crevel's real existence used to be spent at the Rue Notre-Dame-de-Lorette, at Mademoiselle Héloïse Brisetout's, but it had been transferred, as we have seen, to the Rue Chauchat.

Every morning, the *former merchant* (all retired shop-keepers call themselves *former merchants*) spent two hours at the Rue des Saussayes to attend to business, and gave the rest of his time to Zaïre, to Zaïre's great annoyance.

Orosmane*-Crevel had a fixed arrangement with Mademoiselle Héloïse; she owed him five hundred francs' worth of happiness every month, with nothing carried over. In addition, Crevel paid for his dinner and all the *extras*.

This contract, with bonuses (for he gave her a lot of presents), seemed economical to the celebrated singer's former lover. On this subject, he would say to widowed merchants who were too fond of their daughters, that it was better to hire horses by the month than to have one's own stable. Nevertheless, if we recall the confidences of the porter of the Rue Chauchat to the Baron, Crevel could not dispense with either the coachman or the groom.

As we see, Crevel had turned his extreme affection for his daughter to the advantage of his pleasures. The immorality of his situation was justified on high moral grounds. Moreover, the former perfumer acquired from his way of life (inevitable but dissolute, in the style of the Regency,* Pompadour,* Maréchal de Richelieu,* etc.) a veneer of superiority.

Crevel adopted the pose of a broad-minded man, a great lord on a small scale, a generous man, not narrow in his ideas, and all for about twelve to fifteen hundred francs a month. This was not due to political hypocrisy, but to bourgeois vanity; nevertheless, the result was the same. At the Stock Exchange Crevel had the reputation of being a man superior to his age and above all of one who enjoyed the pleasures of life.

In this respect, Crevel believed he was vastly superior to good old Birotteau.

30. *A continuation of the preceding chapter*

'Well!' exclaimed Crevel, turning angry at the sight of Cousin Bette. 'So it's you who are arranging Mademoiselle Hulot's marriage to a young count whom you've brought up for her with the greatest care?'

'Anyone would think you don't like the idea,' replied Lisbeth, casting a searching glance at Crevel. 'What's your interest, then, in preventing my cousin from getting married? For you were responsible for the failure of her proposed marriage to Monsieur Lebas' son, so I'm told.'

'You're a good sort, and you don't tell tales,' continued Père Crevel. 'Well, do you think I'll ever forgive *Monsieur* Hulot for the crime of taking Josépha away from me? Especially as he turned an honest girl, whom I would have ended up by marrying in my old age, into a good-for-nothing, a show-girl, an Opera singer. . . . No, no, never!'

'Yet he's a good fellow, is Monsieur Hulot,' said Cousin Bette.

'Likeable, very likeable, too likeable!' Crevel went on. 'I don't wish him any harm; but I want to take my revenge and I'll take it. I'm determined on it.'

'Would that be why you don't come to Madame Hulot's any more?'

'Perhaps . . .'

'Oh, so you were courting my cousin?' said Lisbeth with a smile. 'I suspected as much.'

'And she treated me like a dog, worse than that, like a lackey. I'll put it even better, like a political prisoner. But I'll get there in the end,' he said, striking his forehead with his clenched fist.

'Poor man, it would be terrible to find his wife was deceiving him, after he has been cast off by his mistress.'

'Josépha!' cried Crevel. 'You say Josépha has left him, sent him packing, turned him out? Bravo, Josépha! Josépha, you have avenged me! I'll send you two pearls to wear in your ears, my ex-darling! This is all news to me, for after seeing you the day after the day the beautiful Adeline once again showed me the door, I went to see the Lebas at Corbeil; I've just come back from there. Héloïse kicked up a terrific fuss to make me go to the country and I've found out why she carried on like that. She wanted to have a house-warming party at the Rue Chauchat without me, with artists, third-rate actors, literary chaps. . . . I was tricked! I'll forgive her, for Héloïse amuses me. She's an unknown Déjazet.* What a comic she is, that girl! Here's the note I found yesterday evening:

'Dear old chap, I've pitched my tent in the Rue Chauchat. I've taken the precaution of having the house warmed up by friends. All goes well. Come when you like, Monsieur. Hagar* awaits her Abraham.'

'Héloïse will tell me all the news, for she has all the bohemian gossip at her fingertips.'

'But my cousin has taken this discomfiture very well,' replied Cousin Bette.

'That's not possible,' said Crevel, stopping his walk to and fro like the pendulum of a clock.

'Monsieur Hulot is no longer young,' remarked Lisbeth maliciously.

'I know that,' continued Crevel. 'But we are like each other in one respect; Hulot will not be able to do without an attachment. He is capable of returning to his wife,' he muttered to himself. 'That would be a novelty for him, but farewell to my revenge. You're smiling, Mademoiselle Fischer? Ah, you know something?'

'I'm laughing at your ideas,' replied Lisbeth. 'Yes, my cousin is still beautiful enough to inspire passions. I'd fall in love with her myself, if I were a man.'

'He who has drunk will drink again!' exclaimed Crevel. 'You're making fun of me. The Baron must have found some consolation.'

Lisbeth gave a nod of assent.

'Oh, he's very lucky to replace Josépha overnight,'

continued Crevel. 'But I'm not surprised, for he told me one evening at supper that in his youth he always had three mistresses so as not to be caught without one: the one he was about to leave, the reigning one, and the one he was courting for the future. He must have kept some little shop-girl in reserve in his fishpond! In his deer-park!* He's very much in the style of Louis XV, the lusty fellow! Oh, how lucky he is to be a handsome man! Still, he's getting old, it's beginning to show. He must have taken up with some little working girl.'

'Oh, no!' answered Lisbeth.

'Ah,' said Crevel, 'what wouldn't I give to stop him hanging his hat up! I couldn't possibly take Josépha from him. Women of that kind never come back to their first love. Besides, as they say, a return is never the same as love. But, Cousin Bette, I would gladly give, that is to say I would willingly spend, fifty thousand francs to take that tall, handsome fellow's mistress away from him and show him that a fat old chap with the paunch of a major and the bald pate of a future mayor of Paris doesn't let his lady friend be filched from him without getting his own back!'

'In my situation, I have to hear everything and know nothing,' replied Bette. 'You needn't be afraid to talk to me. I never repeat a word of what people choose to confide in me. Why should I break that rule of my behaviour? No one would ever trust me again.'

'I know,' Crevel replied. 'You are the pearl of old maids. . . . Yet, hang it all, there are exceptions. I wonder, has the family ever made you any allowance?'

'But I have my pride. I don't want to be a charge on anyone,' said Bette.

'Oh, if you were willing to help me get my revenge, I'd invest ten thousand francs in an annuity for you,' the retired merchant went on. 'Tell me, fair cousin, who has taken Josépha's place, and you'll have the wherewithal to pay your rent, and your breakfast in the morning with that good coffee you're so fond of; you'll be able to buy pure Mocha. . . . What about it? Oh, how delicious it is, that pure Mocha!'

'I'm not so keen on the ten thousand franc annuity, which would yield an income of nearly five hundred francs a year, as on observing complete secrecy,' said Lisbeth. 'For you see, my good Monsieur Crevel, the Baron's extremely good to me; he's going to pay my rent.'

'Yes, for a long time! Count on that!' exclaimed Crevel. 'Where will the Baron get the money from?'

'Oh, I don't know. But he's spending more than thirty thousand francs on the flat he's intending to give this little lady.'

'A lady! What, could it be a society woman? The scoundrel, what a fortunate fellow he is! He has all the luck!'

'A married woman and very respectable,' continued Cousin Bette.

'Really!' cried Crevel, his eyes opening wide as much with desire as with the effect of the magic words: *a respectable married woman*.

'Yes,' said Bette, 'talented, musical, 23 years old, a pretty, innocent face, a dazzling white skin, teeth like a puppy's, eyes like stars, a magnificent forehead . . . and tiny feet. I have never seen any like them; they're no wider than her corset busks.'

'And her ears?' asked Crevel, keenly excited by this lover's description.

'Ears fit to be modelled,' she replied.

'Little hands?'

'I tell you, in a word, she's a jewel of a woman, and so virtuous, so modest, so refined! A lovely nature, an angel, distinguished in every way, for her father was a marshal of France.'

'A marshal of France!' exclaimed Crevel, with a violent, excited start. 'Good God! Heavens above! My goodness! In the name of . . .! Oh, the rascal! Excuse me, Cousin, I'm going mad! I'd give a hundred thousand francs, I think.'

'Well, yes, I tell you she's a respectable woman, a virtuous woman. And the Baron has done things in style.'

'He hasn't a penny, I tell you.'

'There's a husband whose career he has furthered.'

'In what way?' asked Crevel with a bitter laugh.

'He's already been appointed assistant-manager, this husband, who'll no doubt turn a blind eye ... and been nominated for the Cross of the Legion of Honour.'

'The Government ought to take care and respect the people it has decorated by not being lavish with the Cross,' said Crevel, looking piqued because of his political views. 'But what has he got so much in his favour, that great hound of an old Baron?' he continued. 'It seems to me that I'm as good as he is,' he added, admiring himself in a glass and taking up his pose. 'Héloïse has often told me, at a time when women don't lie, that I'm marvellous.'

'Oh,' replied Cousin Bette, 'women love fat men; they're nearly all kind. And as between you and the Baron, *I* would choose you. Monsieur Hulot is clever and handsome, he has style, but you, you are reliable, and then, well ... you seem to be even more of a scapegrace than he is!'

'It's incredible how all women, even religious ones, love men who have that look about them,' cried Crevel, coming up to Bette and putting his arm round her waist, he was so delighted.

'That's not where the difficulty lies,' continued Bette. 'You must appreciate that a woman who's doing so well for herself won't be unfaithful to her protector for a mere trifle, and *that* would cost at least a hundred thousand francs, for the little lady sees her husband head of a department two years from now.... It's poverty that's driving the poor little angel into the abyss.'

Crevel walked up and down his drawing-room like a madman.

'He must be very keen on this woman?' he asked after a moment's pause, during which his desire, thus inflamed by Lisbeth, became a kind of frenzy.

'Judge for yourself,' replied Lisbeth. 'I don't think he's had *that* from her yet,' she said, clicking her thumbnail against one of her huge white teeth, 'and he's already spent about ten thousand francs on presents.'

'Oh, what a joke if I got in before him!' cried Crevel.

'My goodness! It's very wrong of me to tell you all this gossip,' continued Lisbeth, as if stricken with remorse.

'No. I want to make your family blush with shame. Tomorrow I shall invest a sum in the 5-per-cents, to provide an annuity for you of six hundred francs a year, but you must tell me everything: the name and the address of this Dulcinea.* I may as well tell you, I've never had a real lady, and the greatest of my ambitions has been to have one for a mistress. Mahomet's houris are nothing in comparison with what I imagine society women to be like. In fact that's my ideal, my mania, and so much so, you see, that Baroness Hulot will never be 50 years old to me,' he said, unwittingly repeating the thought of one of the cleverest wits of the last century.* 'Listen, my good Lisbeth, I have decided to sacrifice a hundred, two hundred ... Hush! Here come the young people. I see them crossing the courtyard. I shall deny having learned anything from you, I give you my word of honour; for I don't want you to lose the Baron's confidence, quite the contrary. He must be terribly in love with this woman, my old crony!'

'Oh, he's crazy about her,' said Cousin Bette. 'He couldn't raise forty thousand francs to settle his daughter but he has dug them up for his passion.'

'And do you think she loves him?' asked Crevel.

'At his age ...' replied the old maid.

'Oh, what a fool I am!' exclaimed Crevel. 'After all, I put up with Héloïse's artist, just as Henri IV let Gabrielle have Bellegarde.* Oh, old age! old age!—Hello, Célestine, how are you, my pet, and where's the little fellow? Oh, there he is. Upon my word, he's beginning to look like me. How are you, Hulot my boy? All right? ... We're going to have another marriage soon in the family.'

Célestine and her husband made a sign, indicating Lisbeth, and the daughter unashamedly asked her father:

'But whose?'

Crevel put on a knowing look, implying that he was going to cover up his indiscretion.

'Hortense's,' he replied. 'But it's not quite settled yet.

I've just been visiting the Lebas, and they were talking of Mademoiselle Popinot for our young councillor at the Paris royal court. He's very keen to become president of a provincial court. . . . Let's go in to dinner.'

31. *Caliban's last attempt to keep Ariel*

At seven o'clock Lisbeth was already on an omnibus on her way home, for she was longing to see Wenceslas, whose dupe she had been for about three weeks; she was bringing him her basket piled high with fruit by Crevel himself, whose affection for *his* Cousin Bette was greater than ever.

She climbed the stairs to the attic so fast that she was quite out of breath, and found the artist busy finishing the decoration of a box that he wanted to give to his beloved Hortense.

On the border of the lid were hydrangeas with Cupids playing amongst them. In order to raise the money for the box, which was to be made of malachite, the poor lover had made two candelabra for Florent and Chanor, two masterpieces, of which he sold them the copyright.

'You've been working too hard lately, my dear boy,' said Lisbeth, wiping his forehead, which was damp with sweat, and kissing him. 'Such exertion in the month of August seems dangerous to me. Really, your health may suffer for it. . . . Look, here are some peaches and plums from Monsieur Crevel's dinner-party. . . . Don't worry so much. I've borrowed two thousand francs and unless we have bad luck, we'll be able to pay them back if you sell your clock. All the same, I have some doubts about my money-lender, for he has just sent me this official document.'

She placed the writ of arrest for debt under the sketch of the Maréchal de Montcornet.

'For whom are you making these lovely things?' she asked, picking up the red wax sprays of hydrangeas that Wenceslas had put down so that he could eat the fruit.

'For a jeweller.'

'Which jeweller?'

'I don't know. It was Stidmann who asked me to knock it up for him, because he's busy.'

'But these are *hortensias*,' she said in a hollow voice. 'Why have you never modelled anything in wax for me? Was it so difficult, then, to design a brooch, a box, anything at all, as a keepsake?' she said, casting a terrible glance at the artist, whose eyes were fortunately lowered. 'Yet you say you love me!'

'Can you doubt it, Mademoiselle?'

'Oh, that's a very cool *Mademoiselle*! Listen, you have been my only thought since I saw you dying there. When I saved your life, you gave yourself to me. I've never spoken to you of that commitment, but *I* was committed in my own mind. I said to myself: "Since this lad gives himself into my hands, I want to make him happy and rich." Well, I've succeeded in making your fortune!'

'But how?' asked the poor artist, overjoyed.

'This is how,' continued the woman from Lorraine.

Lisbeth could not deny herself the unrestrained pleasure of looking at Wenceslas, who was gazing at her with a filial love mingled with his overflowing love for Hortense, and this misled the old maid. On seeing the fires of passion in a man's eyes for the first time in her life, she thought that it was she who had set them alight.

'Monsieur Crevel says he will advance us a hundred thousand francs to start a business if you are willing to marry me. He has odd ideas, that fat old fellow. What do you think of it?' she asked.

The artist, who had turned pale as death, looked at his benefactress, the light gone from his eyes, which revealed all his thoughts. He stood there, stunned and amazed.

'I've never been told so plainly before that I'm horribly ugly,' she went on with a bitter laugh.

'Mademoiselle,' Steinbock replied, 'my benefactress will never be ugly in my eyes. I have a very great affection for you, but I'm not yet 30, and . . .'

'And I'm 43,' she replied. 'My cousin Hulot, who is 48, still arouses violent passions. But *she* is beautiful!'

'Fifteen years between us, Mademoiselle! What kind of couple would we make? For our own sakes, I think we ought to think very seriously. My gratitude will certainly be as great as your goodness to me. Besides, your money will be repaid in a few days.'

'My money!' she cried. 'You treat me as if I were a heartless usurer.'

'Forgive me,' said Wenceslas, 'but you talk about it so often. . . . Yet it was you who made me, so don't destroy me.'

'You want to leave me, I see,' she said, shaking her head. 'But who has given you the strength to be so ungrateful, you who are as malleable as papier mâché? Could it be that you don't trust me—me, your good angel? . . . I who have so often spent the night working for you! I who have devoted my whole life's savings to you! I who, for four years, shared my bread, the bread of a poor working-woman, with you and who have lent you everything, even my courage!'

'Mademoiselle, enough, enough!' he said, going down on his knees and stretching out his hands to her. 'Don't say another word. In three days, I'll explain, I'll tell you everything. Let me be happy,' he said, kissing her hands. 'I am in love and I am loved.'

'Very well, be happy, my child,' she said, raising him up.

Then she kissed his forehead and hair with the frantic emotion that a condemned man must feel as he appreciates every moment of his last morning.

'Oh, you are the noblest and the best of women; you are as good as the woman I love,' said the poor artist.

'I still love you enough to tremble for your future,' she continued, gloomily. 'Judas hanged himself. All ungrateful people come to a bad end. When you leave me, you won't do any more worthwhile work. I know I'm an old maid and I don't want to stifle the flower of your youth, your poetry as you call it, in my arms which are as tough as vine shoots, but don't you think we could stay together without getting married? Listen, I have a head for business. I can make a fortune for you in ten years of work, for my name is thrift. But with a young wife, who will bring nothing but expense, you will squander everything; you will work only to make her happy. Happiness creates nothing but memories. When *I* think of you, I spend hours with my arms dangling idly.... So, Wenceslas, stay with me.... Look, I understand everything. You shall have mistresses, pretty women like that little Madame Marneffe who wants to meet you and who will give you the kind of happiness you can't find with me. Then you'll get married when I've got together an income of thirty thousand francs a year for you.'

'You're an angel, Mademoiselle, and I'll never forget this moment,' answered Wenceslas, wiping away his tears.

'Now you are as I want you to be, my child,' she said, looking at him rapturously.

Vanity is so strong in us that Lisbeth believed she had triumphed. She had made such a big concession in offering Madame Marneffe! She experienced the keenest emotion of her life. For the first time she felt joy flooding her heart. To experience another such moment, she would have sold her soul to the devil.

'I am committed,' he replied, 'and I love a woman who is incomparable. But you are and always will be the mother I have lost.'

These words fell like an avalanche of snow upon a blazing crater.

Lisbeth sat down and gazed despondently at the young man's distinguished good looks, at his artist's brow and beautiful hair, at everything which aroused her repressed feminine instincts, and little tears, immediately wiped away, filled her eyes for a moment. She looked like one of those slender statues that medieval sculptors have placed over tombs.

'I'm not going to curse you,' she said, getting up abruptly. 'You're only a child. May God protect you.'

She went downstairs and shut herself in her room.

'She's in love with me,' Wenceslas said to himself. 'Poor woman! How heatedly eloquent she was! She's crazy!'

This final effort of an unimaginative, matter-of-fact nature to retain the image of beauty and poetry had been so violent that it can only be compared to the desperate exertion of a shipwrecked sailor as he makes a last attempt to reach the shore.

32. *Failed revenge*

Two days later, at half past four in the morning, when Count Steinbock was fast asleep, he heard a knock at his attic door. He went to open it and saw two badly dressed men come in. They were accompanied by a third man whose dress indicated a bailiff in poor circumstances.

'You are Monsieur Wenceslas Count Steinbock?' asked this third man.

'Yes, Monsieur.'

'My name is Grasset, Monsieur, successor to Monsieur Louchard, sheriff's officer . . .'

'Well?'

'You are under arrest, Monsieur. You must come with us to the Clichy prison. Please get dressed. We've done this with due consideration for you, as you see. I haven't brought any police, and there's a cab downstairs.'

'You're properly caught,' said one of the bailiff's men, 'so we count on your causing no trouble.'

Steinbock got dressed, went downstairs with a bailiff's man holding each arm, and was put in the cab, the driver setting off without any order being given, as a man who knows where to go. In half an hour the poor foreigner found himself well and truly locked up without having made the slightest protest, so great was his surprise.

At ten o'clock, he was summoned to the prison office. There he found Lisbeth, who, all in tears, gave him money so that he could live comfortably and have a room large enough to work in.

'My child,' she said. 'Don't tell anyone about your

arrest. Don't write to a living soul; that would ruin your future. This blot on your reputation must be concealed. I'll soon have you set free. I'll raise the money.... Don't worry. Write down what I should bring you for your work. I'll die or you'll soon be free.'

'Oh, I'll owe you my life twice over!' he cried. 'For I'd lose more than my life if I was thought to be disreputable.'

Lisbeth left with joy in her heart. In keeping her artist locked up she hoped to destroy his plans for marriage to Hortense by saying that he was married, had been pardoned thanks to *his wife's* efforts, and had left for Russia.

To carry out this plan, she went to the Baroness's house about three o'clock, although it was not her usual day for dining there. But she wanted to enjoy the tortures that her young cousin would endure at the time that Wenceslas normally came.

'Are you staying to dinner, Bette?' asked the Baroness, concealing her disappointment.

'Oh, yes.'

'Good!' answered Hortense. 'I'll go and tell them to serve it on time, for you don't like to be kept waiting.'

Hortense signed to her mother not to worry, for she intended to tell the footman to send Monsieur Steinbock away when he arrived; but, as the footman was out, Hortense had to give her order to the maid, and the maid went up to her room to fetch her needlework so as to do it as she waited in the ante-room.

'And what about my admirer?' Cousin Bette asked Hortense. 'You don't talk about him any more.'

'Oh, now that you raise the subject, what's happened to him, for he's famous now?' Hortense asked. 'You must be pleased; everyone's talking of Monsieur Wenceslas Steinbock,' she added, whispering in her cousin's ear.

'Far too much,' answered Bette aloud. 'Monsieur is getting quite unsettled. If it were only a question of enticing him away from the pleasures of Paris, I know my power. But they say that, to attract so gifted an artist to his own court, the Emperor Nicholas is going to pardon him.'

'Oh, nonsense,' replied the Baroness.

'How do you know that?' asked Hortense, whose heart suddenly almost stopped beating.

'Well, a person to whom he is bound by the most sacred ties, his wife, told him so in a letter he got yesterday. He wants to go. Oh, he'd be very foolish to leave France for Russia.'

Hortense looked at her mother, her head falling to one side, and the Baroness was just in time to catch her daughter as she fainted, white as the lace of her fichu.

'Lisbeth, you've killed my daughter!' cried the Baroness. 'You were born to bring us misfortune.'

'But how am I to blame for this, Adeline?' asked the Lorraine peasant woman, getting up and assuming a threatening attitude which the Baroness, in her distress, did not notice.

'I was wrong,' replied Adeline, supporting Hortense. 'Ring the bell.'

At that moment the door opened. The two women looked round simultaneously and saw Wenceslas Steinbock, who, in the maid's absence, had been admitted by the cook.

'Hortense!' cried the artist, rushing forward to the group formed by the three women.

And he kissed his fiancée's brow before her mother's eyes, but so respectfully that the Baroness could not be angry. It was a better antidote to a faint than any English smelling-salts. Hortense opened her eyes, saw Wenceslas, and her colour returned. A moment later she had entirely recovered.

'So this is what you were concealing from me,' said Cousin Bette, smiling at Wenceslas and appearing to guess the truth from the embarrassment of her two cousins.

'How did you manage to steal my admirer from me?' she asked Hortense as she led her into the garden.

Hortense naïvely told her cousin the romantic story of her love. She said that her parents, convinced that Bette would never marry, had allowed Count Steinbock's visits. Only, like a fully fledged Agnès,* Hortense ascribed to chance the purchase of the group and the arrival of the artist who, according to her, had wanted to know the name of his first customer.

Steinbock soon came out to join the two cousins and thanked the old maid effusively for his prompt deliverance. Lisbeth replied to Wenceslas, jesuitically, that as the creditor had made her only vague promises, she did not expect to obtain the artist's release till the following day and that their money-lender, ashamed of an unjust persecution, had, no doubt, taken the initiative. The old maid, moreover, seemed to be pleased and congratulated Wenceslas on his good fortune.

'Naughty boy!' she said in front of Hortense and her mother. 'If, two evenings ago, you had confessed to me that you loved my cousin Hortense and that she loved you, you would have spared me many tears. I thought you were deserting your old friend, your mentor, while, on the contrary, you are going to be my cousin. From now on, you will be linked to me by ties, weak ones it is true, but sufficient for the feelings I have for you.'

And she kissed Wenceslas on the forehead. Hortense flung herself into her cousin's arms and burst into tears.

'I owe you my happiness,' she said. 'I'll never forget it.'

'Cousin Bette,' the Baroness added, kissing Lisbeth in her ecstatic delight at seeing things turn out so well, 'the Baron and I are greatly indebted to you and we'll repay you. Come and talk things over in the garden,' she said, leading the way there.

So, to all appearances, Lisbeth played the part of the good angel of the family. She found herself the darling of Crevel, Hulot, Adeline, and Hortense.

'We don't want you to go on working,' said the Baroness. 'Assuming you can earn forty sous a day, except Sundays, that makes six hundred francs a year. And how much do your savings amount to?'

'Four thousand five hundred francs.'

'Poor Cousin!' said the Baroness.

She raised her eyes to heaven, so greatly was she touched° by the thought of all the hardships and privations represented by this sum of money, the savings of thirty years.

Lisbeth, misunderstanding Adeline's exclamation, saw in it the mocking disdain of a woman who had risen in the world and her hatred was enhanced by a formidable dose of gall, just when her cousin was relinquishing all mistrust of the tyrant of her youth.

'We'll increase that amount by ten thousand five hundred francs,' continued Adeline. 'We'll invest it so that the interest will go to you, the capital to revert to Hortense. That will give you an income of six hundred francs a year.'

Lisbeth appeared to be overjoyed. When she returned to the house, holding her handkerchief to her eyes, wiping away tears of joy, Hortense told her of all the favours that were being rained down on Wenceslas, the darling of the whole family.

33. *The way many marriage contracts are made*

When the Baron came home, he found all his family complete, for the Baroness had officially called Count Steinbock *son* and fixed the marriage for a fortnight later, subject to her husband's approval. So, as soon as he set foot in the drawing-room, the Councillor of State was assailed by his wife and daughter, who ran to meet him, the one to have a private word with him and the other to kiss him.

'You have gone too far, Madame, in pledging me in this way,' the Baron said severely. 'The marriage is not settled,' he said, with a look at Steinbock, whom he saw turn pale.

'He knows of my arrest,' the unhappy artist said to himself.

'Come, children,' added the father, leading his daughter and her future husband into the garden.

And he went and sat down with them on one of the moss-covered benches of the summerhouse.

'Monsieur le Comte, do you love my daughter as much as I loved her mother?' the Baron asked Wenceslas.

'More, Monsieur,' replied the artist.

'The mother was a peasant's daughter and had no fortune at all, not a farthing.'

'Give me Mademoiselle Hortense just as she is, without even a trousseau . . .'

'What an idea!' said the Baron with a smile. 'Hortense is the daughter of Baron Hulot d'Ervy, Councillor of State, a Director at the War Department, Grand Officer of the Legion of Honour, brother of Count Hulot of immortal fame and soon to be a Marshal of France. And . . . she has a dowry!'

'It's true that I seem to be ambitious,' said the enamoured artist, 'but even if my dear Hortense were a workman's daughter I would marry her.'

'That's what I wanted to know,' continued the Baron. 'Leave us now, Hortense, and let me have a chat with Monsieur le Comte. You see that he sincerely loves you.'

'Oh, father, I knew very well that you were joking,' replied the happy girl.

'My dear Steinbock,' said the Baron, speaking graciously and with great charm of manner when he was alone with the artist, 'I settled a dowry of two hundred thousand francs on my son. The poor boy hasn't had a farthing of it; he never will. My daughter's dowry will be two hundred thousand francs, for which you will give me a receipt . . .'

'Yes, Monsieur le Baron . . .'

'Not so fast,' said the Councillor of State. 'Just listen to me. One cannot ask of a son-in-law the devotion one is entitled to expect of a son. My son knew all that I could do and what I would do for his future. He will be a minister and will easily find his two hundred thousand francs. As for you, young man, that's another matter! You will receive sixty thousand francs in 5-per-cent Government stock in your wife's name. From this sum will be taken a little annuity to be paid to Lisbeth, but she won't live long. She's consumptive, I know. Don't tell this secret to anyone; let the poor woman die in peace. My daughter will have a trousseau worth twenty thousand francs. Her mother will contribute six thousand francs' worth of her own diamonds to it.'

'Monsieur, you overwhelm me,' said Steinbock, dumbfounded.

'As for the remaining hundred and twenty thousand francs . . .'

'Say no more, Monsieur,' said the artist. 'All I want is my beloved Hortense.'

'Will you listen to me, impetuous young man? As for the hundred and twenty thousand francs, I don't have them but you will get them . . .'

'Monsieur!'

'You will get them from the Government in orders I shall obtain for you, I give you my word of honour. You see you are going to have a studio at the Sculpture Depot. Exhibit a few fine statues and I'll get you elected to the Institute. There is good will in high places towards my brother and me, so I hope to be successful when I ask for sculpture work for you at Versailles worth a quarter of the amount. You will also receive some orders from the City of Paris and you will get some from the House of Peers. You will have so many, my dear boy, that you will have to employ assistants. In this way, I'll fulfil my obligations. Consider whether a dowry paid in this way will suit you. Think whether you have the strength . . .'

'I feel strong enough to make a fortune for my wife single-handed, if all else fails,' said the high-minded artist.

'That's what I like!' exclaimed the Baron. 'Splendid youth, full of confidence! I'd have overthrown armies for a woman! Come,' he said, clapping his hand on the young sculptor's. 'You have my consent. Next Sunday the contract, and the following Saturday to the altar; it's my wife's birthday.'

'All's well,' the Baroness said to her daughter, who was glued to the window. 'Your fiancé and your father are embracing.'

When he returned home that evening, Wenceslas discovered the explanation of the mystery of his release. At the porter's lodge he found a large sealed parcel containing the documents relating to his debts with an official receipt made out at the bottom of the writ and accompanied by the following letter.

'My dear Wenceslas,—I came to see you at ten o'clock this morning in order to introduce you to a Royal Highness who would like to meet you. There, I learned that the English had taken you away to one of their little islands, whose capital is called *Clichy's Castle*.

'I went immediately to see Léon de Lora, and told him, jokingly, that you couldn't leave your present country abode for want of four thousand francs, and that your future would be compromised if you didn't present yourself to your royal patron. Luckily Bridau, a man of genius who has experienced poverty himself and knows your story, was there. They made up the sum between them, my lad, and on your behalf I went to pay the Philistine who committed the crime of *lèse-génie* by having you locked up. As I had to be at the Tuileries at twelve, I couldn't see you inhaling the air of freedom. I know you are an honourable man; I answered for you to my two friends. But go and see them tomorrow.

'Léon and Bridau don't want your money. Each of them will ask for a group and they're quite right. That's the opinion of one who would like to be able to call himself your rival, but is only your friend.'

STIDMAN

P.S. I told the prince you wouldn't be back from your travels till tomorrow, and he said "Very well, tomorrow."'

Count Wenceslas went to bed between the purple sheets, unmarred by a single crease of faded pink, which popular Favour provides for us. That limping goddess walks even more slowly for men of genius than Justice and Fortune because Jupiter has decreed that she should wear no bandage over her eyes. Easily taken in by the displays of charlatans, attracted by their fancy dress and their trumpets, watching and paying for their parades, she wastes the time she ought to spend seeking out men of merit in their hiding-places.

We must now explain how Monsieur le Baron Hulot managed to raise the money for Hortense's dowry and meet the frightening expenses of the delightful flat where Madam Marneffe was to be installed. His financial plans bore the mark of the talent that leads spendthrifts and men dominated by an obsession into quagmires where many misadventures bring about their destruction. Nothing illustrates more clearly the strange power inspired by vice to which we owe those extraordinary feats that from time to time are performed by ambitious men, by sensualists, in short by all the servants of the devil.

34. *A magnificent example of a devoted follower*

On the morning of the previous day, an old man, Johann Fischer, unable to pay back the thirty thousand francs he had raised for his nephew, found that he would have to file a petition for bankruptcy unless the Baron repaid him. The venerable, white-haired old man of 70 had such blind confidence in Hulot, who, for this Bonapartist, was a ray of Napoleon's sun, that he was walking calmly up and down with the banker's clerk in the front room of the little ground-floor premises, rented for eight hundred francs a year, from which he directed his grain and forage business.

'Marguerite has gone to get the money very near here,' he said.

The clerk, in grey and silver-braided uniform, knew the old Alsatian's honesty so well that he was willing to leave him his bills for thirty thousand francs, but the old man made him stay, telling him that it had not yet struck eight o'clock.

A cab stopped at the door. The old man rushed out into the street and held out his hand, in sublime confidence, to the Baron, who gave him thirty bank notes.

'Go three doors further on, I'll explain later,' said old Fischer. 'Here you are, young fellow,' said the old man, coming in and counting out the money to the bank's representative, whom he then accompanied to the door.

When the man from the bank was out of sight, Fischer called back the cab where his eminent nephew, Napoleon's right hand, was waiting, and said as he led him into the house:

'Do you want them to know at the Bank of France that you paid me thirty thousand francs for bills which you endorsed? As it is, it's too bad that they should bear the signature of a man like you!'

'Let's go to the bottom of your garden, Uncle Fischer,' said the high official. 'You're in good health,' he continued, sitting down in a vine arbour and scrutinizing the old man like a dealer in human bodies scrutinizing a substitute for army service.

'Good enough to invest in an annuity,' replied the little old man, who was spare, thin, wiry, and keen-eyed.

'Does the heat upset you?'

'On the contrary.'

'What do you think of Africa?'

'A fine country! The French went there with the Little Corporal.'

'To save us all, you may have to go to Algeria,' said the Baron.

'But what about my business?'

'A War Ministry clerk who is retiring and hasn't enough to live on will buy your business.'

'What am I to do in Algeria?'

'Supply food for the army, grain and forage. I have your commission signed. You will buy your supplies in the country for 70 per cent less than the price you will enter on your accounts to us.'

'Where shall I get them from?'

'By raids and levies, and from the caliphates. Algeria is a country that is still very little known, although we have been there for eight years; it contains huge quantities of grain and forage. Now, when this produce is in Arab hands, we take it from them under a host of pretexts. Then, when we have it, the Arabs try to take it back. There is a lot of fighting over grain, but no one knows how much has been stolen on both sides. There isn't time in the open field to measure out wheat in hectolitres as they do in the Paris market, and hay as in the Rue d'Enfer. The Arab chiefs, as well as our Spahis, prefer cash and so sell these crops at a very low price. But the Army administration has fixed requirements, so it sanctions purchases at exorbitant prices, calculated on the difficulty of obtaining supplies and on the risks of transport. That's Algeria from the Army contractor's point of view. It's chaos, modified by the scribblings of every new administration. We administrators won't be able to see clearly what's going on there for about ten years, but private individuals have sharp eyes. So I'm sending you there to make your fortune. I'm placing you there as Napoleon used to place a poor marshal at the head of a kingdom where he could secretly protect smuggling. I'm ruined, my dear Fischer. A year from now, I'll need a hundred thousand francs.'

'I see no harm in taking them from the Arabs,' the Alsatian replied calmly. 'That sort of thing used to be done under the Empire.'

'The purchaser of your business will come and see you this morning and will give you ten thousand francs,' continued Baron Hulot. 'That's all you need, isn't it, to go to Africa?'

The old man nodded his assent.

'As for funds out there, don't worry,' the Baron went on. 'I'll keep the rest of the money paid for your business here; I need it.'

'Everything I have is yours, even my life,' said the old man.

'Oh, there's nothing to fear,' continued the Baron, crediting his uncle with greater perspicacity than he in fact had. 'As far as collecting levies are concerned, your reputation for honesty won't suffer. Everything depends on those in authority, and as I appointed them I'm sure of them. This, Uncle Fischer, is a mortal secret. I know you and I have spoken frankly without beating about the bush.'

'I'll go,' said the old man. 'And for how long?'

'Two years. You'll make a hundred thousand francs for yourself to go and live happily in the Vosges.'

'It will be done as you wish. My honour is yours,' said the little old man calmly.

'That's how I like a man to behave. Still, you won't go

till you've seen your great-niece happily married. She's going to be a countess.'

Levies, raiding the raiders, and the price paid by the War Ministry clerk for Fischer's business could not immediately raise the sixty thousand francs for Hortense's dowry plus the trousseau costing about another five thousand francs, as well as the forty thousand francs already spent or about to be spent on Madame Marneffe. And how had the Baron obtained the thirty thousand francs that he had just brought? In this way.

A few days earlier, Hulot had taken out life insurance policies with two companies, for three years, for one hundred and fifty thousand francs.

Armed with the insurance policies for which the premiums had been paid, he had spoken as follows to Monsieur le Baron de Nucingen, peer of France; Hulot was riding back with the Baron in his carriage on the way to dine at Nucingen's house, after a sitting of the House of Peers.

'Baron, I need seventy thousand francs and I'm asking you to lend them to me. You'll appoint a nominee to whom I'll make over the assignable portion of my salary. It amounts to twenty-five thousand francs a year, that's seventy five thousand francs. You'll say, "You may die."'

The Baron nodded his assent.

'Here is an insurance policy for a hundred and fifty thousand francs, which will be handed over to you until eighty thousand francs have been paid,' replied the Baron, taking a paper from his pocket.

'*Put subbose you're tismissed*,' said the millionaire Baron, with a laugh.

The other Baron, the contrary of a millionaire, became thoughtful.

'*Ton't worry. I only raise the opjection to boint out to you dat id's rather goot of me do gif you ze money. You bust pe very hart ub, for the Pank has your signadure.*'

'I'm arranging my daughter's marriage,' said Baron Hulot, 'and I've no money, like everyone else who continues in Government service in an ungrateful age when five hundred bourgeois, sitting on benches, will never know how to reward devoted servants generously the way the Emperor did.'

'*Gome now, you hat Chosépha!*' replied the Peer of France. '*Dat exsblains eferyding! Bedween ourselfs, de Tuc t'Hérufille tit you a real zerfice py bulling dat leech off your burse. "I haf known dat misfordune ant gan symbadize*",' he added, thinking he was quoting a line of French verse.* '*Dake a vrient's atvice: shud up shob, or you'll gome a gropper.*'

This dubious transaction was arranged through the intermediary of a little money-lender called Vauvinet, one of those shady dealers who hang around large banking houses like the little fish that seem to attend upon sharks. The apprentice profiteer promised Monsieur le Baron Hulot— so eager was he to obtain the patronage of such an eminent personality—to raise thirty thousand francs for him in bills of exchange in ninety days, pledging himself to renew them four times and not to put them into circulation.

Fischer's successor was to give forty thousand francs for the business, but with the promise of the contract to supply forage in a department near Paris.

Such was the terrible maze into which his passions were leading a man who, until then, had been of the utmost integrity, one of the most able administrators of the Napoleonic regime: misappropriation of public funds in order to pay for usury, usury required to pay for his passions and for his daughter's marriage.

This ingeniously contrived prodigality, all these efforts, were expended to appear great in the eyes of Madame Marneffe, to be the Jupiter of that middle-class Danaë.* A man would not have to deploy more energy, intelligence, or enterpise in making an honest fortune than the Baron did in plunging head first into a hornets' nest. He attended to the affairs of his department, he harried the decorators, he supervised the workmen, he checked minutely the tiniest details of the Rue Vaneau establishment. Although he was completely absorbed by thoughts of Madame Marneffe, he still went to meetings of the House. He was everywhere at once and neither his family nor anyone else noticed his preoccupations.

35. *In which the tail-end of an ordinary novel comes in the middle of this story which is only too close to reality, touches on the amatory, and is frighteningly moral.*

Adeline, amazed at learning her uncle was saved and at seeing a dowry included in the marriage contract, felt a kind of anxiety mingled with her happiness at the arrangement of Hortense's marriage on such honourable terms. But the day before his daughter's marriage, planned by the Baron to coincide with the day when Madame Marneffe was to take possession of her flat in the Rue Vaneau, Hector put an end to his wife's astonishment by this ministerial announcement.

'Adeline, our daughter is now about to be married, so all our worries on that score are at an end. The moment has come for us to withdraw from society, for I'll now stay barely three more years in my position; at the end of that period I'll have qualified for my retirement pension. Why should we continue with expenses that are no longer necessary? Our rent is six thousand francs a year; we have four servants; we spend thirty thousand francs a year. If you want me to fulfil my obligations, for I have mortgaged my salary for three years in exchange for the sums required to establish Hortense and to pay your uncle . . .'

'Oh, you were quite right to do so, my dear,' she said, interrupting her husband and kissing his hands.

This confession put an end to Adeline's fears.

'I have a few little sacrifices to ask of you,' he continued, withdrawing his hands and kissing his wife on the forehead. 'I have been told of a very nice first-floor flat in the Rue Plumet; it's handsome, with fine wood panelling, and costs only fifteen hundred francs a year. You'd need only one maid for yourself there, and as for me, I'd be satisfied with a boy.'

'Yes, my dear.'

'By maintaining a simple household, though keeping up appearances, you'll spend barely six thousand francs a year, apart from my personal expenses that I'll take care of.'

The generous woman, entirely happy, threw her arms round her husband's neck.

'What joy to be able to show you again how much I love you,' she cried. 'And what a resourceful man you are!'

'We'll have our family to dinner once a week and, as you know, I don't often dine at home. Without anyone taking exception, you can dine twice a week with Victorin and twice with Hortense, and as I think I'll be able to make it up completely with Crevel, we'll have dinner with him once a week. These five dinners and our own will fill the week, allowing for some invitations outside the family.'

'I'll make savings for you,' said Adeline.

'Oh, you are the pearl of women,' he exclaimed.

'My good divine Hector! I'll bless you to my dying day for having made such a good marriage for our dear Hortense,' she replied.

It was in this way that the household of the beautiful Madame Hulot began to be reduced, and she herself to be deserted in accordance with the solemn promise made to Madame Marneffe.

Portly little Père Crevel, naturally invited to be present at the signing of the marriage contract, behaved as if the scene with which this story opens had never taken place, as if he had no grievance against Baron Hulot. Célestin Crevel was cordial, still a little too much the ex-perfumer, but, now that he was a major, he was beginning to assume a majestic bearing. He spoke of dancing at the wedding.

'Fair lady,' he said graciously to Baroness Hulot, 'people like us know how to forget. Don't banish me from your home, and deign to adorn my house sometimes by coming there with your children. Don't worry. I'll never say a word of what lies at the bottom of my heart. I behaved like a fool, for I should lose too much if I never saw you again.'

'Monsieur, a virtuous woman has no ears for the speeches you refer to, and if you keep your word you may be sure that I shall be delighted to see an end to dissension of a kind that is always distressing in families.'

'Well, you big sulky fellow,' said Baron Hulot, forcibly taking Crevel off to the garden, 'you avoid me everywhere, even in my own house. Should two lovers of the fair sex quarrel over a petticoat? Really, that's just too stupid.'

'Monsieur, I'm not as handsome a man as you, and my scant powers of attraction prevent me from making good my losses as easily as you do.'

'You're being sarcastic,' replied the Baron.

'That is the privilege of the vanquished against the victors.'

Begun on this tone, the conversation concluded with a complete reconciliation. But Crevel insisted on his right to take his revenge.

Madame Marneffe wanted to be invited to Mademoiselle Hulot's wedding.

In order to see his future mistress in his drawing-room, the Councillor of State had to invite the staff of his department down to and including the assistant-managers. This meant that he had to give a big ball. As a good housekeeper, the Baroness calculated that an evening party would cost less than a dinner and would allow them to invite more people. So Hortense's wedding created quite a stir.

The Maréchal Prince de Wissembourg and the Baron de Nucingen were the witnesses on behalf of the bride, the Counts de Rastignac and Popinot for Steinbock. Moreover, since Count Steinbock had become famous, the most distinguished of the Polish exiles had sought his company, so that the artist felt obliged to invite them.

The Council of State, the Baron's Government department, and the Army, which wanted to do honour to the Comte de Forzheim, were to be represented at the highest level. The Hulots calculated that they had to send two hundred invitations. Who then can fail to understand little

Madame Marneffe's concern to appear in all her glory in the midst of such an assembly?

A month earlier, the Baroness had sold her diamonds, using the money to furnish her daughter's house, but retaining the finest stones for the trousseau. This sale brought in fifteen thousand francs, of which five thousand were used for Hortense's trousseau. What were ten thousand francs towards furnishing the young couple's flat, if we consider the requirements of modern luxury? But young Monsieur and Madame Hulot, Père Crevel, and the Comte de Forzheim gave valuable presents, for the old uncle had kept a sum in reserve to buy the silverware.

Thanks to all this help, a fastidious Parisian woman would have been satisfied with the young couple's furnishings and equipment in the flat they had chosen in the Rue Saint-Dominique near the Esplanade des Invalides. Everything in it was in harmony with their love, so pure, so open, and so sincere on both sides.

At last the great day arrived, for it was to be as great a day for the father as for Hortense and Wenceslas: Madame Marneffe had decided to have her house-warming party the day after her lapse from virtue and the wedding of the two lovers.

Who has not, at least once in his life, been at a wedding ball? Everyone can think back to his own memories and will certainly smile as he recalls all those people in their Sunday best, with faces to match their conventional dress. If ever a social event proves the influence of environment, surely a wedding party does. Indeed, those who are dressed up for the day have such an effect on the others that people who are quite used to formal dress look as if they belong to the group for whom the wedding is a landmark in their lives. Then remember those solemn old men who are so indifferent to everything that they have not changed their everyday black suits; and the old married men whose faces show the sad experience of life, which the young are just beginning. And there are the pleasurable excitements of the occasion, like the bubbles of carbon dioxide in the champagne, and the envious girls, and the women taken up with the success of their wedding outfits, and the poor relations whose meagre finery is in contrast to the people in full dress rig, and the gluttons who think only of the supper, and the card-players only of playing cards. All types are there, rich and poor, the envious and the envied, the realists and the idealists, all gathered together like the flowers in a bouquet around one rare flower, the bride. A wedding ball is the world in miniature.

36. *The two brides*

When the party was in full swing, Crevel took the Baron by the arm and whispered to him in the most natural possible way.

'Pon my soul, what a pretty little woman that is in pink who is peppering you with her glances.'

'Who?'

'The wife of the assistant-manager whose career you're promoting. goodness knows how, Madame Marneffe.'

'How do you know that?'

'Look here, Hulot, I'll try to forgive the wrongs you've done me if you'll take me to her place, and I'll receive you at Héloïse's. Everyone is asking who that charming creature is. Are you sure that no one from your office will explain how her husband's appointment came to be signed? Oh, you lucky rascal, she's worth more than a department. . . . Oh, I'd gladly work in her office. . . . Come now, *let us be friends, Cinna!*'*

'More than ever, and I promise you to be really obliging. In a month's time I'll have you asked to dinner with that little angel. . . . For we are dealing with angels, my old friend. I advise you to follow my example and leave the devils.'

Cousin Bette, now settled in the Rue Vaneau, in a pretty little third-floor flat, left the ball at ten o'clock and came home to look at her bonds representing an income of twelve hundred francs in two certificates, the one in

Countess Steinbock's name, the other in the younger Madame Hulot's.

So the reader will now understand how Monsieur Crevel could speak of Madame Marneffe to his friend Hulot and know a secret of which the rest of the world was ignorant. For with Monsieur Marneffe away, Cousin Bette, the Baron, and Valérie were the only ones to know of this private arrangement.

The Baron had been unwise in giving Madame Marneffe a dress far too splendid for the wife of an assistant-manager. The other wives were jealous of Valérie's dress and beauty. There were whisperings behind the fans, for the Marneffes' financial difficulties has been talked about in the department. The clerk had been seeking help just when the Baron had become enamoured of his wife. Moreover, Hector was not able to conceal his delight at seeing Valérie's success; modest and dignified, she was envied and subjected to that careful scrutiny which women dread so much when they enter a new social milieu for the first time.

After seeing his wife, daughter, and son-in-law to their carriage, the Baron managed to slip away without being noticed, leaving his son and daughter-in-law with the task of playing host and hostess. He got into Madame Marneffe's carriage and saw her home. But he found her silent and thoughtful, almost melancholy.

'My happiness makes you very sad, Valérie,' he said, drawing her towards him in the back of the cab.

'How do you expect a poor woman not to be thoughtful, my dear friend, when she has her first lapse from virtue, even though her husband's infamous conduct leaves her free? Do you think that I have no feelings, no faith, no religion? Your joy this evening was extremely indiscreet, and you drew attention to me in a thoroughly unpleasant way. Really, a schoolboy would have been less stupid than you. So all those ladies have torn me to pieces with their sideways glances and cutting remarks. What woman does not value her reputation? You have ruined me. Oh, I'm certainly yours now. And the only way I can excuse my fault is by being faithful to you. You monster,' she said, laughing and letting him kiss her. 'You knew very well what you were doing. Madame Coquet, the wife of our office manager, came and sat down beside me to admire my lace. "It comes from England," she said. "Is it very expensive, Madame?" "I've no idea," I replied. "This lace was my mother's. I'm not rich enough to buy lace like that!"'

Clearly, Madame Marneffe had finally so fascinated the old Empire beau that he thought he was the first to persuade her to be unfaithful and had aroused in her a passion strong enough to make her forget all her duties. She said she had been deserted by the odious Marneffe after three days of marriage and from the most frightful motives. Since then, she had lived like the most virtuous of maidens and had been glad to do so, for marriage seemed to her something horrible. This explained her present sadness.

'What if love should be like marriage?' she said, weeping.

These coquettish lies, which are reeled off by nearly all women in Valérie's situation, gave the Baron a glimpse of the roses of the seventh heaven. So Valérie stood on ceremony, while the lovesick artist and Hortense waited, perhaps impatiently, for the Baroness to give her final blessing and last kiss to her daughter.

At seven in the morning, the Baron, blissfully happy—for in Valérie he had found all the innocence of a young girl combined with the most consummate devilry—returned to relieve young Monsieur and Madame Hulot of their thankless task. The dancers, men and women almost strangers to the house, who end up at all weddings by taking over the party, were still performing those final interminable country dances called *cotillons*; the *bouillote* players were glued to their tables; Père Crevel was winning six thousand francs.

The newspapers distributed by the newsvendors contained the following little item in their Paris gossip columns.

'The marriage of Monsieur le Comte de Steinbock and Mademoiselle Hortense Hulot, daughter of Baron Hulot d'Evry, Councillor of State and a Director at the War Ministry, niece of the celebrated Comte de Forzheim, took place this morning at the church of Saint-Thomas-d'Aquin.

'The ceremony drew a large gathering. Among the guests could be seen some of our artistic celebrities: Léon de Lora, Joseph Bridau, Stidmann, Bixiou; eminent officials from the War Ministry and the Council of State, and several members of both Houses; also the most distinguished of the Polish exiles, Counts Paz, Laginski, etc.

'Monsieur le Comte Wenceslas de Steinbock is the great-nephew of the famous general of Charles XII, King of Sweden. The Young Count, having taken part in the Polish rebellion, sought refuge in France, where his well-deserved reputation as a sculptor made it possible for him to obtain limited naturalization papers.'

So, in spite of Baron Hulot's appalling financial difficulties, his daughter's wedding lacked nothing that public opinion demands, not even newspaper publicity, and it was, in every respect, like young Hulot's to Mademoiselle Crevel. This festivity toned down the comments that were being made about the director's financial situation, and the dowry given to his daughter also explained his need to have recourse to borrowing money.

Here ends what is, in a way, the introduction to this story. The narrative so far is to the drama which completes it, as the premises to a syllogism, as the exposition to every classical tragedy.

37. *Moral reflections on immorality*

In Paris, when a woman has decided to make a profession of selling her beauty, it does not mean that she will make a fortune. One can meet lovely, quick-witted creatures there, who eke out a squalid existence and end in misery a life begun in pleasure. The reason is this. It is not enough to decide to adopt the shameful career of the courtesan, intending to pocket all the benefits while retaining the external appearance of a respectable middle-class wife.

Vice does not achieve its triumphs easily. It is like Genius in this respect, that they both require a conjunction of favourable circumstances to bring about the combined effect of fortune and talent. Without the extraordinary phases of the Revolution there would have been no Emperor; he would have been no more than a second Fabert.*

Venal beauty without admirers, without fame, without the cross of dishonour which is earned by the fortunes squandered on it, is a Correggio* in a garret; it is genius dying in an attic.

So a Laïs* in Paris must first of all find a rich man who conceives such a passion for her that he will pay her price. Above all, she must maintain a high standard of elegance which is her trade-mark, she must have such good breeding that it flatters a man's vanity, and she must have a wit as sharp as Sophie Arnould's,* which arouses the rich from their apathy. Finally she must arouse the desire of libertines by appearing to be faithful to one, whose happiness is then envied by the others.

These conditions, which women of that kind call *luck*, are quite hard to come by in Paris, although the town is full of millionaires and idlers, of the bored and the capricious. In this way Providence has no doubt protected the homes of clerks and the lower middle-class, whose difficulties are at least doubled by the environment in which they live and work.

Nevertheless, there are still enough Madame Marneffes in Paris for Valérie to represent a type in this history of manners.

Some of these women are motivated by a combination of real passion and financial necessity, like Madame Colleville, who was attached for so long to one of the most famous orators of the left, the banker Keller; others are impelled by vanity, like Madame de la Baudraye,* who in a way remained virtuous, despite eloping with Lousteau; some are led astray by their need for fine clothes, others by the impossibility of providing for a household on an obviously inadequate salary. The niggardliness of the State or, if you like, of the two Houses, is the cause of many misfortunes and the source of a great deal of corruption. At the present time, much pity is expended on the lot of the working-classes; they are represented as being cruelly exploited by the manufacturers. But the State is a hundred times harder than the greediest industrialist. As far as salaries are concerned, it carried economy to the point of absurdity. If you work hard, industry will pay you according to what you do; but what does the State give to so many obscure and devoted workers?

To stray from the path of honour is an unforgivable sin in a married woman, but there are degrees in this kind of behaviour. Some women, far from being depraved, hide their lapses from virtue and remain apparently respectable women, like the two whose activities have just been recalled, while others add to their misdemeanours by shamelessly trading on them. So Madame Marneffe is, in a way, representative of those ambitious married courtesans who, right from the start, accept depravity and all that it implies and have decided to make their fortunes while having a good time, with no scruples about the means. But, like Madame Marneffe, such women nearly always have their husbands as agents and accomplices.

These Machiavellis in petticoats are the most dangerous women, and of all the evil kinds of Parisian female, they are the worst. A true courtesan, like Josépha, Madame Schontz, Malaga, Jenny Cadine, etc., in the openness of her situation carries a warning as clear as the red lamp of a house of prostitution or the bright lights of a gambling den. Then a man knows that is the way to his ruin. But the simpering respectability, the semblance of virtue, the hypocritical behaviour of a married woman who never lets anything be seen but ordinary household needs and appears to deny herself any extravagance, leads a man to unspectacular ruin, all the more strange in that he can excuse it without being able to explain it. It is sordid household expenses, not gay extravagance, that eat up fortunes. The father of a family goes unostentatiously to his ruin and without even satisfied vanity to console him in his poverty.

This tirade will pierce the hearts of many families like an arrow. Madame Marneffes can be seen at all levels of society and even at royal courts; for Valérie is a sad reality, modelled from life down to the smallest detail. Unfortunately her portrait will cure no one of the addiction to loving sweetly smiling angels with dreamy looks, innocent faces, and a strong-box for a heart.

38. *In which we can see the result of Crevel's opinions*

In 1841, about three years after Hortense's marriage, it was commonly held that Baron Hulot d'Ervy had settled down, had 'taken off his harness', as Louis XV's first surgeon* put it, and yet Madame Marneffe was costing him twice what he had spent on Josépha. But, though always well dressed, Valérie affected the simplicity of a minor official's wife. She reserved her luxury for her dressing-gowns and indoor clothes. In this way she sacrificed her Parisian vanity to her beloved Hector. Nevertheless, when she went to the theatre, she always appeared wearing a pretty hat and a very smart outfit. The Baron took her there in a carriage to a carefully chosen box.

The flat, which occupied all the second floor of a modern building in the Rue Vaneau, between a courtyard and a garden, exuded respectability. Its luxury consisted of chintz curtains and handsome, comfortable furniture. The exception was the bedroom, which displayed the lavishness of the Jenny Cadines and the Madame Schontzes. There were lace curtains, cashmere draperies, brocade door hangings, a mantelpiece with ornaments designed by Stidmann, and a little cabinet crammed with lovely things. Hulot did not want to see his Valérie in surroundings any less magnificent than a Josépha's gold and pearl-studded sink of iniquity.

Of the two main rooms, the drawing-room had been furnished in red damask and the dining-room with carved oak. But, carried away by the desire to have everything in keeping, by the end of six months the Baron had added more durable luxury to the ephemeral, giving her valuable household equipment such as silverware costing more than twenty-four thousand francs.

In two years Madame Marneffe's house had acquired the reputation of being a very pleasant place. People played cards there. Valérie herself soon became known as an agreeable, witty woman. To explain her changed circumstances, the rumour was spread of an enormous legacy left to her in trust by her natural father, Marshal Montcornet.

With an eye to the future, Valérie had added religious hypocrisy to her social hypocrisy. She was punctilious in her attendance at Sunday services and enjoyed all the respect due to her piety. She collected for the Church, did charitable work, gave consecrated bread, and did some good in the neighbourhood, all at Hector's expense.

So everything in her household was conducted with perfect propriety. Many people, then, affirmed the purity of her relationship with the Baron, pointing out the age of the Councillor of State, to whom they attributed a platonic liking for Madame Marneffe's pretty wit, charming manners, and entertaining conversation, rather like the late Louis XVIII's appreciation of a well-turned love letter.

The Baron used to leave at midnight with everyone else and return a quarter of an hour later. Here is the secret of this profound secret.

The porters of the house were Monsieur and Madame Olivier, who, through the Baron's influence—he was a friend of the landlord in search of a caretaker—had left their ill-paid post in gloomy quarters at the Rue du Doyenné for the well-paid one in magnificent quarters at the Rue Vaneau. Now Madame Olivier, a former linen-maid in Charles X's household, who had lost *that position* with the fall of the legitimate monarchy, had three children. The eldest, already a lawyer's junior clerk, was the idol of the Olivier couple. This Benjamin, threatened with six years military service, was about to see his brilliant career interrupted, when Madame Marneffe managed to obtain his exemption from military service because of one of those physical defects which medical boards are able to discover when some power in the War Ministry whispers a word in their ear.

Olivier, a former huntsman of Charles X, and his wife would therefore have crucified Jesus again for Baron Hulot and Madame Marneffe.

What could people say, for they knew nothing of the earlier episode of the Brazilian, Monsieur Montès de Montéjanos? Nothing. Moreover, people are very indulgent to the mistress of a house where they enjoy themselves. What is more, Madame Marneffe added to all her charms the highly prized advantage of having hidden power. So Claude Vignon, who had become secretary to the Maréchal de Wissembourg and dreamed of becoming a member of the Council of State as Master of Appeals, was a frequent visitor to her drawing-room, as were some easygoing deputies who liked a game of cards.

Madame Marneffe's circle had been built up slowly and carefully. Into it were received only people of similar views and habits, interested in supporting each other and in proclaiming the infinite merits of the mistress of the house.

Remember this adage—complicity in vice is the real Holy Alliance* in Paris. Interests always diverge in the end but the corrupt always understand each other.

Within three months of moving to the Rue Vaneau, Madame Marneffe had received Monsieur Crevel, who there and then became Mayor of his district and Officer of the Legion of Honour.

Crevel hesitated a long time; it meant giving up the famous uniform of the National Guard, in which he used to preen himself at the Tuileries, thinking he was as good a soldier as the Emperor. But ambition, encouraged by Madame Marneffe, was stronger than vanity.

Monsieur le Maire had considered his liaison with Mademoiselle Héloïse Brisetout quite incompatible with his political stance. Long before his accession to the bourgeois throne of the Mayoralty, his love-affairs had been wrapped in profound mystery.

But Crevel, as you might have guessed, had paid for the right of taking his revenge for the theft of Josépha with an investment bringing in an income of six thousand francs a year in the name of Valérie Fortin, wife of Monsieur Marneffe, but retaining her own financial assets.

Valérie, inheriting perhaps from her mother the kept woman's special gifts, understood at a glance this grotesque adorer's character.

The words 'I've never had a society woman', which Crevel had used to Lisbeth and which had been repeated by Lisbeth to her dear Valérie, had counted for a lot in the transaction to which she owed her six thousand francs a year in 5-per-cents. Since then, she had never allowed her prestige to diminish in the eyes of César Birotteau's former travelling salesman.

Crevel had married the daughter of a Brie miller for money. She was, moreover, an only child whose inheritance made up three quarters of the ex-perfumer's fortune, for retailers usually get rich less from their business than from the alliance of shopkeeping and agriculture. A great many farmers, millers, stock-breeders, and market-gardeners round Paris dream of the glamour of the shop-counter for their daughters and see in a retailer, jeweller, or money-changer a son-in-law more after their own hearts than a solicitor or a barrister, whose social standing makes them uneasy. They are afraid of being despised later on by these leading lights of the bourgeoisie.

Madame Crevel, rather an ugly woman, very common and stupid, who died none too soon, had given her husband no joys other than those of paternity.

So, in the early days of his business career, tied by the duties of his situation and restrained by lack of means, this libertine had played the role of Tantalus.* In touch, to use his own expression, with the most respected society women, he would see them to the door with the servile bows of a shopkeeper, while admiring their grace, their way of wearing fashionable clothes, and all the indefinable signs of what is called *good breeding*. To reach the heights of one of these queens of society was a desire which had been conceived in his youth and had lain buried in his heart ever since.

To win Madame Marneffe's *favours* was not only the realization of a dream, but also a matter of pride, of vanity, of self-esteem, as we have seen. His ambition increased with success. He experienced enormous mental satisfaction, and when the mind is pleased, the heart benefits, happiness is increased tenfold. In addition, Madame Marneffe offered Crevel sophisticated pleasures that he had never before experienced, for neither Josépha nor Héloïse had loved him, while Madame Marneffe thought it necessary to deceive completely a man in whom she saw an inexhaustible cash-box.

The deceptions of mercenary love are more charming than the real thing. True love involves fierce little quarrels that cut to the quick, but a quarrel for fun is, on the contrary, a caress for the dupe's vanity. And the infrequency of his encounters with Valérie kept Crevel's desire for her in a state of ardent passion. He was continually coming up against Valérie's virtuous severity; she would feign remorse and talk of what her father must be thinking of her in his heroes' paradise.

He had to conquer a kind of coldness which the subtle hussy made him think he overcame; she seemed to yield to the shopkeeper's violent passion. But, as if ashamed, she would always reassume her proud airs of virtuous respectability, neither more nor less than an Englishwoman, and always crushed Crevel beneath the weight of her dignity, for, right from the start, he had swallowed the tale of her virtue. Moreover, Valérie had love-making skills which made her indispensable to Crevel as well as to the Baron.

In public, she presented the fascinating combination of modest, pensive innocence, of impeccable propriety with a wit enhanced by courtesy, grace and charming créole manners. But in private she outdid the courtesans; she was amusing, entertaining, and richly inventive.

Such a contrast appeals enormously to a man of Crevel's stamp. He is flattered to be the sole author of this farce; he believes it is played exclusively for him and he laughs at the delightful hypocrisy, while admiring the actress.

39. *Handsome Hulot dismantled*

Valérie had taken over Baron Hulot in quite a remarkable way. She had induced him to grow old by one of those subtle forms of flattery which can usefully serve to illustrate the diabolical cleverness of this kind of woman.

Even in the strongest constitutions, there comes a moment when, as in a besieged fortress which has put up a brave showing for a long time, the true situation becomes apparent. Foreseeing the approaching disintegration of the old Empire beau, Valérie thought it advisable to hasten the process.

'Why do you bother, my old veteran?' she said, six months after their clandestine and doubly adulterous union. 'Do you have pretensions to further conquests? Do you want to be unfaithful to me? I'd find you much more attractive if you'd stop using make-up. For my sake, sacrifice your artificial charms. Do you think it's two sous' worth of polish on your boots, your rubber belt, your tight waistcoat, and your false hair-piece that I love in you? Besides, the older you look, the less I'll be afraid of seeing my Hulot carried off by a rival.'

So, believing in Madame Marneffe's divine friendship as much as in her love, and expecting to end his days with her, the Councillor of State had followed this confidential advice and no longer dyed his whiskers and hair.

After receiving Valérie's touching declaration, the tall, handsome Hector appeared one fine morning completely white-haired. Madame Marneffe easily convinced her dear Hector that she had seen the white line formed by the growth of the hair a hundred times.

'White hair suits your face admirably,' she said when she saw him. 'It has a softening effect. You look infinitely nicer; you look charming.'

Once started on this course, the Baron in the end left off

his leather waistcoat and his corset; he discarded all his harness. His stomach sagged, his obesity became obvious. The oak tree became a tower, and the heaviness of his movements was all the more alarming in that the Baron was ageing enormously in the role of Louis XII.*

His eyebrows were still black and were a vague reminder of the handsome Hulot, just as in some segments of feudal walls a faint detail of sculpture remains to give a glimpse of what the castle was like in its heyday. This discrepancy made the expression of his eyes, still lively and youthful, all the more strange in his tanned face, for there, where Rubens-like flesh tones had bloomed for so long, livid patches and long, deep wrinkles revealed the struggles of a passion in rebellion against nature. Hulot, at this time, was one of those fine human ruins whose virility is proclaimed by bushy tufts of hair in the ears and nose and on the fingers, giving an effect like that of moss growing on the almost everlasting monuments of the Roman Empire.

How had Valérie managed to keep Crevel and Hulot side by side in her home, when the vindictive Major wanted to triumph openly over Hulot?

Without giving an immediate reply to that question, which will be answered in the course of the drama, we may note that Lisbeth and Valérie between them had invented a complicated device whose powerful mechanism helped to achieve this end.

Marneffe, seeing his wife's beauty enhanced by the milieu where she reigned supreme like the sun of a solar system, seemed, in the eyes of the world, to have felt a renewal of his passion for her; he had become crazy about her. If his jealousy made the worthy Marneffe a kill-joy, it gave an exceptional value to Valérie's favours. Nevertheless Marneffe showed a trust in his director which degenerated into an almost ridiculous affability. The only person whose presence he resented was precisely Crevel.

Marneffe, destroyed by the debaucheries peculiar to great capital cities, described by the Roman poets but for which our modern sense of decency has no name, had become as hideous as a wax anatomical model. But this walking specimen of disease, dressed in fine cloth, was supported on spindle-shanks clad in elegant trousers. His shrivelled chest was clothed in perfumed white linen, and musk smothered the fetid odours of human decay.

This hideous personification of vice in its death throes, yet wearing red-heeled shoes (for Valérie dressed Marneffe in conformity with his status, his decoration, and his post), terrified Crevel, who found it difficult to meet the assistant-manager's pale eyes. Marneffe was the Mayor's nightmare.

When he realized the extraordinary power which Lisbeth and his wife had conferred upon him, the evil rascal used it for his own enjoyment; he played on it as on a musical instrument. And as drawing-room gambling was the last resource of a mind as worn out as his body, he fleeced Crevel, who felt obliged *to go easy* with the respectable official whom *he was deceiving*.

Seeing Crevel tremble like a child in the presence of this hideous, vile mummy, whose corruption was a closed book to the Mayor, seeing him above all so profoundly despised by Valérie, who laughed at Crevel as if he were a clown, the Baron felt he had reason to believe himself so safe from all rivalry that he frequently invited Crevel to dinner.

Valérie, protected by these two passions standing sentinel on either side of her, and by a jealous husband, attracted all eyes, excited everyone's desire in the circle where she shone.

So, while keeping up appearances, in about three years she had succeeded in realizing the very difficult conditions of the success that courtesans strive for but so rarely achieve, with the aid of scandal, of their flaunting behaviour, and of the brilliance of their lives in the glare of publicity. Like a well-cut diamond charmingly set by Chanor, Valérie's beauty, formerly buried in the mine of the Rue du Doyenné, was worth more than its real value; it aroused some men's unhappy love. Claude Vignon was secretly in love with Valérie.

This retrospective explanation, very necessary when we meet people again after an interval of three years, is, as it were, Valérie's balance-sheet. Here now is that of her partner Lisbeth.

40. *One of the seven plagues of Paris*

In the Marneffe household, Cousin Bette had the position of a relative who has combined the duties of companion and housekeeper. But she did not experience the double humiliation which, most of the time, afflicts the poor creature unfortunate enough to have to accept these equivocal situations.

Lisbeth and Valérie offered the touching sight of one of those friendships between women which are so close and so unlikely that Parisians, always too quick to jump to conclusions, immediately dismiss them as scandalous. The contrast between the cold, masculine temperament of the Lorraine peasant and Valérie's warm creole nature gave substance to the calumny.

In addition, Madame Marneffe had unwittingly added weight to the gossip by the care she took of her friend with a view to furthering a matrimonial project which, as we shall see, was to complete Lisbeth's vengeance.

A revolutionary change had taken place in Cousin Bette. Valérie, who had insisted on choosing the old maid's clothes, had profited greatly from it.

This strange woman, her slender figure now properly corseted, used bandoline* lotion for her well-smoothed hair, accepted her dresses as the dressmaker delivered them, and wore elegant little boots and grey silk stockings which were, moreover, included in the tradesmen's bills to Valérie and paid for by whoever was entitled to settle them.

Thus refurbished, but still wearing the yellow cashmere shawl, Bette would have been unrecognizable to anyone seeing her again after that three-year interval. This other diamond, a black one, the rarest of all diamonds, cut by a skilled hand and mounted in the setting that suited it, was appreciated at her full value by a few ambitious clerks.

Those who saw Bette for the first time shuddered

involuntarily at the sight of her wild poetic beauty, which Valérie had skilfully brought out by her care for the dress of this bloodstained Nun,* by artistically framing in thick bands of hair her spare, olive-skinned face with shining eyes as black as the hair, and by making the most of her stiff figure.

Bette, like a Virgin by Cranach* or Van Eyck,* or like a Byzantine Virgin, that had stepped out of their frames, retained the stiffness, the formality of those mysterious figures, first cousins of Isis* and the sheathed divinities of the Egyptian sculptors. She was like a walking statue of granite, basalt, or porphyry.

Secure from want for the rest of her days, Bette was always charming; she brought cheerfulness with her wherever she went to dine. The Baron, moreover, paid the rent of the little flat, furnished, as we know, with the discarded furniture of her friend Valérie's boudoir and bedroom.

'After starting life like a famished goat, I am ending it like a lioness,' she would say.

She continued to do the most difficult pieces of ornamental embroidery for Monsieur Rivet, only, as she said, not to waste her time. And yet, as we shall see, her life was extremely busy. But one of the ingrained ideas of country-bred people is never to give up their means of livelihood; in this they are like the Jews.

Every morning, very early, Cousin Bette went herself to the central market with the cook. In Bette's plan, the household expenses which were ruining Baron Hulot were to enrich her dear Valérie and did in fact do so.

What mistress of a household has not, since 1838, experienced the disastrous effects of the anti-social doctrines spread amongst the lower classes by inflammatory writers?

In every home, the financial burden caused by servants is the heaviest of all financial burdens.

With a few very rare exceptions, which deserve the Montyon prize,* cooks, male and female, are domestic thieves, brazen, salaried thieves, for whom the government complaisantly acts as receiver, thus encouraging the propensity for theft which is almost sanctioned amongst cooks by the old joke about the *shopping-basket handle*.* Where formerly these women used to try to steal forty sous for their lottery tickets, today they take fifty francs for the savings-bank.

And those cold-blooded puritans, who amuse themselves by carrying out philanthropic experiments in France, think they have made the working classes moral!

Between the masters' tables and the market, the servants have set up their secret toll, and the city of Paris is not as efficient at collecting its entry dues as they are at levying theirs on everything. In addition to the 50-per-cent tax they charge on provisions, they demand handsome presents from the shopkeepers. Even the most important tradesmen tremble before this secret power. They pay up without a word: coachmakers, jewellers, tailors, the lot.

If anyone tries to supervise them, the servants reply with insolence or with the costly stupidities of pretended clumsiness. Today they make enquiries about the employers as in the past the employers used to enquire about them.

This evil, which has truly reached a peak and against which the law-courts are beginning to act severely, but to no effect, can only be eradicated when wage-earning servants are compelled by law to have a workman's record book. The evil would then end as if by magic. If all servants were obliged to produce their books and the masters had to enter the reasons for dismissal, corruption would undoubtedly be powerfully held in check.

The people who are concerned with the high politics of the day have no idea of the extent of the dishonesty of the lower classes in Paris; it is equalled only by their consuming jealousy.

There are no statistics about the alarming number of 20-year-old workmen who marry cooks of 40 or 50, enriched through theft. One shudders at the thought of the consequences of such unions, from the threefold standpoint of criminality, degeneration of the race, and unhappy homes.

As for the purely financial harm resulting from domestic thefts, this is enormous from the political point of view.

The cost of living, which is doubled in this way, precludes any extras in many households. The extras! They constitute half the trade of a country, as they do the elegance of life. Books and flowers are as necessary as bread to many people.

Lisbeth, who was well aware of this terrible scourge of Parisian households, had it in mind to take charge of Valérie's housekeeping, when she promised her support during the terrible scene in which they had sworn to be like two sisters.

So she had brought, from the heart of the Vosges, a relative on her mother's side, a former cook to the Bishop of Nancy, a pious, extremely honest old maid. Nevertheless, since she feared her lack of experience of Paris, and above all the evil counsels which destroy so many unstable loyalties, Lisbeth accompanied Mathurine to the central market and tried to train her how to buy.

To know the real prices of things so as to command the salesman's respect, to serve unusual dishes like fish, for instance, when they are not dear, to be aware of the prices of foodstuffs, and to know when a price-rise is imminent so as to buy before it occurs, such housewifely expertise is essential to domestic economy.

As Mathurine was paid good wages and was constantly being given presents, she was sufficiently attached to the household to be pleased when she secured a bargain. So for some time she had been as good as Lisbeth, who thought she was sufficiently trained and reliable not to need to be accompanied to the market except on days when Valérie had guests, which, by the way, was quite often. And for this reason.

The Baron had begun by maintaining the strictest decorum, but very soon his passion for Madame Marneffe had become so ardent and so demanding that he wanted to be away from her as little as possible. He began by dining there four times a week, but then thought it delightful to dine there every day. Six months after his daughter's marriage, he paid Madame Marneffe two thousand francs a month for his board. She would invite anyone that her dear

Baron wished to entertain. In any case, dinner was always prepared for six, so the Baron could always bring three without warning.

By her careful housekeeping, Lisbeth solved the very difficult problem of maintaining a lavish table for the sum of a thousand francs and at the same time giving a thousand francs a month to Madame Marneffe.

41. *Cousin Bette's hopes*

As Valérie's wardrobe was amply paid for by both Crevel and the Baron, the two friends made another thousand francs a month out of that. And so this pure, innocent young woman had already acquired savings of one hundred and fifty thousand francs. She had put her annual allowances and her monthly perquisites together, investing them and increasing them by vast profits due to the generosity with which Crevel allowed the capital of *his little duchess* to share in the success of his own financial operations. Crevel had initiated Valérie into the jargon and speculation procedures of the stock exchange and, like all Parisian women, she soon became more adept than her master.

Lisbeth, who never spent a farthing of her twelve hundred francs, whose rent and clothes were paid for, who never took a sou out of her pocket, also had a little capital of five to six thousand francs, which Crevel, in a fatherly way, invested profitably for her.

Nevertheless, the Baron's love and Crevel's were a heavy burden on Valérie. On the day when the story of this drama is resumed, Valérie, irritated by one of those incidents which, in life, act like the bell whose ringing makes swarming bees settle, went up to Lisbeth's room; there she indulged in one of those comforting, long-winded laments in which women use words rather like cigarettes to allay life's little miseries.

'Lisbeth, my love, I have to spend two hours with Crevel this morning. How very tiresome! Oh, how I wish I could send you in my place!'

'Unfortunately, that can't be done,' said Lisbeth with a smile. 'I shall die a virgin.'

'Belonging to those two old men! There are moments when I'm ashamed of myself! Oh, if my poor mother could see me!'

'You talk as if I were Crevel,' replied Lisbeth.

'Tell me, my dear little Bette, you don't despise me, do you?'

'Oh, if I had been pretty, what adventures I would have had!' exclaimed Lisbeth. 'That justifies your conduct.'

'But you would have listened only to your heart,' said Madame Marneffe with a sigh.

'Bah!' replied Lisbeth. 'Marneffe is a corpse they have forgotten to bury. The Baron is virtually your husband, Crevel is your admirer. As I see it, that's perfectly in order for any married woman.'

'But that's not the trouble, my dear, darling girl. You choose not to understand me.'

'Oh, I understand you perfectly,' exclaimed the Lorraine peasant, 'for the implications of what you've said form part of my revenge. But what do you expect of me? I'm working on the matter.'

'To love Wenceslas so much that it's making me grow thin, and not to be able to see him!' said Valérie, stretching out her arms. 'Hulot suggests to him that he should come to dinner here, but my artist refuses. He doesn't know how he's idolized, that monster of a man! What's his wife? A pretty piece of flesh! Yes, she's beautiful, but I, I know it instinctively, I am more seductive.'

'Don't worry, my little girl, he will come', said Lisbeth in the tone nurses use to impatient children. 'I'm determined on that.'

'But when?'

'Perhaps this week.'

'Let me kiss you.'

As can be seen, these two women were as one. Everything Valérie did, even her most heedless actions, her pleasures, her fits of the sulks, were decided upon only after careful deliberation between them.

Lisbeth, who found this courtesan existence strangely exciting, advised Valérie in everything and pursued the course of her vengeance with pitiless logic.

Besides, she adored Valérie; she had made her her daughter, her friend, her beloved. She found in her the docility of the créole, the yielding nature of the voluptuary. She chatted with her every morning with much more pleasure than she had had in talking to Wenceslas; they could laugh over the mischief they were jointly planning, over the folly of men, and count up together the accumulating interest of their respective piles of treasure.

In carrying out her plan and in her new friendship, Lisbeth had indeed found much more ample scope for her activity than in her insensate love for Wenceslas. The pleasures of satisfied hatred are the keenest and the most ardent that the heart can experience. Love is, in a way, the gold and hatred the iron of that mine of emotions that lies within us.

And then, in Valérie, Lisbeth saw beauty in all its glory, a quality she adored as we adore everything we cannot have. It was a beauty much more approachable than that of Wenceslas, who had always been cold and unresponsive to her.

By the end of nearly three years, Lisbeth was beginning to see some progress in the underground tunnelling which absorbed all her life and to which she devoted her mental energy. Lisbeth was the thinker, Madame Marneffe the doer. Madame Marneffe was the axe, Lisbeth was the hand that wielded it. And with swift blows that hand was demolishing the family which daily became more odious to her, for we hate more and more, as we love more each day, when we love.

Love and hatred are emotions which feed on themselves, but, of the two, hatred is the more long-lasting. Love is bounded by our limited strength; it derives its power from life and generous giving. Hatred is like death and avarice, it is a kind of active abstraction, above people and things.

Lisbeth, having embarked on the life that suited her, brought into play all her faculties. She ruled, like the

Jesuits, as a power behind the scenes. As a result, her appearance had been completely regenerated. Her face glowed. Lisbeth dreamed of becoming Madame la Maréchale Hulot.

This scene, in which the two friends bluntly told each other their most private thoughts without beating about the bush, took place just after Lisbeth's return from the market, where she had been to buy the materials for an elegant dinner.

Marneffe, who coveted Monsieur Coquet's post, was entertaining him and the virtuous Madame Coquet, and Lisbeth was hoping to have the office manager's resignation arranged by Hulot that very evening at the Baroness's house where she was to dine.

'You'll come back to pour out tea for us, Bette dear?' asked Valérie.

'I hope so.'

'What do you mean, you hope so? Have you reached the stage of going to bed with Adeline to drink her tears while she's asleep?'

'If only I could!' replied Lisbeth, with a laugh. 'I wouldn't say no. She is paying for her happiness and that makes me happy; I remember my childhood. It's my turn now. She'll be in the gutter, but *I* shall be Comtesse de Forzheim!'

42. *The extremities to which libertines reduce their legitimate wives*

Lisbeth went off to the Rue Plumet, where for some time she had been in the habit of going as one goes to the theatre, in order to indulge her emotions.

The dwelling selected by Hulot for his wife comprised a large, spacious hall, a drawing-room, a bedroom, and a dressing-room. The dining-room was off the drawing-room on one side. Two servants' rooms and a kitchen on the third floor completed the accommodation, which was, however, not unworthy of a Councillor of State and a Director at the War Ministry. The house, the courtyard, and the staircase were imposing.

The Baroness, who had to furnish her drawing-room, her bedroom, and the dining-room with the relics of her splendour, had taken the best of the worn-out furniture from the house in the Rue de l'Université.

The poor woman was, moreover, attached to these dumb witnesses of her happiness; for her they had an almost consoling eloquence. In her memories, she caught glimpses of flowers, just as, on the carpets, she could see circles of roses which were barely visible to others.

As one entered the enormous hall where twelve chairs, a barometer, a big stove, and long white calico curtains bordered with red reminded one of the dreary waiting-rooms in government offices, one's heart sank; one could feel the solitude in which this woman lived. Sorrow, like pleasure, creates an atmosphere of its own. At a first glance into any home, one knows whether love reigns there or despair. Adeline was to be found in a huge bedroom, furnished with beautiful Jacob Desmalters* furniture in speckled mahagony, with Empire ormolu ornaments that managed to look even colder than Louis XVI bronzes. And one shuddered at seeing this woman seated in a Roman armchair before her work-table decorated with sphinxes, her colour gone, affecting a show of cheerfulness, preserving her Imperial air as carefully as she did the blue velvet dress that she wore in the house. Her proud spirit sustained her body and maintained her beauty.

By the end of the first year of her exile in this apartment, the Baroness had measured the full extent of her misfortune. 'Even though my Hector has banished me here, he has still given me a much better life then a simple peasant woman has any right to expect,' she said to herself. 'He wants me to live like this; his will be done! I am Baroness Hulot, the sister-in-law of a Marshal of France. I have led a blameless life, my two children are settled, I can wait for death wrapped in the immaculate veils of a virtuous wife, in the crape of my vanished happiness.'

Hulot's portrait, in the uniform of a Commissary General of the Imperial Guard, painted by Robert Lefebvre* in 1810, hung above the work-table. When a visitor was announced, Adeline would put away in a drawer of the table a copy of the *Imitation of Christ* which she read constantly. This blameless Magdalen, too, listened to the voice of the Holy Spirit in her desert.

'Mariette, my dear, how is my good Adeline?' Lisbeth asked the cook who came to open the door for her.

'Oh, she seems all right, Mademoiselle. But, between ourselves, if she persists in her ideas, she'll kill herself,' Mariette whispered to Lisbeth. 'Really, you ought to make her promise to eat more. Yesterday, Madame told me to give her two sous' worth of milk and a little roll in the morning, and for dinner either a herring or a little cold veal. She had a pound of veal cooked to last a week, for the days when she dines alone here, of course. She doesn't want to spend more than ten sous a day on her food. That's not sensible. If I were to tell Monsieur le Maréchal of this fine plan, he might quarrel with Monsieur le Baron and disinherit him. But you, on the other hand, are so kind and so clever, you'll be able to put things right.'

'Well, why don't you talk to Monsieur le Baron?' asked Lisbeth.

'Oh, my dear Mademoiselle, it's about three weeks since he was here, in fact all the time since we last saw you. Besides, Madame has forbidden me on pain of dismissal ever to ask Monsieur for money. But, as for troubles, oh, poor Madame has had plenty of them. It's the first time Monsieur has neglected her for so long. Every time the bell rang, she used to rush to the window. But for the last five days she hasn't left her chair. She spends her time reading. Whenever she goes to see Madame la Comtesse, she says to me, "Mariette," she says, "if Monsieur comes, tell him I'm at home and send the porter to me. His errand will be well paid."'

'Poor cousin!' said Bette. 'Her situation breaks my heart. I speak of her to my cousin the Baron every day. What more can I do? He says, "You're right, Bette. I'm a wretch.

My wife's an angel and I'm a monster. I'll go tomorrow."
And he stays with Madame Marneffe. That woman is
ruining him but he adores her. He feels alive only when
he's with her. I do what I can. If I weren't there and if I
hadn't Mathurine with me, the Baron would have spent
twice as much. And as he has almost nothing left, he might
have blown his brains out already. Well, you know,
Mariette, her husband's death would kill Adeline; I'm sure
of that. At least I try to make both ends meet there and to
prevent my cousin getting through too much money.'

'Oh, that's what my poor mistress says. She's well aware
of how much she owes you,' replied Mariette. 'She was
saying that for a long time she misjudged you.'

'Oh!' said Lisbeth. 'Did she say anything else?'

'No, Mademoiselle. If you want to give her pleasure,
talk to her about Monsieur. She thinks you're fortunate to
see him every day.'

'Is she alone?'

'Beg pardon, Mademoiselle, the Marshal's there. Oh, he
comes every day and she always tells him that she has seen
Monsieur that morning, that he comes home very late at
night.'

'And is there a good dinner today?' asked Bette.

Mariette found it difficult to meet the peasant woman's
eye and she was hesitating to reply, when the drawing-
room door opened and Marshal Hulot emerged in such a
hurry that he bowed to Bette without looking at her and
dropped some papers. Bette picked up the papers and ran
to the stairs, for there was no point in calling after a deaf
man. But she contrived not to overtake the Marshal, came
back, and furtively read the following note, written in
pencil:

'My dear brother,—My husband has given me my allowance for
the quarter, but my daughter Hortense needed it so badly that I
have lent her the whole amount, which is barely enough to get
her out of her difficulties. Can you lend me a few hundred francs?
For I don't want to ask for any more money. It would hurt me
too much if he were to reproach me.'

'Oh,' thought Lisbeth, 'to humble her pride to this extent, what a desperate situation she must be in!'

43. *The grieving family*

Lisbeth went in, found Adeline in tears, and flung her arms round her neck.

'Adeline, my dear, I know everything!' said Cousin Bette. 'Look, the Marshal dropped this paper, he was so upset, for he was dashing away like a greyhound. How long is it since that dreadful Hector gave you any money?'

'He gives me my allowance regularly,' replied the Baroness, 'but Hortense needed money, and . . .'

'And you had nothing with which to pay for our dinner,' said Bette, interrupting her cousin. 'Now I understand why Mariette looked so embarrassed when I mentioned the meal to her. You are behaving like a child, Adeline. Look, let me give you my savings.'

'Thank you, Bette,. You are kind,' replied Adeline, wiping away a tear. 'This little difficulty is only temporary and I have made arrangements for the future. My expenses will be no more than two thousand four hundred francs a year after this, including the rent, and I'll have enough. But whatever you do, don't say a word to Hector. How is he?'

'Oh, he's as strong as the Pont-Neuf and as merry as a lark. He thinks of nothing but his bewitching Valérie.'

Madame Hulot was looking at a tall silver fir which she could see through the window and Lisbeth could read nothing in the expression of her cousin's eyes.

'Did you tell him that today is the day we all dine here?'

'Yes, but what does *he* care! Madame Marneffe is giving a big dinner. She's hoping to arrange Monsieur Coquet's resignation. And that takes precedence over everything. Look, Adeline, listen to me. You know how fiercely independent I am. Your husband will certainly ruin you, my dear. I thought I could be useful to you all by staying with that woman, but there's no limit to the creature's depravity. She will extract favours from your husband that will make him dishonour you all.'

Adeline started as if she had been struck by a dagger.

'But, my dear Adeline, I'm sure of it. I must try to open your eyes. Now, let's think of the future. The Marshal is old, but he'll last a long time yet. He has a handsome salary. When he dies, his widow will receive a pension of six thousand francs. With that amount, I would undertake to look after you all. Use your influence over the old chap to get him to marry me. It's not that I care about being Madame la Maréchale. I don't bother about that sort of nonsense any more than I do about Madame Marneffe's conscience. But you would all have your daily bread. I see that Hortense is in want of hers, since you give her yours.'

The Marshal appeared. The old soldier had done his errand so quickly that he was wiping his brow with his neckerchief.

'I've given Mariette two thousand francs,' he whispered to his sister-in-law.

Adeline blushed to the roots of her hair. Tears hung on her eyelashes, which were still long, and she silently pressed the hand of the old man, whose face beamed with the joy of a happy lover.

'I was intending to spend that sum on a present for you, Adeline,' he continued. 'Instead of paying me back, choose yourself whatever you would like best.'

He came forward to take the hand that Lisbeth was holding out to him, and in his pleasure he absent-mindedly kissed it.

'That looks promising,' Adeline said to Lisbeth, smiling in so far as she could.

Just then, Adeline's son and his wife arrived.

'Is my brother dining with us?' asked the Marshal curtly.

Adeline took a pencil and wrote these words on a slip of paper:

'I expect him. This morning he promised me to dine here. But if he doesn't come, it will be because the Marshal has kept him, for he's overwhelmed with work.'

And she gave him the note. She had invented this way of

conversing with the Marshal, and a supply of slips of paper and a pencil were laid ready on her work-table.

'I know he's overwhelmed with work because of the Algerian situation,' replied the Marshal.

At this moment Hortense and Wenceslas came in, and when the Baroness saw her family around her she gave the Marshal a look whose meaning was understood only by Lisbeth.

Happiness had greatly improved the appearance of the artist, who was adored by his wife and flattered by society. His face had become almost full, his elegant figure showed off the advantages bestowed by heredity on all real aristocrats. His premature fame, his importance, the deceptive praise that society showers on artists as thoughtlessly as we say 'good morning' or talk about the weather, gave him the consciousness of his own worth that degenerates into fatuity when talent goes. In his own eyes, the Cross of the Legion of Honour added the final touch to the great man he believed himself to be.

After three years of marriage, Hortense's attitude to her husband was like a dog's to its master. She reacted to all his movements with a look which was like an enquiry; she kept her eyes fixed on him, like a miser on his treasure; her admiring self-effacement was touching. One could see in her the spirit and teaching of her mother. Her beauty, as great as ever, was now changed, though poetically, by the gentle shades of a secret melancholy.

When she saw her cousin come in, Lisbeth thought that complaints, too long repressed, were going to break through the flimsy veil of discretion. From the start of the honeymoon, Lisbeth had thought that the young couple's income was too small for so great a passion.

As she kissed her mother, Hortense whispered to her a few heart-to-heart words, whose secret was revealed to Bette by their shakes of the head.

'Adeline, like me, is going to work for her living,' thought Cousin Bette. 'I'll see that she keeps me informed of what she's going to do. At last those pretty fingers, like mine, will know what it is to be forced to work.'

At six o'clock, the family went into the dining-room. Hector's place was set.

'Leave it,' the Baroness said to Mariette. 'Monsieur sometimes comes late.'

'Oh, my father's coming,' said young Hulot to his mother. 'He promised me he would, as we separated at the Chamber.'

44. *The dinner*

Lisbeth, like a spider at the centre of its web, watched all their faces. She had known Hortense and Victorin since they were born and, for her, their faces were like glass through which she could read their young souls. And from certain glances directed furtively by Victorin at his mother, she realized that some misfortune was about to fall upon Adeline and that he was reluctant to reveal it to her.

The eminent young lawyer was sad at heart. His deep veneration for his mother could be seen in the unhappy looks he gave her.

Hortense, too, was obviously preoccupied with her own sorrows, and Lisbeth had known for a fortnight that her young cousin was experiencing the first anxieties that lack of money arouses in honest people, in young women on whom life has always smiled and who conceal their worries.

So, right from the start, Cousin Bette guessed that the mother had given nothing to her daughter. The scrupulous Adeline had then descended to the deceitful language that necessity suggests to borrowers.

Hortense's preoccupation and her brother's, together with the Baroness's profound melancholy, made the dinner-party a sad one, especially as the old Marshal's deafness cast a chill over it in any case.

Three people enlivened the party, Lisbeth, Célestine, and Wenceslas. Hortense's love had aroused in the artist the Polish animation, the intellectual liveliness typical of Gascons, the attractive high spirits characteristic of these

Frenchmen of the North. His state of mind and the expression of his face made it clear that he believed in himself, and that poor Hortense, faithful to her mother's teaching, hid all the domestic worries from him.

'You must be very pleased,' Lisbeth said to her young cousin as they left the table. 'Your mother has come to the rescue by giving you her own money.'

'Mama!' replied Hortense in astonishment. 'Oh, poor Mama! I'd like to make some money for her! You don't know, Lisbeth, but I have an awful suspicion that she works in secret.'

They were just crossing the great, dark, unlit drawing-room, following Mariette, who was carrying the dining-room lamp into Adeline's bedroom, when Victorin touched the arms of Lisbeth and Hortense. They both understood the meaning of his gesture, and letting Wenceslas, Célestine, the Marshal, and the Baroness go into the bedroom, they stayed behind in a window bay.

'What's the matter, Victorin?' asked Lisbeth. 'I'm sure it's some disaster caused by your father.'

'Alas, yes,' replied Victorin. 'A money-lender called Vauvinet has bills of my father's amounting to sixty thousand francs and wants to sue him. I wanted to talk to my father in the Chamber about this deplorable business but he refused to understand me. He almost avoided me. Ought we to tell our mother?'

'No, no,' said Lisbeth. 'She has too many sorrows. It would be a death-blow to her. We must spare her. You don't know what straits she is in. But for your uncle, you'd have had no dinner here tonight.'

'Oh, good heavens, Victorin, we are monsters,' Hortense said to her brother. 'Lisbeth tells us what we ought to have guessed. My dinner is choking me!'

Hortense could say no more. She put her handkerchief over her mouth to stifle a sob. She was crying.

'I've told this Vauvinet to come and see me tomorrow,' continued Victorin. 'But will he be satisfied with my mortgage guarantee? I don't think so. People of that sort want ready cash in order to get an exorbitant interest from money-lending.'

'Let's sell our capital,' Lisbeth said to Hortense.

'What would that amount to? Fifteen or sixteen thousand francs,' replied Victorin. 'We need sixty thousand.'

'Dear Cousin,' cried Hortense, kissing Lisbeth with the fervour of an innocent heart.

'No, Lisbeth, keep your little capital,' said Victorin, pressing the Lorraine peasant's hand. 'I'll see tomorrow what the man has up his sleeve. If my wife agrees, I'll be able to prevent or delay the proceedings. For it would be terrible to see my father's reputation attacked. What would the Minister of War say? My father's salary, which has been pledged for the last three years, won't be available till December. So that can't be offered as security. This Vauvinet has renewed the bill eleven times, so just think of the sums my father has paid in interest! We must close such a bottomless pit.'

'If only Madame Marneffe were to leave him,' said Hortense bitterly.

'Oh, God forbid!' said Victorin. 'Father might go elsewhere, and with her, the greatest expenses have already been incurred.'

What a change in these children, formerly so respectful, in whom the mother had for so long maintained veneration for their father! Already they had judged him for themselves.

'But for me,' said Lisbeth, 'your father would be even more completely ruined than he is.'

'Let's go in,' said Hortense. 'Mama is shrewd and she'll suspect something. As our good Lisbeth says, let's hide it all from her. Let's be cheerful.'

'Victorin, you don't know what your father will do to you with his passion for women,' said Lisbeth. 'Think about making sure that you will have some resources in the future by marrying me to the Marshal. You should all talk to him about it this evening. I shall leave early on purpose.'

Victorin went into his mother's room.

'Well, my poor little one,' whispered Lisbeth to her young cousin. 'And you, what are you going to do!'

'Come and have dinner with us tomorrow, and we'll talk,' replied Hortense. 'I don't know which way to turn. You know how to deal with the difficulties of life. You'll advise me.'

While the combined family tried to preach marriage to the Marshal and Lisbeth was on her way back to the Rue Vaneau, there occurred one of those incidents which give new energy to the vice of women like Madame Marneffe by forcing them to deploy all the resources of depravity. Let us admit at least this fact: in Paris, life is too rushed for vicious people to do evil because they choose to. They use vice as a defensive weapon; that is all.

45. *Back from the dead with a fortune*

Madame Marneffe, whose drawing-room was full of her faithful adherents, had just set the usual games of whist going, when the footman, a retired military man recruited by the Baron, announced, 'Monsieur le Baron Montès de Montéjanos.'

Valérie had a violent emotional shock, but she rushed hurriedly to the door, exclaiming, 'My cousin!' And when she came up to the Brazilian she whispered to him, 'Be a relative of mine, or all is over between us.'

'Well, Henri,' she continued aloud, bringing the Brazilian to the fireplace, 'so you weren't shipwrecked, as I was told. I mourned you for three years.'

'How are you, my dear fellow?' said Monsieur Marneffe, holding out his hand to the Brazilian, whose bearing was that of a real Brazilian millionaire.

Monsieur le Baron Henri Montès de Montéjanos, on whom the equatorial climate had bestowed the kind of physique and complexion that we all ascribe to the stage Othello, looked gloomy and forbidding, but this was merely an outward appearance, for he had a very gentle and affectionate nature, which predestined him to the kind of exploitation that weak women practise on strong men.

The scorn expressed in his face, the muscular strength proclaimed by his well-proportioned build, all his powers were brought into play only against men, a form of flattery that goes to women's heads so much that men all put on ridiculous matador airs whenever they give an arm to their mistresses.

The Baron's figure was superbly set off by a blue coat with solid gold buttons and by his black trousers; his fine leather boots were irreproachably polished, his gloves were fashionable. The only Brazilian thing about his dress was a huge diamond, worth about a hundred thousand francs, which shone like a star in his sumptuous silk cravat, worn with a half-open white waistcoat, revealing an incredibly fine-textured shirt. His forehead, bulging like a satyr's, a sign of stubborn tenacity in passion, was surmounted by jet-black hair, thick as a virgin forest; beneath it gleamed a pair of light-coloured eyes, so wild and tawny that you would have thought the Baron's mother had been frightened by a jaguar when she was carrying him.

This magnificent specimen of the Portuguese in Brazil took up his stance with his back to the fireplace, in a pose that revealed Parisian habits. With his hat in one hand, his arm resting on the velvet overmantel, he leaned towards Madame Marneffe to talk to her in a low voice, caring very little about the frightful bourgeois who, to his mind, were inopportunely cluttering up the drawing-room.

The Brazilian's dramatic entry, his pose and manner aroused identical feelings of curiosity mingled with anxiety in Crevel and the Baron. They both had the same expression, showing the same foreboding.

And the simultaneous reactions aroused in these two genuinely passion-stricken men was so comical that it amused those who had wit enough to realize that a secret had been revealed.

Crevel, irretrievably bourgeois and very much the shop-keeper although he was Mayor of Paris, remained fixed in his attitude longer than his fellow-sufferer, so that the

Baron caught a fleeting glimpse of Crevel's involuntary self-revelation.

It was another stab in the heart of the elderly lover, who decided to have it out with Valérie.

'This evening we must settle the matter,' Crevel, too, said to himself, as he arranged his cards.

'*You have a heart*,' cried Marneffe, 'and you've just revoked.'

'Oh, I'm sorry,' replied Crevel, trying to take back his card. 'This Baron seems to me unnecessary,' he continued to himself. 'That Valérie should live with *my* Baron, that's my vengeance and I know how to get rid of him. But this cousin, that's one Baron too many. I don't want to be made a fool of. I want to know how he is related to her.'

That evening, by one of those lucky chances that happen only to pretty women, Valérie was charmingly dressed. Her dazzlingly white bosom was encased in russet-coloured lace which set off the matt satin of her beautiful shoulders; she had managed to keep her lovely contours slender in the way only Parisian women can (by what means no one knows). She wore a black velvet dress which seemed about to slip off her shoulders at any moment, and had a lace headdress trimmed with clusters of flowers. Her arms, at once slender and rounded, emerged from puffed sleeves filled with lace. She looked like one of those lovely fruits artistically arranged on a beautiful plate that make the knife-blade itch to be cutting it.

'Valérie, I have come back still faithful to you,' the Brazilian was saying to the young woman in a low voice. 'My uncle is dead and I am twice as rich as I was when I left. I want to live and die in Paris beside you and for you.'

'Lower your voice, Henri, for heaven's sake.'

'Oh, nonsense! I want to speak to you this evening, even if I have to throw all this crowd out of the window, especially after I've spent two days looking for you. I'll stay behind after the others have gone, shan't I?'

Valérie smiled at her so-called cousin and said:

'Remember that you're the son of a sister of my

mother's, who married your father during Junot's campaign in Portugal.'*

'I, Montès de Montéjanos, great grandson of one of the conquerors of Brazil,* tell a lie!'

'Not so loud, or we'll never see each other again.'

'But why?'

'All dying men are engulfed by a final desire, so Marneffe has conceived a passion for me.'

'That wretch?' said the Brazilian, who knew his Marneffe. 'I'll settle him.'

'How violent you are!'

'But where does all this luxury come from?' asked the Brazilian, noticing at last the splendours of the drawing-room.

She began to laugh.

'What bad taste, Henri,' she said.

She had just become aware of two burningly jealous glances which so affected her that she was forced to look at the two suffering hearts.

Crevel, who was playing against the Baron and Monsieur Coquet, had Monsieur Marneffe for his partner. The pairs were equally matched, for Crevel and the Baron were both distracted and were piling mistake upon mistake.

The two old men in love had both, in one moment, revealed the passion that Valérie had managed to make them conceal for three years. But neither had she been able to conceal the joy in her eyes at seeing again the man who had first made her heart beat faster, the object of her first love. The rights of such happy mortals last the whole lifetime of the woman over whom they have acquired them.

Amidst these three devouring passions, one based on the insolence of money, another on the right of possession, and the third on youth, strength, wealth, and priority, Madame Marneffe remained calm and clear-headed, like General Bonaparte when, at the siege of Mantua,* he had to take on two armies in order to continue the blockade of the city.

46. *The age at which a ladies' man becomes jealous*

The expression of jealousy on Hulot's face made him as terrible as the late Marshal Montcornet at the start of a cavalry charge on a Russian square. As a handsome man, the Councillor of State had never known jealousy, just as Murat* had never experienced fear. He had always been quite sure of victory. His failure with Josépha, the first in his life, he attributed to her greed for money. He said he was conquered by a million and not by a dwarf, as he called the Duc d'Hérouville. The venom and the giddiness which abound in this mad emotion had in a moment suffused his heart.

Moving in the manner of Mirabeau,* he turned from his whist-table towards the fireplace, and when he dropped his cards to direct a challenging look at the Brazilian and Valérie, the frequenters of the salon experienced the mixture of fear and curiosity which is inspired by violence threatening to break out at any moment.

The pretended cousin looked at the Councillor of State as if he were studying a large Chinese vase. This situation could not continue without leading to a frightful scene.

Marneffe was afraid of Baron Hulot as much as Crevel was afraid of Marneffe, for he did not at all like the idea of dying an assistant-manager. Dying men believe in life as convicts do in liberty. This man was determined to be an office manager at any price. Alarmed with good reason by the performance of Crevel and the Councillor of State, he got up and slipped a word in his wife's ear. To the company's great astonishment, Valérie went into her bedroom with the Brazilian and her husband.

'Has Madame Marneffe ever spoken to you about this cousin?' Crevel asked Baron Hulot.

'Never,' replied the Baron, getting up. 'That's enough for this evening,' he added. 'I've lost two louis; here they are.'

He threw two gold coins on to the table and went and sat down on the divan with a look which everyone interpreted as a hint to go. After making a few remarks, Monsieur and Madame Coquet left the room, and Claude Vignon, in despair, followed their example. These two departures gave the lead to the less perceptive members of the company, who realized they were in the way.

The Baron and Crevel remained alone without addressing a word to each other.

Hulot, who finally had ceased to be aware of Crevel, went on tiptoe to listen at the bedroom door, but he gave a great leap backwards, for Monsieur Marneffe opened the door, looking quite unruffled, and seemed surprised to find only two people.

'And what about tea?' he asked.

'But where's Valérie?' replied the Baron, furious.

'My wife?' said Marneffe. 'Oh, she's gone up to your cousin's flat; she'll be coming back.'

'And why has she deserted us for that stupid Nanny?'

'Well, Mademoiselle Lisbeth came back from dining with Madame la Baronne, your wife, with some kind of stomach upset, and Mathurine asked Valérie for tea; she's just gone to see what's the matter with your cousin,' said Marneffe.

'And her cousin?'

'He's gone.'

'Do you really believe that?' asked the Baron.

'I saw him to his carriage,' replied Marneffe with a horrible grin.

The sound of a carriage could be heard in the Rue Vaneau.

The Baron, who had no faith at all in Marneffe's word, left the room and went up to Lisbeth's flat. A thought came into his mind of the kind the heart inspires when it is inflamed by jealousy.

Marneffe's base nature was so well known to him that he assumed a shameful complicity between husband and wife.

'But what's become of these ladies and gentlemen?' asked Marneffe, when he found he was alone with Crevel.

'When the sun goes to bed, so does the poultry yard,' replied Crevel. 'Madame Marneffe disappeared, so her admirers have departed. What about a game of piquet?' he added, for he was determined to stay.

He, too, believed the Brazilian was in the house. Monsieur Marneffe accepted. The Mayor was as shrewd as the Baron; he could stay in the house indefinitely, playing with the husband, who, since the suppression of public gambling, had to content himself with the restricted, petty gaming played in private houses.

Baron Hulot went quickly upstairs to his Cousin Bette's flat. But he found the door closed, and the usual enquiries through the door took long enough to allow alert, astute women to stage the scene of an attack of indigestion dosed with an abundance of tea. Lisbeth was in such pain that Valérie was greatly alarmed, so she paid hardly any attention to the Baron's furious entrance. Illness is one of the screens that women put most frequently between themselves and a stormy quarrel.

Hulot looked furtively round the room, but he saw no place in his Cousin Bette's bedroom suitable for hiding a Brazilian.

'Your indigestion, Bette, does credit to my wife's dinner,' he said, looking closely at the old maid, who was in the best of health and doing her best to simulate the rumbles of a belching stomach as she drank tea.

'You see how fortunate it is that our dear Bette lives in my house. But for me, the poor girl would have died,' said Madame Marneffe.

'You look as if you think I'm perfectly well,' added Lisbeth, turning to the Baron, 'and that would be disgraceful.'

'Why?' asked the Baron. 'Do you know the reason for my visit?'

And he glanced surreptitiously at the door of a dressing-room from which the key had been removed.

'What you're saying is Greek to me,' Madame Marneffe

replied, with a heart-rending look of misunderstood affection and fidelity.

'But it's for your sake, my dear cousin, yes, it's your fault that I'm in the state you see me in,' said Lisbeth fiercely.

This outburst diverted the Baron's attention and he looked at the old maid in great astonishment.

'You know I'm fond of you,' continued Lisbeth. 'I'm here, that says it all. I'm expending all the strength I have left in looking after your interests and our dear Valérie's. Her household costs ten times less than any other house run on the same scale. But for me, cousin, instead of two thousand francs a month, you'd have to pay three or four thousand.'

'I know all that,' replied the Baron impatiently. 'You look after us in all sorts of ways,' he added, going over to Madame Marneffe and putting his arm round her neck. 'Isn't that so, my dear little beauty?'

'Upon my word,' said Valérie, 'I think you're mad.'

'Well, you don't doubt my attachment,' continued Lisbeth, 'but I love my cousin Adeline, too, and I found her in tears. She hasn't seen you for a month. No, that won't do. You leave poor Adeline without any money. Your daughter Hortense nearly died when she learned that it was only thanks to your brother that we could have any dinner. There was no bread in your house today. Adeline has made the heroic resolution to be self-supporting. She said to me, "I'll follow your example!" That upset me so much after dinner, that in thinking of what my cousin's situation was in 1811, and what it is thirty years on in 1841, I couldn't digest my dinner. I tried to get over the trouble, but when I got home I thought I'd die.'

'You see, Valérie,' said the Baron, 'what my adoration of you has led me to! To domestic crimes!'

'Oh, I was right to remain an old maid,' Lisbeth exclaimed, with a fierce joy. 'You're a good and kind man, Adeline's an angel, and this is the reward of her blind devotion.'

'An old angel,' Madame Marneffe said quietly, looking

half affectionately and half mockingly at her Hector, who was studying her carefully in the way an examining magistrate studies an accused man.

'Poor woman!' said the Baron. 'It's more than nine months now since I gave her any money, yet I find some for you, Valérie. But at what a price! No one will ever love you as I do, and what sorows you give me in return!'

'Sorrows?' she replied. 'What do you call happiness, then?'

'I don't know what your relationship has been with this so-called cousin, whom you've never mentioned to me,' continued the Baron, paying no attention to Valérie's remarks. 'But when he came in, I felt as if a knife had stabbed my heart. However blinded I may be, I'm not that blind. I read your eyes and his. In short, sparks were emitted from that ape's eyes which were reflected in you and your look. . . . Oh, you've never looked at me like that, never! As for this mystery . . . Valérie, it's going to be cleared up. You are the only woman who has made me know what jealousy is, so don't be surprised at what I'm saying. But another mystery which has burst through its cloak, one that seems to me infamous . . .'

'Go on, go on,' said Valérie.

'. . . is that Crevel, that lump of stupid flesh, loves you and you receive his attentions favourably enough for this idiot to reveal his passion to the whole world.'

'That makes three! Have you noticed any others?' asked Madame Marneffe.

'There may be more,' said the Baron.

'Monsieur Crevel may love me, that's his right as a man. If I were favourable to his passion, that would be to behave like a coquette or like a woman who leaves a lot to be desired. Well, love me with all my faults or leave me. If you give me back my liberty, neither you nor Monsieur Crevel will ever come here again. I'll take my cousin, so as not to lose the charming habits you say I have. Goodbye, Monsieur le Baron Hulot.'

With that, she got up, but the Councillor of State gripped her arm and made her sit down. The old man was no longer able to replace Valérie. She had become a need for him, more overwhelming than the necessities of life, and he would rather remain in uncertainty than be given the slightest proof of Valérie's infidelity.

'Dear Valérie,' he said, 'don't you see what I'm suffering? I'm only asking you to clear yourself. Give me a good explanation.'

'Well, wait for me downstairs, for I imagine you don't want to stay while I do things for your cousin that her state of health requires.'

Hulot went away slowly.

'You old libertine!' cried Cousin Bette. 'You don't even ask me for news of your children. What will you do for Adeline? For a start, *I* am going to take her my savings tomorrow.'

'One ought to give one's wife at least good-quality white bread,' said Madame Marneffe with a smile.

The Baron, without taking offence at the way Lisbeth spoke to him—she gave him orders as dictatorially as Josépha had done—left like a man who was very glad to avoid an awkward question.

Once the door was bolted, the Brazilian came out of the dressing-room where he had been waiting, and he appeared, his eyes full of tears, in a pitiable state. Clearly, Montès had heard everything.

47. *First scene of clever feminine play-acting*

'You don't love me any more, Henri, I can see that,' said Madame Marneffe, hiding her face in her handkerchief and bursting into tears.

It was an exclamation of real love. A woman's cry of despair is so persuasive that it draws out the pardon which every lover has in the bottom of his heart when the woman is young and pretty and wearing a dress which is so low-cut that she could emerge from the top of it in the costume of Eve.

'But why don't you leave everything for me, if you love me?' asked the Brazilian.

This native of America, logical like all children of nature, immediately resumed the conversation at the point where he had left it, putting his arm round Valérie's waist again.

'Why?' she asked, raising her head and dominating Henri with a gaze full of love. 'Because, my pet, I'm married. Because we're in Paris and not in the savannas or the pampas, in the wide open spaces of America. My dear Henri, my first and only love, do listen to me. This husband of mine, who's just an ordinary assistant-manager at the War Ministry, wants to be an office manager and an officer of the Legion of Honour. Can I stop him from being ambitious? Now, for the same reason that he used to leave us completely free (it's nearly four years ago now, do you remember, naughty boy?), Marneffe is now forcing Baron Hulot on me. I shan't be able to get rid of that horrible official, who puffs like a grampus, has hairs like fins in his nostrils, is 63 years old, has aged ten years in his efforts to keep young, and whom I detest, till the day after Marneffe is appointed officer manager and officer of the Legion of Honour.'

'What else will your husband get?'

'A thousand crowns.'

'I'll give him that as an annuity,' Baron Montès went on. 'Let's leave Paris and let's go . . .'

'Where?' said Valérie, making one of those pretty pouting faces with which women tease men they are sure of. 'Paris is the only town where we can live happily. I set too much store by your love to let it fade away by living alone with you in a desert. Listen, Henri, you're the only man in the whole world whom I love. Get that into your tiger's skull.'

Women always persuade men they have made into sheep that they are lions with a will of iron.

'Now, just listen to me. Monsieur Marneffe hasn't five years to live. He's diseased to the very marrow of his bones. Out of twelve months of the year, he spends seven taking medicine and infusions; he live in flannel. In short, the doctor says, he can be mown down at any time. An illness that would be harmless to a healthy man will be fatal to him. His blood is vitiated, his life is fundamentally affected. For five years, I haven't let this man kiss me once, for he is the personification of disease. One day, and that day isn't far off, I'll be a widow. Well, I've already had a proposal from a man with an income of sixty thousand francs a year, and he's as much in my power as this piece of sugar, but I declare to you that even if you were as poor as Hulot, as leprous as Marneffe, and were to beat me, it's you I want for my husband, only you I love and whose name I want to bear. And I'm ready to give you all the pledges of love you want.'

'Well then, tonight . . .'

'But, you child of Rio, my beautiful jaguar come for me from the virgin forests of Brazil,' she said, taking his hand, kissing and caressing it, 'have a little respect for the woman you want to make your wife. Shall I be your wife, Henri?'

'Yes,' said the Brazilian, conquered by her unrestrained passionate language.

And he went down on his knees.

'Come, Henri,' said Valérie, taking both his hands and looking steadily right into his eyes. 'Will you swear to me, here, in the presence of Lisbeth, my best and only friend, my sister, to take me for your wife at the end of my year of widowhood?'

'I swear.'

'That's not enough. Swear by your mother's ashes and by her eternal salvation, by the Virgin Mary, and by your hopes as a Catholic.'

Valérie knew that the Brazilian would keep his oath, even if she were to sink to the depths of the filthiest social mire. The Brazilian took the solemn oath, his nose almost touching Valérie's white bosom and his eyes fascinated. He was intoxicated as a man is when he sees a beloved woman again after being at sea for a hundred and twenty days.

'Now, put your mind at ease. Treat Madame Marneffe with the respect due to the future Baroness de Montéjanos. Don't spend a farthing on me, I forbid it. Stay here, in the front room, and rest on the little sofa. I'll come myself and tell you when you can leave your post. Tomorrow morning we'll have breakfast together and you can leave about one o'clock as if you had come to visit me at twelve. Don't worry. The porters are as devoted to me as if they were my father and mother. I'm going down to my own flat to serve tea.'

'She signed to Lisbeth, who went with her as far as the landing.

There Valérie whispered in the old maid's ear. 'That nigger has come a year too soon, for I'll die if I don't avenge you on Hortense!'

'Don't worry, my dear, sweet little demon,' said the old maid, kissing her on the forehead. 'Love and Vengeance, hunting together, will never lose. Hortense is expecting me tomorrow; she's penniless. To get a thousand francs, Wenceslas would give you a thousand kisses.'

48. *A scene befitting a porter's lodge*

On leaving Valérie, Hulot had gone downstairs to the porter's lodge and appeared without warning before Madame Olivier.

'Madame Olivier?'

On hearing this imperious summons and seeing the gesture which reinforced it, Madame Olivier came out of her lodge and went as far as the courtyard where the Baron took her aside.

'You know that if anyone can help your son to acquire a legal practice one day, it's me. It's thanks to me that he's now third clerk in a solicitor's office and finishing his law studies.'

'Yes, Monsieur le Baron. And Monsieur le Baron can count on our gratitude. Not a day goes by without my praying to God for Monsieur le Baron's happiness.'

'Not so many words, my good woman,' said Hulot. 'I want deeds to prove it.'

'What do you want me to do?' asked Madame Olivier.

'A man came here tonight in a carriage. Do you know him?

Madame Olivier had of course recognized Montès. How could she have forgotten him? Whenever he left the house in the Rue du Doyenné a little too early in the morning, Montès would slip a five-franc piece into her hand.

If the Baron had applied to Monsieur Olivier, he might have learned everything. But Olivier was asleep. In the lower classes, the wife is not only superior to the husband but nearly always controls him. For a long time now, Madame Olivier had made up her mind what to do if there should be a clash between her two benefactors; she looked on Madame Marneffe as the stronger of the two powers.

'Do I know him?' she replied. 'No, definitely no. I have never seen him before.'

'What! Madame Marneffe's cousin never came to see her when she lived in the Rue du Doyenné?'

'Oh, so he's her cousin,' exclaimed Madame Olivier. 'He may have come, but I didn't recognize him. At the first opportunity, I'll look at him carefully.'

'He's coming downstairs,' said Hulot quickly, interrupting Madame Olivier.

'But he's gone,' replied Madame Olivier, who understood everything. 'The carriage isn't there.'

'Did you see him go?'

'As plainly as I can see you. He said to his servant, "To the embassy!"'

At this reassuring speech, the Baron uttered a sigh of happiness. He took Madame Olivier's hand and shook it.

'Thank you, dear Madame Olivier. But that's not everything. What about Monsieur Crevel?'

'Monsieur Crevel? What do you mean? I don't understand,' said Madame Olivier.

'Just listen to me. He's in love with Madame Marneffe.'

'Oh no, Monsieur le Baron. He can't be,' she said clasping her hands together.

'He's in love with Madame Marneffe,' the Baron repeated very imperiously. 'What do they do about it? I don't know, but I am determined to know and you will find out. If you can put me on the scent of that intrigue, your son will be a solicitor.'

'Monsieur le Baron, don't get in such a state,' continued Madame Olivier. 'Madame loves you and loves only you. Her maid knows that very well and we say that you are the most fortunate man in the world in that way, for you know what Madame's worth. Oh, she's quite perfect. She gets up at ten o'clock every day; then she has breakfast. Well, then she takes an hour to dress and by that time it's two o'clock. Then she goes for an outing to the Tuileries in full view of everyone. She's always home by four o'clock in time for your arrival. Oh, she's as regular as a clock. She has no secrets from her maid. And Reine hasn't any from me, either. Reine can't have any because of her relationship with my son, with whom she's very friendly. So you see that if Madame had connections with Monsieur Crevel, we would know.'

The Baron went back upstairs to Madame Marneffe's flat with a beaming face, convinced he was the only man this frightful courtesan loved, but she was as deceitful, though as beautiful and gracious, as a siren.

Crevel and Marneffe were beginning a second game of piquet. Crevel was losing, as men always lose when their minds are not on their game. Marneffe, who knew the reason for the Mayor's lack of concentration, was taking advantage of it unscrupulously. He was looking at the cards on the table and discarding accordingly; then, knowing his opponent's hand, he was playing certain to win.

Playing for stakes of twenty sous, he had already robbed the Mayor of thirty francs when the Baron returned.

'Well, well,' said the Councillor of State, surprised to find no one else there. 'You are alone! Where are they all?'

'Your good mood put them all to flight,' replied Crevel.

'No, it was the arrival of my wife's cousin,' replied Marneffe. 'These ladies and gentlemen thought that Valérie and Henri must have things to say to each other after a three-year separation, so they discreetly retired. If I'd been there, I'd have made them stay. But, as it happens, I'd have done the wrong thing, for Lisbeth usually serves tea about half past ten, and her not being well has upset everything.

'Is Lisbeth really not well then?' asked Crevel, who was furious.

'So they say,' replied Marneffe with the immoral unconcern of a man for whom women no longer exist.

The Mayor had looked at the clock and, judging from the time, he reckoned that the Baron had spent forty minutes in Lisbeth's room. Hulot's happy expression seriously compromised Hector, Valérie, and Lisbeth.

'I've just seen her. She's in great pain, poor thing,' said the Baron.

'So the sufferings of others give you pleasure, my good friend,' continued Crevel tartly. 'For you've come back to us with a face beaming with glee. Is Lisbeth dangerously ill? They say your daughter is her heir. You're like a new man. You left with a face like the Moor of Venice and you come back looking like Saint-Preux.* I'd very much like to see Madame Marneffe's face!'

'What do you mean by that speech?' Monsieur Marneffe asked Crevel, gathering up his cards and laying them down in front of him.

The dull eyes of Valérie's husband, decrepit at 47, lit up, a faint colour suffused his cold, flabby cheeks, he half-opened his toothless mouth, and his blackened lips became coated with a cheese-like foam, white as chalk. The rage of an impotent man, whose life hung on a thread and who, in a duel, would have nothing to risk while Crevel would have everything to lose, frightened the Mayor.

'I'm saying that I'd like to see Madame Marneffe's face,' replied Crevel, 'and with all the more reason because yours at this moment is very unpleasant, my dear Marneffe. On my word of honour, you are horribly ugly, my dear Marneffe.'

'Do you realize that you are being discourteous?

'A man who wins thirty francs in forty-five minutes never looks handsome to me.'

'Oh, if you'd seen me seventeen years ago,' continued the assistant-manager.

'Were you good-looking?'

'That's what ruined me. If I'd looked like you, I'd be a peer and a mayor.'

'Yes,' said Crevel with a smile. 'You've been in the wars too much. And of the two metals to be won by cultivating the god of commerce, you've taken the bad one, the silver drug!'*

And Crevel burst out laughing. If Marneffe took offence when his honour was at risk, he always took these coarse, vulgar jokes well. They were the small change of conversation between Crevel and himself.

'Eve has cost me dear, that's true. But, damn it all, short and merry, that's my motto.'

'I prefer long and happy,' replied Crevel.

49. *Second scene of clever feminine play-acting*

Madame Marneffe came in and saw her husband playing cards with Crevel and the Baron; there were only the three of them in the drawing-room. Merely from the civic dignitary's appearance she realized all the thoughts that had been agitating him and she decided immediately on her course of action.

'Marneffe, my pet,' she said, going over to her husband, leaning on his shoulder, and running her pretty fingers through his drab grey hair, re-arranging it but not managing to cover his head with it. 'It's very late for you; you ought to go to bed. You know that tomorrow you must take a laxative; the doctor said so, and Reine will bring you some herb broth at seven o'clock. If you want to go on living, stop your piquet now.'

'Shall we stop at five points?' Marneffe asked Crevel.

'Alright. I've got two already,' Crevel replied.

'How long will it take?' asked Valérie.

'Ten minutes,' replied Marneffe.

'It's eleven o'clock already,' said Valérie, 'and really, Monsieur Crevel, anyone would think you wanted to kill my husband. In any case, be quick about it.'

This double-edged speech made Crevel, Hulot, and even Marneffe himself smile.

Valérie went over to talk to her Hector.

'Leave now, my dear,' Valérie whispered to Hector. 'Take a walk in the Rue Vaneau and come back when you see Crevel leave.'

'I'd rather leave the flat and come back to your room by the dressing-room door. You could tell Reine to open it for me.'

'Reine's upstairs looking after Lisbeth.'

'Well, suppose I went back up to Lisbeth's room?'

There was danger on all sides for Valérie. Foreseeing that Crevel would demand an explanation, she did not want Hulot in her room where he could hear everything. And the Brazilian was waiting for her at Lisbeth's.

'Really, you men, when you get an idea into your heads, you would set a house on fire to get into it,' Valérie said to Hulot. 'Lisbeth is in no state to receive you. Are you afraid of catching cold in the street? Go out . . . or goodnight!'

'Goodnight, gentlemen,' said the Baron aloud.

Once piqued in his old man's vanity, Hulot was eager to prove that he could behave like a young man and wait for the appointed hour in the street, so he left.

Marneffe said goodnight to his wife and, with a show of affection, took her hands. Valérie pressed her husband's hand significantly, meaning, 'Get rid of Crevel for me.'

'Goodnight, Crevel, I hope you won't stay long with Valérie,' said Marneffe. 'Oh, I'm jealous! It's caught me late in life, but it's got me, and I'll come back to see if you've gone.'

'We've got business to discuss, but I shan't stay long,' said Crevel.

'Talk quietly. What do you want of me?' said Valérie in an undertone, giving Crevel a look of mingled haughtiness and contempt.

At this haughty look, Crevel, who rendered great services to Valérie and wanted to make the most of the fact, became humble and submissive once more.

'This Brazilian . . .'

Appalled by Valérie's fixed, contemptuous stare, Crevel,
stopped short.

'Well?' she said.

'This cousin . . .'

'He's not my cousin, she continued. 'He's my cousin to
the outside world and to Monsieur Marneffe. And if he
were my lover, you wouldn't have the right to say a word.
A shopkeeper who buys a woman to avenge himself on a
man, is, in my judgement, beneath a man who buys her
out of love. You weren't in love with me. You saw in me
only Monsieur Hulot's mistress, and you bought me as
one buys a pistol to kill one's enemy. I was hungry, so I
agreed.'

'You haven't kept your side of the bargain,' replied
Crevel, reverting to his tradesman's standpoint.

'Oh, you want Baron Hulot to know that you've taken
his mistress from him, so that you can have your revenge
for his taking Josépha away. Nothing proves to me more
clearly how contemptible you are. You say you love a
woman, you treat her like a duchess, and you want to
dishonour her! Well, my dear, you're right. This woman
isn't a patch on Josépha. That young lady has the courage
of her shame, while *I* am a hypocrite who ought to be
publicly whipped. Ah well, Josépha is protected by her
talent and her wealth. *My* only defence is my good
reputation. I'm still a respectable and virtuous middle-class
wife, but if you make a scandal, what will become of me?
If I had money, it wouldn't matter. But now I have an
income of fifteen thousand francs at most, isn't that right?'

'Much more than that,' said Crevel. 'I've doubled your
savings in the last two months in Orléans railway shares.'

'Well, you need an income of at least fifty thousand
francs to be anyone in Paris; you can't give me enough to
pay for the position I'll lose. All I ask is for Marneffe to be
appointed an office-manager; he'd have a salary of six
thousand francs. He has twenty-seven years' service, so
that in three years I'd be entitled to a pension of fifteen
hundred francs if he died. You, whom I've loaded with

kindness, stuffed with happiness, you can't wait! And you call that love!' she exclaimed.

'If I began from selfish motives, since then I've become your lap-dog. You trample on my heart, you crush me, you stun me, and I love you as I've never loved anyone before. Valérie, I love you as much as I love Célestine! For you I'd do anything. Listen, instead of coming twice a week to the Rue du Dauphin, come three times.'

'Is that all? You're growing young again, my dear.'

'Let me give Hulot his marching orders, humiliate him, get rid of him for you,' said Crevel, ignoring this insulting remark. 'Don't let that Brazilian in again. Be all mine. You won't regret it. To start with, I'll give you a share certificate worth eight thousand francs a year, but as an annuity. I won't give you the capital until you've been faithful to me for five years.'

'Still making bargains! Tradesmen will never learn to give! You want to organize relays of love for yourself all through your life with share certificates. Oh, you shop-keeper, you hair-oil dealer! You put a price ticket on everything. Hector told me that the Duc d'Hérouville had brought Josépha an income of thirty thousand francs in a paper cone of sugared almonds. I'm worth six times as much as Josépha. Oh, to be loved!' she said, twisting her ringlets round her fingers and going to look at herself in the glass. 'Henri loves me; he'd kill you like a fly, at one flicker of my eyelids! Hulot loves me; he's making his wife destitute. Go and be a good family man, my dear. Oh, you've got three hundred thousand francs for your scrapes, over and above your fortune, quite a pile, and all you think of is to make it more.'

'For you, Valérie, for I offer you half of it,' he said, going down on his knees.

'Oh, you're still there!' exclaimed the hideous Marneffe, appearing in his dressing-gown. 'What are you doing?'

'He's apologizing to me, my dear, for an insulting proposal he's just made me. Since he could get nothing from me, Monsieur thought up the idea of buying me!'

Crevel would have liked to sink down to the cellar through a trap-door, as happens on the stage.

'Get up, my dear Crevel,' said Marneffe with a smile. 'You're ridiculous. I can see from the look on Valérie's face that I'm in no danger.'

'Go to bed and sleep in peace,' said Madame Marneffe.

'How clever she is!' thought Crevel. 'She's adorable! She's saved me!'

When Marneffe had gone back to his own room, the Mayor took Valérie's hands, kissed them, and let a few tears fall on them.

'Everything in your name,' he said.

'That's what I call love,' she murmured in his ear. 'Well, love for love. Hulot is downstairs, in the street. The poor old chap is waiting for me to place a candle in one of my bedroom windows as a sign to him to come up. I give you permission to tell him that I love only you. He'll never believe you. Take him to the Rue du Dauphin, give him proofs, overwhelm him with evidence. You have my permission; in fact I order you to do it. I'm fed up with the old sea-lion; I can't stand him any more. Keep your man at the Rue du Dauphin for the whole night. Kill him with slow torture. Take your revenge for the abduction of Josépha. It may be the death of Hulot but we'll save his wife and children from devastating ruin. Madame Hulot has to work for her living!'

'Oh, poor lady! Upon my word, that's awful,' cried Crevel, his natural kindliness coming to the fore.

'If you love me, Célestin,' she whispered into Crevel's ear, touching it lightly with her lips, 'keep him there, or I'm lost. Marneffe is suspicious. Hector has the key of the carriage entrance door and expects to come back.'

Crevel clasped Madame Marneffe in his arms and left in a seventh heaven of delight. Valérie accompanied him lovingly to the landing. Then, like a woman enthralled, she went down as far as the first floor and then to the bottom of the stairs.

'My own Valérie! Go back upstairs, Don't compromise

yourself in the eyes of the porters. Go, my life and my fortune. Everything is yours. Go back, my duchess.'

'Madame Olivier!' Valérie called softly when the door banged shut.

'What, Madame, you here?' said Madame Olivier in amazement.

'Bolt the big door, top and bottom, and don't open it again.'

'Very good, Madame.'

Once the door had been bolted, Madame Olivier related how the high official had stooped to trying to bribe her.

'You behaved like an angel, my dear Madame Olivier. But we'll talk about that tomorrow.'

Valérie reached the third floor with the speed of an arrow, gave three taps on Lisbeth's door and went back to her own room where she gave her orders to Mademoiselle Reine; for a woman never misses the opportunity of a Montès arriving from Brazil.

50. *Crevel takes his revenge*

'No, by heaven! It's only society women who can love like that.' Crevel said to himself. 'How she came down the stairs, lighting them up with the beams from her eyes, and *I* was drawing her on! Josépha never . . . Josépha, she's *scum*!' cried the former commercial traveller. 'What was that I said? *scum*. . . . My God! I might come out with that some day at the Tuileries. No, if Valérie doesn't see to my education, I'll never be anybody. And I'm so anxious to give the impression of being a real lord. Oh, what a woman! She upsets me like an attack of colic when she looks at me coldly! What grace! What intelligence! Never did Josépha give me such emotions! And what concealed perfections! Ah, there's my man.'

In the darkness of the Rue de Babylone he caught sight of Hulot, his tall figure a little bowed, stealing along by the timbers of a house in course of construction, and he went straight up to him.

'Good morning, Baron, for it's past midnight, my dear fellow. What the devil are you doing there? You're taking a walk in a nice, fine drizzle. At our age, that's not wise. Would you like me to give you a piece of good advice? Let's both go back to our own homes, for, between ourselves, you won't see a light at the window.'

When he heard this last remark, the Baron realized that he was 63 years old and that his coat was wet.

'But who can have told you that?' he asked.

'Valérie! Yes indeed, *our* Valérie, who wants to be only *my* Valérie. We're neck and neck, Baron. We'll play the final round whenever you like. You can't get annoyed. You know that I always stipulated my right of revenge. You took three months to take Josépha from me. *I've* taken Valérie from you in . . . Let's not talk about that,' he continued. 'Now I want her all to myself. But we'll stay good friends all the same.'

'Crevel, be serious,' replied the Baron in a voice choking with rage. 'It's a matter of life and death.'

'Well, well, what a way to take it! Baron, don't you remember what you said to me on Hortense's wedding-day? "Should two lady-killers like us fall out over a skirt? It's behaving like grocers, like nobodies." And we, we agree, are blue-waistcoated Regency* aristocrats, of the rococo Pompadour* era, eighteenth-century men quite like the Maréchal de Richelieu* and, if I may say so, the hero of *Les Liaisons dangereuses*.'*

Crevel could have gone on piling up his literary allusions for a long time. The Baron was listening as deaf men listen when they first become deaf.

Seeing by the gaslight that his enemy's face had turned pale, the victor stopped short. It was a thunderbolt for the Baron after Madame Olivier's assurances and Valérie's parting look.

'My God! There are so many other women in Paris,' he exclaimed at last.

'That's what I told you when you took Josépha from me,' replied Crevel.

'Look here, Crevel, it's impossible. Give me proofs. Have you a key to let yourself in, as I have?'

And the Baron, who had reached the house, pushed a key into the lock. But he found the door immovable and tried in vain to make it give.

'Don't make a disturbance at night,' Crevel said calmly. 'You see, Baron, *I've* got much better keys than yours.'

'Give me proofs! Give me proofs!' repeated the Baron, exasperated by a misery that nearly sent him out of his mind.

'Come with me and I'll give you proofs,' Crevel replied.

And, following Valérie's instructions, he led the Baron towards the quay, along the Rue Hillerin-Bertin.

The unfortunate Councillor of State went along like a businessman the day before he has to file his petition for bankruptcy. He was lost in conjectures about the causes of the depravity hidden in the depths of Valérie's heart and he thought he was the victim of some practical joke.

As they crossed the Pont-Royal, he saw his existence so empty, so utterly finished, in such financial confusion, that he was on the point of giving in to the evil idea that occurred to him of throwing Crevel into the river and of throwing himself in afterwards.

51. *Master Crevel's little house*

When they reached the Rue du Dauphin, which at that time had not yet been widened, Crevel stopped before a small door. The door opened on to a long passage paved with black and white flagstones that formed an entrance hall; at the end of it was a staircase and a porter's lodge lit by a small inner courtyard of a kind frequently found in Paris. The courtyard, which was shared with the next-door property, was an unusual example of unequal division.

Crevel's little house, for he was the owner, had an annexe with a glass roof, built on the neighbouring ground. The height of this structure was restricted by court order and so it was completely hidden from view by the lodge and the protruding staircase.

This place, like so many one sees in Paris, had long been used as storeroom, back premises, and kitchen for one of the two shops facing on to the street. Crevel had separated these three ground-floor rooms from the rest of the property let to the shop, and Grindot had transformed them into a small, compact house.

There were two ways of entering the house. The first was through the shop of a furniture dealer, to whom Crevel let it by the month at a low rent, so that he could penalize him for any indiscretion. The second was by a door so skilfully hidden in the passage wall that it was almost invisible.

The little dwelling, consisting of a dining-room, a drawing-room, and a bedroom, lit from above, standing partly on the neighbouring ground and partly on Crevel's was therefore almost impossible to find. With the exception of the second-hand furniture dealer, the tenants were unaware of the existence of this little paradise.

The porter's wife, who was paid to be Crevel's accomplice, was an excellent cook. So Monsieur le Maire could go in and out of his compact little house at any hour of the night without fear of being spied on.

By day, a woman dressed as a Parisian dresses to go shopping and provided with a key, ran no risks in going to Crevel's place. She could look at the second-hand furniture, discuss the prices, go into the shop, and leave it, without arousing the least suspicion if anyone should meet her.

When Crevel had lit the candlesticks in the sitting-room, the Baron was quite amazed at the elegant luxury with which it had been intelligently furnished. The former perfumer had given Grindot *carte blanche* and the old architect had excelled himself by the creation of a room in the Pompadour style, which, incidentally, had cost sixty thousand francs.

'I would like a duchess who comes in here to be agreeably surprised,' Crevel had said to Grindot.

He had wanted the loveliest of Parisian Edens in which to enjoy his Eve, his society lady, his Valérie, his duchess.

'There are two beds,' Crevel told Hulot, pointing to a divan from which a bed could be pulled out like a drawer from a chest-of-drawers. 'Here's one; the other is in the bedroom. So we can both spend the night here.'

'Show me the proofs,' said the Baron.

Crevel took a candlestick and led his friend into the bedroom, where on a small couch, Hulot saw a magnificent dressing-gown belonging to Valérie; she had worn it in the Rue Vaneau to show it off before using it in Crevel's little house. The Mayor undid the lock of a secret drawer in a pretty little inlaid table of the kind called *bonheur du jour*, rummaged in it, picked up a letter, and handed it to the Baron.

'Look, read that.'

The Councillor of State read the following little note, written in pencil.

'I waited for you in vain, you old rogue. A woman like me never waits for a retired perfumer. No dinner had been ordered and there were no cigarettes. You'll pay me for all this.'

'Isn't that her writing?'

'My God!' said Hulot, collapsing into a chair. 'I recognize everything she's worn; there are her caps and her slippers. Oh, my goodness, how long have you . . .?'

Crevel nodded to show he understood, and picked up a bundle of bills from the little inlaid writing-table.

'Look at these, old chap. I paid the contractors in December 1838. Two months before that, in October, this delightful little house was first used.'

The Councillor of State bowed his head.

'How on earth do you manage it? For I know what she does with her time, hour by hour.'

'But what about her walk in the Tuileries?' said Crevel, rubbing his hands and gloating.

'Well?' continued Hulot, in a daze.

'Your so-called mistress goes to the Tuileries. She is supposed to be having an outing there from one till four.

But, hey presto! In a trice she's here. You know your Molière? Well, Baron, there's nothing imaginary in your title.*

Hulot, no longer able to have any doubts, remained ominously silent. Disasters drive all strong, intelligent men to philosophize. Morally, the Baron was like a man seeking his way in a forest by night.

The gloomy silence, the change which had come over his dejected countenance, alarmed Crevel, who had not wanted to cause his old crony's death.

'As I was saying to you, old chap, we're quits now. Let's play the deciding game. Don't you want to finish the rubber? May the cleverest man win!'

'Why, out of ten beautiful women, are at least seven depraved?' said Hulot, talking to himself.

52. *Two brothers-in-arms*

The Baron was too upset to find the answer to his question. Beauty is the greatest of human powers. All autocratic, unbridled power, with nothing to counterbalance it, leads to abuse, to mad excess. Despotism is power gone mad. In women, despotism takes the form of satisfying their whims.

'You've nothing to complain of, my good friend. You have a very beautiful wife and she's virtuous.'

'I deserve my lot,' Hulot said to himself. 'I've not appreciated my wife. I make her suffer and she's an angel! Oh, my poor Adeline! You're well and truly avenged. She suffers in silence, alone. She should be adored. She deserves my love. I ought . . . for she's still lovely, pure, and virginal again . . . But was there ever a woman more worthless, more vicious, more treacherous than this Valérie?'

'She's a good-for-nothing,' said Crevel, 'a scoundrel who should be whipped on the Place du Châtelet. But, my dear Canillac,* we may be blue-waistcoated, Maréchal de Riche-lieu fashion plates, Pompadour, du Barry, rakes, and

thoroughly eighteenth century, but we don't have a Lieutenant of Police any more.'

'How does one make oneself loved?' Hulot wondered,
not listening to Crevel.

'It's silly of men like us to want to be loved, my friend,'
said Crevel. 'We can only be tolerated, for Madame
Marneffe is a hundred times more corrupt than Josépha.'

'And grasping! She's cost me ninety-two thousand
francs!' exclaimed Hulot.

'And how many centimes?' asked Crevel with the insolence of a businessman who thinks the sum trifling.

'It's obvious you don't love her,' said the Baron sadly.

'*I've* had enough,' replied Crevel, 'for she's had more
than three hundred thousand francs from me.'

'Where is it? Where does it all go?' asked the Baron,
holding his head in his hands.

'If we had made an arrangement between us, like those
young fellows who club together to keep a twopenny
street-girl, she would have cost us less.'

'That's an idea,' replied the Baron. 'But she'd still deceive
us, for what, my stout friend, do you make of that
Brazilian?'

'Oh, you old fox, you're right. We've been tricked like
. . . like shareholders!' said Crevel. 'All women of her sort
are limited liability companies.'

'So it was she who told you about the light in the
window?' said the Baron.

'My dear fellow,' continued Crevel, taking up his stance,
'we've been *swindled*! Valérie is a . . . She told me to keep
you here. . . . Now I see the light. . . . She's got her
Brazilian. Oh, I give her up, for if you were to hold her
hands she would find a way of deceiving you with her feet.
She's utterly vicious, she's a rogue.'

'She's worse than a prostitute,' said the Baron. 'Josépha
and Jenny Cadine were entitled to deceive us; *their* charms
are their profession.

'But *she* pretends to be a saint, a prude,' said Crevel.
'Look here, Hulot, go back to your wife, for your finances
are not in a good state. People are beginning to talk about

certain bills of exchange made out to a little money-lender who specializes in lending to street-girls, one Vauvinet. As for me, that's me cured of respectable women. Besides, at our age, what need have we of these hussies, who, to be honest, cannot fail to deceive us? You have white hair and false teeth, Baron. And I look like Silenus.* I'm going to apply myself to making money. Money can't cheat. Though the Treasury is available to everyone every six months, at least it gives you interest, and that woman makes you spend. With you, my old crony, Gubetta,* I might accept an irregular ... no, a rationally agreed situation. But a Brazilian who may be bringing dubious colonial goods from his country ...'

'Woman,' said Hulot, 'is an inexplicable creature.'

'I can explain her,' said Crevel. 'We're old. The Brazilian is young and handsome.'

'Yes, that's true,' said Hulot. 'I admit we're getting old. But, my friend, how are we to give up the sight of these lovely creatures undressing, fingering their curls, looking at us with a knowing smile as they fix their curl-papers, putting on all their little tricks, reeling off their lies, saying they are unloved when they see us harassed by business affairs, and entertaining us in spite of everything?'

'Yes, upon my word, it's the only pleasure in life,' exclaimed Crevel. 'When a little puss smiles at you and says, "My darling pet, you don't know how nice you are! I must be differently constituted from other women, who go crazy about youngsters with goatee beards, fellows who smoke and are as ill-bred as lackeys! For because they're young they think they can be impudent! Anyway they're here today and gone tomorrow. You think I'm a flirt but I prefer men of 50 to those brats; one can keep older men for a long time. They're devoted and know that women are not so easy to come by; and they appreciate us. That's why I love you, you old rascal." And while they're making confessions of this kind, they're petting and caressing you. . . . But they're as false as Town Hall promises.'

'Lies are often better than the truth,' said Hulot, recalling some charming scenes evoked by Crevel's imitation of

Valérie. 'They have to embroider their lies, to sew spangles on their stage costumes.'

'And then, after all, we have them, the liars,' said Crevel crudely.

'Valérie's a fairy,' cried the Baron. 'She can change an old man into a young one.'

'Oh, yes,' continued Crevel, 'she's an eel that slips through your fingers. But such a pretty eel! White and sweet like sugar! As amusing as Arnal,* and full of new tricks!'

'Oh, yes, she's very clever,' exclaimed the Baron, no longer thinking of his wife.

The two comrades went to bed the best of friends, recalling Valérie's perfections one by one, the intonations of her voice, her wheedling ways, her gestures, her amusing antics, her flashes of wit, her effusions of affection. For this artist in love had some rapturous moments, like a tenor who sings a melody one day better than another. And they both fell asleep lulled by these tempting, diabolical reminiscences lit up by the fires of hell.

At nine o'clock the next morning, Hulot spoke of going to the Ministry; Crevel had business in the country. They went out together and Crevel held out his hand to the Baron, saying;

'No ill-feeling, is there? For neither of us is going to think any more of Madame Marneffe.'

'Oh, that's all over and done with!' replied Hulot with an expression almost of horror.

53. *Two crazy fanatics*

At half past ten, Crevel was going up Madame Marneffe's staircase four steps at a time. He found the shameless creature, the adorable enchantress, wearing the smartest of morning-gowns, partaking of a nice, dainty breakfast in the company of Baron Henri Montès de Montéjanos and Lisbeth.

In spite of his shock at seeing the Brazilian, Crevel asked

Madame Marneffe to give him two minutes in private. Valérie went into the drawing-room with Crevel.

'Valérie, my angel,' said the lovesick Crevel, 'Monsieur Marneffe hasn't long to live. If you'll be faithful to me, when he dies we'll get married. Think it over. I got rid of Hulot for you. So just consider whether that Brazilian can be worth a Mayor of Paris, a man who, for your sake, would aim to reach the highest office and who has already, an income of more than eighty thousand francs a year.'

'I'll think about it,' she said. 'I'll be at the Rue du Dauphin at two o'clock and we'll talk it over. But be sensible. And don't forget the transfer of shares you promised me yesterday.'

She returned to the dining-room, followed by Crevel, who was flattering himself that he had found the way to have Valérie all to himself, when he caught sight of Baron Hulot, who, during this short interview, had come in with the same purpose in mind.

The Councillor of State, like Crevel, asked for a moment's private conversation. Madame Marneffe got up to go back to the drawing-room, smiling at the Brazilian as if to say, 'They're mad. Can't they see you?'

'Valérie, my dear,' said the Councillor of State, 'this cousin is a cousin from America . . .'*

'Oh, that's enough!' she cried, interrupting the Baron. 'Marneffe never has been, never will be, never can be my husband. The first, the only man I've ever loved has come back, unexpectedly. It's not my fault! But take a good look at Henri and then look at yourself. Then ask yourself if a woman can hesitate, especially when she's in love. My dear, I'm not a kept woman. From today, I no longer intend to be like Susanna between two old men. If you care for me, you and Crevel will be our friends. But everything else is over between us, for I'm 26 years old and from now on I intend to be a saint, a woman of worth and dignity . . . like your wife.'

'So that's the situation, is it?' said Hulot. 'That's how you welcome me, when I was coming like a pope with my hands full of indulgences! Well, your husband will never be an office-manager or an Officer of the Legion of Honour.'

'That remains to be seen!' said Madame Marneffe, giving Hulot a significant look.

'Don't let's quarrel,' continued Hulot in despair. 'I'll come this evening and we'll come to an understanding.'

'In Lisbeth's room, all right.'

'Very well, in Lisbeth's room,' said the lovesick old man.

Hulot and Crevel went downstairs together without saying a word to each other till they reached the street. But on the pavement they looked at each other and began to laugh bitterly.

'We're two crazy old men,' said Crevel.

'I've got rid of them,' Madame Marneffe said to Lisbeth as she sat down to table again. 'I've never loved, don't love, and never shall love anyone but my jaguar,' she added, smiling at Henri Montès. 'Lisbeth, my dear, do you know, Henri has forgiven me all the shameful activities to which poverty reduced me.'

'It's my fault,' said the Brazilian, 'I ought to have sent you a hundred thousand francs.'

'Poor boy!' cried Valérie. 'I ought to have worked for a living, but my fingers weren't made for that. Ask Lisbeth.'

The Brazilian went away the happiest man in Paris.

About noon, Valérie and Lisbeth were chatting together in the magnificent bedroom where the dangerous Parisian was putting those finishing touches to her dress which a woman prefers to attend to herself.

Behind bolted doors and drawn door-curtains, Valérie related, down to the last detail, all the events of the previous evening and night and of that morning.

'Are you pleased, my pet?' she asked Lisbeth when she had finished her tale. 'Which should I be, one day, Madame Crevel or Madame Montès? What do you think?'

'Crevel hasn't more than ten years to live, rake that he is,' replied Lisbeth, 'but Montès is young. Crevel will leave you an income of about thirty thousand francs. Let Montès wait. He'll be happy enough as long as he remains the Benjamin. So, when you're about 33, if you take care to keep your looks, you can marry your Brazilian and cut a fine figure with sixty thousand francs a year of your own, especially if you're under the wing of a marshal's wife.'

'Yes, but Montès is a Brazilian. He'll never get anywhere,' remarked Valérie.

'We live in an age of railways, when foreigners in France end up by occupying high positions,' said Lisbeth.

'We'll see, when Marneffe's dead,' continued Valérie, 'and he hasn't long to suffer.'

'These recurring attacks of illness are like the remorse of his physical being,' said Lisbeth. 'But now I'm going to see Hortense.'

'Well, you go, my angel,' replied Valérie, 'and bring me my artist. To think that, in three years, I haven't gained an inch of ground. That's a disgrace to both of us. Wenceslas and Henri, those are my only two passions. One is love, the other is just a whim.'

'How beautiful you look this morning,' said Lisbeth, putting her arm round Valérie's waist and kissing her on the forehead. 'I enjoy all your pleasures, your money, your clothes. I only began to live on the day we became sisters.'

'Wait a minute, my tigress,' said Valérie, laughing. 'Your shawl is askew. . . . After three years, you still don't know how to wear a shawl, in spite of my lessons. Yet you want to be Madame la Maréchale Hulot!'

54. *Another view of a legitimately married couple*

Wearing prunella ankle boots and grey silk stockings, equipped with a dress of magnificent Levantine silk, her braided hair surmounted by a very pretty black velvet bonnet lined with yellow satin, Lisbeth went off to the Rue Saint-Dominique by way of the Boulevard des Invalides, wondering whether Hortense's despondency would finally deliver that strong spirit into her power and whether Slavonic instability, caught at a moment when such natures are susceptible to anything, would make Wenceslas's love waver.

Hortense and Wenceslas lived on the ground floor of a house at the corner of the Rue Saint-Dominique and the Esplanade des Invalides.

The flat, once in harmony with the honeymoon, now had a half-new, half-faded look which could be called the autumn of furnishings. Newly-weds are destructive; without realizing it or meaning to be so, they are wasteful of everything around them, as they are of their love. Wrapped up in themselves, they don't worry about the future which, later on, will preoccupy the mother of a family.

Lisbeth came upon her cousin Hortense just as she had finished dressing a little Wenceslas herself before sending him into the garden.

'Hullo, Bette,' said Hortense, opening the door to her cousin, herself.

The cook had gone to market; the maid, who was also the nanny, was doing some washing.

'Hullo, dear,' replied Lisbeth, kissing Hortense. 'Well,' she whispered to her, 'is Wenceslas at his studio?'

'No, he's talking to Stidmann and Chanor in the drawing-room.'

'Can we be alone?' asked Lisbeth.

'Come to my room.'

The chintz hangings of Hortense's room, with their pattern of pink flowers and green leaves on a white ground, were, like the carpet, constantly exposed to the sun and so had faded. The curtains had not been washed for a long time. The smell of Wenceslas's cigar pervaded the room, for, having become an aristocrat of the art world and being born a nobleman, he dropped tobacco ash on the arms of chairs, on the prettiest pieces of furniture, as a loved one from whom anything is tolerated, as a rich man who pays no attention to middle-class carefulness.

'Well, let's talk about your affairs,' commanded Lisbeth, seeing her beautiful cousin sit silent in the chair into which she had dropped. 'But what's the matter? You look a little pale to me, my dear.'

'Two more articles have appeared, slating my poor Wenceslas. I've read them, but I've hidden them from him, for he would be completely discouraged. The statue of Marshal Montcornet is considered downright bad. They exempt the bas-reliefs but only with horrible treachery, to praise Wenceslas's talent for ornament so as to give more weight to the opinion that serious *art* is inaccessible to him. I begged Stidmann to tell me the truth and he drove me to despair by confessing to me that his own opinion agreed with that of all the artists and critics and of the public. He told me there, in the garden, before lunch, that if, next year, Wenceslas doesn't exhibit a masterpiece, he should abandon large-scale sculpture and confine himself to romantic subjects, small figures, jewellery, and high-class goldsmith's work. This opinion distressed me greatly, for Wenceslas would never accept it. He feels his own gifts; he has so many wonderful ideas.'

'You can't pay tradesmen with ideas,' remarked Lisbeth. 'I used to wear myself out telling him so. You need money for that. Money can ony be got by completed work, which people like well enough to buy. When it's a question of earning a living, it's better for a sculptor to have on his *workbench* the model of a candlestick, or a fender, or a table rather than a group or a statue, for everyong needs those things, while he may have to wait months on end for the buyer of groups and his money.'

'You're right, dear Lisbeth. Do tell him so, for I haven't the courage. Besides, as he told Stidmann, if he goes back to making ornaments and small items, he'll have to give up all thoughts of the Institute and great artistic creations, and we won't get the three hundred thousand francs for work that Versailles, the city of Paris, and the ministry were holding in reserve for us. That's what we lose because of those frightful articles dictated by rivals who would like to inherit our commissions!'

'And that's not what you dreamed of, my poor little darling,' said Bette, kissing Hortense on the forehead. 'You wanted a nobleman at the head of the world of art, the leading sculptor. But that's just romantic imagining, you

know. That dream demands an income of fifty thousand
francs a year and you have only two thousand four
hundred as long as I'm alive, three thousand after my
death.'

Tears rose in Hortense's eyes and Bette lapped them up
with a look as a cat drinks milk.

55. *What makes great artists*

Here is the story of that honeymoon in brief; the account
will perhaps not be lost on artists.

Intellectual work, the pursuit of achievement in the high
regions of the mind, is one of the greatest of human
endeavours. What most deserves glory in art (for in that
word we must include all mental creativity) is, above all,
courage, a courage of which ordinary people have no idea
and which, perhaps for the first time, is revealed here.

Driven by the terrible pressure of poverty, kept by Bette
in a situation like that of a horse kept blinkered to prevent
it from seeing to the right or left of its path, goaded on by
that strict old maid, the personification of Necessity, a
kind of underling of Fate, Wenceslas, a born poet and
dreamer, had passed from the conception of a work to its
execution, crossing the abysses that separate these two
hemispheres of art without taking any account of the leaps.

To think, to dream, to conceive beautiful works of art,
is a delightful occupation. It is like smoking magic cigars,
like living the life of a courtesan who heeds only her own
caprices. The work then appears in all its initial charm, in
the wild delight of its invention, with its flower-like
colours and perfumes and the sweet-tasting juices of a fruit
savoured in anticipation. Such are the pleasures of
conception.

He who can describe his plan in words is already deemed
to be an extraordinary man. All writers and artists have
this ability. But to produce! To bring to birth! To work
hard at rearing the child, to put it to bed every night well-
fed with milk, to kiss it every morning with the inexhaust-

ible love of a mother, to lick it clean, to dress it a hundred times in the prettiest of jackets which it tears again and again; but not to be discouraged by the convulsions of this mad life and to turn it into the living masterpiece which speaks to all eyes in sculpture, to all minds in literature, to all memories in painting, to all hearts in music, that is the task of execution! The hand must be ready at every moment to work in obedience to the mind. And the mind is not creative to order, any more than love flows uninterruptedly.

The habit of creation, the indefatigable maternal love which makes a mother (that natural masterpiece so well understood by Raphael), in short, that intellectual maternity which is so difficult to acquire, is remarkably easy to lose. Inspiration gives genius its opportunity. It runs, not on a razor's edge, but on the very air and takes wing with the quick alarm of a crow. It wears no scarf that the poet can grasp; its hair is a flame; it flies away like those beautiful pink and white flamingoes that are the despair of huntsmen. So work is a wearing struggle that is both feared and loved by the fine and powerful constitutions that are often shattered by it. A great poet of our own day said, speaking of this appalling toil, 'I begin it with despair and leave it with sorrow.'

Let the ignorant be informed! If the artist does not throw himself into his work, like Curtius* into the gulf beneath the Forum, like a soldier against a fortress, without hesitation, and if, in that crater, he does not work like a miner under a fall of rock, if, in short, he envisages the difficulties instead of conquering them one by one, following the example of lovers in fairy-tales who, to win their princesses, struggle against recurring enchantments, the work remains unfinished, it expires in the studio, where production remains impossible and the artist looks on at the suicide of his own talent.

Rossini, a genius akin to Raphael, affords a striking example in the contrast between the poverty of his youth and the affluence of his maturity.

That is the reason for the same reward, the same

triumph, the same laurel wreath being granted to great poets and great generals.

Wenceslas, by nature a dreamer, had expended so much energy in producing, learning, and working under Lisbeth's despotic command, that love and happiness brought a reaction. His true character reappeared. Laziness and indifference, Slavonic weakness of character, regained possession of the receptive pathways of his heart, from which the schoolmaster's rod had banished them.

56. *Effect of the honeymoon on the arts*

During the first months of their marriage, the artist was in love with his wife. Hortense and Wenceslas indulged in the adorable childlike antics of happy, legitimate, boundless love. Hortense was then the first to excuse Wenceslas from all work, proud of thus being able to triumph over her rival, sculpture. In any case, a woman's caresses put the muse to flight and weaken the worker's fierce, determined resolution.

Six or seven months went by, the sculptor's hands forgot how to hold the chisel. When it became apparent that work was necessary, when the Prince de Wissembourg, president of the committee of subscribers, wanted to see the statue. Wenceslas gave the idler's usual answer, 'I'm just going to start work on it.' And he soothed his dear Hortense with deceptive words, with the magnificent plans which an artist sees in his cigar smoke.

Hortense loved her poet more than ever. She saw in her mind's eye a sublime statue of Marshal Montcornet. Montcornet was to be the idealization of intrepid courage, the model cavalry officer, the personification of bravery in the style of Murat.* Indeed, at the mere sight of this statue, one would be able to understand how the Emperor had won all his victories. And the execution would be so splendid! The pencil fell in with the artist's wishes; it was in line with his words.

As for the statue, it turned out to be a ravishing little Wenceslas.

Whenever there was talk of going to the Gros-Caillou studio to work on the clay and complete the model, the prince's clock required Wenceslas's presence at Florent and Chanor's workshop, where the figures were being carved, or the day was grey and gloomy. One day there would be business to attend to, on another there would be a family dinner, not to mention the days when the artist felt his talent falter or did not feel well. And, finally, there were the days when he had a happy time with his adored wife.

In order to obtain the model, the Maréchal Prince de Wissembourg had to get annoyed and say he would reconsider his decision. It was only after innumerable complaints and many harsh words that the subscribers' committee was able to see the plaster cast. After each day at work Steinbock would come home visibly tired out, complaining of having to do a mason's work and of his physical weakness.

During this first year the couple was reasonably well off.

Countess Steinbock, doting madly on her husband, in the happiness of requited love, inveighed against the Minister of War. She went to see him and told him that great works could not be manufactured like cannon and that the state ought to take its orders from genius as Louis XIV, François I, and Leo X* had done. Poor Hortense, believing she had a Phidias* in her arms, treated her Wenceslas with the maternal indulgence of a woman who carries love to the point of idolatry.

'Don't hurry,' she told her husband. 'Our whole future depends on this statue. Take your time. Create a masterpiece.'

She would come to the studio. Steinbock, in love, would lose five hours out of seven with his wife, describing his statue to her instead of working at it. So it took him eighteen months to complete the work which was of capital importance to him.

When the plaster had been cast and the model actually existed, poor Hortense, who had witnessed her husband's tremendous exertions and seen his health suffer from the fatigue which afflicts a sculptor's back, arms, and hand—Hortense thought the work admirable. Her father, who knew nothing about sculpture, and the Baroness, who was equally ignorant, proclaimed it a masterpiece. Then they brought the War Minister to see it, and influenced by them he was pleased with the plaster cast, which had been carefully placed on its own in a favourable light against a green cloth background.

Alas! At the 1841 Exhibition, unanimous disapproval in the mouths of people antagonized by an idol they had been so quick to put upon a pedestal, degenerated into howls of mockery. Stidmann wanted to enlighten his friend; he was accused of jealousy. In Hortense's eyes, the newspaper articles were shrieks of envy.

Stidmann, being a good fellow, had articles written which refuted the critics and in which it was said that sculptors modified their works a great deal between the plaster model and the marble, and it was the marble that was put on show.

'Between the plaster model and the marble statue,' wrote Claude Vignon, 'one can ruin a masterpiece or transform a poor work into a great one. The plaster is the manuscript, the marble is the book.'

In two and a half years, Steinbock had produced a statue and a child. The child was exquisitely beautiful, the statue was appalling.

The prince's clock and the statue paid the young couple's debts. By then Steinbock had formed the habit of going into society, to the theatre, to the Italian Opera. He spoke eloquently about art; in the eyes of society people he maintained his position as a great artist by his conversation and his critical pronouncements.

There are gifted people in Paris who spend their lives *talking* their works and who are satisfied with a drawing-room celebrity. Steinbock, in imitation of these charming eunuchs, acquired an aversion for work which increased daily. He noticed all the difficulties of the work as soon as he tried to start on it, and the ensuing discouragement weakened his will. Inspiration, the frenzy that accompanies intellectual creation, flew swiftly away at the sight of this sick lover.

57. Of sculpture

Sculpture is like dramatic art, at once the most difficult and the easiest of all the arts. Copy a model and the work is completed, but to impart a soul into it, to construct a type by making the representation of one man or one woman, that is to commit Prometheus' sin.* Successes of this order have been achieved in the annals of sculpture, just as there have been poets in the course of human history. Michelangelo, Michel Columb, Jean Goujon, Phidias, Praxiteles, Polyclitus, Puget, Canova, Albrecht Dürer, are the brothers of Milton, Virgil, Dante, Shakespeare, Tasso, Homer, and Molière. Their work is so magnificent that one statue is enough to make a man immortal, just as the characters of Figaro,* Lovelace,* and Manon Lescaut* were enough to immortalize Beaumarchais, Richardson, and the Abbé Prévost.

Superficial people (and there are far too many of them among artists) have said that the only worthwhile sculpture is in the nude, that it died with Greece, and that modern dress makes it impossible.

But, for one thing, sculptors of ancient times made sublime statues fully draped, like the *Polymnia*,* the *Julia*,* etc. and we have not found a tenth of their works. And then, true art lovers have but to go to Florence to see Michelangelo's *Thinker*, or to Mainz Cathedral to see the *Virgin* of Albrecht Dürer who, out of ebony, has made a living woman beneath her triple layer of robes, with hair as softly waving and as easy to dress as any a lady's maid ever combed. Let the ignorant hasten to see these works and they will all realize that genius can put its stamp on a coat, a suit of armour, or a dress, and place a body within them, just as much as a man bears the mark of his temperament and habits on his clothes. Sculpture is the

continual creation of this achievement, which in painting
has one name and one name only, Raphael! The solution
to this terrible problem is to be found in constant, unremitting work, for the material difficulties must be so completely mastered, the hand must be so disciplined, so alert
and obedient, that the sculptor can have a heart-to-heart
struggle with the intangible moral element that he must
idealize in giving it material form.

If Paganini,* who expressed his soul through the strings
of his violin, had spent three days without practising, he
would have lost what he called the *register* of his instrument; that is what he called the bond that existed between
the wood, the bow, the strings, and himself. If that union
were dissolved, he would suddenly become an ordinary
violinist.

Ceaseless work is the law of art, as it is of life, for art is
the creation of an ideal of life. So great artists, like true
poets, do not wait for order or customers. They produce
today, tomorrow, all the time. Consequently they have a
habit of work, a perpetual awareness of their difficulties,
which keeps them in partnership with the muse and her
creative forces. Canova used to live in his studio just as
Voltaire lived in his study. Homer and Phidias must have
lived in this way.

Wenceslas Steinbock was set on the difficult road trav-
elled by these great men, a road which leads to the great
heights of fame, when Lisbeth had kept him in chains in
his garret. Happiness, in the shape of Hortense, had
returned the poet to the state of idleness which is normal
to artists, for *their* idleness is an occupation. It is like the
pleasure of a pasha in his harem; they fondle ideas, they
become drunk at the springs of the intellect. Great artists
like Steinbock, totally absorbed in reverie, have rightly
been called *dreamers*. These opium-eaters all sink into
poverty, whereas, if they had been sustained by harsh
circumstances, they would have been great men. These
demi-artists are, moreover, charming; people like them and
make them drunk with praise. They appear superior to real
artists, who are taxed with egotism, unsociability, and

rebellion against social conventions. And this is the reason
why.

Great men belong to their creations. Their detachment
from all other concerns, their devotion to work, stamps
them as egotists in the eyes of fools who would like to see
them dressed in smart clothes like men about town,
performing the evolutions called social duties. People
would like the lions of Atlas to be combed and perfumed
like a marchioness's lapdogs.

These men, who rarely encounter their few equals, fall
into solitary, exclusive ways. They become incomprehensible to the majority, which is composed, as we know, of
the foolish, the envious, the ignorant, and the superficial.
Do you now understand a woman's function in the life of
one of these impressive, exceptional beings? A wife must
be both what Lisbeth had been for five years and, in
addition, give love, a humble, discreet love, always available, always smiling.

Hortense, having learned from her sufferings as a mother
and harried by dire necessity, realized too late the mistakes
which, out of excessive love, she had involuntarily committed; but like a true daughter of her mother, she was broken-
hearted at the thought of worrying Wenceslas. She loved
her dear poet too much to be his tormentor and she saw
the time coming when poverty would catch up with her,
her son, and her husband.

58. *In which can be seen the power of that socially disruptive force, poverty.*

'Oh, come, come, my dear,' said Bette, seeing tears well up
in her young cousin's lovely eyes, 'you mustn't give way
to despair. A glassful of your tears wouldn't pay for one
plate of soup! How much do you need?'

'About five or six thousand francs.'

'I've got at most three thousand,' said Lisbeth. 'And
what's Wenceslas doing just now?'

'It's been suggested that, in co-operation with Stidmann, he should make a dessert service for the Duc D'Hérouville for six thousand francs. Monsieur Chanor would then undertake to pay the four thousand francs that Wenceslas owes to Léon de Lora and Bridau; it's a debt of honour.'

'What! You've had the money for the statue and the bas-reliefs for the monument to Marshal Montcornet, and you haven't paid that!'

'But,' said Hortense, 'for the past three years we've been spending twelve thousand francs a year and I've an income of two thousand. Once all the expenses were paid, the Marshal's statue brought in no more than sixteen thousand francs. Indeed, if Wenceslas doesn't work, I don't know what will become of us. Oh, if I could learn to make statues, I'd make quick work with the clay!' she said, stretching out her lovely arms.

It was clear that the mature woman fulfilled the promise of the young girl. Hortense's eyes sparkled; determined, impetuous blood flowed in her veins. She bewailed the fact that she had to spend her energy looking after her son.

'Oh, my dear child, a wise girl should marry an artist only when he has made his fortune, not when it has still to be made.'

Just then they heard the steps and voices of Stidmann and Wenceslas, who were seeing Chanor to the door. Soon after, Wenceslas came in with Stidmann.

Stidmann, an artist who was well in with the world of journalists, famous actresses, and well-known courtesans, was a fashionable young man, whom Valérie wanted to have in her circle and whom Claude Vignon had already introduced to her.

Stidmann had just seen the end of his relationship with the celebrated Madame Schontz, who had married and gone to live in a provincial town some months before. Valérie and Lisbeth, who had been told of this break by Claude Vignon, thought it advisable to attract Wenceslas's friend to the Rue Vaneau. As Stidmann, out of tact, did not often visit the Steinbocks, and since Lisbeth had not been present when Claude Vignon introduced him to

Valérie a short while previously, she saw him now for the first time. As she scrutinized the famous artist, she noticed the way he looked at Hortense and that made her envisage the possibility of giving him as a consolation to Countess Steinbock if Wenceslas should be unfaithful to her.

As a matter of fact, the thought had occurred to Stidmann that if Wenceslas were not his friend, Hortense, the superb young Countess, would make an adorable mistress. But this inclination, restrained by a sense of honour, kept him away from the house. Lisbeth noticed his significant embarrassment, of the kind that afflicts a man in the presence of a woman with whom he has forbidden himself to flirt.

'That's a very attractive young man,' she murmured to Hortense.

'Oh, do you think so?' she replied. 'I've never noticed it.'

'Stidmann, my dear fellow,' Wenceslas said quietly to his friend, 'we don't stand on ceremony with each other. You see, we've got some business to discuss with this old maid.'

Stidmann bowed to the two cousins and took his leave.

'It's settled,' Wenceslas said, coming back into the room after seeing Stidmann to the door. 'But the work will take six months and meanwhile we have to live.'

'I've got my diamonds,' cried young Countess Steinbock with the superb impulsive generosity of a woman in love.

Tears came into Wenceslas's eyes.

'Oh, I'm going to work,' he said, going over to sit beside his wife and taking her on his knee. 'I shall make extras on the side, wedding presents, bronze groups.'

'But, my dear children, you know you are my heirs and, believe me, I'll leave a nice little pile especially if you help me to marry the Marshal,' said Lisbeth. 'If we could manage it quickly, I'd take you and Adeline into my house as boarders. Oh, we could live very happily together. For the moment, be advised by my long experience. Don't resort to the pawnshop; that brings ruin on the borrower. I've seen again and again that when the time for renewal comes round, people who are hard up haven't the money needed to pay the interest and everything is lost. I can get someone to lend you the money at only 5 per cent on your note of hand.'

'Oh, that would save us!' said Hortense.

'Well, my dear, Wenceslas should go to see the person who would oblige him at my request. It's Madame Marneffe. If you flatter her, for like all social climber's she's vain, she'll help you out of your difficulty in the most obliging way. Come to her house, my dear Hortense.'

Hortense looked at Wenceslas with an expression like that of the condemned as they mount the scaffold.

'Claude Vignon introduced Stidmann there,' replied Wenceslas. 'It's a very pleasant house.'

Hortense bowed her head. A single word can convey what she felt; it was not a stab of pain, it was a sickness.

'But, my dear Hortense, you must learn what life is like,' exclaimed Lisbeth, understanding Hortense's eloquent gesture. 'If you don't, you'll be like your mother, banished to a deserted room where you'll weep like Calypso after the departure of Ulysses, in an age when there's no Telemachus,'* she added, repeating one of Madame Marneffe's witticisms. 'You must look on people in society as tools you make use of, that you pick up or lay down according to their usefulness. Make use of Madame Marneffe, my dears, and drop her later. Are you afraid that Wenceslas, who adores you, will conceive a passion for a woman four or five years older than you, as faded as a bundle of lucerne hay, and . . .'

'I'd rather pawn my diamonds,' said Hortense. 'Oh, never go to that house, Wenceslas! It's hell!'

'Hortense is right,' said Wenceslas, kissing his wife.

'Thank you, my dear,' said the young wife, overjoyed. 'You see, Lisbeth, my husband's an angel. He doesn't gamble, we go everywhere together, and if only he could settle down to work . . . no, I'd be too happy. Why should we be seen at my father's mistress's house, at the house of a woman who's ruining him and who is the cause of the sorrows that are killing our heroic Mama?'

'My dear child, that's not what is responsible for your

father's ruin. It was his singer who ruined him and then your marriage,' replied Cousin Bette. 'Goodness me, Madame Marneffe's very useful to him, I should say. . . . But I mustn't say anything.'

'You defend everybody, dear Bette.'

Hortense was called into the garden by her child's cries and Lisbeth remained alone with Wenceslas.

'You have an angel for a wife, Wenceslas,' said Cousin Bette. 'Love her well; never give her any cause for sorrow.'

'Yes, I love her so much that I conceal our situation from her. But to you, Lisbeth, I can talk about it. . . . The fact is that even if we were to pawn my wife's diamonds we shouldn't be any further forward.'

'Well, borrow from Madame Marneffe,' said Lisbeth. 'Persuade Hortense to let you come, or, indeed, go there without her knowledge.'

'That's what I was thinking when I refused to go so as not to upset Hortense,' replied Wenceslas.

'Listen, Wenceslas, I love you both too much not to warn you of the danger. If you go there, hold on to your heart with both hands, for that woman's a demon. All the men who see her, adore her; she's so enticingly corrupt. She's as fascinating as a masterpiece of art. Borrow her money, but don't leave your heart as a guarantee. I'd never forgive myself if you were to be unfaithful to my cousin. Here she is!' exclaimed Lisbeth. 'Say no more; I'll arrange the matter for you.'

'Give Lisbeth a kiss, my love,' Wenceslas said to his wife. 'She's going to help us out of our difficulties by lending us her savings.'

And he nodded towards Lisbeth in a way she understood.

'I hope you'll set to work then, my darling,' said Hortense.

'Yes,' replied the artist, 'right away tomorrow.'

'It's the word "tomorrow" that ruins us,' said Hortense, smiling at him.

'Oh, my dear, you know yourself that every day there's

been something to prevent my working, things getting in the way, business to be attended to.'

'Yes, you're right, my love.'

'I have here,' continued Steinbock, touching his forehead, 'such ideas! . . . Oh, but I'm going to astound my enemies. I intend to make a dinner service in the sixteenth-century German style, the imaginative style. I'll make curled-up leaves full of insects, with children sleeping amongst them, and I'll mingle with them new fantasies, true fantasies which are the substance of our dreams. I've got them all in my mind. It will be intricate, light, and elaborate all at once. Chanor went away filled with admiration. I need encouragement, for the last article about the Montcornet statue really shattered me.'

When Wenceslas and Lisbeth were alone for a moment in the day, the artist arranged with the old maid to go and see Madame Marneffe the next day, for either his wife would have agreed to his going or he would go secretly.

59. *Reflections on beauty spots*

Valérie, informed of this success that very evening, insisted that Baron Hulot should invite Stidmann, Claude Vignon, and Steinbock to dinner; for she was beginning to tyrannize over him as such women know how to tyrannize over the old men who trot around the town, and invite anyone who is necessary to the interest or vanity of their hard-hearted mistresses.

The next day, Valérie put on her armour, dressing in the way Parisian women contrive to do when they want to make the most of all their advantages. She studied her appearance for her work, as a man about to fight a duel rehearses his feints and his parries. She had not a line nor a wrinkle. Her skin had never been so soft, white, and delicate and her beauty spots imperceptibly attracted the eye.

People think that eighteenth-century beauty spots have been forgotten or are out of fashion; they are mistaken.

Today women more skilful than those of past ages, use daring devices to incite men to turn their opera-glasses on them.

One woman is the first to invent the knot of ribbons with a diamond placed in the centre, and she monopolizes all eyes for a whole evening. Another revives the hair-net or sticks a dagger in her hair in a way that makes you think of her garter. Another wears black velvet wristbands. And yet another turns up in a coif with pinners. These supreme efforts, the Austerlitzes* of coquetry or love, then become fashionable in lower spheres, just when their happy creators are looking round for new ideas.

For that evening, when Valérie was concerned to be successful, she arranged three beauty spots. First she had her hair rinsed with a lotion which, for a few days, turned her fair hair ash-blonde. Madame Steinbock was a golden blonde, and Valérie wanted to be completely unlike her. This new colour gave Valérie's appearance a piquancy and strangeness which made her faithful admirers so concerned that Montès said to her: 'But what's the matter with you this evening?'

Then she put on a black velvet neck-band, wide enough to set off the whiteness of her bosom.

The third beauty spot could be compared to the black silk patches that our grandmothers used to wear. Valérie placed the prettiest little rosebud in the middle of her bodice, just above the whalebone, in the daintiest of little hollows. It was enough to make any man under 30 lower his eyes.

'I look good enough to eat,' she said to herself, practising her poses in front of the mirror, exactly like a ballet dancer doing her exercises.

Lisbeth had gone to the market and the dinner was to be one of those extra special dinners that Mathurine used to cook for her bishop when he entertained the prelate of the neighbouring diocese.

60. *A fine entrance*

Stidmann, Claude Vignon, and Count Steinbock arrived almost all at the same time, about six o'clock.

Any ordinary or, if you like, unsophisticated woman would have hurried to greet the man whose presence she had so ardently desired, when his name was announced. But Valérie, who had been waiting in her room since five o'clock, left the three guests alone together, certain that she would be the subject of their conversation or of their secret thoughts.

She herself, in supervising the arrangement of her drawing-room, had prominently displayed those delightful trinkets that Paris produces and that no other city could, keepsakes bound in enamel and set with pearls, bowls full of charming rings, masterpieces of Sèvres or Dresden china mounted with exquisite taste by Florent and Chanor, and statuettes and albums as well, all those wildly expensive baubles which are ordered from the makers by passion in its first frenzy or in its last reconciliation.

Success, moreover, had gone to Valérie's head. She had promised Crevel to be his wife if Marneffe died.

The love-stricken Crevel had accordingly transferred to the name of Valérie Fortin ten thousand francs a year, the total profit earned from his railway investments over the last three years, all the earnings from the capital of a hundred thousand crowns that he had offered to Baroness Hulot. So Valérie had an income of thirty-two thousand francs a year.

Crevel had just let himself in for another promise worth even more than the gift of his profits. In the paroxysm of passion in which his *duchess* had engulfed him from two o'clock to four (he gave Madame *de* Marneffe this title so as to complete his illusions), for Valérie had excelled herself at the Rue du Dauphin, he thought he ought to encourage the promised fidelity by holding out the prospect of a pretty little house, which a rash speculator had built for himself in the Rue Barbette and which was now going to be sold. Valérie envisaged herself in this charming house, with its courtyard and garden, and her own carriage.

'What virtuous life can produce all this in so short a time and so easily?' she had asked Lisbeth as she finished dressing.

Lisbeth was dining that day with Valérie so that she could say to Steinbock the things that no one can say about herself.

Madame Marneffe, radiant with happiness, entered the room with graceful modesty; she was followed by Bette, who, dressed all in black and yellow, served as a foil, to use the language of the studio.

'Good evening, Claude,' she said, giving her hand to the celebrated former critic.

Like so many others, Claude Vignon had become a politician, a new word used for an ambitious man on the first stage of his career path. The politician of 1840 fills, in a way, the role of the *abbé* of the eighteenth century. No *salon* would be complete without its politician.

'My dear, this is my young cousin, the Comte de Steinbock,' said Lisbeth, introducing Wenceslas, whom Valérie appeared not to notice.

'Oh yes, I recognized Monsieur le Comte,' replied Valérie, with a gracious inclination of the head to the artist. 'I often used to see you at the Rue du Doyenné. I had the pleasure of being at your wedding. My dear,' she said, turning to Lisbeth, 'it would be difficult to forget your ex-child, even if one had seen him only once. Monsieur Stidmann is very kind,' she continued, greeting the sculptor, 'to have accepted my invitation at such short notice. But necessity knows no law. I knew you were a friend of these two gentlemen. Nothing is more lifeless or dreary than a dinner-party where the guests don't know each other, so I drafted you for their sakes. But you'll come another time for mine, won't you? Do say yes.'

Then she walked to and fro for a few minutes with Stidmann, appearing to be entirely engrossed with him.

One after the other, Crevel, Baron Hulot, and a deputy called Beauvisage were announced.

A provincial Crevel, Beauvisage was one of those people sent into the world to swell the crowd, and he voted under the banner of Giraud, the Councillor of State, and of Victorin Hulot. These two politicians were trying to form a kernel of progressives in the solid block of the Conservative party. Giraud used to come sometimes in the evening to visit Madame Marneffe, and she nurtured hopes of having Victorin Hulot as well. But so far the puritanical lawyer had found pretexts for resisting his father and father-in-law. To frequent the house of the woman who was the cause of his mother's tears seemed to him a crime. Victorin Hulot was to the puritans in politics what a truly pious woman is to the ostensibly devout.

Beauvisage, a former hosier from Arcis, wanted to *adopt the Parisian style*. On the fringe of the Chamber, he was learning the ropes in the drawing-room of the delightful, charming Madame Marneffe, where, greatly admiring Crevel, he had, at Valérie's instigation, accepted him as model and master. He consulted him about everything; he asked him for his tailor's address; he imitated him; he tried to adopt a pose like him. In short, Crevel was his great man.

Valérie, surrounded by these three public figures and by the three artists, well supported by Lisbeth, seemed to Wenceslas all the more an exceptional woman in that Claude Vignon sang Madame Marneffe's praises with the enthusiasm of a man in love.

'She's Madame de Maintenon* dressed up as Ninon,'* said the former critic. 'You need only to be witty for an evening for her to like you, but to be loved by her is a triumph which can satisfy a man's pride and fill his life.'

By her apparent coldness and indifference to her former neighbour, Valérie wounded his vanity, but without realizing it, for she did not know the Polish temperament.

61. *On Poles in general and on Steinbock in particular*

There is a childish side to the Slav as there is to all those originally primitive peoples that have made an irruption into the civilized nations rather than become really civilized themselves. This race has spread like a flood and covered an immense area of the surface of the globe. In inhabits deserts where the spaces are so vast that it has plenty of room. People don't get in each other's way there as they do in Europe, but civilization is impossible without the continual friction of minds and interests. The Ukraine, Russia, the plains of the Danube, in short the Slav peoples are a bridge between Europe and Asia, between civilization and barbarism.

And the Poles, the richest section of the Slav people, have in their character the childishness and fickleness of immature nations. They have courage, intellect, and strength, but, as they lack firmness of purpose, this courage, strength, and intellect have no method or intelligent control, for the Pole is as unstable as the wind that dominates this vast swampy plain. He may be as impetuous as tornadoes which twist up houses and carry them away, but he is also like terrible mountain avalanches and he will get lost in the first pond he comes across, dissolved into water.

Men always take on something of the surroundings in which they live. Continually at war with the Turks, the Poles acquired from them a taste for oriental splendour. They often sacrifice the necessities of life to make a show; they wear jewellery like women, and yet their climate has given them the tough constitution of Arabs.

And so the Poles, sublime in their suffering, have worn out the arms of their oppressors by allowing themselves to be beaten again and again, thus re-enacting, in the nine-teenth century, the performance of the early Christians. If you were to introduce 10 per cent of English guile into the

Polish character, which is so frank and open, the noble white eagle would be reigning in all those regions where the two-headed eagle has slipped in. A little Machiavellianism would have prevented Poland from saving Austria, who has partitioned her, from borrowing from Prussia, the usurer who has undermined her, and from splitting herself up at the time of the first partition. At Poland's christening a Fairy Carabossa,* forgotten by the good spirits who endowed that attractive nation with the most brilliant qualities, must have come and said, 'Keep all the gifts that my sisters have bestowed upon you, but you will never know what you want.' If, in its heroic duel with Russia, Poland had won, the Poles would be fighting amongst themselves today, as formerly they used to do in their Diets to prevent one another from being king. The day when that nation, composed entirely of full-blooded courageous men, has the good sense to seek out a Louis XI* from her own flesh and blood, and to accept from him tyrannical rule and a hereditary monarchy, it will be saved.

What Poland was in politics, most Poles are in their private lives, especially when disaster strikes. So Wenceslas, who for three years had adored his wife and knew that to her he was a god, was so piqued to find that Madame Marneffe barely noticed him, that it became a point of honour with him to obtain some attention from her.

In comparing her with his wife, he gave Valérie the advantge.

Hortense was a lovely morsel of flesh, as Valérie said to Lisbeth, but Madame Marneffe had a spirited demeanour and the piquancy of vice. Devotion like Hortense's is a feeling that a husband thinks is his due. The awareness of the immense value of a single-minded love is soon lost, just as a debtor imagines after a while that the money lent him is his own. This sublime loyalty becomes a kind of daily bread for the heart, and infidelity is as seductive as a sweetmeat.

A disdainful woman, above all a dangerous woman, stimulates curiosity, as spices enchance the flavour of good food. Moreover contempt, so well simulated by Valérie, was a novelty for Wenceslas after three years of easily available pleasures. Hortense was the wife and Valérie was the mistress. Many men want to have these two editions of the same work, although it is a clear proof of inferiority in a man if he is unable to make his wife his mistress. The need for variety in this respect is a sign of inadequacy.

Fidelity will always be the essence of love, the indication of an enormous power, the power that makes the poet. A man should find all women in his wife, as the starveling poets of the seventeenth century made Irises and Chloës* of their Manons.*

'Well,' said Lisbeth to her young cousin when she saw that he was fascinated, 'what do you think of Valérie?'

'She's too charming,' replied Wenceslas.

'You wouldn't listen to me,' continued Cousin Bette. 'Oh, my dear Wenceslas, if we had stayed together, you would have been that siren's love. You would have married her as soon as she was widowed, and you would have had her forty thousand francs a year.'

'Really?'

'Certainly,' replied Lisbeth. 'But now take care. I warned you of the danger. Don't get burned at the candle. Give me your arm. Dinner is served.'

No words could have been more demoralizing, for you have only to point out a precipice to a Pole and he will immediately throw himself over it. That nation has the mentality of a cavalry regiment. It thinks it can break through all obstacles and emerge victorious.

The effect of the spur which Lisbeth applied to her cousin's vanity was increased by the sight of the dining-room, which was gleaming with magnificent silver, and where Steinbock could see all the refinement and elegance of Parisian luxury.

'I would have done better to marry Célimène,'* he said to himself.

62. *Commentary on the story of Delilah*

During dinner, Hulot was charming; he was pleased to see his son-in-law there and even more happy because he was certain of a reconciliation with Valérie, whose fidelity he thought he had ensured by the promise of her husband's succeeding to Coquet's post.

Stidmann responded to the Baron's affability with flashes of Parisian wit and the liveliness of the artist.

Steinbock did not want to be outshone by his friend. He too exerted himself and came out with flashes of wit. He made an impression and was pleased with himself. Madame Marneffe smiled at him several times, showing that she thoroughly understood him.

The good food and heady wines completed the effect of immersing Wenceslas in what must be called the slough of pleasure. Excited by a drop too much wine, he stretched out on a divan, under the spell of a feeling of well-being that was both physical and spiritual, and that Madame Marneffe brought to new heights by sitting down beside him, light, perfumed, lovely enough to damn the angels.

She bent over towards Wenceslas. She almost touched his ear. She spoke to him in a low voice.

'We can't talk business this evening, unless you're willing to stay behind after the others have gone. You, Lisbeth, and I between us will arrange things to suit you.'

'Oh, you're an angel, Madame,' said Wenceslas, also in low tones. 'I was a great fool not to listen to Lisbeth.'

'What did she tell you?'

'She claimed in the Rue du Doyenné that you were in love with me.'

Madame looked at Wenceslas, seemed embarrassed, and got up abruptly.

A woman who is young and pretty never arouses in a man the idea of immediate success with impunity. This movement, that of a virtuous woman repressing a passion kept in the bottom of her heart, was a thousand times more eloquent than the most passionate declaration.

Wenceslas's desire was thus so keenly stimulated that he redoubled his attentions to Valérie. A woman in the public eye is a woman desired. This is the source of the terrible power of actresses. Madame Marneffe, knowing that she was under scrutiny, behaved like an actress who is being acclaimed. She was charming and her triumph was complete.

'I'm no longer surprised at my father-in-law's follies,' Wenceslas said to Lisbeth.

'If you talk like that, Wenceslas,' his cousin replied, 'I'll repent all my life that I got you the loan of those ten thousand francs. Are you going to be like all the others,' she said, indicating the other guests, 'madly in love with that creature? Just think, you would be your father-in-law's rival. And anyway, think of all the sorrow you would cause Hortense.'

'That's true,' said Wenceslas. 'Hortense is an angel. I'd be a monster.'

'One in the family is quite enough,' replied Lisbeth.

'Artists ought never to get married!' exclaimed Steinbock.

'Oh, that's what I told you in the Rue du Doyenné. *Your* children are your groups, your statues, your great works.'

'What are you talking about over there?' asked Valérie, coming and joining Lisbeth. 'Pour out the tea, Cousin.'

Steinbock, out of Polish boastfulness, wanted to appear on familiar terms with this drawing-room fairy. With an insolent look at Stidmann, Claude Vignon, and Crevel, he took Valérie by the hand and forced her to sit down beside him on the divan.

'You're behaving far too much like a great lord,' she said, offering little resistance.

And she began to laugh as she dropped down beside him, not without revealing the little rosebud which decorated her bodice.

'Alas, if I were really a great lord, I wouldn't be coming here as a borrower,' he said.

'Poor fellow! I remember how you used to work all night at the Rue du Doyenné. You were a bit of a fool. You got married as a starving man pounces on bread. You don't know Paris. Look at the position you're in now. But you turned a deaf ear to Bette's devotion as well as to the love of a Parisian who knew her Paris by heart.'

'Don't say another word,' exclaimed Steinbock. 'I'm beaten.'

'You shall have your ten thousand francs, my dear Wenceslas, but on one condition,' she said, playing with his magnificent wavy locks.

'What's that?'

'Well, I don't want any interest.'

'Madame!'

'Oh, don't be cross. You'll give me a bronze group instead. You've begun the story of Samson, now finish it. Make a group of Delilah* cutting the hair of the Jewish Hercules. But you, who'll be a great artist if you listen to me, I hope you'll understand the subject. The important thing is to express the power of the woman. Samson counts for nothing in that situation. He is the dead body of strength. Delilah is passion, that is the ruin of everything. Just as that *replica* . . . is that what you call it?' she added tactfully as she saw Claude Vignon and Stidmann who, noticing that the conversation was turning on sculpture, had come up to them. '. . . as that replica of Hercules at Omphale's* feet is much more beautiful than the Greek myth. Did the Greeks copy the Jews? Or did the Jews get this symbol from the Greeks?'

'Ah, Madame, there you raise an important question, that of the dates of composition of the different books of the Bible. The great and immortal Spinoza,* so stupidly classed as an atheist and who proved the existence of God mathematically, claimed that Genesis and, as it were, the political part of the Bible date from Moses' time, and he used philological proofs to show that other passages were interpolated. And so he was stabbed three times at the door of the synagogue.'

'I didn't know I was so learned,' said Valérie, irritated at the interruption of her tête-à-tête.

'Women know everything by instinct,' replied Claude Vignon.

'Well, will you promise me?' she asked Steinbock, taking his hand with all the hesitancy of a young girl in love.

'You're a lucky man, my dear fellow, if Madame has asked you for something,' exclaimed Stidmann.

'What is it?' asked Claude Vignon.

'A little group in bronze; Delilah cutting Samson's hair,' replied Steinbock.

'That's difficult,' remarked Claude Vignon, 'because of the bed.'

'On the contrary, it's extremely easy,' replied Valérie with a smile.

'Well, do some sculpture for us yourself!' said Stidmann.

'Madame is the subject for sculpture,' replied Claude Vignon, with a meaningful look at Valérie.

'Well,' she went on, 'this is my idea of the composition. Samson has woken up with no hair, as many dandies with false hair-pieces do. The hero is sitting on the edge of the bed, so you've only to indicate the base hidden by sheets and bedclothes. He sits like Marius* on the ruins of Carthage, his arms crossed, his head shaved—Napoleon on Saint Helena if you like! Delilah is kneeling, rather like Canova's *Madeleine*. After a woman has ruined her man, she adores him. As I see it, the Jewess was afraid of Samson when he was terrible and powerful, but she must have loved him when he had become like a child again. So Delilah deeply regrets her crime; she would like to give her love his hair back. She hardly dares look at him, but she looks at him smiling, for she perceives her pardon in Samson's weakness. This group, and one of the ferocious Judith,* would explain all womankind. Virtue cuts off the head; Vice only cuts off the hair. Watch out for your hair-pieces gentlemen!'

And she left the two artists, quite dazzled, singing her praises along with the critic.

'No one could be more delightful!' cried Stidmann.

'Oh, she's the cleverest and most attractive woman I've ever met. it's so rare to see wit together with beauty,' said Claude Vignon.

'If you, who had the honour of knowing Camille Maupin* intimately, make such judgements, what are we to think?' responded Stidmann.

'If you want to make Delilah a portrait of Valérie, my dear Count, I'll pay you a thousand crowns for a copy of the group. Oh yes, dammit, *I'll fork out* a thousand crowns,' said Crevel who had just left the card-table for a moment and had heard everything.

'I'll fork out? What does that mean?' Beauvisage asked Claude Vignon.

'Madame would have to deign to pose for me,' Steinbock said to Crevel, indicating Valérie. 'You ask her.'

63. *He is young, Polish, and an artist. What do you expect him to do?*

Just then, Valérie herself brought Steinbock a cup of tea. This was more than a mark of attention; it was a special favour. There is a whole language in the way a woman performs that office, and women are well aware of this. And so it is interesting to study their movements, their gestures, their looks, and the pitch and intonation of their voices, when they perform this apparently simple act of courtesy.

From the question, 'Do you drink tea?' 'Would you like some tea?' 'A cup of tea?' asked coldly, and the order to the nymph presiding over the tea-urn to bring it, to the eloquent poem of the odalisque coming from the tea-table, cup in hand, and offering it submissively to her heart's pasha, in a caressing voice and with a look full of voluptuous promise, a physiologist can observe the whole range of feminine feelings, from aversion or indifference to Phèdre's declaration to Hippolyte.* In this situation a woman can, at will, make herself disdainful to the point of insult, or as humble as an oriental slave.

Valérie was more than a woman; she was the serpent in female form. She completed her devil's work by coming up in Steinbock with a cup of tea in her hand.

'I'll take as many cups of tea as you'd like to give me, for the sake of having them offered to me like this,' the artist whispered to Valérie, getting up and lightly touching her fingers with his.

'What's that you were saying about posing?' she asked, giving no indication that his outburst of feeling, so ardently awaited, had gone straight to her heart.

'Père Crevel is going to buy a copy of your group for a thousand crowns.'

'Ha! A thousand crowns for a group?'

'Yes, if you'll pose for Delilah,' said Steinbock.

'He won't be present, I hope,' she rejoined. 'Then the group would be worth more than all his money, for Delilah should be a little décolleté.'

Just as Crevel would strike an attitude, so all women have a victorious demeanour, a studied pose which makes them irresistibly admired. You can see them in a drawing-room, spending their time looking at the lace of their bodices or adjusting the shoulders of their dresses, or else making play with the brilliance of their eyes by gazing up at the cornices.

Madame Marneffe, however, did not triumph face to face as other women do. She turned away abruptly to go back to Lisbeth at the tea-table. This dancer's movement with the swing of her dress, which had conquered Hulot, charmed Steinbock.

'Your vengeance is complete,' Valérie whispered to Lisbeth. 'Hortense will cry her eyes out and curse the day she took Wenceslas from you.'

'Until I am Madame la Maréchale, I'll have accomplished nothing,' replied the Lorraine peasant. 'But *they* are all beginning to want it. This morning I went to see Victorin.

I forgot to tell you that. The young Hulots have bought back the Baron's notes of hand from Vauvinet. Tomorrow they'll sign a bond for seventy-two thousand francs with interest at 5 per cent, repayable in three years, with a mortgage on their house as security. So the young Hulots will be hard up for the next three years, and it will be impossible for them to raise any more money on that property. Victorin is terribly depressed. He now fully realizes his father's character. And Crevel is quite capable of refusing to see his children again, he will be so angry at this act of devotion.'

'The Baron must have nothing left now,' Valérie whispered to Lisbeth as she smiled at Hulot.

'He has nothing more, as far as I can see, but he'll be able to get his salary again in September.'

'And he has his insurance policy; he's renewed it. Well, I think it's time he made Marneffe an office-manager. I'll get at him this evening.'

'My dear cousin,' said Lisbeth, going over to Wenceslas. 'Do go home, please. You're making yourself ridiculous; you're looking at Valérie in a way that compromises her, and her husband is madly jealous. Don't imitate your father-in-law, but go back home. I'm sure Hortense is waiting up for you.'

'Madame Marneffe told me to stay on after the others so that, between the three of us, we could arrange our little matter of business,' replied Wenceslas.

'No,' said Lisbeth, 'I'll hand the ten thousand francs over to you, for her husband has his eye on you. It would be unwise for you to stay. Bring the note of hand tomorrow at nine o'clock. At that time, that troublesome Marneffe is in his office, and Valérie is left in peace. I hear you've asked her to pose for a group. Come to my room first. Oh yes, I knew you had the making of a libertine. Valérie is very beautiful, but try not to make Hortense unhappy.'

Nothing irritates a married man more than to find his wife at every turn, standing between him and a desire, however fleeting.

64. *The return home*

Wenceslas returned home about one in the morning. Hortense had been waiting for him since about half past nine.

From half past nine to ten o'clock, she had listened to the sounds of carriages, telling herself that Wenceslas had never come home so late before when he dined without her with Chanor and Florent.

She sat sewing beside her son's cot, for she had started economizing on a sewing-woman's wages by doing some of the mending herself.

From ten to half past ten, a suspicion crossed her mind and she said to herself:

'But has he really gone to have dinner with Chanor and Florent as he told me? When he was dressing, he wanted his best tie and his finest tie-pin. He spent as much time on his appearance as a woman who wants to look even better than she really is. But I'm crazy. He loves me. Anyway here he is.'

Instead of stopping, the carriage that the young wife heard went on its way.

From eleven o'clock till midnight, Hortense was a prey to indescribable terrors, caused by the isolation of the neighbourhood where she lived.

'If he walked back,' she said to herself, 'he may have had an accident. People can kill themselves by stumbling over the edge of a kerb or into holes in the road. Artists are so absent-minded. What if he's been stopped by thieves! This is the first time he's left me here alone for six and a half hours. But why am I tormenting myself? He loves only me.'

Men ought to be faithful to the women who love them, if only because of the continual miracles produced by true love in that sublime world which we call *the world of the spirit*. In her relationship to the man she loves, a woman in love is like a hypnotist's subject who has been given the unhappy power at the end of a trance of being aware as a woman of what she has seen in it. Passionate love makes a woman's nervous energy reach the ecstatic pitch in which presentiment is as revealing as a prophetic vision. A woman knows she is betrayed, but she is so much in love that she doubts and does not listen to her own forebodings. And she gives the lie to the voice of her Pythoness's* power.

This extreme love ought to arouse veneration. In noble minds, admiration of that divine phenomenon will always be a barrier between them and infidelity. How can a man fail to love a beautiful, intelligent woman whose heart attains to such expressions of passion?

At one in the morning, Hortense's anxiety had reached such a pitch that she rushed to the door when she recognized Wenceslas's way of ringing the bell. She took him in her arms and pressed him to her heart like a mother.

'At last, you're here!' she said, regaining the use of her tongue. 'After this, dearest, I'll go wherever you go, for I don't want to undergo the torture of waiting for you like this again. I imagined you stumbling against a kerb and breaking your head! Or killed by thieves! No, another time, I know I should go mad. So you had a good time . . . without me? Bad boy!'

'What could I do, my darling good angel? Bixiou was there and he gave us some new orders. And Léon de Lora, whose wit never ceased to flow, and Claude Vignon, to whom I owe the only favourable article that's been written about the Montcornet monument. There was . . .'

'There were no women?' Hortense asked eagerly.

'The worthy Madame Florent . . .'

'You'd told me it was to be at the *Rocher de Cancale** but was it at their house then?'

'Yes, at their house. I made a mistake.'

'You didn't take a cab home?'

'No.'

'So you walked all the way from the Rue des Tournelles?'

'Stidmann and Bixiou walked back with me along the boulevards; we were talking on the way.'

'It must have been very dry on the boulevards and the Place de la Concorde and the Rue de Bourgogne; you're not muddy at all,' said Hortense, scrutinizing her husband's polished boots.

It had been raining, but from the Rue Vaneau to the Rue Saint-Dominique Wenceslas had not had to muddy his boots.

'Look, here's five thousand francs that Chanor has generously lent me,' said Wenceslas, to cut short this quasi-judicial inquiry.

He had made two bundles of his ten thousand-franc notes, one for Hortense and one for himself, as he had five thousand francs' worth of debts that Hortense knew nothing about. He owed money to his assistant and his workmen.

'Now you don't need to worry any more, my dear,' he said, kissing his wife. 'I'm going to start work first thing tomorrow. Oh, tomorrow I'll be off at half past eight, and I'll go to the studio. So I'm going to bed right away so as to get up early. You don't mind, sweetheart?'

The suspicion that had entered Hortense's heart disappeared; she was a thousand miles from the truth. Madame Marneffe! The thought of her never entered her head. She was afraid of the company of courtesans for her Wenceslas. The names of Bixiou and Léon de Lora, two artists known for their licentious lives, had made her anxious.

The next day, entirely reassured, she saw Wenceslas set off at nine o'clock.

'He's at work now,' she said to herself as she began to dress her baby. 'Oh, I can see him at it; he's in good form. Well, if we can't have Michelangelo's glory, we'll have Benvenuto Cellini's.'*

65. The first dagger-blow

Lulled by her own hopes, Hortense believed she had a happy future, and she was talking to her twenty-month-old son in that onomatopoeic langauge which makes children smile, when, about eleven o'clock, the cook, who had not seen Wenceslas go out, showed Stidmann in.

'I'm sorry to disturb you, Madame,' said the artist. 'Oh, has Wenceslas gone out already?'

'He's at his studio.'

'I came to discuss the work we're doing together.'

'I'll send for him,' said Hortense, motioning to Stidmann to take a seat.

The young wife, inwardly thanking heaven for this piece of luck, wanted to detain Stidmann in order to hear some details about the previous evening's party. Stidmann bowed in acknowledgement of the Countess's courtesy. Madame Steinbock rang, the cook appeared and was told to go to the studio for Monsieur.

'You must have had a good time last night,' said Hortense, 'for Wenceslas didn't get home till after one in the morning.'

'A good time? Not exactly,' replied the artist, who had wanted to *do* Madame Marneffe the previous evening. 'One doesn't have a good time in society unless one has some axe to grind there. That little Madame Marneffe is very clever, but she's a flirt.'

'And what did Wenceslas think of her?' asked poor Hortense, trying to stay calm. 'He didn't tell me anything about her.'

'I'll only tell you one thing,' replied Stidmann, 'and that is that I think she's a very dangerous woman.'

Hortense turned as pale as a woman in childbirth.

'So it was really . . . at Madame Marneffe's . . . and not at Chanor's that you dined . . . yesterday . . . with Wenceslas, and he . . .'

Without knowing what harm he was doing, Stidmann realized that there was something wrong. The Countess did not complete her sentence; she fainted away completely. The artist rang and the maid came in.

When Louise tried to help the Countess to her room, she was seized with the horrible convulsions of a very severe nervous attack.

Stidmann, like all those whose unwitting indiscretion

destroys the structure of falsehood erected by a husband for his family, could not believe that his words could have such an effect. He thought the Countess must be in that delicate state of health in which the slightest annoyance becomes a danger.

The cook came in and said, unfortunately in a loud voice, that Monsieur was not in his studio.

In the midst of her attack, the Countess heard this announcement and the convulsions began again.

'Go and fetch Madame's mother,' said Louise to the cook. 'Run!'

'If I knew where Wenceslas was, I'd go and tell him,' said Stidmann in despair.

'He's at that woman's,' cried poor Hortense. 'He dressed very differently from the way he does when he goes to his studio.'

Stidmann hurried to Madame Marneffe's, realizing the truth of this flash of insight, which stemmed from the *second sight* of passion.

At that moment Valérie was posing as Delilah.

Stidmann, too shrewd to ask for Madame Marneffe, went straight past the porter's lodge and quickly up to the second floor, reasoning to himself thus: 'If I ask for Madame Marneffe, she won't be at home. If I ask bluntly for Steinbock, they'll laugh in my face. So I'll go straight to the point.'

Reine appeared when he rang the bell.

'Tell Monsieur le Comte Steinbock to come at once, his wife is dying!'

Reine, as clever as Stidmann, looked at him rather stupidly.

'But, Monsieur, I don't know . . . what you . . .'

'I tell you that my friend Steinbock is here. His wife is dying. It's a sufficiently serious matter for you to disturb your mistress.'

And Stidmann went away.

'Oh, he's there all right,' he said to himself.

And, indeed, Stidmann, who lingered a few moments in

the Rue Vaneau, saw Wenceslas come out, and signed to him to come quickly.

After telling him of the tragedy that was being enacted at the Rue Saint-Dominique, Stidmann scolded Steinbock for not warning him to say nothing about the previous day's dinner.

'I'm done for,' Wenceslas replied, 'but I forgive you. I quite forgot about our appointment this morning and I made the mistake of not telling you that we were supposed to have dined at Florent's. But there we are! That Valérie has driven me out of my mind. But, dear fellow, she's worth as much as fame, she's worth suffering misfortune for. Oh, she's . . . My God! What a dreadful mess I'm in! Give me some advice. What shall I say? What excuses shall I make for myself?'

'Give you advice? I've no idea,' replied Stidmann. 'But your wife loves you, doesn't she? Well then, she'll believe anything. Anyway, tell her you were coming to see me, while I was going to your house. In that way you'll at least be able to conceal this morning's session. Goodbye!'

At the corner of the Rue Hillerin-Bertin, Lisbeth, informed by Reine, hurried after Steinbock and caught up with him, for she was afraid of his Polish naïveté. As she did not want to be compromised, she said a few words to Wenceslas, who, in his joy, kissed her in the middle of the street. She had presumably given the artist a plank to help him bridge his marital strait.

66. *The first quarrel of married life*

At the sight of her mother, who had come with all speed, Hortense had shed floods of tears. Fortunately, the nervous crises then took a different turn.

'Deceived, dear Mama!' she said. 'After giving me his word of honour not to go to Madame Marneffe's, Wenceslas had dinner there yesterday and didn't get home till a quarter past one in the morning. If only you knew—the evening before we had had not a quarrel but an explanation.

I had said such touching things to him. I was jealous; an infidelity would kill me; he ought to respect my weaknesses, since they stemmed from my love for him; I had my father's blood in my veins as well as yours; on first learning of an infidelity, I would be crazy enough to do anything, to take my revenge, to dishonour all of us, him, his son, and myself; and in the end I might kill first him and then myself—and more besides. But he went there and he's there now. That woman has made up her mind to torment us all. Yesterday my brother and Célestine pledged themselves to take up notes of hand for seventy-two thousand francs signed for the benefit of that good-for-nothing. . . . Yes, Mama, they were going to sue my father and put him in prison. Hasn't that horrible woman got enough with my father and your tears? Why take Wenceslas from me! I'll go to her house and stab her with a dagger!'

Madame Hulot, cut to the heart by the terrible secret that Hortense, in her furious outburst, had unwittingly revealed, conquered her own grief with a heroic effort of the kind great mothers are capable of and drew her daughter's head to her breast, covering it with kisses.

'Wait till Wenceslas comes in, my child, and all will be explained. Things may not be as bad as you think. I've been betrayed too, my dear Hortense. You think I'm beautiful; I'm faithful; and yet for the last twenty-three years I've been deserted for women like Jenny Cadine and Josépha and Marneffe. Did you know?'

'You, Mama, you! You've put up with that for twenty . . .?'

She stopped short, appalled by her own thoughts.

'Do as I have done, my child,' continued her mother. 'Be gentle and kind and you'll have an easy conscience. If, on his deathbed, a man says, "My wife has never caused me the least sorrow", God, who hears these last whispered words, counts them in our favour. If I had given way to rages, like you, what would have happened? Your father would have become embittered. Perhaps he would have left me, and he wouldn't have been held back by the fear of distressing me. Our ruin, which today is complete, would have come ten years earlier. We'd have presented to the world the spectacle of a husband and wife living apart— a dreadful and heart-breaking scandal, for it means the death of the family. Neither you nor your brother would have been able to be settled in marriage. I sacrificed myself and put such a brave face on it that, but for this last liaison of your father's, the world would still think I was happy. My opportunist but brave deception has protected Hector up till now; he is still respected. But I can see that this old man's passion is making him go too far. I fear his folly will destroy the screen that I placed between the world and us. But for twenty-three years I've kept up this curtain, weeping behind it, without a mother or anyone to confide in, with no help but religion, and I've maintained the family honour for twenty-three years.'

Hortense listened to her mother with glazed eyes. Her calm voice and the resignation of her acute suffering eased the pain of the young wife's first wound. Tears overwhelmed her and they returned in floods.

In an access of filial piety, overcome by her mother's sublime attitude, she knelt before her, seized the hem of her dress, and kissed it as pious Catholics kiss the holy relics of a martyr.

'Get up, my dear Hortense,' said the Baroness. 'Such a manifestation of my daughter's love and respect wipes out many unhappy memories. Let me hold you to my heart, which is burdened only with your grief. My little girl's happiness was my only happiness, and her despair has broken the tomb-like seal that nothing should have removed from my lips. Yes, I wanted to take my sorrows to the grave like an extra shroud. To soothe your rage, I have spoken. God will forgive me. Oh, if your life were to be like mine, what would I not do? Men, society, luck, nature, even God I think make us pay for love with the cruellest torments. For ten happy years I shall have paid twenty-four years of despair, of never-ending sorrows, of bitterness.'

'You've had ten years, dear Mama, but I've only had three,' said Hortense in the egoism of her love.

'All is not lost yet, dear. Wait for Wenceslas.'

'Mother,' she said, 'he lied, he deceived me. He told me he wouldn't go there and he went. And that in front of his child's cradle.'

'For the sake of their pleasure, my love, men commit the most dastardly actions, infamous deeds, and even crimes. It's in their nature, so it seems. We women are doomed to sacrifice. I thought my misfortunes had come to an end, but they are just beginning, for I didn't expect to suffer all over again in my daughter's suffering. Be brave and say nothing! Swear to me, my dear Hortense, to talk of your sorrows to no one but me, not to let any of them be seen by a third person. Oh, be as proud as your mother!'

Just then Hortense started, for she heard her husband's step.

'It appears that Stidmann came here while I was going to see him,' said Wenceslas, coming in.

'Really?' cried poor Hortense with the savage irony of an injured woman using words as a dagger.

'But yes. We've just run into each other,' replied Wenceslas, pretending to be surprised.

'But yesterday?' Hortense went on.

'Well, I deceived you, my darling, and your mother shall judge between us.'

This frankness was a relief to Hortense's spirit. All really noble women prefer truth to falsehood. They do not want to see their idol degraded. They want to be proud of the man whose domination they accept.

Russians have something of this feeling about their Czar.

'Listen, Mother dear,' said Wenceslas, 'I love my good, sweet Hortense so much that I kept the full extent of our financial difficulties from her. What else could I have done? She was feeding the baby and worries would have been very bad for her. You know what risks a woman is exposed to at that time. Her beauty, her bloom, her health are all in danger. Was that wrong? She thinks we owe only five thousand francs, but I owe five thousand more. The day before yesterday we were in despair. No one in the world will lend money to an artist. People have no more faith in our talents than they have in the products of our imaginations. I knocked in vain on every door. Lisbeth offered us her savings.'

'Poor woman,' said Hortense.

'Poor woman,' said the Baroness.

'But what's Lisbeth's two thousand francs? Everything to her, but nothing to us. And then, as you know, Hortense, our cousin told us about Madame Marneffe who, out of self-respect, since she owes so much to the Baron, won't accept any interest at all. Hortense wanted to pawn her diamonds. That would have given us a few thousand francs, but we needed ten thousand. And those ten thousand were to be had there for a year, without interest! I said to myself, "Hortense won't know anything about it. I'll go and take them." That woman got my father-in-law to invite me to dinner there yesterday, giving me to understand that Lisbeth had spoken to her and I would have the money. Between Hortense's despair and that dinner, I didn't hesitate. How could Hortense at 24, lovely, pure, and virtuous, she who is all my joy and pride, whom I have never left since our marriage, how could she imagine that I would prefer to her—what!—a jaded, faded, seedy woman?' he said, using a horrible studio-slang expression to encourage belief in his contempt, by exaggerating in the way that women like.

'Oh, if your father had only spoken to me like that!' exclaimed the Baroness.

Hortense flung her arms in gracious forgiveness round her husband's neck.

'Yes, that's what I would have done,' said Adeline. 'Wenceslas, my dear, your wife almost died,' she continued in a serious tone. 'You see how much she loves you. She is yours, alas!' And she sighed deeply. 'He can make a martyr or a happy woman of her,' she said to herself, thinking what all mothers think when their daughter's marry. 'It seems to me', she added aloud, 'that I suffer enough to be allowed to see my children happy.'

'Don't worry, dear Mama,' said Wenceslas, overjoyed at seeing the crisis brought to a happy end. 'In two months I'll have given back the money to that horrible woman. What else could I have done!' he went on, repeating with Polish charm this essentially Polish expression. 'There are times when one would borrow from the devil. After all, it's the family's money. And once I'd been invited, would I have got that money, which is costing us so dear, if I'd responded to her courtesy by being rude?'

'Oh, Mama, what harm Papa has done to us!' cried Hortense.

The Baroness put a finger to her lips and Hortense regretted her complaint, the first words of blame she had ever uttered about a father so heroically protected by a sublime silence.

'Goodbye, children,' said Madame Hulot. 'The fine weather's returned. But don't quarrel again.'

67. A suspicion always follows the first dagger-blow

When Wenceslas and his wife had returned to their room after seeing the Baroness out, Hortense said to her husband:

'Tell me about your evening.'

And she studied her husband's face as he told his story, interrupting him with all the questions that spring to a wife's lips in such circumstances. His account made her thoughtful; it gave her a glimpse of the diabolical entertainment that artists must find in such vicious company.

'Tell me everything, Wenceslas dear. Stidmann was there, and Claude Vignon and Vernisset, and who else? In fact, did you have a good time?'

'Me? I was thinking only of our ten thousand francs, and I was saying to myself. "My Hortense will have no more worries."'

The Livonian found the questioning very tiring and he took advantage of a moment of gaiety to say to Hortense:

'And you, my darling, what would you have done if your artist had been found guilty?'

'What would *I* have done?' she said with a decided little toss of the head. 'I would have taken Stidmann as my lover, but without loving him, of course.'

'Hortense,' cried Steinbock, getting up abruptly and with a theatrical gesture, 'you wouldn't have had time. I'd have killed you.'

Hortense flung her arms round her husband, nearly stifled him with her embrace, covered him with kisses, and said:

'Oh, you do love me, Wenceslas! Now I'm not afraid of anything. But no more Marneffe. Don't plunge into such filth again.'

'I swear, my dear Hortense, that I'll go back there only to redeem my note of hand.'

She sulked, but only as women in love sulk when they want the rewards of their sulking.

Worn out by such a morning, Wenceslas let his wife sulk and went off to his studio to make the clay model for the Samson and Delilah group; he had the sketch for it in his pocket.

Hortense, worried that she had been sulking, and thinking Wenceslas was annoyed, came to the studio just as her husband was finishing the clay model with the intense enthusiasm of artists impelled by the power of the imagination.

At the sight of his wife, he quickly threw a damp cloth over the rough model of the group and took Hortense in his arms, saying:

'Oh, we're not cross, are we, my pet?'

Hortense had seen the group and the cloth thrown over it. She said nothing, but before leaving the studio, she turned round, plucked off the rag, looked at the sketch, and asked:

'What's that?'

A group that I had an idea for.'

'And why did you hide it from me?'

'I didn't want to show it you till it was finished.'

'The woman is very pretty,' said Hortense.

And a thousand suspicions sprang up in her heart, as vegetation in India grows up tall and luxuriant from one day to the next.

68. *The discovery of a child*

After about three weeks, Madame Marneffe was greatly irritated by Hortense. Women of her sort have their pride. They want men to kiss the devil's hoof; they never forgive virtue that is not afraid of their power or that fights against them.

Now Wenceslas had not paid a single visit to the Rue Vaneau, not even the one required by courtesy after a woman has posed as Delilah.

Every time Lisbeth had gone to see the Steinbocks, she had found no one at home. Monsieur and Madame were living at the studio.

Lisbeth, who had tracked down the two turtle-doves to their nest at Gros-Caillou, saw Wenceslas working enthusiastically and learned from the cook that Madame never left Monsieur. Wenceslas was being subjected to the despotism of love.

So, on her own behalf, Valérie adopted Lisbeth's hatred of Hortense. Women value lovers for whom they have rivals as men value women who are desired by several nincompoops. These reflections about Madame Marneffe apply, then, just as much to womanizers, who are a kind of male courtesan.

Valérie's whim became an obsession. More than anything she wanted to have her group, and one morning she was planning to go and see Wenceslas at his studio when one of those serious situations arose which for women of her kind, can be called *fructus belli*.*

This is how Valérie announced the news of a quite

personal matter. She was breakfasting with Lisbeth and Monsieur Marneffe.

'Tell me, Marneffe, had you any idea that you were going to be a father for a second time?'

'Really, are you pregnant? Oh, let me give you a kiss.'

He got up and went to the other side of the table. His wife held up her forehead to him in such a way that the kiss skimmed over her hair.

'As a result of that event,' he went on, 'I'll be an office-manager and an Officer of the Legion of Honour. But I don't want Stanislas to be worse off because of it, my dear. Poor little fellow!'

'Poor little fellow!' exclaimed Lisbeth. 'You haven't seen him for seven months. At the school they think I'm his mother, for I'm the only one in the house who bothers about him.'

'A child who costs us a hundred crowns every three months!' said Valérie. 'Besides that child's yours, Marneffe. You certainly ought to pay for his board out of your salary. The new one, instead of bringing in bills from provision merchants, will save us from poverty.'

'Valérie,' replied Marneffe, imitating Crevel's attitude, 'I hope Monsieur le Baron Hulot will take care of his son and not burden a poor clerk with him. I plan to take a very firm line with him. So collect your evidence, Madame. Try to get letters from him in which he tells you of his happiness, for he's being a bit too dilatory about my appointment.'

And Marneffe went off to the Ministry where, thanks to his Director's valuable friendship, he did not need to arrive till about eleven o'clock. In any case, he did not do much there, because of his notorious incompetence and his aversion to work.

Once they were alone together, Lisbeth and Valérie looked at each other for a moment like two augurs,* and simultaneously broke into an immense fit of laughter.

'Tell me, Valérie, is it true or are you just putting on an act?' asked Lisbeth.

'It's physically true,' Valérie replied. 'Hortense gets me

down and last night I had the idea of throwing this child like a bomb into Wenceslas' household.'

Valérie went back to her room, followed by Lisbeth, and showed her the following letter, completely written out.

'My dear Wenceslas, I still believe in your love, although it's now nearly three weeks since I've seen you. Do you despise me? Delilah can't think so. Isn't it rather the tyranny of a woman whom you told me you could no longer love? Wenceslas, you're too great an artist to let yourself be dominated like this. Domesticity is the death of fame. Show that you are still the Wenceslas of the Rue du Doyenné. You failed with the monument to my father. But you are a much better lover than you are an artist. You've been more successful with the daughter. You are a father, my adored Wenceslas. If you don't come and see me in my present condition, your friends will think you're a very nasty fellow. But I love you so madly that I feel I'll never have the strength to revile you. May I call myself always

Your VALÉRIE

'What do you say to my plan of sending this letter to the studio when our dear Hortense is there alone?' Valérie asked Lisbeth. 'Yesterday evening I learned from Stidmann that Wenceslas is to call for him at eleven o'clock to go to Chanor's to discuss some work. So that hussy Hortense will be alone.'

'After a trick like that, I can't openly remain your friend. I'll have to leave your house and let it be thought that I don't see you any more or even speak to you.' replied Lisbeth.

'Obviously,' said Valérie, 'but . . .'

'Oh, don't worry,' Lisbeth replied. 'We'll see each other again when I'm Madame la Maréchale. *They* all want it now. Only the Baron is unaware of the plan. But you'll persuade him.'

'But it's possible that soon I'll be on rather awkward terms with the Baron,' Valérie replied.

'Madame Olivier is the only one we can trust to make sure Hortense will intercept the letter,' said Lisbeth. 'You must send her first to the Rue Saint-Dominique before she goes to the studio.'

'Oh, our little beauty will be at home,' replied Madame Marneffe, ringing for Reine to tell her to go for Madame Olivier.

69. *A second father for the Marneffe child*

Ten minutes after the dispatch of this fatal letter, Baron Hulot arrived. Madame Marneffe flung her arms round the old man's neck with kittenish grace.

'Hector, you're a father!' she whispered to him. 'That's what comes of quarrelling and making up again.'

Seeing a certain look of surprise which the Baron did not conceal quickly enough, Valérie assumed a cold expression which drove the Councillor of State to despair. She made him extract the most convincing proofs from her one by one. When conviction, gently led on by vanity, had made its way into the old man's mind, she told him of Monsieur Marneffe's fury.

'My dear old grumbler,' she said, 'it will be very difficult for you not to appoint the publisher who takes responsibility for your work, our manager if you like, an office manager and an Officer of the Legion of Honour, for you've ruined the man. He adores his Stanislas, a little *monstrico* who takes after him but whom I can't abide. Unless you would rather give Stanislas an annuity of twelve hundred francs, the capital to be his, of course, but the interest in my name.'

'But if I provide an annuity, I prefer it to be in my son's name, and not in the *monstrico*'s', said the Baron.

This unwise remark, from which the words *my son* burst forth like an overflowing river, was transformed after an hour's conversation into a formal promise to settle twelve hundred francs a year on the child to come.

This promise, on Valérie's tongue and in the expression of her face, then became like a drum in a little boy's hands and she was to play on it for three weeks.

70. *The difference between mother and daughter*

Baron Hulot left the Rue Vaneau as happy as a man married for a year, who wants an heir. Meanwhile Madame Olivier had induced Hortense to extract from her the letter that she was to deliver into the Count's own hands.

The young wife paid twenty francs for this letter. The suicide pays for his opium, his pistol, or his charcoal.

Hortense read the letter; she re-read it. She could see only the paper, striped with black lines. There was nothing in the world but that paper; everything was dark around her. The light of the fire that was consuming the edifice of her happiness lit up the paper, while utter darkness surrounded her. The cries of her little Wenceslas at play reached her ears as if he had been at the bottom of a valley and she at the top of a hill. For Hortense, outraged at the age of 24 in all the splendour of her beauty, embellished by a pure and devoted love, this was more than a dagger-blow, it was death. The first reaction had been purely nervous; her body had writhed in the grip of jealousy. But certainty attacked her heart and her body was as nothing.

For about ten minutes Hortense remained in this stunned condition. Her mother's image appeared before her and wrought a complete change. She became calm and cold; she recovered her reason. She rang the bell.

'Get Louise to help you, my dear,' she said to the cook. 'Pack everything here that belongs to me and all my son's things, as quickly as possible. I give you an hour. When everything's ready, get a cab from the square and let me know. Don't ask questions. I'm leaving the house and taking Louise with me. You must stay with Monsieur. Take good care of him.'

She went into her room, sat down at her table, and wrote the following letter:

'Monsieur le Comte,—The letter attached to mine will explain the resolution I have taken.

'When you read these lines, I'll have left your house and taken refuge at my mother's with our child.

'Don't expect me ever to go back on this decision. Don't think it's due to impulsiveness or the thoughtlessness of youth, or to the hasty reaction of outraged young love: you would be utterly mistaken.

'During the last fortnight I have thought a great deal about life and love, about our marriage and our mutual obligations. I have learned the full extent of my mother's devotion; she has told me of her sorrows. She has been heroic every day for twenty-three years. But I don't feel I have the strength to follow her example, not because I have loved you less than she loves my father, but for reasons deriving from my character. Our home would become a hell, and I might lose my head to the extent of dishonouring you, of dishonouring myself, of dishonouring our child. I don't want to be a Madame Marneffe, for in that career a woman of my temperament would perhaps never stop. Unfortunately for me, I am a Hulot and not a Fischer.

'On my own and far from the sight of your disorderly life, I can answer for myself, especially as I shall be occupied with our child, near my strong and noble mother, whose life will have an effect on the passionate impulses of my heart. There I can be a good mother, bring up our son well, and live. If I stayed with you, the wife would kill the mother and incessant quarrelling would embitter my character.

'I would accept death at one blow but I don't want to suffer for twenty-five years like my mother. If, after three years of absolute, constant love, you have been unfaithful to me for your father-in-law's mistress, what rivals would you give me later? Oh, Monsieur, much earlier than my father, you are embarking on a career of loose living and extravagance, which dishonours the father of a family, lessens his children's respect, and ends in shame and despair.

'I am not implacable. Unrelenting feelings do not become frail beings who live under the eye of God. If you win fame and fortune by steady work, if you give up courtesans and an ignoble and defiling way of life, you will again find a wife worthy of you.

'I think you are too much a gentleman to take legal action. You will respect my wish, Monsieur le Comte, in leaving me at my mother's. And, above all, don't ever come there. I have left you all the money that abominable woman lent you. Goodbye!

HORTENSE HULOT

This letter was written with difficulty. Hortense gave way to tears, to the outcries of murdered passion. She kept laying down her pen and picking it up again in an effort to express in simple terms what love usually declaims in ranting terms in such farewell letters. Her heart overflowed in exclamations, laments, and tears, but reason dictated her letter.

Informed by Louise that all was ready, the young wife walked slowly round the little garden, the bedroom, the drawing-room, and looked at everything for the last time. Then she gave the cook pressing instructions to look after Monsieur's welfare, promising to reward her if she were honest.

At last she got into the cab to go to her mother's, heartbroken, weeping so bitterly that it distressed her maid, and covering little Wenceslas with kisses in a frenzied joy that revealed the great love she still had for his father.

The Baroness had already heard from Lisbeth that the father-in-law had a lot to do with her son-in-law's fault, so she was not surprised at her daughter's arrival. She approved of what Hortense had done and agreed that she could stay with her. Seeing that gentleness and devotion had never restrained Hector, for whom her esteem was beginning to diminish, Adeline thought her daughter was right to follow a different course.

In three weeks, the poor mother had received two wounds the pain of which exceeded all her previous suffering. Because of the Baron, Victorin and his wife were in financial difficulties. Then, according to Lisbeth, he was responsible for Wenceslas's going astray; he had corrupted his son-in-law. The dignity of the father of the family, upheld for so long by absurd sacrifices, was degraded. Although they did not grudge their money, the young Hulots became both mistrustful of the Baron and anxious about him. These quite perceptible feelings distressed Adeline deeply; she foresaw the break-up of the family.

71. *A third father for the Marneffe child*

The Baroness put up her daughter in the dining-room, which was quickly transformed into a bedroom thanks to the Marshal's money; the hall became the dining-room, as it is in many households.

When Wenceslas returned home and had finished reading the two letters, he felt a kind of joy mingled with sadness.

Kept under close watch, as it were, by his wife, he had inwardly rebelled against this new imprisonment of the same kind that Lisbeth had imposed on him. Sated with love for three years, he, too, had been thinking during the last fortnight, and he found the family a heavy burden.

He had just been congratulated by Stidmann on the passion he had aroused in Valérie, for Stidmann, with an ulterior motive easy enough to understand, thought it opportune to flatter the vanity of Hortense's husband, in the hope of consoling the victim. So Wenceslas was happy to be able to go back to Madame Marneffe's. But he remembered the complete, unsullied happiness he had enjoyed, Hortense's perfections, her purity, her innocent, wholehearted love, and he regretted her keenly.

He wanted to rush round to his mother-in-law's to obtain forgiveness, but he did as Hulot and Crevel had done; he went to see Madame Marneffe. He brought her his wife's letter, to show her the extent of the disaster she had caused, and to cash in on his misfortune, so to speak, by demanding pleasures from his mistress in compensation.

He found Crevel with Valérie. The Mayor, puffed up with pride, was pacing up and down the drawing-room like a man excited by violent feeling. He kept striking his attitude as if he wanted to speak and did not dare to. His face was beaming, and he kept going to the window and drumming on the panes with his fingers. He gave Valérie touching and tender looks. Fortunately for Crevel, Lisbeth came in.

'Cousin,' he whispered, 'have you heard the news? I'm a father. It seems to me that I love my poor Célestine less. Oh, what it is to have a child by a woman one idolizes! To combine paternity of the heart with paternity of the blood! Oh, but you must tell Valérie. I'll work for that child; I want him to be rich. She told me that, judging from certain signs, she thought it would be a boy. If it's a boy, I want him to be called Crevel. I'll consult my lawyer.'

I know how much she loves you,' Lisbeth said, 'but for the sake of your future and hers, control yourself. Don't keep rubbing your hands all the time.'

While Lisbeth was having this aside with Crevel, Valérie had asked Wenceslas for her letter back, and was whispering words to him which dispelled his sadness.

'You're free now, my dear,' she said. 'Great artists should never marry. Your imagination and your liberty are the essentials of your life. Never mind, I'll love you so much that you'll never regret your wife. But still, if, like many people, you want to keep up appearances, I undertake to make Hortense come back to you in a very short time.'

'Oh, if that were possible!'

'I'm sure it is,' said Valérie, rather piqued. 'Your poor father-in-law is finished in every way. Out of vanity he wants to appear to be loved, wants people to believe that he has a mistress, and he is so vain on that score that I rule him absolutely. The Baroness still loves her old Hector so much (I always feel as if I were talking about the *Iliad*) that the two old folks will persuade Hortense to be reconciled to you. Only, if you don't want to have storms at home, don't let three weeks go by without coming to see your mistress. I was dying for want of you. My dear, a gentleman owes consideration to a woman he has compromised to the degree that I have been compromised, especially when the woman must take great care of her reputation. Stay to dinner, my darling. And remember that

I must behave all the more coldly to you, as you are the author of this all too obvious lapse.'

72. The five Fathers of the Marneffe Church

Baron Montès was announced. Valérie got up and ran to meet him. She whispered to him for a few moments and made the same reservations about her demeanour towards him as she had just done to Wenceslas, for the Brazilian wore a diplomatic expression appropriate to the great news that overwhelmed him with joy. *He* was sure of his paternity!'

Thanks to her strategy based on the vanity of men as lovers, Valérie had at her table, all of them cheerful, lively, and under her spell, four men who thought they were adored by her and whom, including himself, Marneffe jokingly called the five Fathers of the Church.

Only Baron Hulot at first looked worried, and for this reason. Just before leaving his office, he had been to see the Director of Personnel, a general, his comrade for thirty years, and he had talked to him about appointing Marneffe to the post held by Coquet, who agreed to resign.

'My dear fellow,' he said, 'I wouldn't want to ask the Marshal for this favour unless we are in agreement and I have your consent.'

My dear fellow,' replied the Director of Personnel, 'allow me to point out to you that, for your own sake, you ought not to insist on this appointment. I've already given you my opinion. It would cause a scandal in the Department, where there's already too much talk about you and Madame Marneffe. This is quite between ourselves. I don't want to hurt you on a sensitive spot or in any way be disobliging to you, and I'll prove that. If you're absolutely set on this, if you insist on asking for Monsieur Coquet's post (and he will be a real loss to the War Ministry, for he's been in it since 1809), I'll go away for a fortnight so as to leave you a clear field with the Marshal, who loves you like a son. Then I'll be neither for nor against, and I'll have done nothing against my conscience as an administrator.'

'Thank you,' replied the Baron. 'I'll think over what you've just said.'

'If I permit myself these comments, my dear fellow, it's because your personal interests are much more affected than my situation or my professional pride. In the first place, the Marshal is the chief, and then, my dear fellow, we're blamed for so many things, what does one more or less matter? This is not the first time we've been criticized. Under the Restoration, people were appointed just to give them a salary, with no consideration for the work of the Department. . . . We're old comrades.'

'Yes,' replied the Baron, 'and it's just because I don't want it to affect our old and valued friendship that I . . .'

'Well then,' continued the Director of Personnel, seeing the embarrassed expression on Hulot's face, 'I'll go away, old fellow. But take care. You have enemies, that is to say, people who covet your fine salary, and you have only one string to your bow. Oh, if, like me, you were a deputy, you'd have nothing to fear. So watch your step.'

These words, spoken in friendship, made a strong impression on the Councillor of State.

'But tell me, Roger, what's all this about? Don't play the mystery man with me.'

The man whom Hulot called Roger, looked at Hulot, took his hand, and clasped it.

'We've been friends for too long for me not to give you a piece of advice. If you want to retain your position, you must make your own bed to lie on. So, in your situation, instead of asking the Marshal to give Monsieur Coquet's post to Monsieur Marneffe, I'd request him to use his influence to make me a regular member of the Council of State, where I'd die in peace, and, like the beaver, I'd abandon my Director-Generalship to the hunters.'

'What! The Marshal would forget . . .'

'My dear old friend, the Marshal defended you so warmly at the Council of Ministers that they're no longer thinking of giving you the sack. But there was talk of it. So don't give them any pretexts. I don't want to say any more. At the moment, you can make your own conditions, be a Councillor of State and a Peer of France. If you wait too long, if you give them a hold over you, I can answer for nothing. Should I go on leave?'

'Wait a bit. I'll go and see the Marshal, and I'll send my brother to find out how the land lies with the chief,' replied Hulot.

The frame of mind in which the Baron returned to Madame Marneffe's can now be appreciated. He had almost forgotton that he was a father, for Roger, in enlightening him about his position, had acted as a true and good friend.

Nevertheless, Valérie's influence was such that, half way through the dinner, the Baron was in the same mood as the others and became all the more jovial in that he had more worries to suppress. But the unfortunate man did not suspect that in the course of that evening he was going to be placed between his happiness and the danger indicated by the Director of Personnel, that is to say, forced to choose between Madame Marneffe and his post.

73. *Exploitation of the father*

About eleven o'clock just as the party was at its height, for the drawing-room was full of people. Valérie drew Hector aside on to a corner of her sofa.

'My dear old thing,' she whispered to him, 'your daughter is so angry at Wenceslas's coming here that she's walked out on him. She's a headstrong girl, is Hortense. Ask Wenceslas to show you the letter the little fool wrote. This separation of two lovers, of which I'm supposed to be the cause, can do me untold harm, for that's the way virtuous women attack each other. It's scandalous to play the victim in order to cast the blame on a woman whose only fault is to run a pleasant house. If you love me, you will clear me of blame by sending the two turtle-doves back to their home. Anyway, I'm not at all keen to receive your son-in-law. It was you who brought him here; take him away again. If you have any authority in your family, it seems to me that you could very well require your wife to bring about a reconciliation. Tell the good old lady, from me, that if I'm wrongly blamed for causing a rift between a young couple and breaking up a family, and of taking both the father and the son-in-law, I'll live up to my reputation by causing them trouble in my own way. There's Lisbeth talking of leaving me. She prefers her family to me. I can't blame her. She told me she'll only stay here if the young people make it up. That'll put us in a fine mess. Expenses here will be tripled.'

'Oh, as for that,' said the Baron, on hearing of his daughter's scandalous behaviour, 'I'll put that right.'

'And there's something else,' continued Valérie, 'What about Coquet's post?'

'That's more difficult, not to say impossible,' replied Hector, lowering his eyes.

'Impossible, my dear Hector?' Madame Marneffe said in a low voice to the Baron. 'But you don't know what extreme lengths Marneffe will go to. I'm in his power. He's immoral in his own interests, like most men, but he's extremely vindictive, like all petty-minded and impotent men. In the situation you've placed me in, I'm at his mercy. Obliged as I am to patch things up with him for a few days, he's capable of never leaving my room again.'

Hulot started violently.

'He was leaving me alone on condition that he was made an office-manager. It's monstrous, but it's logical.'

'Valérie, do you love me?'

'To ask me that question in the condition I'm in, my dear, is an insult worthy of a lackey.'

'Well, if I try, only try, to ask the Marshal for a post for Marneffe, that would be the end of me and Marneffe would be dismissed.'

'I thought you and the Prince were intimate friends.'

'Indeed we are; he's given me ample proof of it. But, my dear, above the Marshal there are others, the whole Council of Ministers, for example. With a little time and manoeuvring, we'll get there. To succeed, we must wait for the moment when I've been asked to render some service. Then I'll be able to say, "one good turn deserves another".'

'If I tell Marneffe that, my dear Hector, he'll take it out of us in some way or other. Look, tell him yourself he's got to wait. I won't take on that task. Oh, I know what will happen to me. He knows how to punish me. He won't leave my room. Don't forget the twelve hundred francs' annuity for the child.'

Feeling his pleasure threatened, Hulot took Monsieur Marneffe aside. For the first time he dropped the haughty tone he had maintained hitherto, so appalled was he at the prospect of that moribund creature in such a pretty woman's room.

'Marneffe, my dear fellow,' he said, 'we talked about you today. But you can't be promoted office-manager just yet. We need time.'

'I'll be promoted, Monsieur le Baron,' Marneffe replied curtly.

'But, my dear fellow . . .'

'I'll be promoted, Monsieur le Baron,' Marneffe repeated coldly, looking first at the Baron and then at Valérie. 'You've made it necessary for my wife to be reconciled to me and I'll keep her; for, *my dear fellow*, she's charming,' he added, with horrible irony. 'I'm the master here, more so than you are at the Ministry.'

The Baron felt a pain in his heart like a raging toothache and he could barely restrain his tears.

During this short scene, Valérie was quietly informing Henri Montès of Marneffe's supposed intention and so she got rid of him for a time.

Of the faithful four, only Crevel the owner of the cosy little house, was exempted from this measure. His face accordingly wore an air of truly insolent beatitude, in spite of reproofs which Valérie tried to convey to him by frowns and meaningful looks. But his radiant paternity was beaming in every feature.

At a whispered word of reproach from Valérie, he grasped her hand and said:

'Tomorrow, my duchess, you shall have your little house. The sale will be finalized tomorrow.'

'And the furniture?' she asked, smiling.

'I have a thousand shares in the Versailles left-bank railway. I bought them at a hundred and twenty-five francs, and they'll go up to three hundred because of the amalgamation of the two lines—that's a secret I was let into. You'll have furniture fit for a queen! But you'll be only mine from then on, won't you?'

'Yes, my portly Mayor,' said this middle-class Madame de Merteuil * with a smile, 'but behave yourself. Respect the future Madame Crevel.'

'My dear cousin,' Lisbeth was saying to the Baron, 'I'll be at Adeline's early tomorrow, for, you understand, I can't in all decency remain here. I'll go and keep house for your brother the Marshal.'

'I'm going home tonight,' said the Baron.

'Well, I'll come to lunch tomorrow,' replied Lisbeth with a smile.

74. A sad happiness

Lisbeth realized how necessary her presence was to the family scene which was to take place the next day. So she went first thing in the morning to Victorin's and told him of the separation of Hortense and Wenceslas.

When the Baron returned home about half past ten in the evening, Mariette and Louise, who had had a hard day, were closing the door of the flat, so that Hulot did not have to ring the bell.

The husband, very put out by his enforced virtue, went straight to his wife's room. Through the half-open door he saw her kneeling before her crucifix, lost in prayer and in one of those attitudes, full of meaning, that bring glory to painters or sculptors, who, having discovered them, are fortunate enough to portray them well.

Adeline, carried away by her exaltation, was saying

aloud, 'Oh God! Be merciful to us and make him see the light.'

Thus the Baroness was praying for her Hector.

At the sight, so different from the one he had just left, and on hearing these words prompted by what had happened that day, the Baron was touched and let out a sigh. Adeline turned round, her face covered with tears. She believed so absolutely that her prayer had been answered that she jumped up and embraced her Hector with the fervour inspired by passionate happiness.

Adeline had divested herself of all her own feelings as a woman; grief had obliterated even the memory of them. The only emotions left in her were those of maternity, of family honour, and of a Christian wife's pure affection for an errant husband, that saintly tenderness which survives all else in a woman's heart. All this was evident.

'Hector,' she said at last, 'are you coming back to us? Is God taking pity on our family?'

'Dear Adeline!' replied the Baron, coming in and seating his wife on a chair beside him. 'You are the saintliest being I know and for a long time I have thought myself unworthy of you.'

'You would have little to do, my dear, very little, to put things right again,' she said, holding Hulot's hand and trembling so violently that she seemed to be having a nervous spasm.

She dared not go on. She felt that each word would be a reproach and she did not want to mar the happiness with which this conversation was flooding her soul.

'It is Hortense who brings me here,' Hulot went on. 'Our little girl may do us more harm by her hasty action than my absurd passion for Valérie has done. But we'll talk about all that tomorrow morning. Hortense is asleep, Mariette told me; let's not disturb her.'

'Yes,' said Madame Hulot, suddenly filled with deep sadness.

She realized that the Baron had come home not so much because of the wish to see his family as because of some other consideration.

'Don't worry her tomorrow either, for the poor girl is in a pathetic state. She's been crying all day,' said the Baroness.

75. The ravages caused by women like Madame Marneffe in the bosoms of families

The next day, at nine in the morning, the Baron, while waiting for his daughter whom he had sent for, was walking up and down the huge, empty drawing-room. He was trying to think of arguments with which to overcome the most determined kind of obstinacy, that of an injured young wife, unrelenting like all blameless young people who are ignorant of the shameful compromises of society because they know nothing of its passions and interests.

'Here I am, Papa,' said Hortense.

Her voice was trembling, and suffering had turned her pale.

Hulot sat down on a chair, put his arm round his daughter's waist, and made her sit on his knee.

'Well, my child,' he said, kissing her on the forehead, 'so there's been a quarrel in the household and we've acted impulsively? That's no way for a well-brought-up girl to behave. My Hortense ought not to take a decisive step like leaving her home and deserting her husband, entirely on her own, without consulting her parents. If my dear Hortense had come to see her good, kind mother, she would have spared me the acute sorrow that I feel. You don't know the world; it's very spiteful. People may say that it was your husband who sent you back to your parents. Children brought up like you, in their mother's lap, remain children longer than others. They know nothing of life. An innocent spontaneous love like yours for Wenceslas is, unfortunately, quite uncalculating; it's at the mercy of its first impulse. Our little heart takes the lead, the head follows. We'd set fire to Paris to take our revenge without a thought for the assize court. When your old father comes and tells you that you haven't observed the proprieties, you can believe him. And I say nothing, moreover, of the deep sorrow I've been feeling; it's very acute, for you cast the blame on a woman whose heart is unknown to you and whose hostility can have terrible consequences. Alas, you, so frank, innocent, and pure, you have no doubts. Your name may be blackened, you may be slandered. Besides, my dearest little one, you've taken a joke seriously, and I can personally vouch for your husband's innocence. Madame Marneffe . . .'

So far, the Baron, artist in diplomacy that he was, had formulated his remonstrances with great tact. As we see, he had skilfully introduced that name. But when she heard it, Hortense started like someone cut to the quick.

'Listen to me. I'm an experienced man and I've seen it all,' continued the father, preventing his daughter from speaking. 'That lady treats your husband very coldly. You've been the victim of a practical joke, and I'll give you proofs of it You see, yesterday Wenceslas was there to dinner . . .'

'He was there to dinner? . . .' exclaimed the young wife, getting up and looking at her father with a horror-stricken look on her face. 'Yesterday! After reading my letter? Oh, my God! Why didn't I go into a convent instead of getting married? My life is no longer my own; I have a child,' she added, sobbing.

These tears went straight to Madame Hulot's heart. She came out of her room, rushed to her daughter, took her in her arms, and asked those pointless questions of grief, the first that come to the lips.

'Here come the tears,' the Baron said to himself. 'Everything was going so well. Now what's to be done with crying women?'

'My child, listen to your father. He loves us, come now . . .' the Baroness said to Hortense.

'There, there, Hortense, my dear little girl, don't cry; it spoils your beauty,' said the Baron. 'There, there, be reasonable. Go back home like a good girl and I promise you that Wenceslas will never set foot in that house again.

I ask you to make this sacrifice, if to forgive a beloved husband for the most trifling of faults is a sacrifice. I ask this of you by my white hairs, by your love for your mother. You don't want to fill my old age with bitterness and grief?'

Hortense threw herself like a madwoman at her father's feet with a movement of such violent desperation that her loosely secured hair came undone, and she held out her hands to him with a gesture showing her despair.

'Father, you're asking me for my life,' she said. 'Take it if you like, but at least take it pure and spotless. I will indeed gladly let you have it. But don't ask me to die a dishonoured criminal. I'm not like my mother. I'll not swallow insults. If I go back to my husband's house, I may smother Wenceslas in a fit of jealousy, or do something even worse. Don't demand of me something beyond my strength. Don't weep for me while I'm still alive, for the least bad thing that can happen to me is that I should go mad. I feel madness only two steps away from me. Yesterday! Yesterday! He was dining with that woman after he had read my letter! Are other men made like that? I give you my life, but let not my death be shameful. His fault, trifling? To have a child by that woman!'

'A child?' said Hulot, stepping back. 'Well, that's certainly a joke.'

At that moment Victorin and Cousin Bette came in, and were stunned at the sight before them. The daughter was on her knees at her father's feet. The Baroness stood speechless and torn between her feelings as a mother and as a wife, her distraught face covered with tears.

'Lisbeth,' said the Baron, grasping the old maid's hand and pointing to Hortense, 'you can help me. My poor Hortense is out of her mind. She thinks Madame Marneffe loves her husband, while all Valérie wants is simply to have a group by him.'

'Delilah,' cried the young wife. 'The only thing he has done quickly since our marriage. This fine gentleman was not able to work for me, for his son, but he worked for that good-for-nothing with a zeal . . . Oh, put an end to me, Father, for each of your words is a dagger-blow.'

Turning to the Baroness and Victorin, Lisbeth indicated the Baron, who could not see her, with a pitying shrug of the shoulders.

'Listen, Cousin, I didn't know what sort of a woman Madame Marneffe was when you asked me to go and live in the flat above her and to keep house for her,' said Lisbeth, 'but one learns a lot in three years. This creature is a *tart*, and a tart whose depravity can only be compared to her hideous, vile husband's. You're the dupe, the lord who fills the stock-pot for these people, and they will lead you on further than you think. I must speak to you plainly, for you're at the bottom of a pit.'

On hearing Lisbeth speak like this, the Baroness and her daughter looked at her in the way the devout look at the Madonna to thank her for saving their lives.

'She was determined, that horrible woman, to break up your son-in-law's marriage. For what reason? I've no idea, for I'm not clever enough to see my way through these shady intrigues, so perverse, disgusting, and vile. Your Madame Marneffe is not in love with your son-in-law but she wants him on his knees before her as a revenge. I've just treated this wretched woman as she deserved. She's a shameless courtesan. I told her I was leaving her house; I wanted to extricate my honour from that cesspit. I belong to my family, above everything. I heard that my young cousin had left Wenceslas and here I am! Your Valérie, whom you take for a saint, is the cause of this cruel separation. Can I stay with such a woman? Our dear little Hortense may be the victim of a longing, of a kind felt by such women, who would sacrifice a family for the sake of an ornament,' she said meaningfully, touching the Baron's arm. 'I don't think Wenceslas is guilty but I think he's weak and I don't say he wouldn't succumb to such subtle coquetry. I've made up my mind. That woman's fatal to you. She'll land you in the gutter. I don't want to appear to have a share in my family's ruin, I who have been in that house for the sole purpose of preventing it. You're

deceived, cousin. Say quite firmly that you'll have nothing
to do with that vile Monsieur Marneffe's appointment, and
you'll see what will happen. You're in for a good dressing-
down in that event.'

Lisbeth raised up her young cousin and kissed her
ardently.

'My dear Hortense, stand firm,' she whispered to her.

The Baroness kissed her Cousin Bette with the fervour
of a woman who sees herself avenged.

The whole family stood in silence round the father, who
was intelligent enough to understand what the silence
meant. The clear signs of a violent rage spread from his
brow over his whole face. All his veins swelled, his eyes
were suffused with blood, his complexion became blotchy.

Adeline flung herself down on her knees before him and
took his hands:

'My dear, my dear, for pity's sake!'

'You all hate me,' said the Baron, letting slip the cry of
his conscience.

We are all in the secret of our own wrong-doing. We
nearly always suppose our victims feel the hatred that the
desire for revenge ought to arouse in them. And despite
our efforts at hypocrisy, our words or our looks confess,
as the criminal in past ages used to confess in the hands of
the executioner.

'Our children end up becoming our enemies,' he said, in
an effort to retract his confession.

'Father . . .' said Victorin.

'You are interrupting your father!' continued the Baron
in a thundering voice, looking at his son.

'Father, listen,' said Victorin in a firm, clear voice, the
voice of a puritanical deputy. 'I know the respect I owe
you too well ever to fail in it, and you will certainly always
have in me a most submissive and obedient son.'

Everyone who has attended the sittings of the two
Chambers will recognize the language of parliamentary
debate in these tortuous phrases, used to calm irritation
and gain time.

'We're far from being your enemies,' said Victorin. 'I've

quarrelled with my father-in-law, Monsieur Crevel, because I redeemed Vauvinet's bills for sixty thousand francs, and that money's quite certainly in Madame Marneffe's hands. Oh, I don't blame you, father,' he added, at a gesture of the Baron's, 'but I only want to add my voice to Cousin Lisbeth's and to point out to you that though my devotion to you is blind and unlimited, unfortunately there's a limit to our financial resources.'

'Money!' said the enraged old man, collapsing into a chair, overwhelmed by this argument. 'And he's my son! You'll get your money back, Monsieur,' he said, getting up.

He went towards the door.

'Hector!'

Her cry made the Baron turn round and he suddenly revealed to his wife a face bathed in tears. She threw her arms round him with the strength of despair.

'Don't go away like this. Don't leave us in anger. *I* haven't said a word to you.'

At this declaration of sublime devotion, the children flung themselves at their father's feet.

'We all love you,' said Hortense.

Lisbeth, motionless as a statue, was looking at the group with a sardonic smile on her lips.

At this moment Marshal Hulot came into the hall and they could hear his voice. The family realized the importance of concealment and the scene changed abruptly.

The two children got up and they all tried to hide their emotion.

76. *A brief history of favourites*

An argument was taking place at the door between Mariette and a soldier, who became so insistent that the cook came into the drawing-room.

'Monsieur, a regimental quartermaster just back from Algeria says he must speak to you.'

'Tell him to wait.'

'Monsieur,' said Mariette in a low voice to her master, 'he told me to tell you privately that it's something to do with Monsieur Fischer, your uncle.'

The Baron started; he thought that this must be the arrival of funds that, for two months, he had been secretly asking for in order to pay his bills of exchange. He left his family and hurried into the hall. There he saw a typical Alsatian face.

'Are you Monsieur *la Paron Hilotte*?'

'Yes.'

'Himself?'

'Himself.'

The quartermaster, who had been fumbling in the lining of his képi during this conversation, took out a letter. The Baron opened it eagerly, and read the following:

'Dear Nephew, far from being able to send you the hundred thousand francs you ask me for, I am in an untenable position unless you take strong action to save me. We have a Public Prosecutor after us; he talks about morality and blethers on about the administration. It's impossible to get that civilian to keep his mouth shut. If the War Ministry lets these blackcoats eat out of its hand, I'm done for. I can trust the bearer of this letter. Try to get him promoted, for he has served us well. Don't leave me to the crows.'

The letter was like a thunderbolt. In it the Baron saw the beginning of the internal dissension that still rends the government of Algeria between the civil and military authorities, and he had to think up some immediate palliative for the new difficulty that was emerging.

He told the soldier to come back the next day, and after dismissing him, not without fine promises of promotion, he returned to the drawing-room.

'Hail and farewell, Brother,' he said to the Marshal. 'Goodbye, children, goodbye, my dear Adeline. And what's going to become of you, Lisbeth?' he said.

'Oh, I'm going to keep house for the Marshal, for I must spend the rest of my life still being of use to one or other of you.'

'Don't leave Valérie before I've seen you,' Hulot whispered to his cousin. 'Goodbye, Hortense, my little rebel. Try to be sensible. Serious matters have arisen that I must attend to; we'll discuss your reconciliation later. Think about it, my good little pet,' he said, kissing her.

He was so obviously worried as he left his wife and children that they were filled with the gravest apprehensions.

'Lisbeth,' said the Baroness, 'we must find out what's worrying Hector. I've never seen him in a state like that before. Stay two or three days longer in that woman's house. He tells *her* everything, and in this way we'll learn what's brought about such a sudden change in him. Don't worry; we'll arrange your marriage to the Marshal, for it's become essential.'

'I'll never forget your courage this morning,' said Hortense, kissing Lisbeth.

'You've avenged our poor mother,' said Victorin.

The Marshal looked on with some curiosity at these marks of affection lavished on Lisbeth, who went home and described the scene to Valérie.

This sketch will enable the innocent to appreciate the different kinds of havoc that women like Madame Marneffe wreak in families, and the way in which they attack poor, virtuous women, apparently so beyond their reach.

But if, in our imaginations, we transpose these troubles to the higher social level about the throne, in view of what kings' mistresses must have cost, we can estimate what nations owe their sovereigns when they set an example of good morals and family life.

77. *The impudence of one of the five fathers*

In Paris, every ministry is like a little town from which women have been banished. But gossip and calumny go on as if the feminine population were there. After three years, Monsieur Marneffe's position had been, as it were, clarified, exposed to the light of day, and in the office people were wondering: will Monsieur Marneffe be Monsieur Coquet's successor, exactly as in the Chamber people used to ask whether the allowances for the King and the Prince Royal would be passed or not.

The slightest movement in the Personnel Department was watched; everything in Baron Hulot's department was scrutinized. The cunning Councillor of State had won over to his side the victim of Marneffe's promotion, a capable worker, telling him that if he would scheme on Marneffe's behalf he would certainly succeed him, and pointing out that Marneffe was a dying man. So this official was intriguing on Marneffe's behalf.

As Hulot went through the ante-room to his office, full of visitors, he saw Marneffe's pallid face in a corner and Marneffe was the first to be called in.

'What do you want to ask me, my dear fellow?' asked the Baron, concealing his anxiety.

'Monsieur le Directeur, they're laughing at me in the office, for they've just heard that Monsieur le Directeur du Personnel went off on sick leave this morning. He'll be away about a month. To wait for a month, we all know what that means. You're turning me into a laughing-stock for my enemies. It's quite enough to be drummed at on one side; to be drummed at on both sides at once may burst the drum.'

'My dear Marneffe, it takes a lot of patience to get what one wants. You can't be made an office-manager, if ever you are at all, in less than two months from now. At a time when I'm obliged to consolidate my own position, I can't ask for a promotion that will cause a scandal.'

'If you're fired I'll never be an office-manager,' Monsieur Marneffe said coldly. 'Get me appointed; it won't make any difference to you.'

'So I am to sacrifice myself?' asked the baron.

'If that were not so, I'd lose many illusions about you.'

'You're altogether too much Marneffe, Monsieur Marneffe,' said the Baron, getting up and showing the assistant-manager the door.

'I bid you good morning, Monsieur le Baron,' Marneffe replied obsequiously.

'What an infamous scoundrel,' the Baron said to himself. 'That's rather like a summons to pay in twenty-four hours on pain of expropriation.'

78. *Another summons*

Two hours later, the Baron was ending his instructions to Claude Vignon, whom he was planning to send to the Ministry of Justice to get information about the judicial authorities under whose jurisdiction Johann Fischer was, when Reine opened the door of the Director's office and handed him a little note, asking for an answer.

'To send Reine!' the Baron said to himself. 'Valérie's mad. She's compromising us all and compromising that abominable Marneffe's appointment as well.'

He dismissed the Minister's private secretary and read the following:

'Oh, my dear, what a scene I've just endured! If you've given me three years of happiness, I've paid well for it! He came home from the office in a state of fury that made me tremble. I knew he was very ugly, but he looked like a monster. His four natural teeth were chattering and he threatened me with his hateful company if I continued to receive you.

'My poor pet, alas! our door will be closed to you from now on. You see my tears; they're falling on to my paper, they're soaking it! Will you be able to read this, my dear Hector?

'Oh, not to see you again, when I have within me a little of your life, as I believe I have your heart; it's enough to kill me. Think of our little Hector! Don't desert me, but don't bring disgrace upon yourself for Marneffe. Don't give in to his threats. Oh, I love you as I've never loved before. I've recalled all the sacrifices you've made for your Valérie; she is not and never will be ungrateful. You are, you always will be, my only husband. Think no more of the annuity of twelve hundred francs I asked you to give the dear little Hector who will come in a few months' time. I don't want to be any further expense to you. Indeed, what I have will always be yours.

'Oh, if you loved me as much as I love you, my Hector, you'd retire; we'd both leave behind our families, our worries, our social circle where there's so much hatred, and we'd go and live with Lisbeth in some pretty country place, in Brittany, wherever you like. There we'd see no one and we'd be happy, far away from all these people. Your retirement pension and the little I have in my own name will be enough for us. You're getting jealous—well, you'd see your Valérie taken up entirely with her Hector and you'd never have to shout at me as you did the other day.

'I shall never have more than one child, and he will be ours. You can be sure of that, my beloved old soldier.

'No, you can't imagine how furious I am, for you don't know how he treated me and the insults he spat out on your Valérie; his words would soil the paper. But a woman like me, Montcornet's daughter, ought never to have had to hear a single one of them in all her life. Oh, I wish you'd been there, so that I could punish him by letting him see my mad passion for you. My father would have run his sword through the miserable creature, but I can only do what's in a woman's power—that is, love you madly.

'And so, my dear, in my exasperated state, I can't possibly give up seeing you. Yes, I intend to see you secretly, every day. That's how we women are. I share your resentment. For pity's sake, if you love me, don't make him an office-manager; let him die an assistant manager! At this moment, my head's in a whirl; I can still hear his insults. Bette, who wanted to leave me, has taken pity on me. She'll stay a few days longer.

'My dearest love, I don't yet know what to do. I can only think of flight. I've always adored the country, Brittany, Languedoc, anywhere you like, provided I'm free to love you.

'My poor pet, how I pity you! Now you're forced to go back to your old Adeline, that urn of tears, for he must have told you, the monster, that he's going to watch me day and night. He even spoke of the commissioner of police! Don't come here. I realize now that he's capable of anything, for he's using me as a pawn in the vilest kind of speculation. So I'd like to be able to give you back everything I owe to your generosity.

'Oh, my darling Hector, I may have flirted and appeared frivolous to you, but you didn't know your Valérie. She loved teasing you but she loves you more than anything in the world.

'You can't be prevented from coming to see your cousin, so I'll plan with her some way in which we can have a talk.

'My dear pet, for pity's sake, do write me a line to reassure me, since I can't have your dear presence.—Oh, I'd give a hand to have you in my arms on our sofa. A letter will have the effect of a talisman on me. Write me something that expresses all your noble soul. I'll give you back your letter, for we must be prudent. I wouldn't know where to hide it, for he rummages everywhere. But do reassure your Valérie, your wife, the mother of your child.

'To have to write to you, when I used to see you every day! And so I say to Lisbeth, "I didn't know how lucky I was." A thousand kisses, my pet. Love me dearly

Your VALÉRIE.'

'And tears!' Hector said to himself, as he finished this letter. 'Tears which make her name illegible.'

'How is she?' he asked Reine.

'Madame is in bed. She's had a fit of hysterics. The nervous attack has twisted Madame up like a string round a bundle of twigs. It took her after she'd written. Oh, it comes of crying. We could hear Monsieur's voice on the stairs.'

In his distress, the Baron wrote the following letter on his official paper with its printed heading.

'Don't worry, my darling, *he* will die an assistant manager.

'Your idea is excellent. We'll go away and live far from Paris with our little Hector. I'll retire and I'll be able to get a job in some railway company.

'Oh, my sweet love, your letter makes me feel young again. Oh, I'll start life again and I'll make a fortune for our dear little one. As I read your letter, a thousand times more ardent than the letters in *La Nouvelle Héloïse*,* it worked a miracle. I didn't think my love for you could increase. This evening at Lisbeth's you'll see.

Your HECTOR for life!'

Reine went away with this reply, the first letter that the Baron had written to *his sweet love*. Emotions such as these counterbalanced the disasters that were looming on the horizon. But at that moment the Baron, feeling sure he could ward off the blows aimed at his uncle Johann Fischer, was concerned only about the deficit.

One of the traits of the Bonapartist character is faith in the power of the sword and the firm conviction of the superiority of the military over the civilian administration. Hulot didn't care a rap for the Public Prosecutor in Algeria, where the Ministry of War reigned supreme. A man remains what he has always been. How can the officers of the Imperial Guard forget having seen the mayors of the fine cities of the Empire, the Emperor's prefects, small-scale emperors themselves, come to receive the Imperial Guard, to do it honour at the boundaries of the Department it passed through, and, indeed, render it the honours due to a sovereign?

79. *The door shut in his face*

At half past four the Baron went straight to Madame Marneffe's. As he went upstairs his heart was beating like a young man's, for he was mentally asking himself the question, 'Shall I see her? Shall I not see her?' How could he remember the morning scene when his weeping family was prostrate at his feet? Didn't Valérie's letter, placed for ever in a thin wallet next his heart, prove to him that he was loved more than the most lovable of young men?

After ringing the doorbell, the unfortunate Baron heard the shuffling slippers and loathsome cough of the invalid Marneffe. Marneffe opened the door, but only to take up a stance and show Hulot the staircase with a gesture exactly like the one with which Hulot had shown him the door of his office.

'You are altogether too much Hulot, Monsieur Hulot!' he said.

The Baron tried to push past him. Marneffe took a pistol out of his pocket and cocked it.

'Monsieur le Conseiller d'Etat, when a man is as vile as I am—for you think me utterly vile, don't you?—he would be the stupidest of galley-slaves if he didn't get all the benefits of having sold his honour. You want war; it will be fierce and without quarter. Don't come back again or try to get past me. I've informed the commissioner of police of my situation with regard to you.'

And taking advantage of Hulot's dumbfounded amazement, he pushed him out and shut the door.

'What an absolute scoundrel!' Hulot said to himself as he went up to Lisbeth's. 'Oh, now I understand the letter. Valérie and I will leave Paris. Valérie is mine for the rest of my days; she will close my eyes.'

Lisbeth was not at home. Madame Olivier informed Hulot that she had gone to Madame la Baronne's, thinking she would find Monsieur le Baron there.

'Poor woman! I wouldn't have believed she could be as cunning as she was this morning,' the Baron said to himself, recalling Lisbeth's behaviour as he walked from the Rue Vaneau to the Rue Plumet.

At the corner of the Rue Vaneau and the Rue de Babylone, he looked back at the Eden from which Hymen had banished him with the sword of the law in his hand.

Valérie, at her window, was following Hulot with her eyes. When he looked up she waved her handkerchief, but the disgusting Marneffe struck his wife's cap and pulled her violently away from the window. Tears rose in the eyes of the Councillor of State.

'To be so dearly loved! To see a woman ill-treated and to be nearly 70!' he thought.

Lisbeth had come to tell the family the good news. Adeline and Hortense already knew that as he did not want to be dishonoured in the eyes of the whole Ministry by appointing Marneffe an office-manager, the Baron would be turned out by the husband who had become a violent Hulot-phobe.

And so Adeline, in her happiness, had given orders for a dinner that Hector would think better than those Valérie provided, and the devoted Lisbeth helped Mariette to achieve this difficult result.

Cousin Bette was looked up to as an idol. The mother and daughter kissed her hands; they had told her with touching joy that the Marshal agreed to have her as his housekeeper.

'And from there, my dear, to becoming his wife, it's only a step,' said Adeline.

'Anyway, he didn't say no when Victorin spoke to him about it,' added Countess Steinbock.

The Baron was received by his family with such charming, touching marks of affection, so overflowing with love, that he was forced to conceal his distress. The Marshal came to dinner. After dinner Hulot did not leave. Victorin and his wife came in. They all played whist.

'It's a long time since you've given *us* an evening like this,' the Marshal said gravely.

This remark, coming from the old soldier who was so indulgent to his brother and who, in those words, implicitly rebuked him, made a deep impression. It revealed the long, deep wounds of a heart in which all the sorrows he had divined had found an echo.

At eight o'clock the Baron insisted on seeing Lisbeth home himself, promising to return.

'Do you know, Lisbeth, *he* ill-treats her,' he said to her in the street. 'Oh, I've never loved her so much.'

'Oh, I'd never have thought Valérie loved you so much,' replied Lisbeth. 'She's frivolous and flirtatious; she likes to be courted, to have the comedy of love played out for her, as she puts it, but you are the only one to whom she's really attached.'

'What message did she give you for me?'

'This,' continued Lisbeth. 'As you know, she has shown some favours to Crevel. You mustn't hold that against her, for it's put her beyond the reach of poverty for the rest of her days. But she detests him and it's almost over. Well, she's kept the key of some rooms.'

'Rue du Dauphin!' exclaimed Hulot, overjoyed. 'For that alone, I'd forgive her Crevel. I've been there; I know . . .'

'And here's the key,' said Lisbeth. 'Have a duplicate made tomorrow, two if you can.'

'And then?' said Hulot eagerly.

'Well, I'll come to dinner with you again tomorrow. You'll give me back Valérie's key (for Père Crevel may ask back the one he gave her), and you'll go and meet her the day after tomorrow. There you can lay your plans. You'll be quite safe, for there are two exits. If by any chance Crevel, who, as he says, has Regency ways, were to come in by the passage, you would go out by the shop, and vice versa. Well, you old scoundrel, it's to me that you owe all this. What will you do for me?'

'Anything you like.'

'Well, then, don't oppose my marriage to your brother!'

'You, the Maréchale Hulot! You, Comtesse de Forzheim!' cried Hector in amazement.

'Adeline is well and truly a Baroness,' replied Bette in a sharp, formidable tone. 'Listen, you old libertine. You know the state of your affairs. Your family may find itself starving and in the gutter . . .'

'That's what I dread,' said Hector in alarm.

'If your brother dies, who will support your wife and daughter? The widow of a Marshal of France can get a pension of at least six thousand francs, can't she? Well, I want to marry only to make sure that your wife and daughter will have enough to eat, you old fool.'

'I didn't see it in that light,' said the Baron. 'I'll talk to my brother, for we can rely on you. Tell my angel that my life is *hers*.'

And the Baron, having seen Lisbeth go into the house in the Rue Vaneau, returned to play whist and stayed at home.

The Baroness was overjoyed, since her husband seemed to have come back to family life. For about a fortnight he went to the Ministry at nine in the morning and was home at six for dinner; he spent the evening with his family. Twice he took Adeline and Hortense to the theatre.

The mother and daughter had three thanksgiving masses said and prayed God to preserve the husband and father he had restored to them.

80. *An awakening*

One evening, Victorin Hulot, seeing his father go off to bed, said to his mother:

'Well, we are fortunate; my father has come back to us, so my wife and I don't regret the sacrifice of our capital, if only this lasts.'

'Your father is nearly 70,' answered the Baroness. 'He still thinks of Madame Marneffe; I'm aware of that. But soon he won't think any more about her. The passion for women is not like gambling, or speculation, or avarice. There's an end to it.'

The beautiful Adeline—for she was still beautiful in spite of her fifty years and her sorrows—was mistaken in this. Libertines, men whom nature has gifted with the precious faculty of loving beyond the limits usually set for love, are never as old as their chronological age.

During this relapse into virtue, the Baron had been three times to the Rue du Dauphin and there he was never 70 years old. His rekindled passion made him young again and he would have sacrificed his honour, his family, everything, without a regret to Valérie.

But Valérie, completely changed, never spoke to him of money, nor of the annuity of twelve hundred francs to be made to their son. On the contrary, she offered him money; she loved Hulot as a 36-year-old woman loves a handsome law student who is very poor, very poetic, and very much in love.

And poor Adeline thought she had reconquered her beloved Hector!

The lovers' fourth meeting had been fixed at the last moment of the third one, exactly as the next day's programme used to be announced by the Comédie Italienne at the end of the performance. The hour arranged was nine o'clock in the morning.

At about eight o'clock on the day this great happiness was due—and it was the anticipation of it that reconciled the passionate old man to family life—Reine asked to see the Baron.

Hulot fearing a catastrophe, went out to speak to Reine, who would not come into the flat. The faithful maid handed the Baron the following letter:

'My dear old soldier, don't go to the Rue du Dauphin; our nightmare is ill and I have to look after him. But be there this evening at nine o'clock. Crevel is at Corbeil with Monsieur Lebas, and I'm sure he won't bring a princess to his little house. I've made arrangements here to have my night to myself; I can be back before Marneffe wakes up. Send me an answer to this, for perhaps your gloomy old wife doesn't leave you free any more as she used to. They say she's still so beautiful that you're capable of being unfaithful to me. You're such a libertine! Burn my letter. I'm suspicious of everything.'

Hulot wrote this short reply:

'My love, as I've told you, over twenty-five years my wife has never interfered with my pleasures. I'd sacrifice a hundred Adelines for you. At nine o'clock this evening, I'll be in the Crevel temple, awaiting my divinity. May the assistant-manager peg out soon! Then we'd never be separated again. That is the dearest wish of

Your HECTOR'

In the evening the Baron told his wife that he would be going to work with the Minister at Saint-Cloud and that he would come back at four or five in the morning. But he went to the Rue du Dauphin. It was then the end of the month of June.

Few men have really experienced in their lifetime the terrible sensation of going to their deaths; those who return from the scaffold can be counted on the fingers of one hand. But a few have vividly experienced that agony in dreams. They have felt everything, even the knife placed against their neck at the very moment when their awakening comes with the day to deliver them.

Well, the sensation which the Councillor of State experienced at five in the morning in Crevel's elegant, smart bed was far more horrible than that of being laid on the fatal block in the presence of ten thousand spectators who glare at you with twenty thousand flaming eyes.

Valérie was sleeping in a charming attitude. She was beautiful as women are who are beautiful enough to be beautiful even in their sleep. It was art invading nature, in short a picture in real life.

In his recumbent position, the Baron's eyes were three feet from the ground. His eyes, wandering at random, as any man's do when he wakes up and collects his thoughts, fell on the door decorated with flowers painted by Jan,* an artist who doesn't care a rap for fame. Unlike the man condemned to death, the Baron saw not twenty thousand flaming eyes, but those of only one man, whose look was in fact more devastating than the gaze of the ten thousand in the public square.

This sensation in the midst of pleasure is much rarer than that experienced by condemned men, and many a splenetic Englishman would pay a lot for it. The Baron remained in his recumbent position, literally bathed in a cold sweat. He wanted to doubt his senses, but that murderous eye was eloquent. There was a murmur of whispering voices behind the door.

'If it were only Crevel wanting to have a laugh at my expense,' the Baron said to himself, no longer able to doubt the presence of someone in the temple.

The door opened. French law in all its majesty, which on public notices is second only to the King, appeared in the guise of a nice little police commissioner, accompanied by a long-legged justice of the peace, both ushered in by Master Marneffe.

81. *The cards are reshuffled*

The police commissioner, standing firmly in shoes tied with bedraggled laces, was topped by a yellow cranium with scanty hair; he looked a crafty, ribald, facetious fellow, for whom Parisian life held no secrets. His eyes pierced the glass of his spectacles with a shrewd, cynical look.

The justice of the peace, a retired solicitor, an old admirer of the fair sex, envied the man who was being subjected to the law.

'Please excuse the severity of our duty, Monsieur le Baron,' said the commissioner. 'We have been required to act by a complainant. Monsieur le Juge de Paix is present to authorize entry into a private house. I know who you are and who the lady delinquent is.'

Valérie opened her eyes in amazement, uttered the piercing shriek which actresses have invented to represent the onset of madness on the stage, and writhed in hysterics on the bed like a woman possessed of the devil in the Middle Ages, in her sulphur shift, on a bed of faggots.

'Death! . . . My dear Hector, but the police court? Oh, never!'

She leaped up, swept like a white cloud between the three spectators, and crouched under the writing-desk, hiding her face in her hands.

'Lost! Dead!' she screamed.

'Monsieur, if Madame Marneffe goes mad, you would be worse than a libertine, you would be a murderer,' Marneffe said to Hulot.

What can a man do or say when he is taken by surprise in a bed that is not his, that he has not even hired, with a woman who is not his either? He can behave in this way.

'Monsieur le Juge de Paix, Monsieur le Commissaire,' said the Baron with dignity. 'Be so good as to look after this unfortunate lady whose reason seems to me to be in danger . . . and you can make your report afterwards. The doors are no doubt locked and you needn't be afraid that either she or I will escape, given the state we're in . . .'

The two officials acceded to the request of the Councillor of State.

'Come and have a word with me, miserable wretch,' said Hulot aside to Marneffe, taking him by the arm and pulling him over to him. 'It's not I who would be the murderer, but you! You want to be an office-manager and an Officer of the Legion of Honour?'

'More than anything, Monsieur le Directeur,' replied Marneffe with a slight bow.

'You'll be all that. Reassure your wife and send these gentlemen away.'

'Certainly not,' Marneffe replied shrewdly. 'These gentlemen must draw up their official report that you were caught in the act, for without such a document, the basis of my action against you, where should I be? The top of the Civil Service is riddled with swindlers. You've stolen my wife but you haven't made me an office-manager. Monsieur le Baron, I give you just two days to do the necessary. I have letters . . .'

'Letters!' cried the Baron, interrupting Marneffe.

'Yes, letters which prove that the child my wife is carrying at this moment is yours. Do you understand? You ought to provide for my son an income equal to the amount this bastard takes from him. But I'll be modest in my claims; it's not my business, *I*'m not crazy about paternity. A hundred louis a year will do. Tomorrow morning I'll be Monsieur Coquet's successor and put on the list of people who are to be promoted Officers of the Legion of Honour at the July celebrations,* or . . . the official report will be lodged with my charge, in court. I'm behaving generously, don't you think?'

'My goodness, what a pretty woman! What a loss to the world if she goes mad!' said the Justice of the Peace to the police officer.

'She's not mad,' replied the police officer pointedly.

The police are always the embodiment of scepticism.

'Monsieur le Baron Hulot has walked into a trap,' added the police officer, loudly enough for Valérie to hear him.

Valérie gave the officer a look which would have killed him if looks could give vent to the rage they express. The officer smiled. He too had set his trap and the woman had fallen into it.

Marneffe requested his wife to go back to the bedroom and get dressed decently, for he had come to an agreement on all points with the Baron, who put on a dressing-gown and returned to the other room.

'Gentlemen,' he said to the two officials. 'I don't need to ask you to keep this matter secret.'

The two representatives of the law bowed. The police officer tapped twice on the door. His secretary came in, sat down at the little writing-desk, and began to write as the officer dictated to him in a low voice.

Valérie continued to weep bitterly. When she had finished dressing, Hulot went into the bedroom and got dressed. Meanwhile the official report was drawn up.

Marneffe then proceeded to take his wife away, but Hulot, thinking he was seeing her for the last time, implored with a gesture the favour of speaking to her.

'Monsieur, Madame is costing me dear enough for you to allow me to say goodbye to her—in the presence of you all, of course.'

Valérie came up to him and Hulot whispered to her:

'The only thing left to us now is flight. But how can we correspond? We've been betrayed.'

'By Reine,' she replied. 'But, my dear, after this scandal, we ought not to see each other again. I'm dishonoured. Besides, people will say awful things about me and you'll believe them.'

The Baron made a gesture of denial.

'*He won't die an assistant-manager*' Marneffe muttered to the Councillor of State, as he came back to fetch his wife, to whom he said roughly:

'That's enough, Madame. I may be weak towards you but I don't want others to think I'm a fool.'

Valérie left Crevel's little house with such a mischievous parting look at the Baron that he believed she adored him. The Justice of the Peace gallantly gave his hand to Madame Marneffe as he escorted her to the carriage.

82. *A surgical operation*

The Baron, who had to sign the official report, remained in a stunned state, alone with the police commissioner. When the Councillor of State had signed the report, the officer looked at him knowingly over his spectacles.

'You're very fond of that little lady, Monsieur le Baron?'

'Unfortunately for me, as you see.'

'And if she didn't love you, if she deceived you?' continued the officer.

'I've heard about that already, Monsieur, in this house. Monsieur Crevel and I told each other . . .'

'Oh, so you know you're in the Mayor's little house.'

'Certainly.'

The officer raised his hat a little in a respectful salute to the old man.

'You're very much in love, so I'll say no more. I respect an inveterate passion as much as doctors respect an inveterate ill . . . I've seen Monsieur de Nucingen, the banker, the victim of a passion of that kind.'

'He's a friend of mine,' the Baron replied. 'I've often had supper with the lovely Esther. She was worth the two million she cost him.'

'More than that,' said the officer. 'That whim of the old banker cost four people their lives. Oh, these passions are like cholera.'

'What did you want to tell me?' asked the Councillor of State, who took this indirect warning amiss.

'Why should I deprive you of your illusions?' answered the police commissioner. 'It's so rare to have any left at your age.'

'Rid me of them,' cried the Councillor of State.

'The doctor gets cursed later,' replied the officer with a smile.

'Do, please, Monsieur le Commissaire!'

'Well, that woman was in collusion with her husband.'

'Oh!'

'That happens, Monsieur, in two cases out of ten. Oh, we're experts on this kind of thing.'

'What proof have you of her collusion?'

'Oh, first of all, the husband,' said the shrewd police commissioner with the calm of a surgeon accustomed to excising an infected organ. 'Speculation is stamped on his mean, hideous face. But you must value highly a certain letter written by that woman in which the child is referred to?'

'I value the letter so highly that I always carry it with me,' Baron Hulot replied to the police officer, rummaging in his breast-pocket for the little wallet that he always kept on him.

'Leave the wallet where it is,' said the commissioner, in thundering tones like a public prosecutor. 'Here's the letter. I know now all I wanted to know. Madame Marneffe must have been in the secret of what was in the wallet.'

'She, alone, in all the world.'

'That's what I thought. Now here's the proof you were asking me for of that little lady's complicity.'

'It's not possible!' said the Baron, still incredulous.

'When we got here, Monsieur le Baron, that wretched Marneffe went in first and he picked up this letter which his wife had presumably left there,' he said, pointing to the writing-table. 'Obviously that place had been agreed between the husband and wife, providing she managed to filch the letter from you while you were asleep; for the letter the lady wrote to you, together with those you sent to her, is decisive evidence in the police court.'

The officer showed Hulot the letter which Reine had brought him in his office at the Ministry.

'It's one of the papers in the case,' said the police officer. 'Give it back to me, Monsieur.'

'Well, Monsieur,' said Hulot, his face contorted with emotion, 'that woman is the embodiment of organized debauchery. I'm sure now that she has three lovers.'

'That's obvious,' said the police officer. 'Oh, they're not all out on the streets. When they engage in that trade, with carriages, in drawing-rooms, or in their own homes, it's not a matter of francs and centimes. Mademoiselle Esther, whom you mentioned and who poisoned herself, devoured millions. If you take my advice, you'll cut loose from all this, Monsieur le Baron. This last episode will cost you dear. That scoundrel of a husband has the law on his side. Indeed, but for me, that little woman would have caught you again.'

'Thank you, Monsieur,' said the Councillor of State, trying to retain his dignity.

'Monsieur, we're going to lock the house. The farce is over and you can give the key back to Monsieur le Maire.'

83. *Moral reflections*

Hulot returned home in a state of depression verging on collapse and sunk in thoughts of the deepest gloom. He woke his noble, pure, and saintly wife and poured out the story of the last three years into her heart, sobbing like a child whose toy has been taken from him.

This confession of an old man, young at heart, this terrible and heart-rending saga, while it moved Adeline to pity, gave her the keenest inner joy. She thanked heaven for this final blow, for she saw her husband settled for good in the bosom of his family.

'Lisbeth was right,' said Madame Hulot gently, without making useless reproaches. 'She warned us of this in advance.'

'Yes! Oh, if only I had listened to her instead of getting angry, the day I wanted poor Hortense to go home so as not to compromise the reputation of that ... Oh, dear Adeline, we must save Wenceslas. He's in that mire up to the neck.'

'My poor darling, you had no more success with the little middle-class wife than you had with the actresses,' said Adeline, smiling.

The Baroness was alarmed at the change in Hector's appearance. When she saw him unhappy, suffering, bowed under the weight of his troubles, her heart was filled with love and pity. She would have given her life to make Hulot happy.

'Stay with us, Hector dear. Tell me how these women behave so that they bind you to them so firmly. I'll try . . . Why haven't you taught me to be what you want? Am I not clever enough? Men still think I'm beautiful enough to be courted.'

Many married women, devoted to their duties and to their husbands, may well wonder at this point why strong, kindly men, so sympathetic to women like Madame Marneffe, don't make their wives the subject of their fancies and their passions, especially when they are like Baroness Adeline Hulot. This is linked to one of the deepest mysteries of human nature.

Love, when reason runs riot, the manly, serious pleasure of great hearts, and sensual pleasure, the vulgar commodity sold on the market-place, are two different aspects of the same thing. The woman who can satisfy those two great appetites of the two sides of human nature is as rare amongst her sex as great generals, great writers, great artists, and great inventors are in a nation. Men of superior gifts as well as fools, a Hulot as well as a Crevel, feel the need both of the ideal and of sensual pleasure; all go in search of the mysterious hermaphrodite, that rare object which is usually found to be a work in two volumes. This quest is a depravity for which society is to blame. Clearly, marriage must be accepted as a task to be performed. It is life, with its toil and painful sacrifices to be made equally on both sides. Libertines, those treasure-hunters, are as guilty as other wrong-doers who are more severely punished than they. This reflection is not merely an outward show of morality; it explains many incomprehensible misfortunes. The preceding scene has, moreover, its own moral lessons of more than one kind.

84. *Fructus belli; the outcome depends on the Minister for War*

The Baron went without delay to see the Maréchal Prince de Wissembourg, whose high-powered protection was his last resource. Since he had been the old soldier's protégé for thirty-five years, he had access to him at any time and could be admitted to his rooms first thing in the morning.

'Oh, good morning, my dear Hector,' said that great and kindly leader. 'What's the matter? You look worried. And yet the session's finished. That's another one over. I speak of these things now as I used to about our campaigns. In fact, I think the newspapers also call the sessions parliamentary campaigns.'

'Indeed, we've had our troubles, Marshal. But it's the difficulties of the time,' said Hulot. 'What can we do about it? That's what the world is like. Every age has its problems. The greatest misfortune of 1841 is that neither the King nor his ministers have freedom of action as the Emperor had.'

The Marshal gave Hulot one of his eagle-like looks, whose pride, lucidity, and perspicacity showed that, in spite of the years, his fine spirit was still strong and vigorous.

'You want me to do something for you?' he asked, assuming a light-hearted manner.

'I find myself compelled to ask you, as a personal favour, for the promotion of one of my assistant-managers and his appointment as an Officer of the Legion of Honour.'

'What's his name?' asked the Marshal, casting a look like a lightning-flash at the Baron.

'Marneffe.'

'He has a pretty wife. I saw her at your daughter's wedding. If Roger . . . but Roger's no longer here. Hector, my boy, this is connected with your love affairs. What, you're still at it? Oh! You do credit to the Imperial Guard!

That's what comes of having been in the Commissariat; you have reserves! Drop this affair, my dear boy; it's too much a matter of gallantry to become an administrative concern.'

'No, Marshal. It's a bad business, for the law is involved. Do you want to see me brought before the police court?'

'Oh, what the devil,' exclaimed the Marshal, becoming serious. Go on.'

'The fact is that you see me in the state of a fox caught in a trap. You've always been so kind to me that you'll be good enough to extricate me from the shameful situation I'm in.'

Hulot related his misadventure as wittily and cheerfully as he could.

'And, my dear Prince,' he said in conclusion, 'would you be willing to let my brother, whom you are so fond of, die of grief, and one of your Directors, a Councillor of State, be dishonoured? The Marneffe I speak of is a wretched creature; we'll put him on the retired list in two or three years.'

'How you talk of two or three years, my dear fellow!' said the Marshal.

'But, Prince, the Imperial Guard is immortal.'

'I'm the only Marshal left of the first batch,' said the Minister. 'Listen. Hector. You don't know how much I'm attached to you. You shall see. The day I leave the Ministry, we'll leave together. Oh, you're not a deputy, my friend. A lot of people want your job and, but for me, you'd have already lost it. Yes, I've broken many a lance in order to keep you. . . . Well, I'll grant your two requests, for it would be too hard to see you in the dock at your age and in your position. But you've made too many inroads into your credit. If this appointment gives rise to a fuss, it will be held against us. It doesn't matter as far as I'm concerned, but it's another thorn in your side. At the next session, you'll be fired. Your job is held out as a bait to five or six influential men and you've been kept in office only by my subtle reasoning. I said that the day you retired and your job was given to someone else, we'd have five malcontents and one happy man, while if we leave you in a shaky position for two or three years, we'd have our six votes. They began to laugh at the Council meeting and agreed that the veteran of the Old Guard, as they call me, was getting very clever at parliamentary tactics. . . . I tell you this frankly. Besides, you're growing grey. What a lucky fellow you are still to be able to get into such scrapes. Where are the days when Sub-Lieutenant Cottin had mistresses?'

The Marshal rang.

'That police report must be torn up,' he added.

'You're acting like a father, Monseigneur. I didn't dare tell you of my anxiety.'

'I still wish Roger were here,' cried the Marshal on seeing Mitouflet, his door-keeper, come in, 'and I was going to send for him. You can go, Mitouflet. And, my old comrade in arms, you go and have this nomination drawn up and I'll sign it. But that vile schemer won't enjoy the fruit of his crimes for long. He'll be watched and demoted before the whole company at the least fault. Now that you're saved, my dear Hector, go carefully. Don't wear your friends out. The nomination will be sent to you this morning, and your man will be an Officer of the Legion of Honour. . . . How old are you now?'

'I'll be 70 in three months' time.'

'What a lusty fellow you are,' said the Marshal with a smile. 'You're the one who deserves promotion. But damn it all! We're not in the age of Louis XV!'

Such is the effect of the comradeship which binds together the glorious remnants of the Napoleonic phalanx that they think they're still in an army camp, bound to defend each other against all comers.

'Another favour like that one,' Hulot said to himself as he crossed the courtyard, 'and I'm finished.'

The unhappy official went to see Baron de Nucingen, to whom he owed a trifling sum. He managed to borrow forty thousand francs from him by pledging his salary for two more years. But the Baron stipulated that, in the event of Hulot's retirement, the disposable portion of his pension should be applied to the repayment of this amount, interest and capital in full.

This new transaction, like the first, was negotiated in the name of Vauvinet, to whom the Baron signed bills for twelve thousand francs.

The next day the fatal police report, the husband's charge, and the letters were all destroyed. The scandalous promotions of Master Marneffe, barely noticed amid the bustle of the July festivities,* gave rise to no comment in the newspapers.

85. *Another disaster*

Lisbeth, who to all appearances had broken with Madame Marneffe, had been installed in Marshal Hulot's house.

Ten days after these events, the first banns of the old maid's marriage to the distinguished old man were published. To obtain his consent Adeline told him of her Hector's financial catastrophe, while begging him never to mention it to the Baron, who, she said, was in very low spirits, dejected and quite crushed.

'Alas, he's feeling his age,' she added.

So Lisbeth triumphed! She was about to attain the goal of her ambition, she was going to see her plan accomplished, her hatred satisfied. She was looking forward to the joy of reigning over the family which had despised her for so long. She promised herself to patronize her patrons, to be the rescuing angel who would support the ruined family. She called herself *Madame la Comtesse* or *Madame la Maréchale* as she curtsied to herself in the mirror. Adeline and Hortense would end their days in poverty, struggling against want, while Cousin Bette, received at the Tuileries, would play the fine lady in society.

A terrible event toppled the old maid from the social eminence where she had so proudly established herself.

The very day these first banns were published, the Baron received another message from Africa. A second Alsatian came to the door and handed in a letter, having first made sure that he was giving it to Baron Hulot. After giving him the address of his lodgings, he left the high official overwhelmed by the first few lines he read of the following letter.

'My nephew, according to my calculations, you will receive this letter on 7 August. Assuming you take three days to send us the help we're asking for and that it will take a fortnight to reach us, that brings us to 1 September.

If you can carry out the following plan within that time, you will have saved the honour and life of Johann Fischer.

This is what the clerk you gave me as a colleague is asking for. For it seems that I am liable to be brought before an assize court or a court martial. You appreciate that Johann Fischer will never be brought before any tribunal; he will go, by his own act, before God's.

Your clerk seems to me to be a nasty fellow, quite capable of compromising you. But he's as clever as a scoundrel. He claims that you ought to protest more loudly than the others and send us an inspector, a special commissioner instructed to detect the culprits, to discover the abuses, in short to act vigorously. But he will, in the first place, stand between us and the law by raising the question of the conflict of jurisdiction.

If your commissioner arrives here on 1 September with your orders and if you send us two hundred thousand francs to replace in the stores the quantities that we said were in remote districts, we shall be looked on as honourable and irreproachable agents.

You can entrust a money-order, payable to me at an Algerian bank, to the soldier who delivers this letter. He's a reliable man, a relative, incapable of trying to find out what he's carrying. I've taken steps to ensure the lad's safe return. If you can't do anything, I'll die gladly for the man to whom we owe our Adeline's happiness.'

The agonies and the delights of passion, the catastrophe which had just put an end to his career as a ladies' man, had prevented Baron Hulot from thinking of poor Johann Fischer. Yet his first letter gave clear warning of the danger that had now become so pressing.

The Baron left the dining-room in such an agitated state that he collapsed on to the drawing-room sofa. He was stunned, dazed by his violent fall. He stared at a rose pattern on the carpet without noticing that he was holding Johann's fatal letter in his hand.

From her room Adeline heard her husband fall into the chair like a dead weight. The sound was so unusual that she thought he must have had a stroke.

Overcome by a breathtaking, paralysing fear, she looked in her mirror at the reflection through the door into the drawing-room and saw her Hector lying like a man prostrated.

The Baroness approached on tiptoe. Hector heard nothing; she was able to come nearer; she saw the letter, took it, read it, and trembled in every limb. She experienced one of those violent nervous upsets that leave their mark forever on the body. Some days later she became affected by a constant nervous tremor, but after the first moment the need for action gave her the strength that can only be drawn from the very springs of the life-force.

'Hector, come into my room,' she said in a voice that was no more than a whisper. 'Don't let your daughter see you like this. Come, my dear, come.'

'Where can I find two hundred thousand francs? I can have Claude Vignon sent as a special commissioner. He's a bright, intelligent fellow. That could be settled in two days. But two hundred thousand francs! My son hasn't got that amount. His house is mortgaged for three hundred thousand francs. My brother has savings of thirty thousand francs at most. Nucingen would laugh at me. As for Vauvinet, he grudgingly allowed me ten thousand francs to make up the amount for that vile Marneffe's son. No, it's all up with me. I'll have to throw myself at the Marshal's feet, confess to him what the situation is, hear myself called a rotter, and accept his broadside so that I can go under decently.'

'But, Hector, it's not only ruin, it's dishonour,' said Adeline. 'My poor uncle will kill himself. Kill only us, you have the right, but you mustn't be a murderer! Take heart; there must be some way out.'

'None,' said the Baron. 'No one in the Government can

lay his hands on two hundred thousand francs, not even to save a ministry. Oh, Napoleon, where are you now?'

'My uncle! Poor man! Hector, we can't let him kill himself, dishonoured.'

'There might be one way out,' he said, 'but it's very chancy. Yes, Crevel is at daggers drawn with his daughter. . . . Oh, he's got plenty of money; he's the only one who might . . .'

'Listen, Hector. Better to let your wife be destroyed than to allow the destruction of our uncle, of your brother, and of the family honour,' said the Baroness, as an idea suddenly flashed through her mind. 'Yes, I can save you all. Oh, my God! What a disgraceful thought! How could it have entered my head?'

Adeline put her hands together, fell on her knees, and said a prayer. When she got up, she saw such a crazy look of joy on her husband's face, that the diabolical thought returned, and she then fell into a kind of melancholy stupor.

'Go, my dear, hurry to the Ministry,' she cried, arousing herself from her torpor. 'Try to send out a commissioner. You must *wheedle the Marshal*! And when you come back at five o'clock, perhaps you'll find . . . yes, you'll find two hundred thousand francs. Your family, your honour as a man, as a Councillor of State, as a Government official, your integrity, your son, all will be saved. But your Adeline will be lost and you'll never see her again. Hector, my dear,' she said, kneeling before him, clasping his hand and kissing it, 'give me your blessing and bid me goodbye.'

It was so heart-rending that, as he raised his wife, embracing her and kissing her, Hulot said, 'I don't understand you.'

'If you understood,' she replied, 'I'd die of shame or I'd not have enough strength to make this final sacrifice.'

'Lunch is ready,' said Mariette, coming in.

Hortense came in and said good morning to her father and mother. They had to go to lunch and assume facial expressions that belied their feelings.

'Go and start lunch without me; I'll join you,' said the Baroness.

She sat down at her table and wrote the following letter:

'My dear Monsieur Crevel,—I have a favour to ask of you. I shall expect you this morning and I count on your gallant courtesy, which is familiar to me, not to keep me waiting too long.

Your devoted servant,

ADELINE HULOT.'

'Louise,' she said to her daughter's maid, who was serving lunch, 'take this letter down to the porter. Tell him to take it immediately to its address and to ask for an answer.'

The Baron, who was reading the newspapers, handed a Republican paper to his wife, pointed out an article, and said:

'Will there be time?'

Here is the article, one of those terrible snippets with which newspapers spice their political screeds.

'One of our correspondents writes us from Algiers that such serious abuses have come to light in the commissariat of the province of Oran, that judicial inquiries are being made. The malversations are obvious and the guilty have been identified. If severe measures are not taken, we shall continue to lose more men through the misappropriation of funds that affects their rations, than by the swords of the Arabs or the heat of the climate. We await more information before writing further on this distressing subject.

We are no longer surprised at the fear aroused by the establishment of the Press in Algeria, as envisaged by the Charter of 1830.'*

I'll get dressed and go to the Ministry,' said the Baron, leaving the table. 'Time is too precious; there's a man's life in every minute,'

'Oh, Mama, I've no hope left,' said Hortense.

And unable to restrain her tears, she handed her mother a copy of the *Revue des Beaux-Arts*. Madame Hulot saw an engraving of the Delilah group by the Comte de Steinbock, beneath which was printed: *Belonging to*

Madame Marneffe. From the very first lines, the article, signed V, revealed the talent and partiality of Claude Vignon.

'Poor child,' said the Baroness.

Alarmed by her mother's almost indifferent tone, Hortense looked at her and recognized in her expression a grief beside which her own paled; she came over to her mother and kissed her, saying:

'What's the matter, Mama? What's happened? Can we be more unhappy than we are already?'

'It seems to me, my child, that in comparison with what I'm suffering today, my terrible sufferings of the past are as nothing. When will my suffering be at an end?'

'In Heaven, Mother dear,' said Hortense gravely.

'Come, my love, you'll help me dress. . . . But no . . . I don't want you to be concerned with what I wear for this. Send Louise to me.'

86. *A different style of dressing*

When Adeline had returned to her room, she went and scrutinized herself in the mirror. She studied her reflection sadly and questioningly, asking herself:

'Am I still beautiful? Am I still desirable? Am I wrinkled?'

She pushed back her beautiful fair hair and uncovered her temples. The skin there was as fresh as a young girl's.

Adeline went further. She bared her shoulders and was satisfied; she felt a thrill of pride. The beauty of beautiful shoulders is the last to leave a woman, especially when her life has been pure.

Adeline chose the items of her dress with care, but, a pious, chaste woman, she remained chastely dressed in spite of her little attempts at coquetry. What was the use of new, grey silk stockings or satin shoes with built-up soles when she was totally ignorant of the art of putting out a pretty foot at the decisive moment, a little beyond a slightly lifted dress, to open up horizons of desire?

She did indeed put on her prettiest dress of flowered muslin, with a low neck and short sleeves, but, alarmed at the sight of her bare flesh, she covered her beautiful arms with transparent gauze sleeves and veiled her bosom and her shoulders with an embroidered fichu.

Her hair, curled in the English style, seemed to her too suggestive, so she reduced its impact by putting on a very pretty cap. But with or without a cap, would she have known how to play with her golden ringlets so as to show off her tapered fingers and have them admired?

And her only make-up was as follows. The certainty that she was planning a crime, the preparations for a deliberate sin, gave this saintly woman a violent fever which momentarily restored the sparkle of her youth. Her eyes shone; her skin glowed. But instead of assuming a seductive look, she saw herself as looking, in a way, shameless and she was horrified.

At Adeline's request, Lisbeth had related the circumstances of Wenceslas's infidelity and the Baroness had then learned, to her great astonishment, that in one evening, in a moment, Madame Marneffe had made herself the mistress of the bewitched artist.

'How do these women do it?' the Baroness had asked Lisbeth.

Nothing equals the curiosity of virtuous women on this subject; they would like to possess the seductions of vice and yet remain pure.

'Well, they seduce; that's their job,' Cousin Bette had replied. 'You see, my dear. that evening, Valérie was beautiful enough to damn an angel!'

'But tell me how she set about it.'

'There's no theory; there's only practice in that trade,' said Lisbeth sardonically.

The Baroness, recalling this conversation, would have liked to consult Cousin Bette, but there was no time. Poor Adeline, incapable of inventing a beauty-spot, or of placing a rosebud right in the centre of her bodice, or of devising tricks of dress calculated to revive man's dulled passions, was merely dressed with care. One cannot be a courtesan at will!

'Woman is man's meat.' as Molière amusingly observed by the mouth of the discerning Gros-René.* This comparison implies a kind of culinary science in love. The noble, virtuous wife would then be the Homeric meal, flesh thrown on burning coal. The courtesan, on the other hand, would be Carême's* work with its condiments, spices, and studied presentation.

The Baroness could not, did not, know how to *serve up* her white bosom in a magnificent dish of lace in the style of Madame Marneffe. She did not know the secret of certain attitudes, the effect of certain glances. In short, she did not have her secret weapon.

The noble woman might have racked her brains a hundred times, she would still have had nothing to offer a libertine's practised eye. To be an upright and virtuous woman to the outside world, and to turn herself into a courtesan for her husband, is to be a woman of genius, and there are few. There lies the secret of long attachments, inexplicable to women who are not endowed with these complementary and magnificent abilities. Imagine a virtuous Madame Marneffe, and you have the Marchesa de Pescara!* Such great and distinguished women, lovely as Diane de Poitiers* yet virtuous, can be counted on the fingers of one hand.

The scene with which this serious and terrible study of Parisian life began was, then, about to be repeated, with the outstanding difference that the woes prophesied by the Captain of the citizen militia had reversed the roles. Madame Hulot was waiting for Crevel with the same intentions that had brought him smiling at the citizens of Paris from the top of his *milord* three years previously.

Yet, strange to say, the Baroness was faithful to herself and to her love in preparing to commit the worst kind of infidelity, that which, in the eyes of certain judges, is not justified by the force of a passion.

'What can I do to be a Madame Marneffe?' she asked herself, as she heard the door-bell ring.

She restrained her tears; fever gave animation to her features. She promised herself to behave like a real courtesan, poor, noble creature!

'What the devil does that good Madame Hulot want of me?' Crevel wondered as he went up the main staircase. 'Well, no matter, she's going to talk to me about my quarrel with Célestine and Victorin. But I shan't give way.'

As he followed Louise into the drawing-room and looked at the bareness of the *premises* (to use Crevel's word), he said to himself:

'Poor woman! She's stuck here like one of those fine pictures put in the attic by a man who knows nothing about painting.'

Crevel, seeing Count Popinot, Minister of Trade, buy pictures and statues, wanted to make himself celebrated among Parisian Maecenases* whose love of the arts consists of trying to buy for twenty sous works worth twenty francs.

87. *A sublime courtesan*

Adeline gave Crevel a gracious smile and motioned him to a chair facing her.

'Here I am, fair lady, at your service,' said Crevel.

Monsieur le Maire, now a political figure, had taken to wearing black. His face emerged above this apparel like a full moon on top of a screen of dark clouds. His shirt, studded with three enormous pearls worth five hundred francs each, gave a high idea of his capacity . . . his thoracic capacity, and he would say: 'You see in me the future athlete of the Chamber!' His broad plebeian hands were in yellow gloves from early morning. His polished boots showed that he had come in his little brown, one-horse coupé.

In the course of three years, ambition had modified Crevel's pose. Like the great painters, he was on to his second period.

In society, when he went to the Prince de Wissembourg's, to the Prefecture, to Count Popinot's etc., he would hold his hat in his hand in a free and easy way that Valérie had taught him, and put the thumb of his other hand into his waistcoat armhole with a skittish air, while making simpering movements with his head and eyes. This second manner of *striking an attitude* he owed to the teasing Valérie, who, on the pretext of rejuvenating her Mayor, had endowed him with another ridiculous stance.

'I have asked you to come, my dear, kind Monsieur Crevel, for a matter of the utmost importance,' said the Baroness uneasily.

'I can guess what it is,' said Crevel, with a knowing look. 'But you are asking for the impossible. . . . Oh, I'm not an inhuman father, a man, as Napoleon said, *standing fair square* in his avarice. Listen to me, fair lady. If my children were ruining themselves for their own benefit, I'd come to their aid. But to be guarantor for your husband, Madame! It's like wanting to fill the cask of the Danaïdes!* They've mortgaged their house for three hundred thousand francs for an incorrigible father. They've nothing left, the poor creatures, and they've had no fun out of it. All they have to live on now is what Victorin can earn at the Law Courts. Let him jabber away, your distinguished son. Oh, he was to be a minister, that learned little lawyer, the hope of us all! He's a fine tug-boat pilot who stupidly goes aground, for if he borrowed to get on, if he got into debt through entertaining deputies, to get votes and increase his influence, I'd say to him, 'Here's my purse; take what you want, my boy.' But to pay for papa's follies, follies that I predicted to you! Oh, his father has ruined his chances of coming into power. It's I who'll be a minister.'

'Alas, *dear Crevel*, it's not a question of our children, poor devoted things. If you close your heart to Victorin and Célestine, I shall love them so much that perhaps I might soothe the bitter sorrow that your anger brings to their noble hearts. You punish your children for a good deed.'

'Yes, for a good deed badly done. That's a half-crime,' said Crevel, well pleased with this expression.

'To do good, my dear Crevel,' continued the Baroness, 'isn't a matter of giving money from an overflowing purse. It's to put up with hardship because of one's generosity, it's to suffer as a result of one's good deed, to expect ingratitude. Charity that costs nothing goes unnoticed in heaven.'

'Let saints, Madame, go to the workhouse if they want to. They know that for them it is the gate of heaven. But I'm a man of this world; I fear God, but I fear still more the hell of poverty. To be penniless is the last degree of misfortune in our present social order. I'm a man of my time. I respect money.'

'You are right from the worldy point of view,' said Adeline.

She found herself miles away from the point and, as she thought of her uncle, she felt like St Lawrence* on the gridiron, for, in her mind's eye, she saw him shooting himself with a pistol.

She lowered her eyes, and then raised them, full of angelic sweetness, to look at Crevel; but they had none of that enticing sensuality which sparkled in Valérie's.

Three years earlier, Crevel would have been fascinated by that adorable look.

'I have known you to be more generous,' she said. 'You used to speak of three thousand francs like a great nobleman.'

Crevel looked at Madame Hulot; she seemed to him like a lily near the end of its flowering and a vague thought came into his mind. But he respected this saintly creature so much that he pushed these suspicions back into the libertine side of his heart.

'Madame, I've not changed, but a retired businessman behaves and ought to behave like a great nobleman, with method and economy. He does everything in an orderly manner. He opens an account for his dissipations, allows for them, assigns certain profits to that heading, but to break into one's capital—that would be madness. My children will have all that is rightly theirs, their mother's fortune and mine, but they surely don't want their father to be utterly bored, to turn into a monk or a mummy! I lead a gay life; I sail cheerfully down the river. I fulfil all the duties required by the law, by my own heart, and by my family, just as I used to pay all my bills when they fell due. If my children manage their domestic affairs as well as I do, I'll be satisfied. And as for the present, provided my dissipations—for I do indulge in some—cost nothing to anyone except *gogos* (I beg your pardon; you don't know that Stock Exchange slang for gullible fools), they'll have nothing to reproach me with and will still inherit a handsome fortune on my death. Your children will not be able to say as much for their father, who plays around to the ruin of his son and my daughter.'

The more the conversation continued, the further away the Baroness was from her objective.

'You bear a great grudge against my husband, my dear Crevel, and yet you'd have been his best friend if his wife had given in to you.'

She cast a burning glance at Crevel. But then she behaved like Dubois when he kicked the Regent three times,* she went too far, and the licentious thoughts came back with such force to the Regency perfumer that he said to himself:

'I wonder if she wants to avenge herself on Hulot? Does she like me better as Mayor than as National Guardsman? Women are so odd!'

And he struck an attitude in his second manner, looking at the Baroness with a Regency expression.

'One might think', she continued, 'that you're taking your revenge on him for a virtue that resisted you, for a woman whom you used to love enough . . . to . . . buy her,' she added in a low voice.

'For a divine woman,' replied Crevel with a meaningful smile at the Baroness, who lowered her eyes, her lashes wet with tears. 'Yes, you've swallowed many a bitter pill, these last three years. Isn't that so, my beauty?'

'Don't let's talk of my sufferings, *dear Crevel*; they are more than any human being can bear. Oh, if you still loved me, you could rescue me from the abyss I've landed in. Yes, I'm in hell. The regicides who were tortured with red-hot pincers, who were drawn and quartered, were on a bed of roses compared to me, for only their bodies were dismembered, but it is my heart that is torn to pieces.'

Crevel withdrew his hand from his waistcoat armhole; he put his hat on the work-table, abandoned his attitude, and smiled! His smile was so idiotic that the Baroness misunderstood it; she took it for an expression of kindness.

'You see a woman, not in despair, but suffering the death-throes of her honour and resolved to do anything, *my dear*, to prevent crimes . . .'

Fearing that Hortense might come in, she bolted her door; then, with the same brusque movement, she flung herself at Crevel's feet, took his hand, and kissed it.

'Be my saviour,' she said.

She imagined that there were generous strings in his businessman's heart and had a sudden gleam of hope that she might obtain the two hundred thousand francs without losing her honour.

'Buy my heart, you who sought to buy my virtue,' she went on, looking at him wildly. 'Trust my integrity as a woman, my honour; you know how steadfast it is! Be my friend! Save a whole family from ruin, shame, and despair! Save it from wallowing in a sea of filth where the mud will be made of blood! Oh, don't ask me for an explanation!. . . .' she said, as a gesture from Crevel showed he was about to speak. 'Above all, don't say, "I told you so", as friends do who are glad of one's misfortune. Come, do as you are asked by a woman you once loved, whose humiliation at your feet is perhaps an act of supreme nobility. Don't ask for anything in return but expect everything from her gratitude. No, give nothing, but lend me, lend to her you used to call Adeline!'

At this point the tears flowed so profusely, Adeline sobbed so abundantly, that Crevel's gloves were drenched.

The words, 'I need two hundred thousand francs', were barely audible in the flood of tears, just as stones, however big they are, make no impresssion on Alpine torrents swollen by the melting snows.

Such is the inexperience of virtue! Vice asks for nothing,

as we have seen in the case of Madame Marneffe, but contrives to have everything offered to it. Women of that sort become demanding only when they have made themselves indispensable or when it's a matter of working to get all they can out of a man as one *works* a quarry when the stone is becoming scarce, *ruined*, as the quarrymen say.

When he heard the words, 'Two hundred thousand francs', Crevel understood everything.

He gallantly raised the Baroness to her feet, with the insolent words, 'Come now, compose yourself, *little mother*', which Adeline in her distraught state did not hear.

The character of the scene was changing. Crevel was becoming, as he put it, master of the situation.

88. *Crevel pontificates*

Crevel was so impressed by the enormity of the amount that his keen emotion on seeing this beautiful woman in tears at his feet subsided.

But however angelic and saintly a woman may be, when she is weeping bitterly her beauty disappears. As we have seen, the Madame Marneffes of this world grizzle a little sometimes, let a tear trickle down their cheeks; but burst into tears, make their eyes and noses red . . . they never make *that* mistake.

'Come now, *my child*, calm yourself, for heaven's sake,' continued Crevel, taking the beautiful Madame Hulot's hands in his own and patting them. 'Why are you asking me for two hundred thousand francs? What do you want to do with them? Whom are they for?'

'Don't require me to give any explanation, give them to me!. . . . You will have saved three people's lives and your children's honour.'

'And do you think, little mother,' said Crevel, 'that you will find in Paris a man who, on the word of a half-crazy woman, will go, *hic et nunc*, and take out of a drawer or from anywhere two hundred thousand francs which are quietly simmering away there, waiting till she condescends to skim them off? Is that all you know of life and business matters, my lovely one? Your people are very sick; send them the sacraments, for no one in Paris, except her Divine Highness Madame la Banque, the celebrated Nucingen, or some insane miser, as much in love with gold as we other men are with women, can perform a miracle like that. The Civil List, however civil it may be, the Civil List itself would ask you to call back tomorrow. Everyone invests his money and speculates to his best advantage. You are much mistaken, my dear, if you think it's King Louis-Philippe who reigns, but he's not mistaken about that. He knows, as we all do, that above the Charter* there is the holy, venerated, tangible, charming, gracious, beautiful, noble, young, all-powerful hundred-sou piece. Now, my lovely one, money demands interest and it's always busy gathering it. 'God of the Jews, you prevail!'* as the great Racine said. In short, it's the eternal allegory of the Golden Calf.* In Moses' day, there was stockjobbing in the desert. We have returned to biblical times. The Golden Calf was the first register of public loans,' he went on. 'You live too much in the Rue Plumet, my dear Adeline. The Egyptians owed enormous amounts borrowed from the Hebrews and they didn't pursue God's people, but financial capital.'

He looked at the Baroness with an expression which seemed to say, 'See how witty I am!'

'You don't know how much every citizen loves his filthy lucre,' he continued after a pause. 'Now just listen to me carefully; try to understand my line of argument. You want two hundred thousand francs. Nobody can come up with that amount without realizing investments. Do a few sums. To raise two hundred thousand francs *in cash*, you'd have to sell investments bringing in about seven thousand francs a year at 3 per cent. Well, you wouldn't get your money in less than two days. That's the quickest way. To induce someone to part with a fortune (for that's a fortune to many people—two hundred thousand francs!), you'd also have to tell him what it's all in aid of, what you want it for . . .'

'My dear, kind Crevel, it's a question of two men's lives; one will die of grief and the other will kill himself. And it concerns me too, for I shall go mad. Am I not a little mad already?'

'Not as mad as all that,' he said, grasping Madame Hulot's knees. 'Père Crevel has his price, since you deigned to think of him, my angel.'

'It seems that I have to let him grasp my knees,' thought the noble, saintly woman, hiding her face in her hands. 'You offered me a fortune once,' she said, blushing.

'Oh, little mother, that was three years ago,' replied Crevel. 'Oh, you're more beautiful now than I've ever seen you,' he cried, taking hold of the Baroness's arm and pressing it to his heart. 'By heaven, you've a good memory, my dear girl! Well, now you see how wrong you were to be so strait-laced; for the three hundred thousand francs that you high-mindedly refused are in another woman's purse. I loved you then and I love you still, but let's cast our minds back to three years ago. When I said to you, 'You shall be mine!', what was my motive? I wanted to take my revenge on that scoundrel Hulot. Well, your husband, my beauty, took as his mistress a gem of a woman, a pearl, an artful little hussy, then aged 23, for she's 26 now. I thought it would be more amusing, more perfect, more Louis XV, more Maréchal de Richelieu,* more satisfying, to pinch that charming creature from him; in any case she never loved Hulot and for the last three years she has been crazy about your humble servant.'

As he said these words Crevel, from whose hands the Baroness had withdrawn her own, struck his attitude again. He stuck his thumbs in his armholes and flapped his hands against his chest like a pair of wings, thinking that made him desirable and charming. It was as if he were saying, 'This is the man you showed the door to!'

'So there we are, my dear girl, I've had my revenge and your husband knew it. I've proved to him convincingly that he was *fooled*, given *tit for tat* as we say. Madame Marneffe is *my* mistress, and if Master Marneffe dies she will be my wife.'

Madame Hulot looked at Crevel with a fixed, distraught gaze.

'Hector knew that!' she said.

'And he went back to her!' replied Crevel. 'And I put up with it because Valérie wanted to be the wife of an office-manager. But she swore to me that she'd arrange things so that our Baron would be so thoroughly *licked* that he'd never turn up again. And my little duchess (for she was born a duchess, that woman, on my word of honour) has kept her word. She has returned your Hector to you *virtuous in perpetuity*, as she so wittily puts it. The lesson was a good one, that's a fact. The Baron has had some hard knocks. He won't keep any more dancers or respectable women either. He's thoroughly cured, rinsed out like a beer glass. If you'd listened to Crevel instead of humiliating him and throwing him out, you'd have had four hundred thousand francs, for my revenge cost me fully that amount. But I hope I'll get my cash back when Marneffe dies. I've invested in my future wife. That's the secret of my extravagance. I've solved the problem of behaving like a highborn aristocrat on the cheap.'

'You'd give your daughter a stepmother like that!' cried Madame Hulot.

89. *In which the false courtesan arises a saint*

'You don't know Valérie, Madame,' replied Crevel solemnly, striking the attitude of his first period., 'She's a woman of good family, as well as of good standing, and she also enjoys the highest public esteem. Why, yesterday the vicar of the parish was dining at her house. We've given a magnificent monstrance to the church, for she's devout. Oh, she's clever, she's witty, she's delightful, she has everything going for her. As for me, dear Adeline, I owe that charming woman everything. She's sharpened my wits and refined my language, as you see. She improves my wisecracks and helps me with words and ideas. I no longer say anything improper. People see great changes in me;

you must have noticed them. What's more, she has revived my ambition. If I were a deputy, I wouldn't make any *howlers*, for I'd consult my Egeria* even on the smallest matters. All great politicians, Numa as well as our present distinguished minister,* have had their Cumaean Sibyl.* Valérie entertains about a score of duputies; she is becoming very influential, and now that she's going to live in a charming house with her own carriage, she'll be one of the hidden rulers of Paris. She's as good as a railway engine at forging ahead, a woman like that! Oh, I've often been grateful to you for your harshness!'

'It's enough to make one doubt the virtue of God himself,' said Adeline, whose indignation had dried her tears. 'But no, divine justice must be hovering over her head.'

'You don't know the world, fair lady,' continued Crevel, the great politician, deeply hurt. 'The world, my dear Adeline, loves success. Tell me, does it ever come in search of your sublime virtue, whose price is two hundred thousand francs?'

These words made Madame Hulot shudder and she had another attack of nervous trembling.

She realized that the retired perfumer was taking a despicable revenge on her, as he had done on Hulot. Her heart was sickened with disgust, which made her nerves so tense that her throat contracted and she could not speak.

'Money . . . I still need money,' she said at last.

'I was deeply moved when I saw you there, weeping at my feet,' resumed Crevel, brought back by these words to the Baroness's humiliation. 'Well, perhaps you won't believe me, but if I'd had my wallet with me, it would have been yours. Come now, must you really have that amount?'

On hearing this question, pregnant with two hundred thousand francs, Adeline, lured by the prospect of success held out by Crevel in such a Machiavellian manner, forgot the odious insults of this aristocrat on the cheap. All he wanted was to get to the bottom of Adeline's secrets to laugh over them with Valérie.

'Oh, I'll do anything,' cried the unhappy woman. 'I'll sell myself, Monsieur; I'll become a Valérie, if necessary.'

'You'd find that difficult,' Crevel replied. 'Valérie is the perfect specimen of her kind. My dear little mother, twenty-five years of virtue always repel a man, like a neglected illness. And your virtue has turned very mouldy here, my dear girl. But you'll see how fond I am of you. I'm going to make it possible for you to have your two hundred thousand francs.'

Adeline grasped Crevel's hand, held it, and pressed it to her heart, unable to utter a word, and a tear of joy came into her eyes.

'Oh, hang on a minute! There's work to be done first. I, for my part, enjoy my pleasures; I'm a good sort, without prejudices, and I'll tell you quite plainly how things stand. You want to do as Valérie does, all right. But that's not enough; you need a sucker, a shareholder, a Hulot. I know a hefty retired shopkeeper, a hosier, in fact. He's slow-witted and dull, without an idea in his head. I'm educating him and don't know when he'll be fit to do me credit. My man's a deputy; he's stupid and vain, and the tyranny of some sort of female in a turban in the depths of the provinces has kept him in a state of complete virginity as far as the luxuries and pleasures of Paris are concerned. But Beauvisage (that's his name) is a millionaire and, like me three years ago, my dear girl, he would give a hundred thousand crowns for the love of a real lady. Oh yes,' he said, thinking he had understood correctly a gesture of Adeline's, he's jealous of me, you see. Yes, jealous of my happiness with Madame Marneffe, and the fellow's just the chap to sell a property so that he can be the proprietor of a ...'

'Enough, Monsieur Crevel,' said Madame Hulot, no longer concealing her disgust and letting all her shame appear in her face. 'I'm punished now more than my sin deserved. My conscience, so forcibly silenced by the iron hand of necessity, cries out to me at this last insult that such sacrifices are impossible. I've lost all my pride; I'm not getting very angry with you, as I was the last time. I've received a mortal blow, but I won't say to you, 'Go!' I've lost the right to do so. I offered myself to you like a prostitute. Yes,' she continued, in reply to a gesture of protest, 'I've defiled my hitherto unblemished life with an odious intention. And I've no excuse. I knew that. I deserve all the insults that you're heaping upon me. May God's will be done! If he wishes the death of two beings worthy to go to him, I shall pray for them. If he wishes the humiliation of our family, let us bow under the avenging sword, as the Christians we are. I know how to expiate this momentary shame, which will torment me to the end of my days. It is no longer Madame Hulot who is speaking to you, Monsieur, it is the poor humble sinner, the Christian whose heart will in future contain only one feeling, repentance, and who will be entirely devoted to prayer and charity. I can be only the lowliest of women and the first of penitents because of the enormity of my sin. You have been the instrument of my return to reason, to the voice of God which now speaks in me; I thank you.'

She was trembling with the nervous tremor which, from that moment on, never left her.

Her voice was very gentle, in contrast with the feverish tones of the woman resolved on dishonour in order to save her family. The blood deserted her cheeks, she turned pale, and her eyes were dry.

'In any case, I played my part very badly, didn't I?' she went on, looking at Crevel with the gentleness the martyrs must have shown as they looked at the proconsul. 'True love, the holy and devoted love of a wife, has other pleasures than those which are bought in the market of prostitution. But why talk like this?' she said, reflecting on her words and taking another step forward on the path to perfection. 'It sounds as if I'm being ironical, and I'm not. Forgive me. Perhaps, in any case, it was only myself I wanted to hurt.'

The majesty of virtue with its celestial radiance had swept away this woman's momentary impurity. Resplendent in the beauty that was properly her own, she seemed in Crevel's eyes to have grown taller.

At that moment Adeline was sublime, like the figures symbolic of Religion, upheld by a cross, painted by the early Venetians. But she expressed all the greatness of her own misfortune as well as that of the Catholic Church, to which she turned for refuge like a wounded dove.

Crevel was dazzled, dumbfounded.

'Madame, I am at your service with no strings attached,' he said in a burst of generosity. 'Well, the impossible! . . . I'll do it. I'll deposit some shares in the bank, and in two hours you'll have your money.'

'Oh, God, this is a miracle!' said poor Adeline, falling on her knees.

She uttered a prayer with a fervour which touched Crevel so deeply that when Madame Hulot, her prayer said, rose to her feet, she saw tears in his eyes.

'Be my friend, Monsieur,' she said. 'Your heart is better than your deeds and words. God gave you your heart, but you take your ideas from the world and your passions. Oh, I'll love you dearly,' she cried with an angelic ardour whose expression was a strange contrast to her silly little coquetries.

'Don't go on trembling so,' said Crevel.

'Am I trembling?' asked the Baroness, unaware of the infirmity which had come upon her so suddenly.

'Well, yes, look,' said Crevel, taking Adeline's arm and showing her that she had a nervous tremor. 'Come, Madame,' he continued respectfully. 'Calm yourself; I'm going to the bank.'

'Come back without delay. Think, my friend,' she said, revealing her secrets, 'that it's a question of preventing the suicide of my poor Uncle Fischer, who has been compromised by my husband. Now I can trust you and tell you everything. Oh, if we don't arrive in time, I know the Marshal—he's so sensitive that he wouldn't survive more than a few days.'

'I'm away then,' said Crevel, kissing the Baroness's hand. 'But what's poor old Hulot done?'

'He has robbed the State.'

'Oh, my God! I'll hurry, Madame. I understand, and I admire you.'

Crevel went down on one knee, kissed Madame Hulot's dress, and vanished, saying:

'I'll be back soon.'

90. *Another guitar**

Unfortunately, on the way from the Rue Plumet to get his share certificates from his own house, Crevel had to go by the Rue Vaneau and he could not resist the pleasure of going to see his little duchess.

He still looked upset when he arrived. He went into Valérie's room and found her having her hair done.

She studied Crevel in the mirror and, like all women of her kind, even before knowing anything about it, she was shocked to see that he was under the sway of a strong emotion of which she was not the cause.

'What's the matter, my pet?' she asked Crevel. 'Is this the way to come into your little duchess's room? Even if I weren't still a duchess for you, Monsieur, I'd still be your *little lovey-dovey*, you old monster!'

Crevel replied with a sad smile and indicated Reine.

'Reine, my girl, that's enough for today. I'll finish doing my hair myself. Give me my Chinese housecoat, for *my Monsieur* looks to me as if he's well entangled in *a Chinese puzzle*.'

Reine, a girl with a face pitted like a sieve, who seemed to have been made expressly for Valérie, exchanged a smile with her mistress and brought the housecoat.

Valérie took off her dressing-gown, appeared in her slip, and fitted into her housecoat like an adder under its tuft of grass.

'Madame is at home to no one?'

'What a question!' said Valérie. 'Now, tell me, my big puss, have the left-bank shares slumped?'

'No.'

'You think you're not the father of your little Crevel?'

'What nonsense!' replied Crevel in the tone of a man sure that he was loved.

'Well, I'm nonplussed,' said Madame Marneffe. 'When I have to draw a friend's troubles out of him as one draws corks from champagne bottles, I give up. Go away, you're a . . .'

'It's nothing,' said Crevel. 'I need to raise two hundred thousand francs in two hours.'

'Oh, you'll find them all right. Look, I haven't used the fifty thousand francs we got out of the police report on Hulot, and I can ask Henri for fifty thousand francs.'

'Henri! Always Henri!' cried Crevel.

'And do you think, you fat, budding Machiavelli, that I'll dismiss Henri? Does France disarm her fleet? Henri— why, he's a dagger in its sheath, hanging on a nail. That boy', she said, 'is useful in letting me know if you love me. And you don't love me this morning.'

'I, not love you, Valérie!' said Crevel. 'I love you like a million!'

'That's not enough,' she replied, jumping on to Crevel's lap and putting her two arms round his neck as if she were hanging herself on a hat-peg. 'I want to be loved like ten million, like all the gold in the world, and more. Henri would never stay five minutes without telling me what's bothering him. Come, what's the matter, my big darling? Unload all your little troubles. Tell your little lovey-dovey everything, and smartly.'

And she brushed Crevel's face with her hair and tweaked his nose.

'Can a man have a nose like that and keep a secret from his Vava-lélé-ririe?' she went on.

At *Vava*, the nose was pulled to the right, at *lélé* it went to the left, and at *ririe* she put it back into place.

'Well, I've just seen . . .'

Crevel stopped short and looked at Madame Marneffe.

'Valérie, my treasure, will you promise me on your honour . . . you know, our honour, not to repeat a word of what I'm going to tell you?'

'Agreed, Mayor. I raise my hand like this . . . and my foot.'

She posed in such a way as to strip Crevel from head to heel, as Rabelais put it; she was so amusing, with her superb naked form visible through the mist of fine lawn.

'I've just seen virtue in despair.'

'Is there any virtue in despair?' she asked, shaking her head and folding her arms like Napoleon.

'It's poor Madame Hulot. She must have two hundred thousand francs. If she doesn't get them, the Marshal and Père Fischer will blow their brains out, and since that's a little because of you, my little duchess, I'm going to repair the damage. Oh, she's a saintly woman, I know her, she'll pay back the lot.'

At the mention of Hulot and two hundred thousand francs, Valérie darted a look from beneath her long eyelashes like the flash of a cannon in its smoke.

'What did the old lady do to make you sorry for her? She showed you what? Her . . . her religion?'

'Don't make fun of her, my love. She's a very saintly, noble, and devout woman, who deserves respect.'

'And don't *I* deserve respect?' asked Valérie, with an ominous look.

'I'm not saying you don't, replied Crevel, realizing how much his praise of virtue must hurt Madame Marneffe.

'I'm devout too,' said Valérie, moving away and sitting down in an armchair. 'But I don't make a parade of my religion; I go to church secretly.'

She sat in silence and paid no more attention to Crevel.

Greatly perturbed, Crevel went and stood in front of the chair into which Valérie had retreated, but he found her lost in the thoughts he had so foolishly aroused.

'Valérie, my little angel . . .!'

Profound silence. A rather dubious tear was furtively wiped away.

'One word, my lovey-dovey . . .'

'Monsieur!'

'What are you thinking of, my love?'

'Oh Monsieur Crevel, I'm thinking of the day of my

first communion. How lovely I was! How pure! How saintly and immaculate! Oh, if anyone had come and told my mother, 'Your daughter will be a *slut*; she'll deceive her husband. One day, a police commissioner will find her in a little house; she will sell herself to a Crevel to betray a Hulot, two horrid old men . . .' Oh, it's disgusting! She'd have died before the end of the sentence—she loved me so much, poor woman!'

'Calm down.'

'You don't know how much an adulteress must love a man to silence the remorse that gnaws at her heart. I'm sorry Reine has gone. She would have told you that this morning she found me at prayer with tears in my eyes. You see, Monsieur Crevel, *I* don't scoff at religion. Have you ever heard me say a word against it?'

Crevel made a gesture of denial.

'I don't allow people to talk about it in front of me. I make fun of anything you like: royalty, politics, finance, everything that is sacred in the eyes of the world, judges, marriage, love, young girls, old men. But the Church! . . . But God! . . . Oh, there I draw the line. I know very well that I'm doing wrong, that I'm sacrificing my future to you. And yet you don't even suspect the extent of my love!'

Crevel clasped his hands.

'Oh, you'd have to see right into my heart, to measure the extent of my convictions, to realize all that I'm sacrificing for you! I feel I have in me the stuff of which a Magdalen is made. And see what respect I show to the priests. Look how many presents I make to the Church. My mother brought me up in the Catholic faith and I realize what God is. It is to us sinners that he speaks most awesomely.'

Valérie wiped away two tears that rolled down her cheeks.

Crevel was appalled. Madame Marneffe got up, became intensely excited.

'Calm down, my lovey-dovey. You frighten me!'

Madame Marneffe fell on her knees.

'Oh God! I am not bad at heart,' she said, putting her hands together. 'Deign to rescue your lost sheep. Strike her, wound her to save her from the hands that turn her into an infamous adulteress. She will hide her head against your shoulder. She will return filled with happiness to the fold.'

She got up, and looked at Crevel, and Crevel was afraid of Valérie's blank stare.

'And then, Crevel, do you know? Now and again, I'm afraid. God's justice prevails in this world below as well as in the next. What good can I expect from God? His vengeance comes down on the guilty in all sorts of ways. It takes the form of every kind of misfortune. All the misfortunes which fools cannot explain are punishments. That's what my mother told me on her death-bed, speaking of her old age. But if I were to lose you! . . .' she added, clutching Crevel in a wildly fierce embrace . . .' Oh, I'd die!'

Madame Marneffe released Crevel, knelt again in front of her chair, placed her hands together (and in what a ravishing pose), and recited with remarkable fervour the following prayer:

'And you, Sainte Valérie, my good patron saint, why don't you visit more often the bedside of her who is entrusted to your care? Oh, come this evening as you came this morning to inspire me with good thoughts, and I shall leave the path of wickedness. Like Magdalen, I shall give up false joys, the deceptive glamour of the world, even the man I love so much.'

'My lovey-dovey!' said Crevel.

'No more lovey-dovey, Monsieur!' She turned round with the pride of a virtuous wife and, her eyes wet with tears, she appeared dignified, cold, and indifferent.

'Leave me,' she said, repulsing Crevel. 'What is my duty? To belong to my husband; he is dying. And what am I doing? I deceive him at the brink of the grave. He thinks your son is his. . . . I'm going to tell him the truth and begin by asking his forgiveness before asking for God's. We must part. Goodbye, Monsieur Crevel,' she continued, getting up and offering him an ice-cold hand. 'Goodbye, my friend, we shall meet again only in a better world. You owe a few pleasures to me, very sinful ones, but now I want . . . yes, I shall have your esteem.'

Crevel was weeping bitterly.

'You big idiot!' she cried with a peal of diabolical laughter. 'That's what pious women do to wangle two hundred thousand francs out of you. And you, who talk about the Maréchal de Richelieu, the model for Lovelace,* you let yourself be caught by that well-tried gambit, to use Steinbock's language! *I* could extract sums of two hundred thousand francs out of you if I wanted to, you big fool. Keep your money, then. If you've got a surplus, that surplus belongs to me. If you give two sous to that respectable woman who practises religion because she's 57 years old, we'll never meet again and you can take her as your mistress. You'll come back to me the next day all bruised from her bony caresses and saturated with her tears, her trashy little caps, and her lamentations, which must turn her favours into showers of rain.'

'The fact is,' said Crevel, 'that two hundred thousand francs is a lot of money.'

'They have good appetites, these pious women! Oh, would you believe it, they sell their sermons for more than we get for the rarest and the surest thing on earth, pleasure. . . . And what tales they tell! No—oh, I know them; I've seen some of them at my mother's. They think they can do anything for the Church, for . . . Oh, you should be ashamed, my pet, you who are so little of a giver. For you haven't given me two hundred thousand francs, all told.'

'Oh, but I have,' replied Crevel. 'The little house alone will cost that.'

'So then you have four hundred thousand francs,' she said meditatively.

'No.'

'Well, Monsieur, were you intending to lend that old frump the two hundred thousand for my hotel? That's high treason against your lovey-dovey!'

'But just listen to me.'

'If you were giving that money to some stupid philan-thropic enterprise you'd be looked on as a coming man,' she said, becoming more eloquent, 'and I'd be the first to advise you to do so, for you're too simple to write fat books about politics which would make your reputation. You can't write well enough even to knock up long-winded pamphlets. Like everyone in your position, you might cover your name with glory by placing yourself at the head of some social, moral, national, or anything-at-all organization. Benevolence is not an option any more; it's got no reputation now. Young ex-prisoners who are given a better lot than poor honest devils, that's old hat. For two hundred thousand francs I'd like to see you think up something less simple, something really useful. Then you'd be talked about like Edmé Champion* with his little blue cloak, or a Montyon,* and I'd be proud of you. But to throw two hundred thousand francs into a holy-water basin, to lend them to a religious fanatic deserted by her husband for some reason or other—you can be sure there's always a reason; does anyone desert me?—is a stupidity which, in our time, can only germinate in the brain of an ex-perfumer. It smacks of his shop. Two days later, you wouldn't dare look at yourself in the mirror. Go and deposit the money in the sinking fund; be quick, for I won't let you in here again without the receipt for the amount. Go! And be quick about it, right away!'

She pushed Crevel out of the room by the shoulders, seeing avarice bloom once again on his face.

When the outer door of the flat had closed, she said:

'There's Lisbeth well and truly avenged! What a pity she's at her old Marshal's; what a good laugh we'd have had! So the old lady wants to take the bread from my mouth! *I'll* give her a good shaking up.'

91. *A picture of Marshal Hulot*

As he had to live in a style appropriate to the highest military rank, Marshal Hulot had taken up his quarters in a splendid house in the Rue du Montparnasse, where there were two or three princely establishments.

Although he had rented the whole house, he only occupied the ground floor.

When Lisbeth came to keep house, she wanted to sublet the first floor; that, she said, would pay the whole rent and the Count would then be housed almost for nothing. But the old soldier refused.

For some months the Marshal had been troubled by sad thoughts. He had realized his sister-in-law's financial difficulties and he had an idea that she was in distress, though he could not discover the cause. The old man, who had been so serene and cheerful, became taciturn; he thought that one day his house would be a refuge for Baroness Hulot and her daughter, and he was keeping the first floor for them.

It was so well known that the Comte de Forzheim had only modest means of his own that the Minister of War, the Prince de Wissembourg, had insisted that his old comrade should accept a settling-in grant.

Hulot used this grant to furnish the ground floor, where everything was done befitting his rank, for, as he put it, he did not want a marshal's baton in order to carry it on foot.

Since, under the Empire, the house had belonged to a senator, the ground-floor reception rooms had been decorated with great magnificence, all in white and gold with carved woodwork, and were in a good state of preservation. The Marshal had put in handsome old furniture to match. In the coach-house he kept a carriage with two crossed batons painted on the panels, and he hired horses when he had to go *in fiocchi*,* either to the Ministry or to the Palace, for some ceremony or social occasion.

For thirty years he had had as his servant an old soldier

of 60, whose sister was his cook, so he was able to save about thirty thousand francs, which he added to a little hoard intended for Hortense.

Every day the old man walked from the Rue du Montparnasse to the Rue Plumet by the boulevard. Every pensioner from the Invalides, on seeing him coming, invariably stood to attention and saluted him, and the Marshal would reward each old soldier with a smile.

'Who's that man you stand to attention for?' a young workman asked an old captain from the Invalides one day.

'I'll tell you, my lad,' the officer replied.

And the youngster assumed the attitude of a man resigned to listening to a garrulous old fellow.

'In 1809,' said the pensioner, 'we were defending the flank of the *Grande Armée*, commanded by the Emperor, who was marching on Vienna. We came to a bridge defended by a triple battery of cannons, terraced on a sort of cliff, three redoubts, one above the other, trained on to the bridge. We were under the command of Marshall Masséna.* The man you see there was then Colonel of the Grenadier Guards and I was attached to them. Our columns held one bank of the river, the redoubts were on the other. They attacked the bridge three times, and three times they were driven back. . . . "Go and fetch Hulot," the Marshal said. "Only he and his men can crack that nut." So we came up. The last general, who was withdrawing from the bridge, stopped Hulot under fire to tell him how to tackle the job and he was blocking up the road. "I don't need advice, but room to pass," the General said calmly as he crossed the bridge at the head of his column. And then, rattle bang! Thirty cannons opened fire on us.'

'Oh, my goodness!' cried the workman. 'That must have been responsible for a lot of those crutches!'

'If you'd heard him calmly making that remark, as I did, my lad, you'd bow down to the ground before that man. It's not so well known as the bridge at Arcola,* but perhaps it's even finer. And we advanced on the batteries at full speed with Hulot. All honour to those who fell there,' said the officer, raising his hat. 'The *Kaiserlichs** were bewildered by the attack. So the Emperor made the old man you see there a count. He honoured us all in honouring our leader, and the present lot were quite right to make him a marshal.'

'Long live the Marshal!' said the workman.

'Oh, you can shout as loud as you like; the Marshal's deaf from the sound of the cannon.'

This anecdote may give some idea of the respect with which the old soldiers treated Marshal Hulot, whose steadfast republican views won him the affection of ordinary people in the whole neighbourhood.

It was heartrending to see suffering enter that calm, pure, noble soul. The Baroness could only lie and, with feminine skill, hide the whole dreadful truth from her brother-in-law.

In the course of that disastrous morning, the Marshal, who, like all old men, slept little, had got some enlightenment about his brother's situation from Lisbeth, by promising to marry her as a reward for her indiscretion.

Everyone will appreciate the old maid's pleasure at letting confidences be extracted from her, which, ever since she had entered the house, she had wanted to make to her future husband; for in that way she would make her marriage more certain.

'Your brother is incorrigible,' Lisbeth shouted in the Marshal's good ear.

The Lorraine peasant's strong, clear voice enabled her to talk to the old man. She wore out her lungs in her eagerness to show her future husband that he would never be deaf with her.

'He has had three mistresses,' said the old man, 'and he had an Adeline! Poor Adeline!'

'If you take my advice,' shouted Lisbeth, 'you will use your influence with the Prince de Wissembourg to get an honourable position for my cousin. She'll need it, for the Baron's salary is pledged for three years.'

'I'll go to the Ministry and see the Marshal,' he replied. 'I'll find out what he thinks of my brother and ask for his active patronage for my sister. To find a position worthy of her . . .'

'The Paris Ladies' Charitable Association has formed benevolent societies under the patronage of the Arch-bishop. They need to employ adequately paid inspectors to investigate cases of real need. Duties of that kind would suit my dear Adeline; they would be after her own heart.'

'Send for the horses,' said the Marshal. 'I'm going to dress. I'll go to Neuilly,* if necessary.'

'How he loves her! Am I then to find her always and everywhere in my way?' muttered the Lorraine peasant.

'Lisbeth was already the ruler of the household, but out of the Marshal's sight.

She had intimidated the three servants. She had engaged a personal maid and used her old maid's energy to demand accounts of everything, to pry into everything, and to further her Marshal's well-being in every way.

Lisbeth was as republican as her future husband and so he liked her for her democratic ideas. She flattered him, too, with great skill. And so, for the last two weeks, the Marshal, who was living more comfortably and finding himself looked after like a child by its mother, had come to the conclusion that Lisbeth was the match of his dreams.

'My dear Marshal,' she shouted, going to the steps with him, 'put up the windows. Don't sit in a draught, for my sake.'

The Marshal who had never been coddled, old bachelor that he was, smiled at Lisbeth as he went off, although his heart was aching.

92. *The Prince's dressing-down*

At that very moment Baron Hulot was leaving the War Ministry and on his way to the office of the Maréchal, Prince de Wissembourg, who had sent for him.

Although there was nothing out of the ordinary in the Minister sending for one of his Directors, Hulot had such a bad conscience that he thought there was something cold and forbidding in Mitouflet's face.

'How is the Prince, Mitouflet?' he asked, as he shut his office door and overtook the doorkeeper, who had gone ahead.

'He must have a bone to pick with you, Monsieur le Baron,' replied the doorkeeper, 'for his voice, his look, and his face are set stormy.'

Hulot turned pale and said no more. He went through the hall and the reception rooms and arrived, his heart beating apprehensively, at the Minister's office door.

The Marshal, then aged 70, his hair completely white, his face weather-beaten as is usual with old men of his age, had a striking forehead so broad that the imagination could envisage it as a battlefield.

Beneath that stern, snow-crowned dome, and in the shade of the very pronouncd projection of two overhanging eyebrows, shone eyes of a Napoleonic blue, usually sad and filled with bitter thoughts and regrets.

This rival of Benadotte's* had hoped to end his days on a throne. But those eyes became two flashes of lightning when expressing a strong feeling, and then his usually deep voice rang out stridently. In anger the Prince became a soldier again; he spoke the language of sub-lieutenant Cottin; he spared nothing and nobody. Hulot saw the old lion, his hair straggling like a mane, standing by the fireplace, with his back to the chimney-piece, frowning and with an absent look in his eyes.

'I am here at your command, my Prince,' Hulot said courteously, in an unconcerned tone.

The Marshal gazed fixedly at the Director without saying a word during the whole time he took to walk from the door to within a few steps of him.

This leaden stare was like the eye of God. Hulot could not withstand it; he lowered his eyes in embarrassment.

'He knows everything,' he thought.

'Does your conscience tell you nothing?' asked the Marshal in his deep, grave voice.

'It tells me, my Prince, that I was probably wrong to go

foraging in Algeria without mentioning it to you. At my age and with my tastes, after forty-five years of service, I have no personal fortune. You know the principles of the four hundred elected representatives of France. These gentlemen are envious of anyone in an important position; they have cut ministers' salaries and that tells the whole story. What's the point of asking them for money for an old servant of the State? What can you expect from people who pay legal officials so badly? who pay thirty sous a day to workers in the port of Toulon when it's a physical impossibility for a family to live there on less than forty sous? who never think twice about the atrocity of paying clerks salaries of six hundred or ten or twelve hundred francs in Paris but who want our jobs for themselves when the salary is forty thousand? . . . and who now refuse to return to the Crown a piece of Crown property,* what's more one bought with Louis XVI's money, when they were requested to do so for an impoverished prince? If you had no personal fortune, my Prince, they'd leave you high and dry, like my brother, with nothing but your salary, without remembering that you saved the *Grande Armée*, with me at your side, in the marshy plains of Poland.'

'You have robbed the State; you have put yourself in the position of being liable to be tried in the law-courts like that Treasury official.* And you treat the matter so lightly, Monsieur!'

'But what a difference, Monseigneur!' cried Baron Hulot. 'Have I dipped my hands in a cash-box entrusted to me?'

'When a man in your position commits such infamous crimes, he is doubly guilty if he does them clumsily. You shamefully compromised our high-level administration, which up till now has been the most unblemished in Europe. And that, Monsieur, for two hundred thousand francs and a whore!' said the Marshal in a terrible voice. 'You are a Councillor of State, and the private soldier who sells regimental property is punished with death. Here is a tale that Colonel Pourin of the Second Lancers told me one day. At Saverne, one of his men fell in love with a little Alsatian girl, who wanted a shawl. The hussy made such a fuss that the lancer, poor devil, who was about to be promoted quartermaster after twenty years' service, the pride of the regiment, sold things belonging to his company so that he could give her the shawl. Do you know what this lancer did, Baron d'Ervy? He ground down the glass from a window and ate it, took ill, and died eleven hours later in hospital. As for you, Monsieur, try to die of a stroke so that we can save your honour.'

The Baron looked at the old warrior with haggard eyes, and on seeing Hulot's expression, which showed he was a coward, the Marshal became red with anger and his eyes blazed.

'Would you desert me?' Hulot stammered.

93. *A very short encounter between Marshal Hulot, Comte de Forzheim, and his Excellency, Monseigneur le Maréchal Cottin, Prince de Wissembourg, Duc d'Orfano, Minister of War.*

Just then, Marshal Hulot, learning that his brother and the Minister were alone together, took the liberty of walking in and, as deaf men do, went straight up to the Prince.

'Oh,' shouted the hero of the Polish campaign, 'I know what you've come for, my old comrade, but it's no use.'

'No use?' repeated Marshal Hulot, who had heard only those two words.

'Yes, you've come to speak up for your brother, but do you know what your brother is?'

'My brother?' the deaf man asked.

'Well, he's a damned scoundrel, unworthy of you,' shouted the Marshal.

And in his anger the Marshal's eyes darted those flaming looks which, like Napoleon's, broke men's wills and minds.

'That's a lie, Cottin,' replied Marshal Hulot, who had

turned pale. 'Throw down your baton, as I throw down mine. I am at your service.'

The Prince went straight up to his old comrade, looked him straight in the face, and shouted in his ear as he pressed his hand:

'Are you a man?'

'You shall see.'

'Well, keep a grip on yourself! You have to bear the greatest misfortune that could happen to you.'

The Prince turned round, took a file from his table, and put it in Marshal Hulot's hands, shouting to him:

'Read that!'

The Comte de Forzheim read the following letter which was on the file.

TO HIS EXCELLENCY THE PRESIDENT OF THE COUNCIL
(*Confidential*)

Algiers

'My dear Prince,—We have a very unpleasant business on our hands, as you will see from the enclosed documents.

'Briefly, the matter is this. Baron Hulot d'Ervy sent one of his uncles to the province of O. . . to speculate on the purchases of grain and forage, giving him a storekeeper as an accomplice. The storekeeper confessed in order to enhance his own importance and finally ran away. The public prosecutor dealt with the matter strictly, thinking only two minor officials were involved. But Johann Fischer, your Director-General's uncle, finding himself about to be put on trial, stabbed himself in prison with a nail.

'That would have been the end of it all, if this worthy, honest man, apparently deceived by both his accomplice and his nephew, had not taken it into his head to write to Baron Hulot. His letter, seized by the prosecution, so amazed the Public Prosecutor that he came to see me. It would be such a terrible thing to arrest and try a Councillor of State, a Director-General who has such a long record of good and loyal service (for, after the crossing of the Béresina,* he saved us all by reorganizing the administration), that I had the papers sent to me.

'Must the affair take its course? Or, since the main obvious culprit is dead, should we put an end to the legal proceedings by convicting the storekeeper in his absence?

'The public prosecutor agrees to my sending you the papers, and since Baron Hulot d'Ervy is domiciled in Paris, the prosecution will be within the jurisdiction of your higher court. We have thought up this rather dubious way of getting rid of the problem for the moment.

'Only, my dear Marshal, make a decision quickly. People are already talking far too much about this deplorable business, which would do as much harm to us as it will cause to others, if the complicity of the main culprit, known as yet only to the public prosecutor, the examining magistrate, and myself, should leak out.'

There the paper fell from Marshall Hulot's hands. He looked at his brother and saw there was no point in reading the rest of the papers. But he looked for Johann Fischer's letter and handed it to him after reading it at a glance.

'From the prison at O. . .'

Dear Nephew,—When you read this letter, I shall no longer be alive.

'Don't worry; no evidence will be found against you.

'With me dead, and that Jesuit of a Chardin escaped, the law-suit will be stopped.

'The thought of our Adeline's face, made happy by you, makes death easy for me.

'You no longer need to send the two hundred thousand francs. Goodbye.

'This letter will be delivered to you by a prisoner whom I think I can trust.

JOHANN FISCHER'

'I beg your pardon,' Marshal Hulot said to the Prince de Wissembourg with touching pride.

'Come, don't stand on ceremony with me, Hulot,' the Minister replied, pressing his old friend's hand. 'The poor lancer killed no one but himself,' he said with a thunderous look at Hulot d'Ervy.

'How much did you take?' the Comte de Forzheim asked his brother sternly.

'Two hundred thousand francs.'

'My dear friend,' said the Count, turning to the Minister. 'You will have the two hundred thousand francs within forty-eight hours. It shall never be said that a man bearing the name of Hulot defrauded the State of one sou.'

'What nonsense!' said the Marshal. 'I know where the two hundred thousand francs are and I'll have them returned. Hand in your resignation and apply for your pension,' he continued, tossing a double sheet of foolscap paper to the other side of the table, where the Councillor of State, his legs giving way beneath him, had sat down. 'Your trial would bring shame on all of us, so I've had the permission of the Council of Ministers to take the course of action I'm pursuing. Since you accept life without honour, without my esteem, a life of degradation, you'll have the pension you're entitled to. Only make yourself scarce!'

The Marshal rang,

'Is the clerk Marneffe there?'

'Yes, Monseigneur,' said the doorkeeper.

'Tell him to come in.'

'You and your wife,' exclaimed the Minister, on seeing Marneffe, 'have deliberately ruined the Baron d'Ervy, who is sitting here.'

'I beg your pardon, Monsieur le Ministre. We are very poor. I have only my salary to live on and I have two children; the second one will have been placed in my family by Monsieur le Baron.'

'What a scoundrel he looks,' said the Prince to Marshal Hulot, indicating Marneffe. 'That's enough of this Sganarelle* whining,' he continued. 'You will give back two hundred thousand francs or you will go to Algeria.'

'But, *Monsieur le Ministre*, you don't know my wife. She's gone through the lot. Monsieur le Baron used to invite six people to dinner every day. They spent fifty thousand francs a year at my house.'

'Get out,' said the Minister in the terrible voice that used to give the order to charge in the thick of battle. 'You will receive notice of your transfer in two hours. . . . Go.'

'I prefer to hand in my resignation,' said Marneffe insolently, 'for it's too much to be in my shoes and beaten into the bargain. *I* wouldn't be satisfied in that situation.'

And he left the room.

'What an impudent rascal,' said the Prince.

Marshal Hulot, who had remained standing, motionless and deathly pale, looking surreptitiously at his brother, went over to the Prince, took his hand and said again:

'In forty-eight hours the material loss will be made good, but as for honour! Goodbye, Marshal. It's the last blow that kills. Yes, it will kill me,' he murmured.

'Why the devil did you have to come this morning?' returned the Prince, deeply moved.

'I came on behalf of his wife,' replied the Count, pointing to Hector. 'She is destitute, now more than ever.'

'He has his pension,'

'It's pledged to a money-lender.'

'He must be possessed by the devil,' said the Prince, shrugging his shoulders. 'What philtre do such women make you swallow to deprive you of your wits?' he asked Hulot d'Ervy. 'How could you, you who know the meticulous care with which the French administration writes down everything, records everything, gets through reams of paper to note the receipt or expenditure of a few centimes, you who used to deplore the requirement of hundreds of signatures for trifles, to free a soldier, to buy curry-combs, how could you possibly hope to conceal a theft for long? And what about the newspapers? and the people who're jealous of you? and the people who would like to steal? Do these women deprive you of common sense? Do they put blinkers on your eyes? Or are you made differently from the rest of us? You should have left government service the moment you ceased to be a man and became a slave to your temperament. If you add such follies to your crime, you'll end up . . . I don't want to say where.'

'Promise me to look after her, Cottin,' said the Comte de Forzheim, who heard nothing and was thinking only of his sister-in-law.

'Set your mind at ease,' said the Minister.

'Well, thank you and goodbye. Come, Monsieur,' he said to his brother.

The Prince looked, apparently calmly, at the two brothers, so different in their attitude, build, and character, the brave man and the coward, the self-indulgent and the disciplined, the honest man and the speculator, and he said to himself:

'That coward will not know how to die, but my poor Hulot, the soul of integrity, has death in his knapsack.'

He sat down in his chair and resumed reading the despatches from Africa with a gesture which revealed both a military commander's self-control and the profound pity inspired by the sight of battlefields; for in reality, no men are more humane than soldiers, who appear to be so tough and whose familiarity with war gives them that impassive firmness, so essential on the battlefield.

94. *A theory about press reports*

The next day, several newspapers contained, under various headings, the following items:

'M. le Baron Hulot d'Ervy has just sent in his resignation. The irregularities in the accounts of the Algerian administration, which have come to light with the death and flight of two officials, have a bearing on the decision of this highly placed administrator. On learning of the crimes committed by employees, in whom, unfortunately, he had placed his trust, Monsieur le Baron Hulot had a stroke when he was still in the Minister's office.

M. Hulot d'Ervy, the Marshal's brother, has had forty-five years' service. This decision, which he has been urged in vain to reconsider, has been regretted by all those who know M. Hulot, whose personal qualities are equal to his talents as an administrator. No one has forgotten the devotion of the chief Commissary of the Imperial Guard at Warsaw, nor the extraordinary energy with which he organized the various supply services of the army hastily raised by Napoleon in 1815.

Yet another of the glorious figures of the Imperial era is about to leave the stage. Since 1830, M. le Baron Hulot has been one of the indispensable luminaries in the Council of State and the War Ministry.'

'ALGIERS. The affair known as the forage case, to which some newspapers have attached an absurd importance, has been brought to an end by the death of the chief culprit. The man Johann Wisch killed himself in prison and his accomplice has fled. But he will be tried in default.

Wisch, a former army contractor, was an honest man with a good reputation; he could not bear the thought of being duped by one Chardin, the absconding storekeeper.'

And amongst the Paris news items could be read the following:

'In order to prevent any future irregularity, M. le Maréchal, Minister of War, has decided to institute a Commissariat department in Africa. An office-manager, M. Marneffe, is tipped to be the head of this organization.'

'The succession to Baron Hulot arouses many ambitions. It is said that his Directorship has been offered to M. le Comte Martial de la Roche-Hugon, a deputy and brother-in-law of M. le Comte de Rastignac. M. Massol, Master of Appeals, will be appointed Councillor of State, and M. Claude Vignon Master of Appeals.'

Of all kinds of false rumours, the most dangerous for opposition newspapers is the official one. However shrewd journalists may be, they are at times, wittingly or unwittingly, the dupes of those among them who, like Claude Vignon, have risen from the newspaper world to the high regions of power.

It takes a newspaper man to get the better of a newspaper.

So, to misquote Voltaire, we may say:

'The Paris news item is not what a deluded people thinks.'*

95. *The brother's dressing-down*

Marshal Hulot drove home with his brother, who sat in the front seat of the carriage, respectfully leaving the inside to his older brother.

The two brothers did not exchange a word. Hector was shattered. The Marshal was absorbed in his thoughts, like a man who is summoning up all his strength and concentrating it in order to support a crushing weight.

When they reached his house, he led his brother to his study without saying a word but with a commanding gesture.

The Emperor Napoleon had given the Count a magnificent pair of pistols made at Versailles; on the case was engraved the inscription: *Presented by the Emperor Napoleon to General Hulot*. He took it out of the desk where he kept it, indicated it to his brother, and said:

'There's your medicine.'

Lisbeth, who was looking through the half-open door, hurried to the carriage and ordered the coachman to drive at full speed to the Rue Plumet.

In about twenty minutes she brought back the Baroness, whom she had told of the Marshal's threat to his brother.

Without looking at his brother, the Count rang for his servant, the old soldier who had served him for thirty years.

'Beaupied,' he said, 'fetch my lawyer, Count Steinbock, my niece Hortense, and the Treasury stockbroker. It's now half past ten and I must have them all here by twelve. Take cabs and go *faster than that* . . .' he said, reverting to a Republican expression that was often on his lips in former times.

And he assumed the fierce expression which kept his soldiers in order when he was searching the thickets of Brittany in 1799 (see *Les Chouans*).*

'You will be obeyed, Marshal,' said Beaupied, giving a military salute.

Without paying any attention to his brother, the old man went back into his study, took a key that was concealed in a desk, and opened a malachite box mounted on steel, a gift from the Emperor Alexander.

On the Emperor Napoleon's orders, General Hulot had gone to return to the Russian Emperor personal property captured at the Battle of Dresden, in exchange for which Napoleon was hoping to get Vandamme.*

The Czar rewarded General Hulot magnificently by

giving him the malachite box, and told him that he hoped one day to extend the same courtesy to the Emperor of the French. But he kept Vandamme.

The Imperial Arms of Russia were inlaid in gold on the lid of the box, which was ornamented entirely with gold. The Marshal counted out the bank notes and the gold it contained. He had a hundred and fifty-two thousand francs. He made a gesture expressing his satisfaction.

At that moment Madame Hulot came in, in a state fit to melt the heart even of politically biased judges.

She threw herself into Hector's arms, looking frantically from the box of pistols to the Marshal.

'What have you against your brother? What has my husband done to you?' she said in such ringing tones that the Marshal heard her.

'He has dishonoured us all,' replied the old soldier of the Republic, with an effort that re-opened one of his wounds. 'He has robbed the State. He has made my name hateful to me; he makes me want to die; he has killed me. I have only enough strength left to make restitution. I have been humiliated before the Condé* of the Republic, before the man I esteem above all others and whom, unjustly, I accused of lying, the Prince de Wissembourg. Is *that* nothing? That's the state of his account with his country!'

He wiped away a tear.

'And now for his family,' he continued. 'He snatches from you the bread I was saving for you, the fruit of thirty years' savings, the hoard acquired from the privations of an old soldier. That's what I was intending for you,' he said, pointing to the bank notes. 'He has killed his Uncle Fischer, a noble and worthy son of Alsace, who could not, as he did, endure the thought of a stain upon his peasant name. Above all, God in his wonderful mercy allowed him to choose the most angelic of women. He had the incredible good fortune to marry an Adeline, but he has betrayed her, filled her cup with sorrows. He has left her for whores, street-walkers, dancing-girls, and actresses, for Cadines, Joséphas, and Marneffes. And this is the man whom I regarded as my son, my pride. Go, unhappy creature, if you can accept the disgraceful life you have made for yourself. Leave my house! As for me, I haven't the strength to curse a brother I've loved so much. I'm as weak, as far as he is concerned, as you are, Adeline. But let him never come into my presence again. I forbid him to attend my funeral, to follow my coffin. Let him bear the shame of his crime, even if he feels no remorse.'

The Marshal, who had turned deadly pale, dropped on to the couch in his study, exhausted by this solemn speech.

And for the first time in his life, perhaps, two tears fell from his eyes and trickled down his cheeks.

'Poor Uncle Fischer!' exclaimed Lisbeth, putting a hand-kerchief to her eyes.

'Brother,' said Adeline, kneeling down in front of the Marshal. 'Live for my sake! Help me in the work I shall undertake of reconciling Hector to life, of making him atone for his sins.'

'Him!' said the Marshal. 'If he lives, he's not come to the end of his crimes. A man who failed to appreciate an Adeline, and who has extinguished in his heart the feelings of a true republican, the love of family, of country, and of the poor that I tried to inculcate in him, that man is a monster, a swine. Take him away, if you still love him, for I hear a voice within me, crying to me to load my pistols and blow his brains out. By killing him, I'd save you all and I'd save him from himself.'

The old man got up with such a terrifying gesture that poor Adeline cried:

'Come, Hector!'

She gripped hold of her husband, led him away, and left the house, dragging the Baron along with her; he was in such a sorry state that she had to put him in a cab to convey him to the Rue Plumet, where he took to his bed.

Completely prostrated, he stayed there several days, refusing all food and not saying a word.

By dint of tears, Adeline persuaded him to swallow some broth. She watched over him, sitting by his bedside, and of all the feelings that had once filled her heart, there remained only a profound pity.

96. *A fine funeral*

At half past twelve, Lisbeth showed the lawyer and Count Steinbock into her dear Marshal's study; she was so alarmed at the changes that were taking place in him that she had stayed there with him.

'Monsieur le Comte,' said the Marshal, 'I request you to sign the authorization required by my niece to sell a share certificate of which, at present, she possesses only the capital. Mademoiselle Fischer, you will agree to this sale by renouncing your entitlement to the interest.'

'Yes, dear Count,' said Lisbeth without hesitating.

'Good, my dear,' replied the old soldier. 'I hope to live long enough to reward you. I did not doubt you; you are a true republican, a daughter of the people.'

He took the old maid's hand and kissed it.

'Monsieur Hannequin,' he said to the lawyer, 'draw up the necessary document in the form of a power of attorney and let me have it between now and two o'clock, so that the stock can be sold on the stock exchange today. My niece, the Countess, holds the title. She will be here presently. She will sign the document when you bring it, and so will Mademoiselle. Monsieur le Comte will go back with you to sign it in your office.'

The artist, at a sign from Lisbeth, bowed respectfully to the Marshal and left the room.

The next day, at ten in the morning, the Comte de Forzheim sent in his name to the Prince de Wissembourg and was admitted immediately.

'Well, my dear Hulot,' said Marshal Cottin, holding out the newspapers to his old friend. 'As you see, we have saved appearances. Read these.'

Marshal Hulot put the papers on his old comrade's desk and handed him two hundred thousand francs.

'Here is the amount my brother took from the State,' he said.

'But this is crazy,' cried the Minister. 'We can't possibly

arrange such a restitution,' he added, speaking into the ear-trumpet the Marshal offered him. 'We'd have to admit your brother's peculations and we've done everything possible to conceal them.'

'Do what you like with the money, but I don't want a farthing stolen from State funds to be in the Hulot family's fortune,' said the Count.

'I'll seek the King's orders on the matter. Let's say no more about it,' replied the Minister, realizing the impossibility of overcoming the old man's sublime obstinacy.

'Goodbye, Cottin,' said the old man, taking the Prince de Wissembourg's hand. 'I feel as if my heart were frozen.'

Then, after taking a step towards the door, he turned round and looked at the Prince, whom he saw deeply moved; he opened his arms to him, and the Prince and the Marshal embraced.

'I feel as if I were saying goodbye to the whole *Grande Armée* in your person.'

'Goodbye, then, my good old comrade,' said the Minister.

'Yes, goodbye, for I'm going where all the old soldiers we have mourned have gone.'

At that moment Claude Vignon came in.

The two old remnants of the Napoleonic army gravely saluted each other, banishing all traces of emotion.

'You must have been pleased with the newspapers, my Prince,' said the future Master of Appeals. 'I managed things so that the Opposition sheets believed they were publishing our secrets.'

'Unfortunately, it's all of no use,' replied the Minister, looking at the Marshal as he left through the reception room. 'I've just said a last farewell which has caused me great pain. Marshal Hulot hasn't three days to live; I saw that clearly yesterday. That man, of perfect integrity, a man whom even the bullets respected in spite of his daring ... look ... in that chair ... he received his death-blow, and at my hand, from a piece of paper. Ring and order my carriage. I'm going to Neuilly,'* he said, putting the two hundred thousand francs away in his ministerial briefcase.

Despite Lisbeth's care, three days later the Marshal was dead.

Such men are the pride of the causes they have espoused.

For the Republicans, the Marshal was the ideal of patriotism, and so they all attended his funeral, which was followed by a huge crowd. The Army, the Government, the Court, ordinary people, everybody came to pay homage to his noble virtue, his perfect integrity, and his unsullied renown.

It's not just anyone who has ordinary people at his funeral.

These funeral ceremonies were marked by one of those manifesations of delicacy, good taste, and feeling which now and then recall the virtues and the glory of the French nobility.

For, walking behind the Marshal's coffin, could be seen the old Marquis de Montauran, the brother of the man who, during the Chouan uprising* of 1799, had been the opponent—the unsuccessful opponent—of Hulot. The Marquis, as he lay dying from the bullets of the Blues, had entrusted the interests of his young brother to the soldier of the Republic (see *Les Chouans*). Hulot had carried out the dying nobleman's verbal testament so conscientiously that he succeeded in saving the property of the young man, who was at that time an émigré.

Thus the soldier who nine years earlier had conquered Madame* was not denied the homage of the old French aristocracy.

This death, which occurred four days before the last publication of her marriage banns, was for Lisbeth the thunderbolt which burns up the harvest together with the barn in which it has been stored.

As often happens, the Lorraine peasant had succeeded only too well. The Marshal had died from the blows inflicted on his family by her and Madame Marneffe. The old maid's hatred, which seemed to be assuaged by success, was increased by the disappointment of all her hopes.

Lisbeth went to Madame Marneffe's and wept with rage;

for she was without a home, the Marshal having restricted his tenancy to his lifetime.

To console Valérie's friend, Crevel took charge of her savings and amply increased them; he invested the capital at 5 per cent in Célestine's name, the interest to be paid to Lisbeth.

Thanks to this transaction, Lisbeth had an annuity of two thousand francs.

When the inventory of the Marshal's assets was made, a note was found for his sister-in-law, his niece Hortense, and his nephew Victorin, bidding them pay, between the three of them, an annuity of twelve hundred francs to Mademoiselle Lisbeth Fischer, the woman who was to have been his wife.

97. *Departure of the prodigal father*

Seeing that the Baron was hovering between life and death, Adeline managed to conceal the Marshal's death from him for some days. But Lisbeth came in, wearing mourning, and the fatal truth was disclosed to him eleven days after the funeral.

This terrible blow restored the sick man's energy; he got up from his bed and found his whole family, wearing black, together in the drawing-room. They fell silent when he appeared.

In a fortnight Hector, who had become as thin as a ghost, appeared before his family as a shadow of his former self.

'We must come to a decision,' he said in a faint voice, sitting down in an armchair and looking round at the family group from which Crevel and Steinbock were missing.

'We can't stay here any longer,' Hortense was saying just as her father came in. 'The rent is too high.'

'As far as accommodation is concerned,' said Victorin, breaking the painful silence, 'I can offer *my mother . . .*'

On hearing these words, which seemed to exclude him,

the Baron raised his eyes, which had been gazing at the flowers on the carpet without seeing them, and gave the lawyer a wretched look.

A father's rights are always so sacred, even when he has behaved shamefully and been stripped of his honour, that Victorin stopped short.

'Your mother . . .', the Baron repeated. 'You are right, my son.'

'The rooms above ours, in our wing,' said Célestine, completing her husband's sentence.

'Am I a nuisance to you, my children?' asked the Baron, with the gentleness of a man condemned by his own conscience. 'Oh, don't worry about the future. You won't need to complain of your father any more; you won't see him again till the day you no longer have to blush for him.'

He took Hortense in his arms and kissed her forehead. He opened his arms to his son, who threw himself into them despairingly, guessing his father's intentions. The Baron motioned to Lisbeth, who came up to him; he kissed her brow.

Then he retreated to his room, where Adeline, in a state of acute anxiety, followed him.

'My brother was right, Adeline,' he said, taking her hand. 'I am unworthy of family life. I didn't dare bless my poor children except in my heart; their behaviour has been superb. Tell them that all I could do was to embrace them, for coming from a dishonoured man, from a father who has been the murderer and scourge of his family, instead of being its pride and protector, a blessing might be disastrous. But I shall bless them from afar, every day. As for you, God alone, for he is all-powerful, can reward you as you deserve. I ask your forgiveness,' he said, kneeling before his wife, taking her hands and drenching them with tears.

'Hector! Hector! You have sinned greatly, but divine pity is infinite and you can make amends for everything by staying with me. Rise up with Christian feeling in your heart. I am your wife and not your judge. I belong to you; do what you like with me; take me with you wherever you go. I feel within me the strength to console you, to make life bearable for you by the power of my love, care, and respect. Our children are settled; they don't need me any more. Let me try to be your amusement, your entertainment. Let me share the hardships of your exile, of your poverty, to lighten them. I'll always be of some use, even if only to spare you the expense of a servant.'

'Do you forgive me, my dear, beloved Adeline?'

'Yes, my dear, but get up.'

'Well, with your forgiveness, I'll be able to live,' he continued, getting up. 'I went back into our bedroom so that our children shouldn't witness their father's humiliation. Oh, to see every day, in front of their eyes, a father as criminal as I am, there's something dreadful about that which degrades paternal authority and destroys the family. So I can't stay amongst you. I'm leaving you, to spare you the odious spectacle of a father devoid of dignity. Don't resist my departure, Adeline. To do so would be for you yourself to load the pistol with which I'd blow out my brains. And don't follow me into my retreat; you would deprive me of my only remaining source of strength, that of remorse.'

Hector's determined tones reduced the half-fainting Adeline to silence.

The Baroness, who was so great in the midst of so many disasters, drew her courage from her close union with her husband, for she saw him as returned to her; she envisaged the sublime mision of consoling him, of returning him to family life, reconciling him with himself.

'Do you want to let me die, then, of despair, anxiety, and worry, Hector?' she said, seeing the source of her strength about to be taken from her.

'I'll come back to you, my angel descended from heaven especially for me. I'll return, if not rich, at least in comfortable circumstances. Listen, my dear Adeline. I can't stay here, for a host of reasons. First of all, my pension, which will be six thousand francs, is pledged for four years, so that I have nothing. And that's not all. I'm going to be in danger of arrest in a few days because of bills held by

Vauvinet. So I must stay away until my son, with whom I'll leave precise instructions, has redeemed them. My disappearance will make that transaction much easier. When my retirement pension is free of liability, when Vauvinet is paid, I'll come back to you. You would give away the secret of my hiding-place. Don't worry, Adeline, don't cry. It'll only be for a month.'

'Where will you go? What will you do? What will become of you? Who will look after you, for you're no longer young? Let me disappear with you; we'll go abroad,' she said.

'Well, we'll see.' he replied.

The Baron rang and ordered Mariette to collect all his things and pack them quickly and secretly.

Then, after kissing his wife with an effusive affection to which she was unaccustomed, he begged her to leave him alone for a moment to write out the instructions Victorin needed, promising not to leave the house till nightfall, and not without her.

As soon as the Baroness had returned to the drawing-room, the wily old man went through the dressing-room into the hall and left the house, giving Mariette a piece of paper on which he had written:

'Send on my baggage by rail to Corbeil, addressed to Monsieur Hector, bureau restant, Corbeil.'

The Baron was already driving across Paris in a cab, when Mariette came to show the Baroness the note, saying that Monsieur had just gone out.

Adeline rushed into the bedroom, trembling more than ever. Her children heard a piercing shriek and followed her in alarm. They lifted up the Baroness, who had fainted, and had to put her to bed; for she was attacked by a nervous fever which kept her for a month suspended between life and death.

'Where is he? were the only words that could be got out of her.

Victorin's inquiries were fruitless.

And this is why.

98. *In which Josépha reappears*

The Baron had himself driven to the Place du Palais Royal. He had regained all his mental agility in order to carry out a plan thought out during the days he had stayed in bed overwhelmed with distress and grief, and having crossed the Palais Royal he hired a splendid carriage in the Rue Joquelet.

Following the order he had been given, the coachman turned into the Rue de la Ville l'Évêque and into the court-yard of Josépha's house, whose gates were opened for this magnificent carriage at the coachman's shout.

Josépha, prompted by curiosity, looked to see who was there. Her footman told her that an invalid old man, unable to leave his carriage, begged her to come down for a moment.

'Josépha, it's me!'

The famous singer recognized her Hulot only by his voice.

'Why, it's you! My poor old fellow! My word, you look like one of those twenty-franc pieces, clipped by German Jews, that money-changers won't take.'

'Alas, yes,' replied Hulot. 'I've been at death's door. But you, you are still beautiful! Are you kind as well?'

'That depends; everything is relative,' she said.

'Listen,' continued Hulot. 'Can you put me up in a servant's room in the attic for a few days? I'm absolutely broke, without hope, without bread, without a pension, without a wife, without children, without a roof over my head, without honour, without courage, without a friend, and worst of all, liable to be arrested for non-payment of bills of exchange.'

'Poor old chap! That's a lot of withouts! Are you without breeches—a *sans-culotte*—as well?'

'You're making fun of me; I'm done for!' exclaimed the Baron. 'Yet I was counting on you, as Gourville* did on Ninon.'

'Was it a society lady, as people say, who was responsible for the state you're in?' asked Josépha. 'Those wenches know better than we do how to pluck the turkey. Oh, you look like a carcass that's been picked clean by the crows. I can see the daylight through you!'

'There's no time to waste, Josépha!'

'Come in, old boy. I'm on my own and my servants don't know you. Dismiss your carriage. Is it paid for?'

'Yes,' said the Baron getting down leaning on Josépha's arm.

'If you like, you can say you're my father,' said the singer, touched by pity.

She sat Hulot down in the magnificent drawing-room where he had last seen her.

'Is it true, old boy, that you've killed your brother and your uncle, ruined your family, mortgaged your children's house up to the hilt, and embezzled Government funds in Africa, for the benefit of the princess?'

The Baron bowed his head sadly.

'Well, I like that!' exclaimed Josépha, getting up full of enthusiasm. 'That's a wholesale *conflagration*. It's Sardan-apalus!* It's grand! It's perfect! You may be a rotter but you have a heart. Personally, I prefer a spendthrift like you, who's crazy about women, to those cold, soulless bankers who are supposed to be virtuous but who ruin thousands of families with their railways that are gold for them but iron for their dupes. You've ruined only your own family; you've affected only yourself. And then, you have an excuse, both physical and moral.'

And striking a tragic pose, she recited:

'*C'est Vénus tout entière à sa proie attachée.*' *

'And there you are!' she added, with a pirouette.

Hulot found his sins absolved by vice; vice smiled at him from the midst of its unbridled luxury. There, as for a jury, the magnitude of the crimes was an extenuating circumstance.

'Is your society lady pretty, at least?' asked the singer, trying, as her first act of charity, to distract Hulot, whose grief went to her heart.

'Indeed, nearly as pretty as you!' replied the Baron tactfully.

'And . . . game for anything, so they say? What did she do for you then? Is she more amusing than me?'

'Let's talk no more about her,' said Hulot.

'They say she's ensnared my Crevel, young Steinbock, and a magnificent Brazilian.'

'That's quite likely.'

'She's living in a house Crevel gave her, that's as pretty as this one. That hussy, she's my major-domo; she finishes off the men I've had first go at. And that's why I'm so curious to know what she's like, old man. I caught a glimpse of her in a carriage in the Bois de Boulogne, but only from a distance. . . . Carabine told me she's a consummate gold-digger. She's trying to eat up Crevel, but she'll only be able to nibble at him. Crevel's a *skinflint*, an amiable skinflint who always says *yes* but does only what he wants. He's vain, he's ardent, but his money's cold. Fellows of that sort are good only for a thousand to three thousand francs a month, but they draw back at any big expenditure, like donkeys at a river. It's not like you, old boy; you're a man of passion; you could be induced to sell your country! So you see, I'm ready to do anything for you. You're my father; you gave me my start in life. It's a sacred duty. What do you need? Do you want a hundred thousand francs? I'll work myself to death to get them for you. As for giving you board and lodging, that's nothing. Your place will be set here every day. You can have a nice room on the second floor and you'll get a hundred crowns a month pocket-money.'

The Baron, moved by this welcome, showed a final spark of noble feeling.

'No, my dear, no, I didn't come here for you to keep me,' he said.

'At your age, it's quite a triumph,' she said.

'Here's what I want, child. Your Duc d'Hérouville has huge estates in Normandy and I'd like to be his manager under the name of Thoul. I'm capable and honest, for a man's taking money from his government doesn't mean that he'll steal from a cash-box.'

'I'm not so sure,' said Josépha. 'He who's drunk once will drink again.'

'In fact, all I want is to live incognito for three years.'

'That can be arranged in a moment, this evening, after dinner,' said Josépha. 'I've only to ask. The Duke would marry me if I were willing, but I have his money and I want more than that . . . I want his esteem. He's a duke of the old school. He's as great as Louis XIV and Napoleon put together, although he's a dwarf. And then I've done the same for him as Schontz* did for Rochefide: thanks to my advice, he's just gained two million. But listen to me, old chap. I know you; you're fond of women, and once you're there you'll run after the little Norman girls, who are fine lasses. You'll get your bones broken by the lads or the fathers, and the Duke will be forced to give you the sack. Can't *I see*, by the light in your eye when you look at me, that the *young man* within you isn't dead yet, as Fénélon* said. That job wouldn't do for you. You can't break with Paris and us girls just at will, you see. You'd die of boredom at Hérouville.'

'What's to become of me?' asked the Baron, 'for I only want to stay with you long enough to reach a decision.'

'Well, would you like me to fix you up according to my ideas? Listen, you old stoker!'

99. *A peg to hang on*

'You can't live without women. That makes up for everything. At the foot of la Courtille, Rue Saint-Maur-du-Temple, I know a poor family which has a treasure: a little girl, even prettier than I was at 16. Oh, there's a glint in your eye already! She works sixteen hours a day embroidering luxury materials for silk-merchants, and she earns sixteen sous a day, one sou an hour, a pittance. And, like the Irish, she lives on potatoes, but fried in rat fat, with bread five times a week. She drinks Ourcq water* out of the town pipes, because Seine water is too dear. And she can't set up her own business, because she hasn't got six or seven thousand francs. She would commit a *hundred* horrors to get seven or eight thousand francs. Your wife and family bore you, don't they? Besides, one can't put up with being a nobody where one used to be worshipped like a god. A penniless, dishonourd father can only be stuffed and put in a glass case.'

The Baron could not help smiling at this outrageous flippancy.

'Well, little Bijou is coming tomorrow to bring me an embroidered housecoat, a beauty. They've spent six months working at it; no one else will have material like that. Bijou is fond of me because I give her nice titbits and my old dresses. Then I send the family vouchers for bread, wood, and meat, and they would break anyone's shins for me if I wanted them to. I try to do a little good. Oh, I know what I suffered when I was hungry! Bijou has poured out her little secrets into my heart. There's the makings of a dancer at the Ambigu-Comique* in that little girl. Bijou dreams of wearing beautiful dresses like mine and, above all, of riding in a carriage. I'll say to her, "Little one, would you like a gentleman of . . ." *But how old are you?*' she asked, interrupting herself. 'Seventy-two?'

'I'm ageless now!'

'"Would you like a gentleman of 72?", I'll say to her, "very well turned out, who doesn't take snuff, sound as a bell, who's as good as a young man? You'll get married to him in the thirteenth district* and he'll be very nice to you. He'll give you seven thousand francs to set up your own business. He'll furnish a flat for you all in mahogany, and then if you're good he'll take you to the theatre sometimes. He'll give you a hundred francs a month for yourself and fifty francs for household expenses." I know Bijou; she's just as I was at 14. I jumped for joy when that ghastly Crevel made me those same appalling propositions. Well, old man, you'll be stowed away there for three years. She's well-behaved and honest, and she'll retain her illusions for three or four years, not more.'

Hulot did not hesitate. He had made up his mind to refuse. But to show his gratitude to the kind-hearted, good-natured singer, who was doing good according to her lights, he appeared to hesitate between vice and virtue.

'Goodness me! You're as cold as the pavement in December,' she went on, in surprise. 'Come now, you'll be giving happiness to a whole family, made up of a tottering grandfather, a mother who's wearing herself out with work, and two sisters, one very ugly, who between them earn thirty-two sous and ruin their eyesight in the process. That makes up for the distress you've caused in your own home. You can redeem your sins and have a good time like a lorette at Mabille.'*

To put an end to this temptation, Hulot went through the motions of counting out money.

'Don't worry about ways and means,' resumed Josépha. 'My Duke will lend you ten thousand francs: six thousand for an embroidery business in Bijou's name, three thousand for furniture. And every three months you'll find a note of hand for six hundred and fifty francs. When you get your pension back, you'll give the Duke back that seventeen thousand francs. Meanwhile you'll be as happy as a sand-boy, and buried in a hole where the police can't find you. You'll wear a big beaver coat and you'll look like a well-off householder of the district. Call yourself Thoul if you fancy. I'll tell Bijou you're a bankrupt uncle of mine from Germany and you'll be cosseted like a god. How about it, Papa? Who knows? Perhaps you'll regret nothing. If by chance you're bored, keep some of your smart togs and you could come here, invite yourself to dinner, and spend the evening.'

'But I wanted to become a virtuous and orderly character! Look, get me a loan of twenty thousand francs, and I'll off to America to make my fortune, like my friend d'Aiglemont* when Nucingen ruined him.'

'You!' cried Josépha. 'Leave morals to grocers, to ordinary clodhoppers, to French citizens who have nothing but their virtue to distinguish them. You were born to be something better than a mug. You are as a man what I am as a woman, a rogue of genius.'

'I'll sleep on it. We'll talk of all this tomorrow.'

'You'll have dinner with the Duke. My d'Hérouville will receive you as courteously as if you had saved the State, and you can make up your mind tomorrow. Come on, cheer up, old man. Life's like a suit of clothes. when it's dirty, we brush it; when it's torn, we mend it. But we stay clothed as best we can.'

This philosophy of vice and her good spirits dissipated Hulot's burning sorrows.

At noon the next day, after a delicious lunch, there appeared before Hulot's eyes one of those living master-pieces that only Paris in the whole world can produce; for only there is the continual concubinage of luxury and poverty, of vice and virtue, of repressed desire and recur-rent temptation, which makes the town the successor to Nineveh, Babylon, and Imperial Rome.

Mademoiselle Olympe Bijou, a young girl of 16 had the sublime face that Raphael painted for his Virgins. Her innocent eyes were saddened by excessive work, dark, dreamy eyes with long lashes, their natural moisture dried up by wearing, nightly toil, eyes dulled by fatigue. But she had a complexion like fine porcelain, of an almost unhealthy pallor, and her mouth was like a half-open pomegranate. She had a heaving bosom, a rounded figure, pretty hands, remarkably white teeth, and luxuriant black hair. All this beauty was done up in cotton at seventy-five francs a meter, trimmed with an embroidered collar, mounted on leather shoes without nails, and ornamented with gloves at twenty-nine sous.

The child, unconscious of her worth, had put on her best clothes to come to the fine lady's house. The Baron, gripped once more by the claws of sensuality, felt all his life flowing out through his eyes. He forgot everything at the sight of this sublime creature.

He was like the hunter who espies game; even in an emperor's presence, he takes aim at it.

'And she's guaranteed brand-new, virtuous with nothing

to eat. That's Paris. That's what I was like,' Josépha whispered to him.

'Agreed,' replied the old man, getting up and rubbing his hands.

When Olympe Bijou had gone, Josépha looked at the Baron mischievously.

'If you don't want trouble, Papa, be as strict as a judge on the bench. Keep a tight rein on the child; be a Bartholo.* Beware of the Augustes, the Hippolytes, the Nestors, the Victors,* of all the *ors*.* Damn it all! Once she's properly clothed and fed, if she raises her head, you'll be led by the nose like a Russian. I'll see about getting rooms ready for you. The Duke does things handsomely. He'll lend you, that is to say give you, ten thousand francs. He'll deposit eight thousand with his lawyer, who'll be instructed to pay you six hundred francs every quarter, for I fear you'll squander it. Aren't I nice!'

'Adorable!'

Ten days after Hector had deserted his family they were gathered all in tears round Adeline, who was lying in bed at death's door, and was saying in a faint voice, 'What is he doing?'

Under the name of Thoul, he was by then living with Olympe as head of an embroidery business with the unusual name of Thoul and Bijou.

100. *The Marshal's legacy*

The misfortune that implacably dogged his family gave Victorin the last touch that perfects or demoralizes a man. He was perfected. In the great storms of life we imitate the sea-captains who, in a hurricane, lighten the ship by throwing heavy cargo overboard.

The lawyer lost his personal arrogance, his obvious self-assurance, and his oratorical pomposity. In short, he became as a man what his mother was as a woman. He resolved to make the best of his Célestine, who, to be sure, was not the realization of his dreams, and he adopted a sound view of life, appreciating that its universal law obliges us to put up with the *less than perfect* in everything.

He vowed then to fulfil all his duties, so appalled was he by his father's behaviour. These feelings were reinforced at his mother's bedside on the day that her life ceased to be in danger.

This first stroke of good fortune did not come alone.

Claude Vignon, who came every day on behalf of the Prince de Wissembourg to enquire after Madame Hulot's health, asked the re-elected deputy to go with him to see the Minister.

'His Excellency wants to discuss your family affairs with you,' he said.

The Minister had known Victorin Hulot for a long time, and so received him with characteristic cordiality that augured well.

'My dear boy,' said the old warrior, 'I vowed to your uncle, the Marshal, in this very room, to take care of your mother. That saintly woman, I'm told is on the road to recovery. The time has come to dress your wounds. I have two hundred thousand francs here for you which I'm going to give you.'

The lawyer made a gesture worthy of his uncle the Marshal.

'Set your mind at rest,' said the Prince with a smile. 'It's money left in trust. My days are numbered; I shan't be here for ever, so take the money and stand in for me in the bosom of your family. You can use the money to pay off the mortgages on your house. These two hundred thousand francs belong to your mother and sister. If I were to give that money to Madame Hulot, I fear that her devotion to her husband would lead her to waste it, and the intention of those who return it is that it should provide for the maintenance of Madame Hulot and her daughter, the Comtesse de Steinbock. You are a virtuous man, the worthy son of your noble mother, the true nephew of my friend the Marshal. You are warmly appreciated here, my dear boy, as well as elsewhere. So be your family's guardian angel; accept this legacy from your uncle and from me.'

'Monseigneur,' said Hulot, taking the Minister's hand and pressing it, 'men like you know that words of thanks are meaningless; gratitude is proved by deeds.'

'Prove yours,' said the old soldier.

'What must I do?'

'Accept my proposals,' said the Minister. 'We want to give you a legal appointment in the War Ministry, which, in the engineering section, is overburdened with litigation arising from the Paris fortifications. We'd also like to appoint you as consultant lawyer to the Prefecture of Police and adviser to the Civil List Board. These three appointments will give you a salary of eighteen thousand francs and will not deprive you of your independence. You will still be able to vote in the Chamber according to your political views and your conscience. Act quite freely as far as that's concerned. We'd be very put out if we didn't have a national opposition! And lastly, a note from your uncle, written a few hours before he breathed his last, indicated to me what I should do to help your mother, whom the Marshal was very fond of. Mesdames Popinot, de Rastignac, de Navarreins, d'Espard, de Grandlieu, de Carigliano, de Lenoncourt, and de la Bâtie have created a post of Superintendent of Charities for your dear mother. These ladies, presidents of charitable societies, cannot do everything themselves. They need a reliable lady who can actively supplement their work, visit the unfortunate, find out if the charity has been misapplied, make sure that help has been properly given to those who have asked for it, seek out poor people who are too proud to ask for help, etc. Your mother will fulfil the mission of a good angel. She will have contact only with the parish priests and the charitable ladies. Her salary will be six thousand francs a year and her carriages will be paid for. You see, young man, that, from beyond the grave, a pure, honourable, and upright man can still look after his family. Names such as your uncle's are and ought to be a shield against misfortune in a well-organized society. Follow in your uncle's footsteps; continue steadfastly on that road, for you have started on it already, I know.'

'Such consideration, Prince, does not surprise me in my uncle's friend,' said Victorin. 'I shall try to live up to all your expectations.'

'Go right away and bring comfort to your family. Oh, by the way,' the Prince added, as he shook hands with Victorin, 'is it true that your father has disappeared?'

'Alas, yes.'

'So much the better. The unhappy man showed intelligence in that, a quality, incidentally, he never lacked.'

'He's afraid of bills of exchange he can't pay.'

'Oh, you'll get six months' salary in advance from your new appointments. This payment in advance will no doubt help you to redeem these bills from the money-lender's hands. In any case, I'll see Nucingen and I may be able to free your father's pension without its costing you or my Ministry a farthing. The peer of France hasn't killed the banker; Nucingen is insatiable and he'll ask for some concession or other.'

When he returned to the Rue Plumet, Victorin could then carry out his plan of taking his mother and sister to live in his house.

101. *Great changes*

The distinguished young barrister possessed as his whole fortune one of the finest properties in Paris, a house bought in 1834 in anticipation of his marriage, situated on the boulevard between the Rue de la Paix and the Rue Louis-le-Grand. A speculator had built two houses, one on the street and one on the boulevard; between them, with a garden and a court on either side, stood the magnificent wing of an old house, all that remained of the splendours of the great Verneuil mansion.

Young Hulot, relying on Mademoiselle Crevel's dowry, bought this superb property when it was auctioned, paying five hundred thousand francs down. He lived on the ground floor of the wing, thinking he could pay off the rest of the price by letting the other floors. But although speculations in house property in Paris are safe, returns can be slow or erratic, for they depend on unpredictable circumstances.

As strollers about Paris may have noticed, the boulevard between the Rue Louis-le-Grand and the Rue de la Paix was developed slowly. It was such a big task to clean it up and beautify it that only in 1840 were commercial premises established there, with their splendid window-displays, the money-changers' gold, the fairy-like creations of fashion, and the unbridled luxury of the shops.

In spite of the two hundred thousand francs given to his daughter by Crevel in the days when his vanity was flattered by her marriage and when the Baron had not yet robbed him of Josépha, and in spite of two hundred thousand francs paid by Victorin over seven years, the debt on the property still stood at five hundred thousand francs, because of the son's devotion to his father.

Fortunately the steady rise in rents and the beauty of the situation gave the two houses, at this time, their full value. The speculation was becoming profitable after eight years during which the lawyer had used all his resources to pay the interest and an insignificant amount of the capital.

The shopkeepers themselves were proposing profitable rents for the shops, on condition that they had eighteen-year leases. The flats were increasing in value because of the change in the business centre, which was then becoming established between the Stock Exchange and the Madeleine, and which was in future to be the seat of political power and finance in Paris.

The money handed over by the Minister, together with the salary paid in advance and the key-money agreed to by the tenants, would reduce Victorin's debt by two hundred thousand francs. The two houses, fully let, would bring in a hundred thousand francs a year.

In another two years, during which he would live on his fees, doubled by the salaries of the positions the Marshal had given him, young Hulot would be in an excellent position. It was manna from heaven.

Victorin was able to give his mother the whole first floor

of his wing, and his sister the second, where Lisbeth would have two rooms.

And, run by Cousin Bette, this triple household could meet all its expenses and present an honourable face to the world, as befitted the establishment of a distinguished lawyer. The stars of the law-courts were rapidly disappearing, and young Hulot, gifted with the art of judicious eloquence and of being a man of strict integrity, was listened to by judges and councillors. He studied his cases carefully and said nothing that he could not prove; he did not plead causes indiscriminately and was, in short, a credit to the bar.

Her house in the Rue Plumet was so hateful to the Baroness that she let herself be moved to the Rue Louis-le-Grand.

Thanks to her son, then, Adeline occupied a beautiful suite of rooms. She was spared all the material cares of life, for Lisbeth took on the task of repeating the economic miracles she had performed at Madame Marneffe's; she saw in this a way of wreaking her vengeance on these three noble lives, the objects of a hatred inflamed by the overthrow of all her hopes.

Once a month she went to see Valérie, sent there by Hortense, who wanted news of Wenceslas, and by Célestine, who was extremely worried by her father's open and acknowledged liaison with the woman who had caused the ruin and unhappiness of her mother and sister-in-law.

As can be imagined, Lisbeth took advantage of their curiosity to see Valérie as often as she pleased.

About twenty months elapsed, during which the Baroness's health improved, although her nervous trembling did not leave her. She familiarized herself with her duties, which provided a noble means of distracting her from her grief, as well as nourishment for the spiritual aspirations of her soul.

In these duties, moreover, she saw a way of finding her husband as a result of the chance opportunities they afforded of taking her to every part of Paris.

During this time, Vauvinet's bills were paid and the

pension of six thousand francs, payable to Baron Hulot, was almost redeemed. Victorin paid all his mother's expenses and Hortense's as well, with the ten thousand francs interest on the capital left in trust for them by the Marshal.

As Adeline's salary was six thousand francs, that amount, together with the Baron's pension of six thousand francs, was soon to provide an income of twelve thousand francs a year, free of all encumbrances, for the mother and daughter.

The poor woman would have been almost happy but for her incessant anxiety about the Baron's fate; she would have liked to enable him to share in the good fortune that was beginning to smile on the family. She suffered too from the sight of her deserted daughter and from the terrible blows inflicted on her *in all innocence* by Lisbeth, who gave free rein to her diabolical character.

A scene which took place at the beginning of March 1843 will serve to explain the effects produced by Lisbeth's persistent, underlying hatred, still seconded by Madame Marneffe.

Two great events had taken place in Madame Marneffe's life.

First she had given birth to a still-born child, whose coffin was worth two thousand francs a year to her.

Then, as for Master Marneffe, this is the news that Lisbeth gave the family on her return from a reconnaissance expedition to the Marneffe establishment.

'This morning that frightful Valérie sent for Doctor Bianchon to make sure that the doctors, who yesterday said there was no hope for her husband, weren't mistaken,' she had reported. 'Dr Bianchon said that this very night the disgusting creature would be claimed by the hell that awaits him. Père Crevel and Madame Marneffe saw the doctor out, and your father, my dear Célestine, gave him five gold coins for this good news. When he got back to the drawing-room, Crevel capered about like a dancer; he kissed that woman exclaiming, "So you'll be Madame Crevel at last!" And when she left us alone to return to her place at the bedside of her husband, gasping with the death-rattle, your honourable father said to me, "With Valérie for my wife, I'll become a peer of France. I'll buy an estate I've got my eye on, the estate of Presles, that Madame de Serizy wants to sell. I'll be Crevel of Presles; I'll become a member of the Council of Seine-et-Oise and a deputy. I'll have a son. I'll be everything I want to be." "But what about your daughter?" I said to him. "Bah, she's a girl," he replied, "and she's become too much of a Hulot, and Valérie can't abide that lot. My son-in-law has never been willing to come here; why does he pose as a mentor, a Spartan, a puritan, a philanthropist? In any case, I've settled my accounts with my daughter; she's had all her mother's fortune and two hundred thousand francs more. So I'm at liberty to do as I like. I'll form an opinion on my son-in-law and daughter when I get married. As they behave, so shall I. If they're nice to their stepmother, I'll see. I'm a man, I am!" And he talked a lot of that sort of nonsense, striking an attitude like Napoleon on his column.'

The ten months' official widowhood, decreed by the Napoleonic Code, had expired some days previously. The Presles estate had been bought.

That very morning, Victorin and Célestine had sent Lisbeth to Madame Marneffe's in search of news about the charming widow's marriage to the Mayor of Paris, now a member of the Council of Seine-et-Oise.

102. *The sword of Damocles*

Célestine and Hortense, who had become much more attached to each other by living under the same roof, spent nearly all their time together.

The Baroness, impelled by a moral feeling that made her exaggerate the obligations of her post, devoted herself to the charitable works for which she acted as the intermediary. She was out every day from eleven o'clock till five.

The two sisters-in-law, united by the care of their

children, whom they looked after jointly, stayed at home and worked together. They had got to the stage of thinking aloud, presenting a touching harmony between two sisters, the one happy,* the other melancholy.

Beautiful, overflowing with life, lively, and cheerful, the unhappy sister's demeanour seemed to belie her true situation, just as the melancholy one, gentle and calm, as equable as reason itself, habitually thoughtful and reflective, gave the impression of having secret sorrows. Perhaps this contrast contributed to their warm friendship. Each of these two women supplied the other with what she lacked.

Seated in a little summerhouse in the middle of the garden spared by a caprice of the builder (who had planned to keep these hundred square feet for himself), they were enjoying the first spring shoots of the lilacs. The blossom is a spring festival which can only be fully appreciated in Paris, where, for six months, Parisians forget about vegetation, and live amongst the stone cliffs against which their human ocean ebbs and flows.

'Célestine,' Hortense was saying, in reply to a complaint by her sister-in-law that her husband was in the Chamber on such a fine day, 'I don't think you appreciate your happiness enough. Victorin is an angel and you nag him sometimes.'

'My dear, men like to be nagged. Certain kinds of annoyance are a proof of affection. If your poor mother had been, not demanding but always on the point of being so, you probably wouldn't have had so many misfortunes to grieve over.'

'Lisbeth's not back yet. I'll sing the song about Marlborough!'* said Hortense. 'How I'm longing for news of Wenceslas. What's he living on? He's done no work for two years.'

'Victorin told me he saw him the other day with that hateful woman, and he assumes she keeps him in idleness. Oh, if you wanted to, dear sister, you could still bring your husband back.'

Hortense shook her head.

'Believe me, your situation will soon become intolerable,' continued Célestine. 'To start with, anger, despair, and indignation gave you strength. The appalling misfortunes that have overwhelmed our family since then—two deaths, financial ruin, and Baron Hulot's disasters—have filled your mind and heart. But now that you're living in peace and quiet, you won't find it easy to bear the emptiness of your life. And as you can't and don't want to leave the path of virtue, you'll have to be reconciled to Wenceslas. That's what Victorin thinks and he's very fond of you. There's something stronger than our personal feelings, and that is nature.'

'He's so spineless,' cried the proud Hortense. 'He loves that woman because she keeps him. So she's paid his debts, has she? My God! I think of that man's situation night and day. He is the father of my child and he lives in degradation.'

'Look at your mother, my dear,' continued Célestine.

Célestine belonged to the class of women who, when given reasons good enough to convince Breton peasants, repeat their original argument for the hundredth time. The uninteresting, cold, and commonplace character of her face, her light brown hair arranged in stiff plaits, the colour of her complexion, everything about her indicated that she was a sensible woman with no charm but also with no weakness.

'The Baroness would dearly like to be near her disgraced husband, to comfort him, to hide him in her heart from all eyes,' continued Célestine. 'She's got Monsieur Hulot's room ready for him upstairs as if she might find him any day and settle him in there.'

'Oh, my mother is sublime,' replied Hortense. 'She has been sublime every moment, every day, for twenty-six years. But I haven't got her temperament. What can I do? Sometimes I get angry with myself. Oh, Célestine, you don't know what it is to compromise with infamy.'

'And what about my father?' replied Célestine calmly. 'He's certainly on the path where yours was destroyed. My father's ten years younger than the Baron, and he was in business, it's true, but how will it all end? That Madame

Marneffe has turned my father into her lap-dog; she has control of his fortune and of his ideas, and nothing can open my father's eyes. And now I tremble at the prospect of hearing that his marriage banns have been published. My husband's making a final effort; he regards it as his duty to avenge society and the family, to call that woman to account for all her crimes. Oh, my dear Hortense, noble minds like Victorin's, and hearts like ours, realize too late what the world and its ways are like. This, dear sister, is a secret. I'm telling it you in confidence, for it concerns you. But don't reveal it by a word or gesture to Lisbeth, or your mother, or anyone, for . . .'

'Here's Lisbeth,' said Hortense. 'Well, Cousin, how are things going in the inferno at the Rue Barbet?'

'Badly for you, my dears. Your husband, my dear Hortense, is more infatuated than ever with that woman who, I must admit, is crazy about him. Your father, dear Célestine, is as blind as a king. That's not news; it's what I see every fortnight when I go there, and really I'm fortunate never to have had anything to do with men. They're just animals. Five days from now, my dear, you and Victorin will have lost your father's fortune.'

'Have the banns been published?' asked Célestine.

'Yes,' Lisbeth replied. 'I've just been pleading your cause. I told this monster, who's following in the footsteps of the other one, that if he were willing to get you out of your financial difficulties by paying off the mortgage on your house, you'd be grateful to him and receive your stepmother.'

Hortense made a gesture of alarm.

'Victorin will decide,' replied Célestine coldly.

'Do you know what Monsieur le Maire replied?' Lisbeth went on. "I want to leave them in financial difficulties. Horses are broken only by hunger, lack of sleep, and sugar." Baron Hulot was a better man than Monsieur Crevel. So, my poor children, go into mourning for your inheritance. And what a fortune! Your father paid three million for the estate at Presles and he has thirty thousand francs a year left. Oh, he has no secrets from me! He talks of buying the Navarreins mansion in the Rue du Bac. Madame Marneffe herself has forty thousand francs a year. Oh, here's our guardian angel, here's your mother,' she cried, hearing the sound of a carriage.

Indeed a moment later, the Baroness came down the steps and joined the family group.

At the age of 55, tried by so many sorrows, trembling incessantly as if afflicted with a fever, Adeline, who had become pale and wrinkled, retained her beautiful figure with its superb contours, and her natural dignity.

On seeing her, people would say, 'She must have been very beautiful.' Consumed by the grief of not knowing where her husband was and by her inability to let him share in the seclusion and peace of this Parisian oasis, in the prosperity that his family was about to enjoy, she had the soothing charm of old ruins.

After each gleam of hope was extinguished, after each search proved fruitless, Adeline would fall into a deep depression that was the despair of her children.

The Baroness, who had set off in the morning with fresh hope, was eagerly awaited. A senior administrative officer, under an obligation to Hulot, to whom he owed his good position, said he had caught sight of the Baron in a box at the Ambigu-Comique theatre with a dazzlingly beautiful woman. Adeline had been to see Baron Vernier. The high official, while affirming that he had seen his old patron and asserting that his behaviour towards this woman during the performance suggested a clandestine, unofficial marriage, had told Madame Hulot that her husband had left well before the end of the performance, in order to avoid meeting him.

'He behaved as if he were with a member of his family, and his dress suggested ill-concealed straitened circumstances,' he added in conclusion.

'What news?' the three women asked the Baroness.

'Well, Monsieur Hulot is in Paris, and it's already a glint of happiness for me to know that he is near us,' replied Adeline.

'He doesn't seem to have mended his ways,' said Lisbeth

when Adeline had finished giving an account of her interview with Baron Vernier. 'He'll have set up house with some little working-girl. But where can he be getting money from? I bet he's asked for it from his former mistresses, Mademoiselle Jenny Cadine or Josépha.'

The Baroness's nervous trembling became twice as violent. She wiped away the tears that came to her eyes and looked up sadly towards heaven.

'I can't believe a Grand Officer of the Legion of Honour has sunk so low,' she said.

'For his pleasure,' Lisbeth continued, 'what would he not do? He's stolen from the State; he'll steal from private individuals; perhaps he'll commit murder.'

'Oh, Lisbeth,' cried the Baroness, 'keep such thoughts to yourself.'

103. *Baron Hulot's friend*

Just then, Louise came up to the family group; the two Hulot children and little Wenceslas had joined it to see if there were any sweets in their grandmother's pockets.

'What is it, Louise?' they asked.

'There's a man asking for Mademoiselle Fischer.'

'What kind of man?' said Lisbeth.

'He's in rags, Mademoiselle, and he's got fluff on him like a mattress-maker. He has a red nose and he smells of wine and brandy. He's one of those men who work for barely half a week.'

The effect of this not very attractive description was to make Lisbeth hurry to the courtyard of the house in the Rue Louis-le-Grand, where she found the man smoking such a well-seasoned pipe that it showed he was practised in the art of smoking.

'Why have you come here, Père Chardin?' she asked.

'We agreed that on the first Saturday of each month you would be at the door of Madame Marneffe's house, in the Rue Barbet-de-Jouy. I've just come back after staying there for five hours, and you didn't come.'

'I did go, respected and charitable lady,' replied the mattress-maker, 'but there was a prize game of pool going on at the Café des Savants in the Rue du Côeur-Volant, and every man has a craze for something. Mine is for billiards. But for billiards, I'd be eating off silver plates,' he said, looking for a piece of paper in the pocket of his torn trousers, 'for you must understand that billiards leads to a tot of spirits and a drop of plum brandy. . . . It ruins a man, like all good things, by what goes along with it. I know my orders, but the old man's in such a jam that I've come on to forbidden ground. If our horsehair were all horsehair, you could go to sleep on it, but it's a mixture. God isn't on everyone's side, as they say; he has his preferences. That's his right. Here's the note from your worthy relative, a good friend of the mattress trade. That's his political opinion.'

Père Chardin tried to draw zigzag lines in the air with the forefinger of his right hand.

Lisbeth, without listening to him, read the following two lines:

'Dear Cousin, be my providence! Give me three hundred francs today.

HECTOR

'Why does he want so much money?'

'The *landlord*!' said Père Chardin, who was still trying to draw patterns in the air. 'And then, my son's come back from Algeria through Spain and Bayonne, and . . . he hasn't taken anything, as he usually does, for he's a skilful operator, my son, saving your presence. But what's he to do? He's hungry. But he'll pay you back all we lend him because he wants to set up a limited liability company. He has ideas that will take him far.'

'To the police court!' replied Lisbeth. 'He's my uncle's murderer. I shan't forget that.'

'Him, he wouldn't kill a chicken! He couldn't do it, good lady!'

'Take this. Here's three hundred francs,' said Lisbeth, taking fifteen gold coins from her purse. 'Be off with you and don't ever come here again.'

She went to the gate with the Oran storekeeper's father and drew the porter's attention to the old drunk.

'Any time that man comes, if by any chance he should come again, don't let him in, and tell him I'm not at home. If he wants to know if young Monsieur Hulot or Madame la Baronne Hulot live here, say you don't know anyone of that name.'

'Very well, Mademoislle.'

'You could lose your job if you committed a blunder, even involuntarily,' murmured the old maid in the concierge's ear.

'Cousin,' she said to the lawyer, who was just coming in, 'you're threatened with a great misfortune.'

'What's that?'

'In a few days from now, your wife will have Madame Marneffe for a stepmother.'

'That remains to be seen,' replied Victorin.

For the last six months, Lisbeth had been regularly paying a small allowance to her protector, Baron Hulot, whose protectress she had become. She knew the secret of his whereabouts and she relished Adeline's tears. Whenever Bette saw her cousin cheerful and hopeful, she would say, as we have just seen:

'You can expect to read my poor cousin's name in the newspaper police-court reports some day.'

In this, as previously, she went too far in her thirst for vengeance. She had aroused Victorin's suspicions. Victorin had made up his mind to get rid of this sword of Damocles continually pointed out by Lisbeth, and of the she-devil to whom his mother and the whole family owed so much unhappiness.

The Prince de Wissembourg, who was aware of Madame Marneffe's activities, supported the lawyer's secret undertaking. He had promised him, as a President of Council can promise, the secret help of the police to enlighten Crevel and to save a fortune from the diabolical courtesan, whom he had not forgiven either for Marshal Hulot's death or for the complete ruin of the Councillor of State.

104. *Vice and Virtue*

The words, 'He gets it from his former mistresses', spoken by Lisbeth, occupied the Baroness's mind all night.

Like invalids given up by the doctors, who have recourse to quacks, like those who have fallen to Dante's lowest circle of despair, or like drowning men who clutch at straws for support, she finally came to believe in the degrading action, the merest hint of which had aroused her indignation, and she conceived the idea of applying for help to one of those odious women.

The next morning, without consulting her children, without saying a word to anyone, she went to the house of Mademoiselle Josépha Mirah, a prima donna of the Royal Academy of Music, to find or lose the hope that had begun to gleam like a will o' the wisp.

At noon, the famous singer's maid handed her Baroness Hulot's card, saying that the lady was waiting at the door; she had asked if Mademoiselle could receive her.

'Are the rooms done?'

'Yes, Mademoiselle.'

'Are the flowers fresh?'

'Yes, Mademoiselle.'

'Tell Jean to take a look round and see that everything's in order before showing the lady in, and all of you treat her with the greatest respect. Go, and then come back and help me dress, for I want to be stunningly beautiful.'

She went and looked at herself in her cheval-glass.

'I must dress up to the nines,' she said to herself. 'Vice must be under arms to face virtue. Poor woman! What can she want of me? It upsets me to see *Misfortune's noble victim*! . . .'*

She was just coming to the end of that well-known aria when her maid came in.

'Madame,' said the maid, 'the lady's had an attack of nervous trembling.'

'Offer her some orange-flower water, or rum, or soup.'

'I've done so, Mademoiselle, but she's refused everything; she said it's a little disability she has, due to her nerves.'

'Which room did you show her into?'

'The large drawing-room.'

'Hurry up, my girl! Quick, my prettiest slippers, my flowered housecoat, the one Bijou embroidered, and all the lace paraphernalia. Do my hair up in a way that would amaze any woman. This lady plays the role opposite mine! And let someone tell her ... (for she's a great lady, my girl. She's more than that, she's something you'll never be: a woman whose prayers deliver souls from your purgatory). Let someone tell her that I'm in bed, that I was performing last night, and that I'm just getting up.'

The Baroness, shown into Josépha's large drawing-room, was oblivious of the time she spent there although she waited a good half-hour.

The drawing-room, which had already been refurbished since Josépha had settled into the small house, was hung with brown and gold silk.

The four inter-connecting rooms were resplendent with the luxury that great noblemen used to display in their little houses and that can be seen in so many survivals aptly called *follies*; modern techniques had enhanced this luxury with concealed warm air-vents which maintained a mild temperature.

The dazzled Baroness examined every work of art in utter amazement. In them she found the explanation of the melting down of fortunes in a crucible under which Pleasure and Vanity stoke a consuming fire.

The woman who for twenty-six years had lived among the cold relics of Empire luxury, whose eyes were used to carpets with threadbare flower-patterns, tarnished bronzes, and silk-hangings as worn and faded as her own heart, caught a glimpse of the seductive power of Vice as she beheld its achievements. It was impossible not to look enviously at these beautiful things, at those marvellous creations produced by the contributions of all the great unknown artists who make modern Paris and its European reputation what it is.

Here, the perfection and individuality of every object were amazing. As the models had been broken, the figures, the statuettes, and the sculptures were all originals. That is the last word in modern luxury. The possession of things not vulgarized by two thousand wealthy bourgeois, who think luxury consists in displaying expensive items which cram the shops, that is the mark of true luxury, the luxury of modern great noblemen, those ephemeral stars in the Parisian firmament.

As she gazed at the flower-stands filled with the rarest exotic flowers and decorated with bronze carvings in the style called Boule,* the Baroness took fright at the sight of the wealth the room contained.

Inevitably, the feeling was extended to the person upon whom this profusion of wealth was showered. Adeline reflected that Josépha Mirah, whose portrait, painted by Joseph Bridau,* was prominently displayed in the neighbouring room, was a singer of genius, a Malibran,* and she expected to see a truly lionized star.

She was sorry she had come. But she was impelled by such a powerful natural feeling, by such disinterested devotion, that she summoned up her courage to go through with the interview. And then she was going to satisfy her nagging curiosity, to see at close quarters the charm of such women which enables them to extract so much gold from the meagre deposits in the Parisian soil.

The Baroness looked at herself to see if she was not a blot on this luxury, but she carried herself well in her velvet dress with its inset up to the neck and its beautiful collar of magnificent lace; her velvet hat of the same colour was becoming.

Seeing herself still as imposing as a queen, still a queen even though ruined, she reflected that the nobility of misfortune is fully the equal of the nobility of talent.

She heard doors opening and closing, and at last saw Josépha.

The singer looked like Allori's* *Judith*, who is graven in the memory of all those who have seen her in the Pitti Palace by the door of one of the great salons. She had the same proud bearing, the same sublime features, black hair simply knotted and a yellow housecoat embroidered with a thousand flowers, exactly like the brocade in which the immortal murderess, created by Bronzino's nephew,* is dressed.

'Madame la Baronne, I am overwhelmed by the honour you do me in coming here,' said the singer, who had promised herself to give a good performance as a great lady.

With her own hand, she brought forward a low padded armchair for the Baroness and sat down herself on a folding-chair. She appreciated Madame Hulot's vanished beauty and was moved by deep pity when she saw her shaken by the nervous trembling which the least excitement made convulsive. At a glance she read the story of the saintly life that Hulot and Crevel had described to her in the past. Not only did she abandon all idea of vying with this woman, but she even humbled herself before a greatness that she understood. The sublime artist admired what the courtesan used to mock.

'Mademoiselle, I am brought here by despair, which drives one to resort to every means . . .'

A gesture of Josépha's made the Baroness understand that she had just hurt the feelings of the woman from whom she expected so much, and she looked at the singer.

Her pleading look quenched the flame in Josépha's eyes and the singer finally smiled.

Between the two women there was a dumb exchange of glances that spoke volumes.

'It's two and a half years now since Monsieur Hulot left his family and I don't kow where he is, although I know he's living in Paris,' continued the Baroness with emotion. 'A dream gave me the idea, perhaps an absurd one, that you must have taken an interest in Monsieur Hulot. If you could put me in the way of seeing him again, oh, Mademoiselle, I would pray to God for you every day, so long as I remain on this earth.'

Two large tears that welled up in the singer's eyes foretold her answer.

'Madame,' she said, in a tone of deep humility, 'I injured you without knowing you. But now that, in seeing you, I have the good fortune to catch a glimpse of the most perfect image of virtue on this earth, believe me, I am sensible of the extent of my fault and sincerely repent it; so you can count on me to do all I can to repair it.'

She took the Baroness's hand before Madame Hulot could prevent the gesture, and kissed it with the greatest respect, humbling herself to the extent of going down on one knee.

Then she got up as proudly as when she came on stage in the part of Matilda* and rang the bell.

'Go quickly on horseback and wear the horse out, if necessary,' she said to her footman. 'Find little Bijou, Rue Saint-Maur du Temple. Bring her here. See her into a cab and pay the driver to come here at top speed. Don't lose a minute . . . or I'll dismiss you.'

'Madame,' she said, returning to the Baroness and addressing her in a most respectful tone. 'You must forgive me. As soon as I had the Duc d'Hérouville for my protector, learning that the Baron was ruining his family for me, I sent him back to you. What more could I do? In the theatrical profession we all need a protector to start with. Our salaries don't cover half our expenses, so we take temporary husbands. I didn't care for Monsieur Hulot, who made me leave a rich man, a conceited creature. Père Crevel would certainly have married me . . .'

'He told me so,' said the Baroness, interrupting the singer.

'Well, you see, Madame, I'd have been a respectable woman today, with only one lawful husband.'

'You have excuses, Mademoiselle,' said the Baroness. 'God will take them into account. But far from coming here to reproach you, I have come, on the contrary to incur a debt of gratitude towards you.'

'Nearly three years ago, I provided for Monsieur le Baron's needs.'

'You!' exclaimed the Baroness, her eyes filling with tears. 'Oh, what can I do for you? I can only pray.'

'I, together with Monsieur le Duc d'Hérouville,' replied the singer. 'He's noble-hearted, a real gentleman.'

And Josépha told the story of Père Thoul's establishment and marriage.

'So, Mademoiselle, thanks to you, my husband has lacked for nothing?' said the Baroness.

'We did all we could to that end, Madame.'

'And where is he?'

'About six months ago, Monsieur le Duc told me that the Baron, known to his lawyer as Monsieur Thoul, had drawn the whole sum of eight thousand francs which was to be remitted to him only in equal quarterly instalments,' replied Josépha. 'Neither Monsieur d'Hérouville nor I have had any news of the Baron. People like us lead such full, busy lives that I couldn't run after Père Thoul. It so happens that, for the last six months, Bijou, who does my embroidery, his . . . what shall I say?'

'His mistress,' said Madame Hulot.

'His mistress,' Josépha repeated, 'hasn't been here. Mademoiselle Olympe Bijou may well have divorced him. Divorce is common in our district.'

105. *Liquidation of the firm of Thoul and Bijou*

Josépha got up, rummaged about among the rare flowers in her flower-stands, and made a charming, lovely bouquet for the Baroness, whose expectations, we may say, were entirely disappointed.

Like those good bourgeois who take men of genius for monsters, eating, drinking, walking, and talking quite differently from other people, the Baroness had been hoping to see Josépha the bewitcher of men, Josépha the singer, the clever courtesan, skilled in the art of love. But she found a calm, well-poised woman, with the dignity of her talent and the simplicity of an actress who knows that in the evening she is queen; and better than all that, she found a young woman who, by her looks, attitude, and behaviour, paid full and unqualified homage to the virtuous wife, the *Mater Dolorosa* of the sacred hymn, and who placed flowers on her wounds, as in Italy they place flowers on the Madonna.

'Madame, Mère Bijou is on her way,' said the footman, returning half an hour later. 'But you mustn't expect little

Olympe. Madame's embroideress has become a respectable woman. She's married . . .'

'A phoney marriage?' asked Josépha.

'No, Madame, really married. She's in charge of a splendid business. She married the owner of a big fancy-goods store in the Boulevard des Italiens; he spent millions on it. She's left her embroidery business to her sisters and mother. She's Madame Grenouville. The fat shopkeeper . . .'

'Another Crevel!'

'Yes, Madame,' said the footman. 'He settled thirty thousand francs a year on Mademoiselle Bijou in her marriage contract. They say her older sister is also going to marry a rich man, a butcher.'

'Your affair doesn't seem to me to be getting on at all well,' the singer said to the Baroness. 'Monsieur le Baron is no longer where I fixed him up.'

Ten minutes later, Madame Bijou was announced. Josépha took the precaution of showing the Baroness into her boudoir and drew the curtain over the door.'

'You would scare her,' she said to the Baroness. 'She wouldn't give anything away, for she'd guess you're interested in her confidences. Let me confess her. You hide there; you'll hear everything. This scene is enacted as often in real life as in the theatre.'

'Well, Mère Bijou,' said the singer to an old woman wrapped up in so-called *tartan* material, who looked like a portress in her Sunday best. 'So you're all happy now. Your daughter's been lucky!'

'Oh, happy! My daughter gives us a hundred francs a month, and she rides in a carriage and eats off silver. She's a millionairess. Olympe could easily have saved me from poverty. At my age, to have to work! Is that a kindness?'

'She's wrong to be ungrateful, for she owes her beauty to you,' Josépha continued. 'But why hasn't she been to see me? It was I who rescued her from poverty by marrying her to my uncle.'

'Yes, Madame, Père Thoul. But he's very old and broken down.'

'What have you done with him, then? Is he with you?

She was very wrong to leave him; he's worth millions now.'

'Oh, goodness me,' said Mère Bijou, 'that's what we told her when she behaved badly to him, and he was the soul of gentleness, poor old chap. Oh, she kept him on the go! Olympe was perverted, Madame.'

'How did that happen?'

'Pardon me for saying so, Madame, but she got to know a fellow paid to clap at the theatre, the great-nephew of an old mattress-maker of the Faubourg Saint-Marceau. This *idler*, like all those good-looking lads hired to promote plays, you know, is the idol of the Boulevard du Temple, where he works for the new shows and *takes care of the entrances* of the actresses, as he says. He spends the morning having lunch; before the performance he has dinner so as to raise his spirits; and he's been fond of drink and billiards ever since he was born. 'That's not a profession,' I told Olympe.'

'Unfortunately, it is a profession,' said Josépha.

'Anyway, Olympe lost her head over this fellow, who, Madame, kept bad company; you can tell that, for he nearly got arrested in the bar where thieves go. But that time Monsieur Braulard, the head of the clapping team, got him off. The fellow wears gold earrings, and lives by doing nothing and sponging on women who are crazy about such good-looking men. He went through all the money Monsieur Thoul gave the child. The business was doing very badly. All that she got from her embroidery went on billiards. And then, Madame, this fellow had a pretty sister, a worthless creature, in the same profession as the brother, in the students' quarter.'

'A street-walker from La Chaumière,'* said Josépha.

'Yes,' said Mère Bijou. 'So Idamore—that's his working name; his real name is Chardin—Idamore imagined that your uncle must have more money than he said he had, and he found a way of sending his sister Élodie—he gave her a theatre name—to us as a worker without my daughter supecting it. Well, bless my soul! She turned the whole place upside down! She got all the other girls into bad ways and you couldn't make them behave themselves again, if you'll pardon my saying so. And she contrived somehow to get Père Thoul for herself, taking him off to we don't know where. That put us in a fix, because of all those bills. Right to this very day we still can't pay them, but my daughter, who's involved with that, looks after them when they become due. When Idamore saw that he'd got hold of the old man through his sister, he deserted my poor daughter and now he's with a young leading lady from the Funambules.* And that's how my daughter came to get married, as you'll see.'

'But do you know where the mattress-maker lives?' asked Josépha.

'Old Père Chardin? As if he lived anywhere! He's drunk from six in the morning. He makes one mattress a month. He spends the whole day in shady bars. He goes in for the pools.'

'What, he goes after the girls? He's a fine cock!'*

'You don't understand, Madame. I mean pools at billiards. He wins three or four every day and he drinks . . .'

'Hen's milk!' said Josépha. 'But Idamore operates on the Boulevard, and if we apply to my friend Braulard we'll find him.'

'I don't know, Madame, since all this happened six months ago. Idamore is one of those fellows who ought to go to the police court and from there to Melun* and then . . . well! . . .'

'To penal servitude!' said Josépha.

'Oh, Madame knows all about it,' said Mère Bijou with a smile. 'If my daughter hadn't known that creature, she, she would be . . . But she was very lucky all the same, you'll tell me, for Monsieur Grenouville fell so much in love with her that he married her.'

'And how did this marriage come about?'

'Because Olympe was in despair, Madame. When she saw she'd been deserted for the young leading lady—oh, she gave her a real good hiding! She fair whacked her!— and that she'd lost Père Thoul, who adored her, she decided she was through with men. Then Monsieur Grenouville, who used to come and buy a lot from us, two hundred embroidered Chinese shawls a quarter, wanted to console her. But whatever the rights or wrongs of it, she wouldn't agree to anything unless the Town Hall and the Church were involved. "I intend to be respectable, or die!" she kept on saying. And she stuck to her guns. Monsieur Grenouville agreed to marry her on condition that she would have nothing more to do with us, and we agreed.'

'For a consideration?' enquired the clear-sighted Josépha.

'Yes, Madame, ten thousand francs, and an allowance for my father who can't work any more.'

'I'd asked her to make Père Thoul happy, and she's thrown him into the gutter. That wasn't right. I'll never take an interest in anyone again. That's what comes of trying to do good works! Clearly good works are a very chancy speculation. Olympe ought at least to have let me know about these goings-on. If you find Père Thoul again within a fortnight, I'll give you a thousand francs.'

'It's very difficult, my good lady, but there's a lot of hundred-sou pieces in a thousand francs, so I'll try and earn your money.'

'Goodbye, Madame Bijou.'

106. *The angel and the devil hunt in company*

When she went into her boudoir, the singer found Madame Hulot in a dead faint. But although she was unconscious, she was still shaking with her nervous tremor, just as the sections of an adder still twitch when it has been cut in pieces.

Strong smelling-salts, cold water, all the usual remedies were lavished upon the Baroness and brought her back to life or, if you will, to the awareness of her sorrows.

'Oh, Mademoiselle, how low he has fallen!' she said, as she recognized Josépha and saw that she was alone with her.

'Take heart, Madame,' replied Josépha, who had sat

down on a cushion at the Baroness's feet and was kissing her hands. 'We'll find him again. And if he's in the mire, well, he'll wash it off. Believe me, for well-bred people, it's a matter of clothes. Let me make up for the wrongs I've done you, for since you came here I see how deeply you're attached to your husband, in spite of his behaviour. Well, there it is! The poor man! He's fond of women. But, you know, if you'd had a little of our *savvy*, you'd have stopped him gallivanting; for you'd have been what we know how to be: *all kinds of women* to a man. The government ought to set up a training school for respectable women. But governments are so prudish! They are led by men who are led by us! I'm sorry for the people they govern. But now we must work for you and not make jokes. So don't worry, Madame. Go home and set your mind at rest. I'll bring your Hector back to you as he was thirty years ago.'

'Oh, Mademoiselle, let's go and see this Madame Grenouville,' said the Baroness. 'She must know something. Perhaps I'll be able to see Monsieur Hulot today and snatch him away immediately from poverty and shame.'

'Madame, I express to you here and now the deep gratitude I shall always feel for the honour you do me; I shall not allow the singer Josépha, the Duc d'Hérouville's mistress, to be seen beside the most beautiful and saintly image of virtue. I respect you too much to appear in public with you. It's not the feigned humility of an actress; it's a homage I pay you. You make me regret that I don't follow your path, Madame, in spite of the thorns that draw blood from your hands and feet. But what can I do? I belong to art as you belong to virtue.'

'Poor girl!' said the Baroness, touched in the midst of her sorrows by a strange feeling of compassionate sympathy. 'I shall pray to God for you, for you are the victim of society, which needs entertainment. When old age comes, say penitential prayers. You will be pardoned if God deigns to hear the prayers of a . . .'

'Of a martyr, Madame,' said Josépha, respectfully kissing the hem of the Baroness's dress.

But Adeline took the singer's hand, drew her towards her, and kissed her on the forehead.

Blushing with pleasure, the singer saw Adeline to her carriage with marks of the humblest respect.

'It must be one of those charitable ladies,' the footman said to the lady's maid, 'for *she* doesn't trust anyone else like that, not even her good friend, Madame Jenny Cadine.'

'Wait a few days, Madame,' Josépha said, 'and you'll see *him* or I'll deny the God of my fathers; and for a Jewess, you know, that's a promise of success.'

107. *Another devil*

While the Baroness was visiting Josépha, Victorin was seeing in his study an old woman of about 75. In order to gain admission to the celebrated lawyer, she had made use of the terrible name of the chief of police.

The servant announced, 'Madame de Saint-Estève.'

'I'm using one of my professional names,' she said as she sat down.

Victorin was gripped by an inner shudder, as it were, at the sight of this dreadful old woman. Although richly dressed, she aroused fear because of the indications of cold malevolence on her dull, horribly wrinkled, pale, sinewy face.

Marat,* had he been a woman of her age, would have been like this Saint-Estève, a living image of the Terror. The bloodthirsty greed of tigers gleamed in her pale eyes. Her squat nose, with nostrils extended to form oval holes breathing hellfire, reminded one of the beaks of the most evil birds of prey. The genius of intrigue was manifest on her low, cruel brow. The long hairs which had grown at random in all the furrows of her face, indicated the masculine quality of her undertakings.

Anyone seeing this woman would have thought that all the painters had failed to portray the face of Mephistopheles.

'My dear Monsieur,' she said in a patronizing tone, 'I

haven't been involved in anything for a long time. What I'm going to do for you is out of consideration for my dear nephew, whom I love more than I would a son. Now, the President of the Council dropped a few words in the ear of the Prefect of Police, but he, after conferring with Monsieur Chapuzot about you, thought the police ought not to appear at all in an affair of that kind. My nephew has been given a free hand, but he will act only in an advisory capacity; he must not be compromised.'

'So you're the aunt of . . .'

'That's right, and I'm rather proud of it,' she replied, interrupting the lawyer, 'for he's my pupil, a pupil who soon became the master. We've examined your affair, and we've *sized it up*. Will you pay thirty thousand francs to be rid of the whole business? I'll settle the matter for you and you needn't pay till the job's done.'

'Do you know the people concerned?'

'No, my dear Monsieur, I await further information from you. We were told: "There's an old idiot who's in the clutches of a widow. This 29-year-old widow has plied her trade as a thief so well that she has obtained an income of forty thousand francs a year from two heads of families. She's on the point of absorbing eighty thousand francs a year by marrying an old chap of 61. She'll ruin a whole respectable family and give this enormous fortune to the child of some lover, by speedily getting rid of her old husband." That's the problem.'

'That's correct,' said Victorin. 'My father-in-law, Monsieur Crevel . . .'

'A former perfumer, a mayor. I live in his district under the name of Ma'am Nourrisson,' she replied.

'The other person is Madame Marneffe.'

'I don't know her,' said Madame Saint-Estève, 'but in three days I'll be in a position to count her underwear.'

'Could you prevent the marriage?' the lawyer asked.

'What stage has it reached?'

'The banns have been published twice.'

'The woman would have to be kidnapped. Today's Sunday. There are only three days, for they'll get married on Wednesday; no, it's not possible. But we can kill her for you.'

Victorin Hulot gave a start of horror as any honest man would on hearing these six words spoken in cold blood.

'Murder!' he said. 'And how will you do it?'

'For the past forty years, Monsieur, we've taken the place of fate,' she replied with fierce pride, 'and we do anything we please in Paris. More than one family, and from the Faubourg Saint-Germain* at that, have told me their secrets, you know. I've made and broken many marriages; I've torn up many wills, I've saved many reputations. There,' she said, pointing to her head, 'I stow away a flock of secrets worth sixty thousand francs a year to me. And you, you'll be one of my lambs, you see. Would a woman like me be what I am if she talked about her ways and means? I act! Everything that happens, my dear sir, will be the work of chance and you won't have the least remorse. You'll be like a man cured by a clairvoyant; at the end of a month they think that nature did it all.'

Victorin broke out into a cold sweat.

The sight of the executioner would have horrified him less than this moralizing, pretentious sister of galley-slaves. As he looked at her wine-coloured dress, she seemed to be dressed in blood.

'Madame, I can't accept the assistance of your experience and your operations, if success is to cost someone's life or if it results in the least criminal act.'

'You're a great baby, Monsieur,' replied Madame Saint-Estève. 'You want to remain upright in your own eyes, but at the same time you want your enemy to be overcome.'

Victorin shook his head in denial.

'Yes,' she continued. 'You want this Madame Marneffe to drop the prey she has in her jaws. And how would you make a tiger let go of its piece of beef? Would you do it by stroking it and saying: *Pussy! Pussy!*? You're not logical. You give the order for battle but you don't want any wounds. Well, I'll make you a present of the innocence you have so much at heart. I've always looked upon virtue as the stuff of which hypocrisy is made. One day, in three months' time, a poor priest will come and ask you for forty thousand francs for a charitable cause, a ruined convent in the Levant, in the desert. If you're satisfied with your lot, give the good fellow the forty thousand francs. You'll pay much more in taxes. It's not much, you know, compared with what you'll gain.'

She stood up on her broad feet, that bulged out of satin slippers which could hardly contain them, and took her leave with a smile and a curtsey.

'The devil has a sister,' said Victorin, getting up from his chair.

He saw out this horrible stranger, who had emerged from the caverns of the secret police as a monster rises from the lowest depths of the Opera house at the wave of a magic wand in a fairy ballet.

When he had finished his work at the law-courts, Victorin went to see Monsieur Chapuzot, the head of one of the most important departments at the Prefecture of Police, to make enquiries about his unknown visitor.

108. *The police*

Seeing Monsieur Chapuzot alone in his office, Victorin Hulot thanked him for his help.

'You sent me an old woman who could serve to personify the criminal side of Paris,' he said.

Monsieur Chapuzot put his spectacles down on his papers and looked at the lawyer with an expression of surprise.

'I should certainly not have taken the liberty of sending anyone to see you without letting you know beforehand or sending a note of introduction,' he replied.

'It was Monsieur le Préfet, then . . .'

'I don't think so,' said Chapuzot. 'The last time Monsieur le Prince de Wissembourg dined with the Minister of the Interior, he saw Monsieur le Préfet and spoke to him about the situation you were in, a deplorable situation; he asked him if it was possible to help you in a friendly way.

Monsieur le Préfet, his interest greatly aroused by his Excellency's evident concern over this family affair, was good enough to consult me on the matter. Ever since Monsieur le Préfet took over the reins of this department, which has been so maligned but is so useful, he has forbidden any interference in family matters. He was right in principle and morally as well, but in practice he was wrong. During the forty-five years that I have been in the service, the police have rendered immense service to families, especially between 1799 and 1815. Since 1830, the press and constitutional government have totally changed the conditions of our existence. So my advice was not to get involved in such an affair and Monsieur le Préfet was so good as to agree with my opinion. The chief of the Criminal Investigation Department received, in my presence, the order not to proceed in the matter, and if by any chance you've seen someone sent by him, I'll reprimand him. It would be grounds for dismissal. It's easy to say: "The police will do this or that!" The police! The police! But, my dear sir, the Marshal, the Council of Ministers, don't know what the police are. Only the police really know the police. The kings, Napoleon, Louis XVIII, knew their own police. But as for ours, only Fouché,* Monsieur Lenoir,* Monsieur de Sartines,* and a few clever prefects have any idea of them. Today everything has changed. We are diminished, disarmed. I have seen the growth of many private misfortunes that I could have prevented with five grains of arbitrary action. We'll be regretted by those very people who have destroyed us, when, like you, they are faced with some moral monstrosity that we ought to be able to clear away as we clear away mud. In public affairs, the police are expected to foresee everything when public safety is at stake, but as for the family, that's sacred. I'd do anything to discover and prevent an attempt on the King's life; I'd make the walls of a house transparent! But to probe into domestic affairs, into private interests!—never, so long as I sit in this office, for I'm afraid . . .'

'Of what?'

'Of the press, Monsieur le Député of the Left Centre.'

'What should I do?' said young Hulot after a pause.

'Well, you represent the family,' continued the Head of Department. 'There's no more to be said. Do as you think best. But to come to your assistance, to make the police an agent of private interests and passions, that's not possible. There, you see, lies the secret of the inevitable persecution, deemed illegal by the magistrates, of the predecessor of our present head of the Criminal Investigation Department. Bibi-Lupin used the police on behalf of private individuals. This concealed an immense social danger. With the means at his disposal, such a man would have been formidable, he would have been a kind of deputy-fate.'

'But in my place?' asked Hulot.

'Oh, you are asking me for an opinion, you who sell opinions!' replied Monsieur Chapuzot. 'Come, come, dear sir, you're making fun of me.'

Hulot bowed to the head of Department and went away without noticing that official's almost imperceptible shrug of the shoulders when he got up to show him out.

'And he wants to be a statesman!' Monsieur Chapuzot said to himself, turning back to his reports.

109. *Change from Père Thoul to Père Thorec*

Victorin returned home, still full of perplexities, which he could confide to no one.

At dinner the Baroness joyfully told her children that within a month their father might be sharing their prosperity and ending his days peacefully in the bosom of his family.

'Oh, I'd gladly give my three thousand six hundred francs a year to see the Baron here,' cried Lisbeth. 'But, dear Adeline, don't count on such happiness in advance, I beg of you.'

'Lisbeth is right,' said Célestine. 'Dear Mother, wait till it happens.'

The Baroness, filled with love and hope, told of her visit to Josépha, thought those poor girls unhappy in their good fortune, and spoke of Chardin, the mattress-maker, the Oran storekeeper's father, thus proving that she was not indulging in a false hope.

At seven o'clock the next morning, Lisbeth was in a cab on the Quai de la Tournelle; she stopped it at the corner of the Rue de Poissy.

'Go to the Rue des Bernardins, number seven,' she told the driver. 'It's a house with an entrance drive and no porter. Go up to the fourth floor and ring at the door on the left, where you'll read: "Mademoiselle Chardin, Laces and cashmere shawls repaired." When someone comes to the door, ask for *the gentleman*. The answer will be: "He's gone out." Then say: "I know, but find him, for his *maid* is there in a cab on the quay and wants to see him!"'

Twenty minutes later an old man, who looked about 80, his hair completely white, his nose reddened by the cold in a pale, wrinkled face like an old woman's, his back bent, shuffled along in felt slippers. He was dressed in a worn alpaca coat, was wearing no decorations, had the sleeves of a knitted waistcoat showing at his wrists and a disturbingly yellow shirt. He approached timidly, looked at the cab, recognized Lisbeth, and came to the door.

'Oh, my dear Cousin,' she said, 'what a state you're in.'

'Élodie takes everything for herself,' said Baron Hulot. 'Those Chardins are foul scum.'

'Do you want to come back to us?'

'Oh, no, no,' said the old man, 'I'd like to go to America.'

'Adeline is on your track.'

'Oh, if only my debts could be paid,' said the Baron with a questioning, furtive look, 'for Samanon is after me.'

'We haven't paid your arrears yet; your son still owes a hundred thousand francs.'

'Poor boy!'

'And it'll be seven or eight months before your pension is free. If you'll wait, I've got two thousand francs here.'

The Baron held out his hand with a gesture of frightening avidity.

'Give them to me, Lisbeth! May God reward you! Give them to me! I know where to go.'

'But you'll tell me, you old monster?'

'Yes, I can wait the eight months, for I've discovered a little angel, a kind, innocent creature who's not old enough yet to be depraved.'

'Think of the police court,' said Lisbeth, who had hopes of seeing Hulot there one day.

'Well, it's the Rue de Charonne,' said Baron Hulot, 'a district where there's no scandal whatever you do. Oh, I'll never be found there. I've disguised myself as Père Thorec, Lisbeth. People will take me for a retired cabinet-maker; the child loves me and I shan't let myself be fleeced any more.'

'No, that's been done already!' said Lisbeth looking at his coat. 'Suppose I drive you there, Cousin?'

Baron Hulot got into the carriage, dropping Mademoiselle Élodie without bidding her goodbye, like a novel one has finished reading.

After half an hour, during which Baron Hulot talked to Lisbeth of nothing but little Atala Judici—for he had gradually come to be possessed by one of those frightful manias that ruin old men—his cousin set him down, with two thousand francs in his pocket, in the Rue de Charonne, in the Faubourg Saint-Antoine, at the door of a house with a suspicious and ominous exterior.

'Goodbye, Cousin. You'll be *Père Thorec* now? Is that right? Don't send me anyone but public messengers and always hire them from different places.'

'Agreed. Oh, I'm very happy.' said the Baron, whose face was lit up with the joy of a quite new happiness to come.

'They won't find him there,' Lisbeth said to herself, as she stopped her cab at the Boulevard Beaumarchais, from where she returned by bus to the Rue Louis-le-Grand.

110. *A family scene*

The next day, after lunch, when all the family were together in the drawing-room, Crevel was announced. Célestine rushed forward, threw her arms round her father's neck, and behaved as if he had been there the day before, although it was his first visit for two years.

'Good afternoon, father,' said Victorin, shaking his hand.

'Good afternoon, children,' said Crevel pompously. 'Madame la Baronne, I pay you my deepest respects. Heavens, how these children grow! They're hard on our heels; they say to us, "Grandpa, I want my place in the sun!" Madame la Comtesse, you're still marvellously beautiful,' he added, looking at Hortense. 'And here's the balance of our treasure, Cousin Bette, the wise virgin. Well, you're all very comfortable here,' he said, after handing out these remarks to each of them, with an accompaniment of hearty laughs that barely disturbed the florid masses of his broad face.

And he looked at his daughter's drawing-room with something like contempt.

'My dear Célestine, I'll give you all my furniture from the Rue des Saussayes; it will go very well here. Your drawing-room needs to be redone. Oh, here's that young rascal, Wenceslas! Well, little ones, are we good children? You must learn to behave well.'

'To make up for those who behave badly,' said Lisbeth.

'That sarcastic remark, my dear Lisbeth, doesn't apply to me any more. I'm going to put an end to the false position I've been in for so long. I've come, like a good head of a family, to tell you, without beating about the bush, that I'm going to get married.'

'You have the right to marry,' said Victorin, 'and for my part, I release you from the promise you made me when you gave me my dear Célestine's hand.'

'What promise?' asked Crevel.

'That you wouldn't get married,' replied the lawyer. 'You will do me the justice of admitting that I didn't ask you for such a commitment and that you undertook it quite voluntarily in spite of my pointing out to you, at the time, that you shouldn't tie yourself in this way.'

'Yes, I remember, dear boy,' said Crevel shamefacedly. 'But, look here, upon my word, dear children, if you're willing to live on good terms with Madame Crevel, you'll have no reason to regret it. I'm touched by your consideration, Victorin. No one's generosity to me goes unrewarded. Now, be nice to your stepmother and come to my wedding.'

'You don't say who your fiancée is, Father,' said Célestine.

'But that's the crucial point of the story,' continued Crevel. 'Let's not play hide-and-seek. Lisbeth must have told you . . .'

'My dear Monsieur Crevel,' replied the Lorraine cousin, 'there are names that are not mentioned here.'

'Well, it's Madame Marneffe!'

'Monsieur Crevel,' the lawyer replied sternly, 'neither my wife nor I will be present at this marriage, but not from interested motives, for I spoke to you sincerely just now. Yes, I'd be very pleased to know that you'd found happiness in this union. But I am affected by considerations of honour and delicacy which you must understand and which I can't elaborate, for they would re-open wounds that are still bleeding here.'

The Baroness signed to the Countess, who picked her son up in her arms, saying:

'Come, Wenceslas, you must have your bath now. Goodbye, Monsieur Crevel.'

The Baroness left the room with a silent bow to Crevel, who could not help smiling at the child's surprise at finding himself threatened with this unexpected bath.

'Monsieur,' exclaimed the lawyer, when he was alone with Lisbeth, his wife, and his father-in-law, 'you are about to marry a woman who is laden with spoils from my father and who has cold-bloodedly led him into his present situation, a woman who, after ruining the father-in-law, lives with the son-in-law, and is the cause of my sister's grievous sorrows. And do you believe that we'll show approval of your folly by my presence? I'm sincerely sorry for you, my dear Monsieur Crevel. You have no family feeling; you don't understand the strong tie of honour that binds its different members to each other. One can't reason with passions—I know that, unfortunately, only too well. Men who are a prey to passions are as deaf as they are blind. Your daughter Célestine is too well aware of her filial duties to utter a word of reproach.'

'That would be a fine way to behave!' said Crevel, trying to cut this reprimand short.

'Célestine would not be my wife if she said a word to you on the matter,' continued the lawyer, 'but I, at least, can try to stop you before you step over the precipice, especially as I have given you proof of my disinterestedness. Indeed, it's not your fortune, it's you yourself that I'm concerned about. And to make my feelings quite clear to you, I can add, if only to set your mind at ease about your future marriage contract, that my financial situation now leaves nothing to be desired.'

'Thanks to me!' cried Crevel, who had become purple in the face.

'Thanks to Célestine's fortune,' the lawyer replied, 'but if you regret having given your daughter, as a dowry coming from you, a sum less than half what her mother left her, we are ready to return it to you.'

'Do you realize, Monsieur my son-in-law,' said Crevel, striking his attitude, 'that when I give Madame Marneffe the protection of my name, she is not obliged to answer to the world for her conduct except as Madame Crevel.'

'That may be very chivalrous,' said the lawyer. 'As far as affairs of the heart and the aberrations of passion are concerned, that's very generous. But I know of no name, or laws, or title that can cover up the theft of three hundred thousand francs shamelessly extorted from my father. I tell you plainly, my dear father-in-law, that your future wife is unworthy of you, that she is deceiving you, and that she is madly in love with my brother-in-law, Steinbock; she's paid his debts.'

'It was I who paid them.'

'All right,' resumed the lawyer. 'I'm very pleased for Count Steinbock, who'll be able one day to repay you. But he is loved, very much loved, frequently loved.'

'He is loved!' said Crevel, his face showing he was thoroughly upset. 'It's cowardly and dirty and petty and vulgar to slander a woman. When you make accusations like that, Monsieur, you have to prove them.'

'I'll give you proofs.'

'I'm waiting for them.'

'The day after tomorrow, my dear Monsieur Crevel, I'll tell you the day and the hour, the moment I'm in a position to reveal the frightful depravity of your future wife.'

'Very good, I'll be charmed,' said Crevel, recovering his composure. 'Goodbye, children, goodbye. Goodbye, Lisbeth.'

'Do go after him,' Célestine whispered to Cousin Bette.

'Well, what a way to go off!' Lisbeth shouted after Crevel.

'Oh,' said Crevel, 'he's come on very well, my son-in-law; he's got into good shape. The Law Courts, the Chamber, legal trickery, and political trickery have made a fine fellow of him! Oh yes, he knows I'm getting married next Wednesday, and on Sunday this gentleman proposes to tell me three days later the time when he'll prove that my wife is unworthy of me. That's quite cunning. I'm going back to sign the contract. Come on, come with me, Lisbeth, do come. They'll know nothing about it. I was going to leave forty thousand francs a year to Célestine, but Hulot has just behaved in a way to alienate my feelings from them for ever,'

'Give me ten minutes, Père Crevel. Wait for me in your carriage at the door. I'll find some pretext for going out.'

'All right. Agreed!'

'My dears,' said Lisbeth, going back to the family in the drawing-room, 'I'll go with Crevel. They're signing the contract this evening and I'll be able to tell you its terms.

It will probably be my last visit to that woman. Your father's furious. He's going to disinherit you.'

'His vanity will prevent him doing that,' replied the lawyer. 'He wanted to own the Presles estate; he'll hang on to it; I know him. Even if he has children, Célestine will still get half of what he leaves. The law doesn't allow him to give away his whole fortune. But these questions are of no consequence to me. I'm thinking only of our honour. Go, Cousin,' he said, shaking Lisbeth's hand. 'Listen carefully to the contract.'

111. *Another family scene*

Twenty minutes later, Lisbeth and Crevel entered the house in the Rue Barbet where, mildly impatient, Madame Marneffe was awaiting the outcome of the step she had ordered Crevel to take.

In the end Valérie had succumbed to the overwhelming love which, once in a lifetime, grips a woman's heart—such was her love for Wenceslas. A failure as an artist, he became such a perfect lover in Madame Marneffe's hands that he was for her what she had been for Baron Hulot.

Valérie held her slippers in one hand, the other was in Steinbock's, her head resting on his shoulder.

A conversation made up of broken phrases, such as the one they engaged in after Crevel's departure, is like those long literary works of our time with title-pages bearing the words: *Copyright reserved*. Such a masterpiece of intimate poetry naturally brought to the artist's lips a regret expressed with some bitterness.

'Oh, what a pity I got married,' said Wenceslas, 'for if I had waited, as Lisbeth told me to, I could marry you now.'

'Only a Pole could want to turn a devoted mistress into a wife,' exclaimed Valérie. 'To exchange love for duty! Pleasure for boredom!'

'I know how fickle you are,' replied Steinbock. 'Haven't I heard you talking to Lisbeth about Baron Montès, that Brazilian?'

'Do you want to get rid of him for me?' said Valérie.

'That would be the only way to prevent you from seeing him,' replied the ex-sculptor.

'You should know, darling,' Valérie replied, 'that I was treating him gently, so as to make a husband of him, for I tell *you* everything! The promises I've made to that Brazilian!—Oh, long before I knew you,' she said in reply to a gesture from Wenceslas. 'Well, those promises, which he's using now as weapons to torment me with, force me to marry almost secretly; for if he learns that I'm marrying Crevel, he's quite capable of . . . of killing me!'

'Oh, as for that fear!' said Steinbock with a contemptuous gesture which meant that *that* danger was insignificant for a woman loved by a Pole.

It is worth noting that in matters of courage, there is not a trace of boastfulness in Poles, for they are truly and unquestionably brave.

'And that fool of a Crevel, who wants to give a party and is indulging his taste for penny-pinching ostentation at my wedding, puts me in an awkward situation; I don't know how to get out of it.'

Valérie could not admit to the man she adored, that since the dismissal of Baron Hulot, Baron Henri Montès had succeeded to the privilege of visiting her at any hour of the night, and that, for all her cleverness, she still had not found an excuse for a quarrel in which the Brazilian would believe that he was entirely in the wrong.

She knew only too well the Baron's almost primitive nature, which was quite like Lisbeth's, so that she could not but tremble as she thought of the Moor of Rio de Janeiro.*

At the sound of carriage wheels, Steinbock, whose arm had been round Valérie's waist, left her side and picked up a newspaper; he appeared to be completely absorbed in it while, with great concentration, Valérie was embroidering slippers for her future husband.

'How they slander *her*!' Lisbeth whispered to Crevel at the door, indicating this tableau to him. 'Look at her hair!

Is it in disarray? To hear Victorin, you could have surprised two turtle-doves in their nest.'

'My dear Lisbeth,' said Crevel, striking his pose, 'to turn an Aspasia* into a Lucretia,* one has only to inspire a passion in her.'

'Haven't I always told you that women love fat libertines like you?' replied Lisbeth.

'Anyway, she'd be very ungrateful if she didn't,' continued Crevel, 'for I've spent a lot of money on this place. Only Grindot and I know how much.'

And he pointed to the staircase.

In the decoration of the house which Crevel looked on as his own, Grindot had tried to vie with Cleretti, the fashionable architect to whom the Duc d'Hérouville had entrusted the decoration of Josépha's villa.

But Crevel, incapable of understanding the arts, had wanted, like all bourgeois, to spend a fixed sum, specified in advance. Limited by an estimate, Grindot found it impossible to realize his architectural dream.

The difference between Josépha's house and the one in the Rue Barbet was that which exists between things with an individual character and those which are commonplace. The objects one admired in Josépha's establishment could be seen nowhere else; the gleaming ornaments in Crevel's could be bought anywhere. These two types of luxury are separated from each other by a river of millions. A unique mirror is worth six thousand francs, a mirror invented by a manufacturer who sells as many copies of it as he can, costs five hundred francs. A genuine Boule* chandelier will fetch up to three thousand francs at a public auction; the same chandelier, moulded, can be produced for a thousand to twelve hundred francs. The one is, in antiques, what a picture by Raphael is in painting; the other is a copy. What do you think a copy of a Raphael is worth?

So Crevel's house was a magnificent example of the luxury of fools, while Josépha's was the finest example of an artist's dwelling.

'War is declared,' said Crevel, going up to his wife-to-be.

Madame Marneffe rang.

'Go and fetch Monsieur Berthier,' she said to the footman, 'and don't come back without him. If you'd been successful, dear old thing,' she said, putting her arms round Crevel, 'we'd have delayed my happiness and had a brilliant party. But when a whole family is opposed to a marriage, my dear, decorum requires that it should be unostentatious, especially when the bride is a widow.'

'On the contrary, *I* want to make a display of luxury in Louis XVI style,' said Crevel, who for some time had been finding the eighteenth century tame. 'I've ordered new carriages. There's the bridegroom's carriage and the bride's, two elegant coupés, a barouche, and a ceremonial coach with a superb box that trembles like Madame Hulot.'

'Oh, *I want*! So you're not my lamb any more? No, no, my pet, you'll do what *I* want. We'll sign the contract here privately, this evening. Then on Wednesday, we'll get married officially, as people really do marry, *on the sly*, as my poor mother used to say. We'll go on foot, dressed very simply, to the church, where there'll be a low mass. Our witnesses will be Stidmann, Steinbock, Vignon, and Massol, all bright fellows who'll be at the town hall as if by chance and who'll put up with listening to a mass for our sakes. Your colleague will marry us, as an exceptional case, at nine in the morning. The mass is at ten o'clock, so we'll be back here for lunch at half past eleven. I've promised our guests that we won't get up from table till the evening. We'll have Bixiou, your old colleague from Birotteau's place, du Tillet, Lousteau, Vernisset, Léon de Lora, Vernou, the cream of witty fellows, who won't know we're married. We'll bamboozle them. We'll get a little tight and Lisbeth will be of the party. I want her to learn about marriage. Bixiou must make advances to her . . . and enlighten her.'

For two hours, Madame Marneffe rattled off nonsense that led Crevel to this wise reflection: 'How can such a high-spirited woman be depraved? Frivolous, yes. But perverse . . . it's not possible!'

'What did your children say about me?' Valérie asked

Crevel at a moment when she held him close to her on her sofa. 'Lots of horrors?'

'They claim that you are guilty of an immoral love for Wenceslas, you, who are virtue itself!' replied Crevel.

'Of course I love my little Wenceslas,' cried Valérie, calling the artist to her side, taking his head in her hands, and kissing him on the forehead. 'Poor boy, with no one to help him and no money, scorned by a carrot-haired giraffe! What do you expect, Crevel? Wenceslas is my poet and I love him in broad daylight as if he were my child. Those virtuous women see evil everywhere and in everything. Oh, that sort, couldn't they even sit beside a man without doing wrong? But I'm like a spoilt child who's never been refused anything; sweets don't excite me any more. Poor women, I pity them! And who ran me down like that?'

'Victorin,' said Crevel.

'Well, why didn't you shut that legal parrot's beak with the tale of *his mama's* two hundred thousand francs?'

'Oh, the Baroness had fled,' said Lisbeth.

'Let them beware, Lisbeth,' said Madame Marneffe, frowning. 'Either they'll receive me at their home, and in style, and visit their stepmother, the lot of them, or I'll bring them down lower than the Baron. Tell them that from me. In the end, I'm resolved to turn nasty. Upon my word, I think evil is the scythe that cuts down good.'

112. *The effects of blackmail*

At three o'clock Maître Berthier, Cardot's successor, read the marriage contract after a short conference with Crevel, for certain provisions depended on the decision young Monsieur and Madame Hulot would take.

Crevel settled on his future wife a fortune comprising: (1) an income of forty thousand francs from certain specified securities; (2) the house with all its furniture; and (3) three million francs in cash. In addition, he gave his future wife unconditionally all that the law allowed him to give, and if there should be no children of the marriage, the spouses left all their assets, possessions, and property respectively to each other.

This contract reduced Crevel's fortune to a capital of two million. If he had children by his new wife, Célestine's share would be reduced to five hundred thousand francs because of the life interest settled on Valérie. That was about a ninth part of his fortune at that time.

Lisbeth came back to dinner at the Rue Louis-le-Grand with despair written on her face. She explained and commented on the marriage contract, but found Célestine as well as Victorin indifferent to the disastrous news.

'You have annoyed your father, my dear children. Madame Marneffe has vowed that you will receive Monsieur Crevel's wife in your home and that you will come to hers.' she said.

'Never!' said Hulot.

'Never!' said Célestine.

'Never!' cried Hortense.

Lisbeth was gripped by a longing to humble the proud stance taken up by all the Hulots.

'She seems to have some weapon she can use against you,' she replied. 'I don't know yet what it's all about, but I'll find out. She spoke vaguely of some story of two hundred thousand francs connected with Adeline.'

Baroness Hulot fell gently back on to the couch where she was sitting, and was seized with an appalling attack of convulsions.

'Go there, children!' the Baroness exclaimed. 'Receive that woman! Monsieur Crevel is a vile wretch! He deserves the worst of punishments. To do what that woman says! Oh, he's a monster! *She knows everything!*'

After these words, mingled with tears and sobs, Madame Hulot summoned the strength to go upstairs to her room, supported by her daughter and Célestine

'What does all this mean?' exclaimed Lisbeth, left alone with Victorin.

The lawyer, rooted to the spot in very understandable amazement, did not hear Lisbeth.

'I am appalled,' said the lawyer, whose face had become threatening. 'Woe to anyone who lifts a finger against my mother; in that case, my scruples have gone. If I could, I would crush that woman like a viper. So, she attacks the life and honour of my mother!'

'She said, but don't repeat this, my dear Victorin, she said she'll bring you all down even lower than your father. She reproached Crevel sharply for not closing your mouth with the secret that seems to terrify Adeline so much.'

They sent for a doctor, for the Baroness's condition grew worse.

The doctor prescribed a large dose of opium and after taking it Adeline fell into a deep sleep. But the whole family was a prey to the keenest alarm.

The next day the lawyer set off early for the Law Courts, and on his way he called at the Prefecture of Police, where he asked Vautrin,* head of the Criminal Investigation Department, to send him Madame de Sainte-Estève.

'We've been forbidden to concern ourselves with your affairs, Monsieur, but Madame de Sainte-Estève is a business woman and she's at your service,' the celebrated head-officer replied.

On his return home, the unhappy lawyer learned that they feared for his mother's reason. Doctor Bianchon, Doctor Larabit, and Professor Augard, assembled in consultation, had just decided to use drastic measures to turn the flow of blood away from the brain.

Just as Victorin was listening to Doctor Bianchon detailing his reasons for hoping that the crisis would pass despite the pessimism of his colleagues, the footman announced the lawyer's client, Madame de Sainte-Estève.

Victorin left Bianchon in the middle of a sentence and rushed downstairs like a madman.

'Is there a streak of contagious madness in this house?' asked Bianchon, turning to Larabit.

The doctors departed, leaving a junior hospital doctor, with instructions from them, to watch over Madame Hulot.

'A whole lifetime of virtue!' were the only words the sick woman had uttered since her disastrous seizure.

Lisbeth did not leave Adeline's bedside, sitting up all night with her. She was the admiration of the two younger women.

'Well, my dear Madame Sainte-Estève,' said the lawyer, showing the horrible old woman into his study and closing the doors carefully, 'how far have we got?'

'Well, my good friend,' she said, looking at Victorin with cold irony, 'so you've given the matter a little thought?'

'Have you done anything?'

'Will you pay fifty thousand francs?'

'Yes,' replied young Hulot, 'for we must get going. Do you know, with a single sentence that woman has endangered my mother's life and reason. So get going.'

'We've got going,' replied the old woman.

'Well?' said Victorin with a convulsive gesture.

'Well, the expense doesn't put you off?'

'On the contrary.'

'You see the cost already amounts to twenty-three thousand francs.'

Young Hulot looked at Madame Sainte-Estève in stunned amazement.

'Oh, you're surely not that simple-minded, you, one of the leading lights of the Law Courts?' said the old woman. 'For that amount we've bought the conscience of a lady's maid and a picture by Raphael. That's not dear.'

Hulot was still in a daze; he stood there wide-eyed.

'Well,' continued Sainte-Estève, 'we've bought Mademoiselle Reine Tousard. Madame Marneffe has no secrets from her.'

'I understand.'

'But if you grudge the money, say so.'

'I'll pay, I'll trust you,' he replied. 'Go ahead. My mother told me that those people deserve the worst of punishments.'

'They don't break people on the wheel any more,' said the old woman.

'You guarantee success?'

'Leave it to me,' replied Sainte-Estève. 'Your vengeance is simmering.

She looked at the clock. It was just six.

'Your vengeance is getting ready; the ovens at the *Rocher de Cancale* have been lit; the carriage horses are pawing the ground; my irons are getting hot. Oh, I know your Madame Marneffe by heart. Everything is ready now; there's poison in the rat-trap. I'll tell you tomorrow if the mouse is poisoned. I think she will be. Goodbye, my boy.'

'Goodbye, Madame.'

'Do you know English?'

'Yes.'

'Have you seen a performance of *Macbeth* in English?'

'Yes.'

'Well, my boy, thou shalt be king! that is to say, thou shalt inherit!' said the frightful witch who was foreseen by Shakespeare and who seemed to know Shakespeare's works.

She left Hulot dumbfounded at the door of his study.

'Don't forget that the case is on for tomorrow,' she said graciously in the manner of an experienced litigant.

She saw two people coming in and wanted to pass in their eyes for a Countess Pimbèche.*

'What a cool customer!' Hulot said to himself as he bowed out his pretended client.

113. *Combabus*

Baron Montès de Montéjanos was a social celebrity, but a celebrity with a mystery attached. Fashionable Paris, the Paris of the turf and the courtesans, admired the foreign nobleman's superb waistcoats, his impeccably polished boots, his incomparable walking-sticks, his much-coveted horses, his carriage driven by completely enslaved, well-beaten negroes.

The extent of his fortune was common knowledge. He had a credit of seven hundred thousand francs with du

Tillet, the well-known banker. But he was always seen alone. If he went to a first night, he always had a seat in the stalls. He frequented no salon. He had never given his arm to a courtesan. His name could never be linked with that of any pretty society woman. To amuse himself he played whist at the Jockey Club.

People were reduced to casting aspersions on his habits and morals, or, what seemed infinitely more amusing, on his personal appearance. They called him Combabus!

Bixiou, Léon de Lora, Lousteau, Florine, Mademoiselle Héloïse Brisetout, and Nathan, having supper one evening at the renowned Carabine's with lots of social celebrities of both sexes, had invented this extremely ludicrous explanation.

Massol, in his capacity as Councillor of State, and Claude Vignon, as a former professor of Greek, had told the ignorant girls the famous anecdote related in Rollin's *Ancient History* about Combabus, the voluntary Abélard* entrusted with the protection of the wife of a king of Assyria, Persia, Bactria, Mesopatamia, and other regions of the personal geography of old Professor Bocage, who completed the work of d'Anville,* the creator of the East of antiquity.

This nickname, which sent Carabine's guests into fits of laughter for a quarter of an hour, was the subject of a host of jokes, too spicy to be included in a work to which the Academy would probably not award the Montyon prize.* But amongst them, the name stood out and remained attached to the shaggy mane of the handsome Baron. Josépha called him a *magnificent Brazilian* as one talks of a magnificent *Catoxantha.**

Carabine, the most celebrated of the courtesans, had a refined beauty and ready wit which had wrested the sceptre of the thirteenth district from the hands of Mademoiselle Turquet, better known under the name of *Malaga*. Mademoiselle Séraphine Sinet (for that was her real name) was to the banker du Tillet what Josépha Mirah was to the Duc d'Hérouville.

Now, at about seven in the morning on the very day

Sainte-Estève prophesied success to Victorin, Carabine had said to du Tillet:

'Be nice and give me a dinner at the *Rocher de Cancale*, and invite Combabus. We want to find out, once and for all, if he has a mistress. I've bet that he has and I want to win.'

'He's still at the *Hôtel des Princes*. I'll call in there,' replied du Tillet. 'We'll have some fun. Let's have all the lads, Bixiou, Lora, in fact the whole gang.'

At half past seven, in the best room of the restaurant where all Europe has dined, there glittered a magnificent service of silver-plate, made expressly for dinner-parties where vanity paid the bill in bank notes. Floods of light produced, as it were, gleaming cascades along the edges of the chased metal. Waiters, whom a provincial would have taken for diplomats were it not for their youth, stood there with the solemn air of men who know they are overpaid.

Five people had arrived and were waiting for nine others.

First there was Bixiou, the salt of every intellectual dish, still going strong in 1843, with a battery of witticisms that were always new—a phenomenon as rare in Paris as virtue.

Then came Léon de Lora, the greatest living landscape and seascape painter, who had the advantage over all his rivals of never having fallen below the level of his early works.

The courtesans found these two kings of wit indispensable. Not a supper, not a dinner, not a party could take place without them.

Séraphine Sinet, known as Carabine, in her role as acknowledged mistress of the Amphitryon* of the party, had been one of the first to arrive. Under the floods of light she displayed the dazzling beauty of her shoulders, unrivalled in Paris, her neck looking as if it had been turned on a lathe, it was so smooth, her face full of fun, and her dress of figured satin, blue upon blue, decorated with enough English lace to feed a whole village for a month.

Pretty Jenny Cadine, who was not performing at her theatre that evening, and whose appearance is too well known to need any description, arrived in a fabulously expensive outfit.

For these ladies, a party is always a Longchamps* of dress at which each of them wants to win a prize for her millionaire by saying in this way to her rivals:

'See how much I'm worth!'

A third woman, presumably just beginning her career, was almost shamefacedly looking at the luxury of the two wealthy, established comrades.

She was simply dressed in white cashmere trimmed with blue lace; her hair had been done up with flowers by an incompetent hairdresser, whose clumsy hand had unintentionally given an unsophisticated charm to her lovely fair hair. Still ill-at-ease in her evening dress, *she had the shyness inseparable from a first appearance*, to use a well-worn phrase. She had arrived from Valognes* to find a market in Paris for a heart-breaking youthful freshness, an artlessness that would arouse desire in a dying man, and a beauty fit to rank with all those that Normandy has already supplied to the different theatres of the capital. The lines of her perfect face portrayed the ideal of angelic purity. Her milky white skin reflected the light as perfectly as a mirror. Her delicate colouring looked as if it had been applied to her cheeks with an artist's brush. She was called Cydalise.*

As we shall see, she was a necessary pawn in the game that *Ma'am* Nourrisson was playing against Madame Marneffe.

'Your arms don't fit your name, child,' Jenny Cadine had said when Carabine introduced her to the 16-year-old masterpiece she had brought to the party.

And indeed Cydalise offered for public admiration lovely, firm arms, with well-textured skin but reddened by a vigorous flow of blood.

'How much is she worth?' Jenny Cadine asked Carabine in a whisper.

'A fortune.'

'What are you going to do with her?'

'Madame Combabus, of course!'

'And what are you going to get for that job?'

'Guess!'

'A beautiful service of silver-plate?'

'I've got three already!'

'Diamonds?'

'I'm selling them!'

'A green monkey?'

'No, a picture by Raphael!'

'What crazy notion have you got into your head?'

'Josépha bores me to tears with her pictures,' replied Carabine, 'and I want to have finer ones than hers.'

Du Tillet came in with the guest of honour, the Brazilian. The Duc d'Hérouville followed them with Josépha.

The singer wore a simple velvet dress.

But around her neck gleamed a necklace worth a hundred and twenty thousand francs, its pearls barely distinguishable from her camelia-white skin. Into her black braided hair she had thrust a single red camelia (a beauty-spot!) with dazzling effect and, just for fun, she had placed eleven rows of pearl bracelets, one above the other, on each arm.

She came up to shake hands with Jenny Cadine, who said:

'Oh, do lend me your mittens!'

Josépha took off her bracelets and offered them on a plate to her friend.

'What style!' said Carabine. 'Quite the duchess! What a show of pearls! Have you plundered the sea to adorn the girl, Monsieur le Duc?' she added, turning to the little Duc d'Hérouville.

The actress took just two bracelets, put the other twenty on the singer's beautiful arms, and kissed them.

Lousteau, the literary scrounger, La Palférine and Malaga, Massol and Vauvinet, and Théodore Gaillard, one of the proprietors of a leading political newspaper, completed the party.

The Duc d'Hérouville, courteous to everyone as a great nobleman always is, gave La Palférine that special greeting which, without implying esteem or intimacy, tells everybody, 'We belong to the same class, the same breed; we are equals.' That greeting, the *shibboleth** of the aristrocracy, was invented to the despair of the wits and the upper middle class.

Carabine placed Combabus on her left and the Duc d'Hérouville on her right. Cydalise was on the other side of the Brazilian, and Bixiou was put next to the Norman girl. Malaga took her place beside the Duke.

114. *A courtesan's dinner-party*

At seven o'clock they attacked the oysters. At eight o'clock, between two courses, they sipped iced punch. Everyone knows the menu of these parties.

At nine o'clock they were chattering away as people chatter after drinking forty-two bottles of different wines, shared between fourteen people. The dessert, the horrible dessert of the month of April,* had been served. The heady atmosphere had affected only the Norman girl, who was humming a Christmas carol.

With the exception of that poor girl, no one had lost the use of his reason; the drinkers, men and women, were the élite of Paris diners-out. Wits were sparkling merrily, eyes, though gleaming, were still full of intelligence, but tongues turned to satire, anecdote, and indiscreet gossip.

The conversation up till then had kept to the vicious circle of racing and horses, of Stock Exchange operations, of the comparative merits of social celebrities and of well-known scandalous stories. But it was threatening to become intimate and to break up into heart-to-heart talks between couples.

It was at this moment that, at winks from Carabine to Léon de Lora, Bixiou, La Palférine, and du Tillet, they began to talk of love.

'Well-bred doctors never talk of medicine, real nobles never talk of their ancestors, men of talent never talk about their works,' said Josépha. 'Why should we talk about our profession? I had the Opera performance cancelled so that

I could come here and it certainly wasn't so that I should *work*. So let's not *put on an act*, my dear friends.'

'They're talking about real love, my dear,' said Malaga, 'of the kind of love that engulfs a man completely, that makes him drag down his father and mother, sell his wife and children, and end up in Clichy.'*

'Talk away then,' replied the singer. 'Not known here.'

Not known here! When this phrase, taken over from street urchins' slang into the vocabulary of courtesans, is reinforced by the expression in the eyes and on the faces of these women, it is, on their lips, a whole poem.

'So I don't love you, Josépha?' said the Duke in a low voice.

'You may love me truly,' the singer whispered to the Duke with a smile. 'But I don't love you with the kind of love they're talking about, with the love which makes the universe all dark without the man one loves. I think you're very nice and I find you useful, but you're not indispensable to me. And if you were to desert me tomorrow, I'd have three dukes for one.'

'Does love exist in Paris?' said Léon de Lora. 'No one here has the time to earn a decent living, so how can one devote oneself to true love that takes possession of a man as water does sugar? You have to be enormously rich to love, for love annihilates a man, rather as it has done to our Brazilian friend here. As I said a long time ago, *extremes coincide*! A true lover is like a eunuch, for women no longer exist on earth for him. He is a mystery; he is like the true Christian in his solitary retreat. Just look at our fine Brazilian!'

The whole table stared at Henri Montès de Montéjanos, who was embarrassed at finding himself the cynosure of all eyes.

'He's been feeding there for the last hour, as unaware as an ox that he's sitting beside the . . . I won't say, in this company, the loveliest, but the freshest young woman in Paris.'

'Everything's fresh here, even the fish. That's what this place is famous for,' said Carabine.

Baron Montès de Montéjanos looked affably at the landscape artist and said:

'Very good. I drink to your health.'

Then he nodded to Léon de Lora, put his glassful of port to his lips, and drank deeply.

'So you're in love,' Carabine said to her neighbour, interpreting the toast in this way.

The Brazilian Baron had his glass filled up again, bowed to Carabine, and repeated the toast.

'To Madame's health,' replied the courtesan in such an amusing tone that the painter, du Tillet, and Bixiou burst out laughing.

The Brazilian remained as unmoved as a bronze statue. His composure irritated Carabine. She knew perfectly well that Montès was in love with Madame Marneffe, but had not expected the absolute trust, the obstinate silence of a man with no doubts at all.

A woman is judged as often by her lover's demeanour as a lover is judged by his mistress's bearing.

Proud of loving Valérie and of being loved by her, there was a tinge of irony in the smile the Baron bestowed on these experienced connoisseurs, and, moreover, he was magnificent to look upon. Wine had not altered his colour, and his eyes, shining with the brilliance peculiar to burnished gold, did not reveal the secrets of his heart.

So Carabine said to herself: 'What a woman! How she has sealed up that heart of yours!'

'He's a rock,' said Bixiou under his breath; he thought it was only a bit of fooling and did not suspect the importance Carabine attached to the demolition of this fortress.

While, on Carabine's right, this apparently frivolous conversation was taking place, on her left the discussion about love was being continued between the Duc d'Hérouville, Lousteau, Josépha, Jenny Cadine, and Massol.

They had reached the stage of considering whether such rare phenomena were the product of infatuation, obstinacy, or true love.

Josépha, thoroughly bored by these theories, wanted to change the subject.

'You're talking of something you know absolutely nothing about. Is there any one of you who has loved a woman enough—and a woman quite unworthy of him—to squander all his fortune, and his children's too, to compromise his future, to tarnish his past, to run the risk of the galleys by robbing the State, to kill an uncle and a brother, to let his eyes be so completely blindfolded that he didn't realize it was being done so as to prevent him from seeing the abyss into which he was thrust as a final jest? Du Tillet has a cash-box under his left breast; Léon de Lora has his wit there; Bixiou would laugh at himself if he loved anyone but himself; Massol has a minister's portfolio instead of a heart; Lousteau has only an internal organ there, for he let Madame de la Baudraye* leave him; Monsieur le Duc is too rich to be able to prove his love by ruining himself; Vauvinet doesn't count, for I exclude the discounter of the human race. So you've never been in love, nor have I, nor Jenny, nor Carabine. For my own part, I've only once seen the phenomenon I've just described. It was our poor Baron Hulot,' she said, turning to Jenny Cadine. 'I'm going to advertise for him like a lost dog, for I want to find him.'

'Well, well!' Carabine said to herself with a sideways look at Josépha. 'So has Madame Nourrisson got two Raphael pictures, since Josépha's playing my game?'

'Poor man!' said Vauvinet. 'He was a great man, quite splendid. What style! What bearing! He had the appearance of François I!* What a volcano! And what skill, what genius he had in getting hold of money! Wherever he is, he's looking for it. He must be extracting some from those walls made of bones that you see in the outskirts of Paris, near the gates, where he's probably hiding.'

'And all that for little Madame Marneffe,' said Bixiou. 'She's a cunning bitch, if ever there was one.'

'She's going to marry my friend Crevel,' du Tillet added.

'And she's crazy about my friend Steinbock,' said Léon de Lora.

These three remarks were three pistol shots that struck Montès full in the chest.

He turned pale and was in such distress that he found it difficult to get up.

'You swine!' he said. 'You ought not to mention the name of an honest woman in the same breath as the names of all your dissolute creatures, let alone making her a target for your jibes.'

Montès was interrupted by cries of 'Bravo' and unanimous applause. Bixiou, Léon de Lora, Vauvinet, du Tillet, and Massol gave the signal; it was a chorus.

'Long live the Emperor!' said Bixiou.

'Let's crown him!' cried Vauvinet.

'A growl for Médor,* hurrah for Brazil!' shouted Lousteau.

'Aha, my copper-coloured Baron, so you're in love with our Valérie,' said Léon de Lora, 'and you're not disgusted with her!'

'It wasn't said in parliamentary language, but it was magnificent!' remarked Massol.

'But, my dearest client, you were recommended to me. I'm your banker. Your innocence will count against me.'

'Oh, tell me, you who are a sensible man . . .' the Brazilian said, turning to du Tillet.

'Thanks on behlf of the whole company,' said Bixiou, bowing.

'Tell me some positive facts,' added Montès, paying no attention to Bixiou's remark.

'As to that,' replied du Tillet, 'I have the honour to tell you that I'm invited to Crevel's wedding.'

'Oh, Combabus is going to defend Madame Marneffe,' said Josépha, solemnly getting up.

She went up to Montès with a tragic air, gave him a friendly little pat on the head, looked at him for a moment with a comic expression of admiration on her face, and shook her head.

'Hulot is the first example of love *at all costs*; here's the second,' she said. 'But he shouldn't count, for he comes from the tropics.'

As Josépha gently tapped the Brazilian's brow, he fell back into his chair and appealed with a look to du Tillet.

'If I'm the butt of one of your Parisian jokes,' he said, 'if you wanted to wrest my secret from me . . .'

And he cast a fiery look round the whole table, including all the guests, in a glance blazing with the Brazilian sun.

'For pity's sake, tell me so,' he continued with a pleading and almost childlike look, 'but don't slander a woman I love.'

'That's all very well,' Carabine replied in a low voice, 'but if you were shamefully betrayed, deceived, tricked by Valérie, if I were to give you proofs in an hour's time at my house, what would you do?'

'I can't tell you here in front of all these Iagos,' said the Brazilian Baron.

Carabine understood him to say *magots*—ugly wretches.

'Well, say no more,' she replied, smiling. 'Don't make yourself a laughing-stock for the wittiest men in Paris, but come to my place and we'll have a talk.'

Montès was shattered.

'Proofs,' he stammered. 'Just think . . .'

'You'll have only too many,' replied Carabine, 'but since mere suspicion goes to your head so much, I fear for your reason.'

'What an obstinate fellow he is; he's worse than the late King of Holland.* Look here, Lousteau, Bixiou, Massol, listen, all of you. Aren't you all invited to lunch by Madame Marneffe for the day after tomorrow?' asked Léon de Lora.

'*Ya*,' replied du Tillet. 'I have the honour to inform you again, Baron, that if by any chance you intend to marry Madame Marneffe, you are thrown out like a parliamentary bill, blackballed by a man called Crevel. My friend, my former colleague, Crevel, has an annual income of eighty thousand livres and you probably haven't made a show of as much as that, for, if you had, I think you'd have been preferred.'

Montès listened with a half-abstracted, half-smiling expression which seemed terrifying to the whole company.

Just then the head-waiter came in and whispered to

Carabine that one of her relatives was in the ante-room and wanted to speak to her. The courtesan got up, left the room, and found Madame Nourrisson veiled in black lace.

'Well, am I to go to your house, my child? Has he taken the bait?'

'Yes, mother dear, the pistol is so well loaded that I'm afraid it'll explode,' replied Carabine.

115. *In which Madame Nourrisson is seen at work*

An hour later Montès, Cydalise, and Carabine, back from the *Rocher de Cancale*, entered Carabine's little drawing-room in the Rue Saint-Georges.

The courtesan saw Madame Nourrisson sitting in an easy-chair by the fire.

'Why, here's my good aunt!' she said.

'Yes, my child. I've come myself to get my little allowance. You might forget me, although you have a kind heart, and I've bills to pay tomorrow. A clothes dealer is always hard up. Who's that you're dragging in after you? The gentleman looks thoroughly upset.'

The repulsive Madame Nourrisson, at this moment completely metamorphosed and looking like a kindly old lady, got up to kiss Carabine, one of the hundred or so courtesans she had launched in the horrible career of vice.

'He's an Othello who hasn't made a mistake, and whom I have the honour to introduce to you; Monsieur le Baron Montès de Montéjanos.'

'Oh, I know Monsieur by repute. They call you Combabus because you love only one woman. In Paris, that's the same as if you had none at all. Well, is it by any chance the object of your love that's troubling you? Madame Marneffe, Crevel's woman? Well, my dear sir, you should thank your stars instead of blaming them. . . . She's a good-for-nothing, that little woman. I know her goings-on!'

'But that's not the point,' said Carabine as Madame

Nourrisson kissed her and slipped a letter into her hand. 'You don't know the Brazilians. They're swaggering fellows who are anxious to be stabbed through the heart! The more jealous they are, the more they want to be. This gentleman talks of slaughtering everybody, but he won't slaughter anybody, because he's in love. Anyway, I've brought Monsieur le Baron back here to give him proofs of his misfortune that I got from little Steinbock.'

Montès was drunk; he was listening as if the matter concerned somebody else. Carabine went to take off her velvet cape and read the facsimile of the following note:

'My pet, *he* is going to have dinner at Popinot's this evening, and will call for me at the Opera about eleven. I'll leave the house about half past five and expect to find you at our paradise, where you'll have dinner sent in from the *Maison d'Or*.* Dress so that you can take me on to the Opera. We'll have four hours to ourselves. You must give me back this little note, not that your Valérie doesn't trust you—I would give you my life, my fortune, and my honour—but I'm afraid of the tricks of chance.'

'There you are, Baron. That's the love letter sent this morning to the Comte de Steinbock. Read the address. The original has just been burned.'

Montès turned the piece of paper over and over, recognized the handwriting, and was struck by a sensible idea, which showed his distraught state of mind.

'But tell me, what do you get out of tearing my heart to pieces, for you must have paid a lot to have this note in your hands long enough to get it lithographed?' he asked, looking at Carabine.

'You big fool!' said Carabine at a sign from Madame Nourrisson. 'Don't you see poor Cydalise here? She's a youngster of 16 who's been so much in love with you for three months that she's quite lost her appetite and is heartbroken because you haven't yet given her even a casual glance.'

Cydalise put a handkerchief to her eyes and looked as if she were crying.

'Although she looks as if butter wouldn't melt in her

mouth, she's furious at seeing the man she's madly in love with, the dupe of a scheming bitch,' continued Carabine, 'and she'd kill Valérie . . .'

'Oh, as to that,' said the Brazilian, 'that's my business!'

'Kill her? You, my dear boy?' said Ma Nourrisson. 'We don't do that sort of thing here nowadays.'

'Oh,' replied Montès, 'but *I* don't belong to this country! I live in a region where I don't give a rap for your laws, and if you give me proofs . . .'

'But isn't this note a proof, then?'

'No,' said the Brazilian, 'I don't believe in writing, I want to see . . .'

'Oh, as for seeing,' said Carabine, who understood perfectly a new sign from her pretended aunt, 'well, we'll enable you to see everything, my dear tiger, but on one condition.'

'What's that?'

'Look at Cydalise.'

At a sign from Madame Nourrisson, Cydalise looked tenderly at the Brazilian.

'Will you love her? Will you establish her in life?' asked Carabine. 'A woman as lovely as that is worth a house and a carriage. It would be monstrous to let her go about on foot. And she has . . . debts. How much do you owe?' asked Carabine, pinching Cydalise's arm.

'She's worth what she's worth,' said Ma Nourrisson. 'It's enough that there's a buyer.'

'Listen,' cried Montès, at last becoming aware of this wonderful masterpiece of feminine beauty, 'will you show me Valérie?'

'And the Comte de Steinbock into the bargain,' said Madame Nourrisson.

The old woman had been watching the Brazilian for the last ten minutes and she saw in him the instrument tuned to the pitch of murder that she required. Seeing, too, that he was blinded enough not to pay any attention to those who were leading him on, she intervened.

'Cydalise, my darling from Brazil, is my niece, so the matter concerns me a little. This whole mess can be cleared

up in ten minutes, for it's from one of my friends that
Steinbock rents the furnished room where your Valérie is
having her coffee, a queer kind of coffee but she calls it her
coffee. So, lets come to an arrangement, Brazil! I love
Brazil; it's a hot country. What will you do for my niece?'

'You old ostrich!' said Montès, struck by the feathers on
Ma Nourrisson's hat. 'You interrupted me. If you show
me . . . show me Valérie and that artist together . . .'

'As you'd like to be with her yourself,' said Carabine.
'That's agreed.'

'Well, I'll take this Norman girl and carry her off . . .'

'Where to?' asked Carabine.

'To Brazil!' replied the Baron. I'll make her my wife.
My uncle has left me ten square leagues of land I can't sell.
That why I still own the place. I've got a hundred negroes
there, nothing but negroes, negresses, and little negroes
bought by my uncle.'

'A slave-dealer's nephew!' said Carabine, making a face.
'That has to be thought about. Cydalise, my child, do you
like niggers?'

'Come, let's be serious, Carabine,' said Ma Nourrisson.
'Hang it all! The gentleman and I are talking business.'

'If I take a Frenchwoman again, I want her all to myself,'
continued the Brazilian. 'I warn you, Mademoiselle, I'm a
king, but not a constitutional king; I'm a czar. I've bought
all my subjects and no one can leave my kingdom, which
is a hundred leagues from any other human habitation. Its
interior is bordered by a country of savages and it is
separated from the coast by a desert as extensive as your
France.'

'I prefer an attic here!' said Carabine.

'That's what I thought,' replied the Brazilian. 'That's
why I sold all my estates and everything I owned in Rio de
Janeiro to come back to Madame Marneffe.'

'One doesn't make journeys like that for nothing,' said
Madame Nourrisson. 'You're entitled to be loved for your
own sake, especially as you're very handsome. Oh, he is
handsome!' she said to Carabine.

'Very handsome, more handsome than the Longjumeau postilion,'* replied the courtesan.

Cydalise took the Brazilian's hand, but he disengaged it as politely as he could.

'I came back to carry off Madame Marneffe,' the Brazilian went on, resuming his tale, 'and do you know why it took me three years to come back?'

'No, savage,' said Carabine.

'Well, she told me so often that she wanted to live alone with me in some deserted spot.'

'He's not a savage any more,' said Carabine, bursting out laughing. 'He belongs to the tribe of civilized mugs.'

'She told me that so often,' said the Baron, untouched by the courtesan's mocking laughter, 'that I had a charming dwelling prepared for her in the middle of that huge estate. I've come back to France to fetch Valérie, and the night I saw her again . . .'

'*Saw her again* is a polite expression,' said Carabine. 'I'll remember it.'

'She told me to wait till that miserable Marneffe died, and I agreed. At the same time I forgave her for accepting Hulot's advances. I don't know if the devil has put on petticoats, but from that moment she has given in to all my whims, to all my demands. Not for a minute, in fact, has she given me grounds for suspicion.'

'Well, that's a bit much!' Carabine said to Madame Nourrisson.

Madame Nourrisson nodded in agreement.

'My faith in that woman was equal to my love,' Montès said, giving way to tears. 'I nearly boxed the ears of everyone at table just now.'

'I saw that quite clearly,' said Carabine.

'If I'm deceived, if that woman marries, if at this moment she's in Steinbock's arms, she has deserved a thousand deaths, and I'll kill her as I'd crush a fly . . .'

'And what about the police, my dear fellow?' asked Madame Nourrisson with an old hag's grin that made one's flesh creep.

'And the police commissioner and the judges and the assize court and the whole hullaballoo?' said Carabine.

'You're a fool, my dear fellow,' continued Madame Nourrisson, who wanted to find out the Brazilian's plans for vengeance.

'I'll kill her,' Montès repeated coldly. 'Well, so you called me a savage! Do you think I'm going to imitate the stupidity of your compatriots who go and buy poison at the chemist's? On the way to your house I thought about my vengeance, in case you were right about Valérie. One of my negroes carries with him the most deadly of animal poisons, a terrible disease which is more efficacious than a vegetable poison and which can be cured only in Brazil. I'll get Cydalise to take it and she'll give it to me. Then when death's in the veins of Crevel and his wife, I'll be beyond the Azores with your cousin. I'll have her cured and I'll make her my wife. We savages have our own way of doing things! Cydalise', he said, looking at the Norman girl, 'is the creature I need. How much does she owe?'

'A hundred thousand francs,' said Cydalise.

'She doesn't say much, but it's to the point,' Carabine whispered to Madame Nourrisson.

'I'm going mad!' the Brazilian exclaimed in a hollow voice, collapsing into an easy-chair. 'It'll be the death of me. But I want to see for myself, for it's impossible! A lithographed note! How do I know it isn't the work of a forger? Baron Hulot love Valérie?' he said, remembering Josépha's words. 'But the proof that he didn't love her is the fact that she's still alive. *I'll* not leave her alive for anyone, if she isn't mine alone!'

Montès was terrifying to see and even more terrifying to hear. He was roaring and writhing; he broke everything he touched; the rosewood shattered like glass.

'How he's smashing everything up!' said Carabine, looking at Nourrisson. 'My dear fellow,' she said, tapping the Brazilian on the arm, 'Roland in a fury* is all very well in a poem, but in a flat it's prosaic and expensive.'

'My dear boy,' said Ma Nourrisson, getting up and taking up her stance opposite the dejected Brazilian. 'I'm of your persuasion. When one loves in a certain way, when one is *hooked until death*, life is answerabe for love. The one who breaks loose tears the whole thing up by the roots, causes total destruction. You have my esteem, my admiration, and my consent, above all for your line of action which is making me pro-negro. But you're in love; you won't go through with it.'

'Me! If she's a faithless hussy, I'll . . .'

'Come now, you talk too much, when all's said and done,' Madame Nourrisson went on, becoming her practical self once more. 'A man who wants to avenge himself, who claims to behave like a savage, acts differently. To see your loved one in her paradise, you must take Cydalise and go in there, as if you'd been shown into the wrong room with your mistress as a result of a maid's error. But don't make a scene. If you want to be avenged, you must behave like a coward, look as if you're in despair, and let yourself be hoodwinked by your mistress. Got the idea?' said Madame Nourrisson, seeing the Brazilian surprised at such a subtle scheme.

'Very well, ostrich,' he replied. 'Very well. . . . I understand.'

'Goodbye, darling,' said Madame Nourrisson to Carabine.

She motioned to Cydalise to go downstairs with Montès and remained alone with Carabine.

'Now, my pet, I'm afraid of only one thing—that he'll strangle her! That would put me in a fix. We must handle only *quiet* affairs. Oh, I think you've earned your Raphael picture, but they say it's a Mignard.* But don't worry; it's much nicer. I've been told that the Raphaels were all black, while this picture is as pretty as a Girodet.'*

'I only care about scoring over Josépha,' cried Carabine, 'and I don't care if it's with a Mignard or a Raphael. Do you know, that gold-digger was wearing such pearls this evening . . . you'd sell your soul for them!'

116. *A little house in 1840*

Cydalise, Montès, and Madame Nourrisson got into a cab
which was waiting at Carabine's door. Madame Nourrisson quietly directed the driver to a house in the same block
as the Italian Opera. They could have got there quite
quickly, for it is only seven to eight minutes' drive from
the Rue Saint-Georges, but Madame Nourrisson told him
to go by the Rue Lepelletier and to drive very slowly so
that they could examine the waiting carriages.

'Brazilian,' said Ma Nourrisson, 'look out for your
angel's carriage and servants.'

The Baron pointed out Valérie's carriage as the cab drove
past it.

'She told her servants to come at ten o'clock and she
took a cab to the house where she is with Count Steinbock.
She had dinner there and in half an hour she'll arrive at the
Opera. It's well worked out. That explains how she's been
able to pull the wool over your eyes for so long,' said
Madame Nourrisson.

The Brazilian made no answer. Transformed into a tiger,
he had recovered the imperturbable composure that had
been so greatly admired at the dinner-party. In short, he
was as calm as a bankrupt the day after his petition has
been filed.

At the door of the fateful house, a two-horse hackney
carriage was waiting, one of those called *General company*
from the name of the firm that runs them.

'Stay in your cab,' Madame Nourrisson said to Montès.
'You can't go in there as if it were a public bar. Someone
will come and fetch you.'

Madame Marneffe's and Wenceslas's paradise was not
the least like Crevel's little house, which he had sold to
Comte Maxime de Trailles, for it seemed to him it was no
longer required.

This paradise, a paradise used by many people, consisted

of a fourth-floor room opening on to the staircase in a house in the same block as the Italian Opera.

On each floor of the house, on each landing, there was a room formerly intended to serve as a kitchen for each flat.

But as the house had become a sort of inn whose rooms were let out for clandestine love-affairs at exorbitant prices, the real Madame Nourrisson, a second-hand clothes dealer in the Rue Neuve-Saint-Marc, had made a sound judgement of the enormous value of these kitchens and had converted each one into a sort of dining-room.

Each of these rooms had thick party-walls on both sides, looked out on to the street, and was completely cut off by very thick folding doors providing a secure lock on the landing side. Tenants could therefore discuss important secrets at dinner without risk of being overheard. For greater security, the windows were provided with Venetian blinds outside and shutters inside.

Because of their special feature these rooms cost three hundred francs a month.

This house, replete with its paradises and its mysteries, was let for twenty-four thousand francs a year to Madame Nourrisson I, who made a profit of twenty thousand a year, taking one year with another, after paying her agent Madame Nourrisson II, for she did not manage the property herself.

The paradise let to Count Steinbock had been hung with chintz. The coldness and hardness of the cheap red-polished tiles could no longer be felt underfoot because of a soft carpet. The furniture consisted of two pretty chairs and a bed in an alcove; just then it was half hidden by a table, on which there were the remains of an elegant dinner, and where two long-necked bottles and an empty champagne bottle in its ice-bucket marked out the fields of Bacchus tilled by Venus.

Sent no doubt by Valérie, there was a comfortable upholstered armchair beside a low fireside chair and a pretty rosewood chest of drawers with its mirror nicely framed in the Pompadour style. A lamp hanging from the ceiling shed a half-light, augmented by the candles standing on the table and on the mantelpiece.

This sketch will give an idea, *urbi et orbi*,* of the sordid dimensions of a clandestine love-affair in the Paris of 1840. How far removed, alas, from adulterous love as symbolized by Vulcan's nets* three thousand years ago.

As Cydalise and the Baron were going upstairs, Valérie, standing in front of the fireplace where a large faggot was blazing, was having her stays laced up by Wenceslas. This is the moment when a woman who is neither too fat nor too thin, like the slender, elegant Valérie, appears divinely beautiful. The pink-tinted, dewy, flesh invites a glance from the sleepiest eyes. The lines of the body, so thinly veiled at such a time, are so clearly defined by the striking folds of the petticoat and the material of the stays that a woman is then irresistible, like everything we are obliged to leave. Her happy, smiling face in the mirror, her foot tapping impatiently, her hand busy repairing the disorder of her curls and her badly rearranged hair, her eyes overflowing with gratitude, then the glow of contentment which, like a sunset, lights up the smallest details of her face, everything makes that moment a mine of memories. Indeed, anyone who casts a backward glance at his youthful errors will recall some of these delightful details and will perhaps understand, without excusing them, the follies of the Hulots and the Crevels.

Women know their power at such a moment so well that they always gather then what can be called the aftermath of the encounter.

117. *The last scene of clever feminine play-acting*

'Come now! After two years, you still don't know how to lace up a woman! You're too much a Pole, by far! It's ten o'clock already, my Wences . . . las!' said Valérie, laughing.

At this moment, a malicious maid adroitly lifted with a knife-blade the latch of the double door which constituted the whole security of Adam and Eve.

She opened the door smartly, for the tenants of these Edens all have only a short time to themselves, and revealed one of those charming genre pictures, after Gavarni,* so often exhibited at the Salon.

'This way, Madame,' said the girl.

And Cydalise entered, followed by Baron Montès.

'But there's someone here! Excuse me, Madame,' said the Norman girl, taken aback.

'What's this? Why, it's Valérie!' cried Montès, slamming the door shut.

Madame Marneffe, prey to an emotion too violent to be concealed, collapsed into a low chair by the fireplace.

Two tears came to her eyes but dried again immediately. She looked at Montès, saw the Norman girl, and burst into a peal of forced laughter. The dignity of a woman outraged effaced the impropriety of her half-clothed state. She went up to the Brazilian and looked at him so proudly that her eyes gleamed like daggers.

'So this', she said, standing in front of the Brazilian and pointing to Cydalise, 'lies behind your fidelity. You, who made me promises that would have convinced a woman with no faith in love! You, for whom I have done so much and even committed crimes! You're right, Monsieur. I'm nothing compared to a girl of that age and beauty. I know what you're going to say,' she continued, pointing to Wenceslas, whose disordered dress was too obvious a proof to be denied. 'That's my business. If I could love you after such infamous treachery—for you've spied on me; you've bought every step of that staircase, and the mistress of the house, and the servant, and perhaps Reine too. Oh, that's a fine thing to do!—if I had a spark of affection left for such a coward, I'd give him reasons that would make him love me more than ever. But I leave you, Monsieur, with all your doubts that will turn into remorse. . . . Wenceslas, my dress.'

She took her dress, put it on, studied herself in the mirror, and calmly finished dressing without looking at the Brazilian, absolutely as if she were alone.

'Wenceslas, are you ready? You go first.'

Out of the corner of her eye and in the mirror, she had been watching the expression on Montès's face; she thought that in his pallor she saw signs of the weakness which makes such strong men captive to the fascination of women. She took him by the hand, going so close to him that he could smell those powerful, beloved perfumes that intoxicate men in love. And feeling his heart beat faster, she looked at him reproachfully.

'I give you my permission to go and give an account of your expedition to Monsieur Crevel. He'll never believe you, so I've a right to marry him. He'll be my husband the day after tomorrow and I'll make him very happy. Good-bye! Try to forget me . . .'

'Oh Valérie!' cried Henri Montès, clasping her in his arms. 'It's impossible. Come to Brazil!'

Valérie looked at the Baron and saw he was her slave again.

'Oh, if you still loved me, Henri! In two years I'd be your wife. But at the moment, your face looks to me a little dubious.'

'I swear to you they made me drunk; false friends planted this woman on me and the whole thing is the result of chance,' said Montès.

'So I could still forgive you?' she asked, smiling.

'And would you still get married?' asked the Baron, prey to a harrowing anxiety.

'Eighty thousand francs a year!' she said with half-comic enthusiasm. 'And Crevel loves me so much that he'll die of it!'

'Oh, I understand you,' said the Brazilian.

'Well, in a few days we'll come to an agreement,' she said.

And she went downstairs in triumph.

'I've no more scruples,' thought the Baron, rooted to the spot for a moment. 'What, she's planning to use that fool's love to get rid of him, just as she counted on Marneffe's death! I'll be the instrument of divine anger!'

118. *Vengeance strikes Valérie*

Two days later, those of du Tillet's guests who had ruthlessly torn Madame Marneffe's reputation to shreds were sitting at her table, an hour after she had turned over a new leaf by changing her name for the glorious name of a Mayor of Paris.

This verbal treachery is one of the commonest kinds of fickle behaviour in Parisian life.

Valérie had had the pleasure of seeing the Brazilian Baron at the church; Crevel, now a fully fledged husband, had invited him in a spirit of boasting triumph.

Montès's presence at lunch surprised no one. All these men about town had long been familiar with the weaknesses of passionate love and the compromises of desire.

Steinbock, beginning to despise the woman he had regarded as an angel, was plunged in a deep melancholy that was considered to be in excellent taste. In this way the Pole seemed to be saying that all was over between himself and Valérie.

Lisbeth came to kiss her dear Madame Crevel, apologizing for not staying to the lunch because of Adeline's poor state of health.

'Don't worry,' she said to Valérie as she left her. 'They'll receive you in their house and you'll receive them in yours. Just through having heard the four words, *two hundred thousand francs*, the Baroness is at death's door. Oh, you have a hold over them all with that story. But you'll tell me all about it, won't you?'

A month after her marriage, Valérie was at her tenth quarrel with Steinbock, who was demanding explanations from her about Henri Montès; he kept reminding her of her remarks in the scene in their paradise and, not content with making withering remarks about Valérie, watched over her so closely that she no longer had a free moment, so hard-pressed was she between Wenceslas's jealousy and Crevel's ardour.

Since Lisbeth, who used to give her excellent advice, was no longer at hand, she lost her temper to such an extent that she bitterly reproached Wenceslas about the money she had lent him.

Steinbock's pride was so thoroughly aroused that he did not return to the Crevels' house. Valérie had achieved her objective; she wanted to get rid of Wenceslas for a while in order to recover her liberty.

Valérie waited until Crevel had to make a trip to the country to see Count Popinot in order to arrange for Madame Crevel's reception at his house; she could thus make an appointment with the Baron, whom she wanted to have with her for a whole day so as to give the Brazilian reasons which would redouble his love.

On the morning of that day, Reine, judging the enormity of her crime by the amount of money she had received, tried to warn her mistress, in whom she was naturally more interested than in people she did not know. But as she had been threatened with being treated as a madwoman and locked up in La Salpêtrière if she were indiscreet, she was nervous.

'Madame is so happy now,' she said. 'Why should you bother any more about that Brazilian? *I* don't trust him!'

'You're right,' she replied. 'So I'm going to get rid of him.'

'Oh, Madame, I'm so pleased. He frightens me, that nigger. I think he might do anything.'

'Don't be silly! It's for him you should be afraid when he's with me.'

Just then Lisbeth came in.

'My dear, darling Nanny, what an age it is since we've seen each other,' said Valérie. 'I'm very unhappy. Crevel bores me to death and Wenceslas has left me; we've quarrelled.'

'I know,' replied Lisbeth, 'and it's because of him that I've come. Victorin met him about five o'clock in the evening just as he was going into a cheap restaurant in the Rue de Valois. He caught him low with hunger, worked on his feelings, and took him back to the Rue Louis-le-

Grand. When Hortene saw Wenceslas looking thin, ill, and badly dressed, she gave him her hand. That's how you let me down!'

'Monsieur Henri, Madame,' the footman whispered to Valérie.

'Leave me now, Lisbeth. I'll explain everything tomorrow.'

But, as we shall see, Valérie was soon to be unable to explain anything to anyone.

119. *The mendicant*

Towards the end of May, Baron Hulot's pension was completely freed by the successive payments that Victorin had made to Baron Nucingen. Everyone knows that the six-monthly pension payments are only made on presentation of a certificate showing that the recipient is still alive, and as no one knew where Baron Hulot lived, the instalments set aside to pay Vauvinet had accumulated at the Treasury. Vauvinet having signed the withdrawal of his claim, it was essential to find the pensioner in order to collect the arrears.

Thanks to Doctor Bianchon's care, the Baroness had regained her health.

By a letter, whose spelling revealed the Duc d'Hérouville's collaboration, the kind-hearted Josépha contributed to Adeline's complete recovery.

This is what the singer wrote to the Baroness after forty days of active investigation.

'Madame la Baronne,—Two months ago, Monsieur Hulot was living with Élodie Chardin, the lace-mender, who had taken him away from Mademoiselle Bijou. But he went away, leaving all his possessions behind, without saying a word, and no one knows where he has gone. I haven't given up hope and I've sent in search of him a man who already thinks he's come across him on the Boulevard Bourdon.

The poor Jewess will keep her promise to the Christian. I hope the angel will pray for the demon. That must sometimes happen in heaven.

I am, with deep respect and always, your humble servant,

JOSÉPHA MIRAH.'

Hearing nothing more of the terrible Madame Nourrisson, seeing his father-in-law married, having restored his brother-in-law to the bosom of the family, experiencing no trouble from his new mother-in-law, and finding his mother in better health every day, Maître Hulot d'Ervy became involved with his political and legal work, carried along by the swift current of Parisian life, in which hours are counted as days.

As he had to write a report for the Chamber of Deputies towards the end of the session, he had to spend a whole night working at it.

He went back to his office about nine o'clock, and as he waited for his servant to bring his shaded lamps, he was thinking of his father. He was reproaching himself for leaving the search for him to the singer, and was planning to see Monsieur Chapuzot the next day about the matter, when he saw at his window in the glow of the twilight the fine head of an old man, bald and fringed with white hair.

'Tell your servant, dear Sir, to admit a poor hermit from the desert, who is collecting money to rebuild a holy almshouse.'

The apparition, which was finding a voice and which suddenly reminded the lawyer of the horrible Nourrisson's prophecy, made him shudder.

'Show the old man in,' he said to his servant.

'He'll make Monsieur's office stink,' the servant replied. 'He's wearing a brown habit that hasn't been changed since he left Syria and he's got no shirt . . .'

'Show the old man in,' repeated the lawyer.

The old man came in. Victorin examined the so-called pilgrim hermit with a suspicious eye and saw a superb specimen of those Neapolitan monks whose habits are just like beggars' rags, whose sandals are tatters of leather, just as the monks themselves are tatters of humanity. The monk was so completely true to life that, although still on his guard, the lawyer rebuked himself for believing in Madame Nourrisson's spells.

'What do you want of me?'

'What you think you ought to give me.'

Victorin took a five-franc piece from a pile of coins and handed it to the stanger.

'As payment on account for fifty thousand francs, that's not much,' said the beggar from the desert.

These words removed all Victorin's doubts.

'And has heaven kept its promises?' asked the lawyer, frowning.

'Doubt is a sin, my son,' replied the hermit. 'If you prefer not to pay till the funeral is over, you're within your rights. I'll come back in a week.'

'The funeral?' exclaimed the lawyer, getting up.

'Steps have been taken,' said the old man as he turned to go, 'and death moves fast in Paris.'

When Hulot, who had bowed his head, began to reply, the nimble old man had disappeared.

'I don't understand a word of all this,' Hulot said to himself. 'But in a week's time, I'll ask him about my father if we still haven't found him. Where does Madame Nourrisson (yes, that's what she calls herself) find such actors?'

120. *Doctor's comments*

The next day, Doctor Bianchon allowed the Baroness to go down into the garden. He had just examined Lisbeth, who had been confined to her room for a month by a mild attack of bronchitis. The experienced doctor, who did not venture to express his full opinion about Lisbeth until he had seen decisive symptoms, accompanied the Baroness to the garden to study the effect of fresh air, after two months of seclusion, on the nervous tremor he was treating. The cure of this nervous condition was a challenge to Bianchon's professional skill.

When they saw the famous great doctor sit down to

spend to a few moments with them, the Baroness and her children politely made conversation with him.

'You have a very busy life—and a very sadly busy one,' said the Baroness. 'I know what it is to spend one's days in the presence of distress and physical pain.'

'Madame, I am not unaware of the sights you are obliged to witness in your charitable work,' replied the doctor. 'But in the end you will get used to them, as we all do. It is the law of society. The confessor, the magistrate, the lawyer, would have an impossible task if their sense of social duty did not predominate over their human feelings. Could we live if this didn't happen? A soldier, too, in wartime is obliged to witness sights even more cruel than those we see. And all soldiers who have been in action are kind. We doctors have the pleasure of successful cures, just as you have the satisfaction of saving a family from the horrors of hunger, depravity, and poverty by bringing its members back to work and to life in society. But what is the consolation of the magistrate, the police officer, and the lawyer, who spend their lives investigating the most nefarious schemes of self-interest, that social monster which knows the regret of failure but is never touched by repentance? One half of society spends its life watching the other half. An old friend of mine, a lawyer now retired, used to say that for the last fifteen years solicitors and barristers have been as mistrustful of their clients as of their clients' opponents. Your son is a lawyer. Has he never been compromised by the man he undertook to defend?'

'Oh, often!' said Victorin with a smile.

'What is the cause of this deep-seated evil?' asked the Baroness.

'Lack of religion and the pervasion everywhere of finance which is nothing but the concrete manifestation of selfishness,' replied the doctor. 'In the old days, money was not everything; it was recognized that superior values took precedence over it. There was nobility, talent, and service to the state. But today the law makes money a general yardstick; it has made it the basis of political qualification. Some magistrates cannot be elected as deputies; Jean-Jacques Rousseau couldn't be elected. The continual division of inheritances means that everyone is forced to think of his own interests from the age of 20. Well, between the necessity of making money and crooked scheming there is no barrier, for there is a dearth of religious feeling in France, in spite of the praiseworthy efforts of those who are striving for a Catholic revival. That's the opinion of all those who study, as I do, the innermost workings of society.'

'You have few pleasures,' said Hortense.

'A true doctor is passionately devoted to science,' replied Bianchon. 'He's sustained by this devotion as well as by the conviction that he's useful to society. For instance, at the moment, you see me filled with a kind of scientific joy, and many superficial people would take me for a heartless man. Tomorrow I'm going to announce a discovery to the Academy of Medicine. At the moment, I'm studying a long-lost disease. What's more, it's a fatal disease and we have no remedy against it in temperate climates, though it's curable in the Indies. It was prevalent in the Middle Ages. It's a fine war that a doctor wages against an enemy like that. For ten days I've been thinking continually about my patients, for there are two of them, husband and wife. Aren't they connections of yours? For, Madame, you are Monsieur Crevel's daughter, aren't you?' he said, turning to Célestine.

'What! Could your patient be my father?' asked Célestine. 'Does he live in the Rue Barbet-de-Jouy?'

'That's right,' replied Bianchon.

'And the disease is fatal?' Victorin repeated, horrified.

'I'm going to my father,' cried Célestine, getting up.

'I positively forbid you, Madame,' Bianchon replied calmly. 'This disease is infectious.'

'But you go there, Monsieur,' replied the young woman. 'Do you think that a daughter's duty is less important than a doctor's?'

'Madame, a doctor knows how to protect himself from

infection, but your unreflecting devotion convinces me that you couldn't be as prudent as I am.'

Célestine got up and went back to her room, where she dressed to go out.

121. *The hand of God and the Brazilian's too*

'Monsieur, have you any hope of saving Monsieur and Madame Crevel?' Victorin asked Bianchon.

'I hope to, but have no faith that I shall,' replied Bianchon. 'The case is inexplicable to me. The disease is peculiar to negroes and native Americans, whose skin structure is different from that of the white races. But I can't establish any link between blacks, Red Indians, or half-castes and Monsieur or Madame Crevel. And though it's a splendid disease for us to study, it's terrible for everyone else. The poor creature, who, they say, was pretty, is well punished at the source of her sins, for today she is horribly ugly, if she can be said to be anything at all. Her teeth and hair are falling out; she looks like a leper; she's an object of horror to herself. Her hands look revolting; they are swollen and covered with greenish pustules. Her loosened nails remain in the sores that she scratches. In fact, all the extremities of her body are being destroyed by running ulcers.'

'But what's the cause of these afflictions?' the lawyer asked.

'Oh,' said Bianchon, 'the cause is in a rapid deterioration of the blood; it is decomposing with frightening speed. I hope to do something about the blood. I've had it analysed. I'm going home to pick up the result of work done by my friend Professor Duval, the famous chemist, so that I can undertake one of those desperate measures that we sometimes attempt against death.'

'This is the hand of God,' said the Baroness, in a tone of deep emotion. 'Although this woman has done me such harm that, in moments of madness, I have called down divine justice on her head, I wish, God knows, that you may succeed, Doctor.'

Victorin Hulot turned dizzy. He looked at his mother, his sister, and the doctor in turn and trembled lest they should read his thoughts. He looked on himself as a murderer. As for Hortense, she thought God was very just.

Célestine came back to ask her husband to go with her.

'If you go there, Madame, and you, Monsieur, stay a foot away from the patients' beds; that's the only precaution you need take. Neither you nor your wife should think of kissing the dying man. So you should accompany your wife, Monsieur Hulot, to see that she doesn't break this rule.'

Adeline and Hortense, left alone, went to keep Lisbeth company. Hortense's hatred of Valérie was so violent that she could not restrain it.

'Cousin, my brother and I are avenged!' she cried. 'That venomous creature must have bitten herself; she's in a state of decomposition!'

'Hortense,' said the Baroness, 'your behaviour isn't Christian at this moment. You ought to pray God that he will deign to inspire the unhappy woman with repentance.'

'What are you saying?' cried Bette, getting up from her chair. 'Are you talking of Valérie?'

'Yes,' replied Adeline, 'there's no hope for her. She's dying of a horrible disease whose very description makes one shudder.'

Cousin Bette's teeth chattered; she broke out into a cold sweat; she gave a violent start, which revealed the depth of her passionate attachment to Valérie.

'I'm going to her,' she said.

'But the doctor has forbidden you to go out.'

'No matter, I'm going. Poor Crevel! What a state he must be in, for he loves his wife.'

'He's dying too,' replied Countess Steinbock. 'Oh, all our enemies are in the devil's hands.'

'In God's, my child!'

Lisbeth got dressed and put on her famous yellow

cashmere shawl, her black velvet hood, and her ankle-boots. Ignoring the remonstrances of Adeline and Hortense, she set off as if impelled by an irresistible force.

122. *Valérie's last bon mot*

Lisbeth reached the Rue Barbet a few moments after Monsieur and Madame Hulot, and found seven doctors, summoned by Bianchon to observe this unique case; he had just joined them. The doctors were standing about in the drawing-room discussing the disease. From time to time, one or other of them went into Valérie's or Crevel's room to have a look and came back with some argument based on his rapid observation.

Two serious opinions divided these princes of science.

One, alone in his opinion, held that it was a case of poisoning and spoke of private revenge, denying that it was a reappearance of the disease known in the Middle Ages.

Three others held the view that it was a decomposition of the lymph and the humours.

The other party, agreeing with Bianchon, maintained that the disease was caused by a degeneration of the blood due to some unknown morbid factor. Bianchon brought the result of Professor Duval's blood analysis.

The treatment, although a last resort and quite experimental, depended upon the answer to this medical question.

On seeing an assistant priest from Saint-Thomas-d'Aquin at her friend's bedside and a Sister of Charity tending her, Lisbeth stood petrified three paces from the bed. Religion found a soul to save in a mass of rotting flesh which, of the five senses of a human being, had retained only that of sight. The Sister of Charity, the only person who had undertaken the task of caring for Valérie, stood at a distance. Thus the Catholic Church, that divine institution, always inspired by the spirit of sacrifice in all things, in its dual form of spirit and flesh, came to the aid of the revolting, putrid, dying woman, lavishing on her its infinite compassion and its inexhaustible wealth of pity.

The terrified servants refused to enter Monsieur's or Madame's bedroom. They thought only of themselves and considered that their master and mistress had been justly smitten.

The stench was so great that, in spite of the open windows and most powerful perfumes, no one could stay long in Valérie's room. Religion alone kept watch there.

How could a woman as intellectually superior as Valérie not have asked herself what interest made these two representatives of the Church stay with her? So the dying woman had listened to the priest's voice. Repentance had made inroads into that perverse soul in proportion to the ravages that the wasting disease had wrought in her beauty. The delicate Valérie had offered much less resistance to the disease than Crevel had, and she was to be the first to die, having been indeed the first to be attacked.

'If I hadn't been ill, I'd have come to look after you,' said Lisbeth at last, after exchanging a glance with her friend's dejected eyes. I've been confined to my room for the last two or three weeks, but when I learned of your condition from the doctor, I came at once.'

'Poor Lisbeth, *you* still love me. I see that,' said Valérie. 'Listen to me. I've only a day or two left to think, for I can't say *to live*. As you see, I haven't a body any more. I'm a heap of mud. They won't let me look at myself in a mirror. I've only got what I deserve. Oh, I'd like to undo all the harm I've done so that I could receive mercy.'

'Oh,' said Lisbeth, 'if you talk like that, you're as good as dead.'

'Don't prevent this woman from repenting; leave her to her Christian thoughts,' said the priest.

'There's nothing left,' Lisbeth, terrified, said to herself. 'I can't recognize her eyes or her mouth. Not one of her features remains. And her mind has gone. Oh, it's frightening!'

'You don't know', Valérie continued, 'what death is, what it is to have to think of the day after your last one, of what you'll find in your coffin; there are worms for the body, but what is there for the soul? Oh, Lisbeth, I feel there is another life and I am possessed by a terror that prevents me from feeling the pain of my rotting flesh. To think that I used to say laughingly to Crevel, making fun of a saint, that God's vengeance assumed every kind of misfortune! Well, I was a prophet. Don't play about with sacred things, Lisbeth. If you love me, follow my example and repent!'

'Me!' said the Lorraine peasant. 'I've seen vengeance everywhere in nature. Insects die to satisfy their need for vengeance when they're attacked. And these gentlemen,' she said, pointing to the priest, 'don't they tell us that God avenges himself and that his vengeance is eternal?'

The priest gave Lisbeth a look full of gentleness and said:

'You are an atheist, Madame.'

'But look what I have come to!' said Valérie.

'But how do you come to be in this rotting state?' asked the old maid, who persisted in her peasant incredulity.

'Oh, Henri sent me a letter which leaves me in no doubt about my fate. He's killed me. To die just when I wanted to live respectably, and to die an object of horror! Lisbeth, give up all idea of revenge. Be kind to that family; in my will, I've already left them everything the law allows me to dispose of. Go, my dear, although you're the only being today who doesn't withdraw from me in horror. I beg you, go away, leave me. I have time left only to give myelf up to God.'

'She's delirious,' Lisbeth said to herself as she stood at the bedroom door.

The most powerful feeling we know, a woman's affection for another woman, did not have the heroic constancy of the Church. Lisbeth, choked by the noxious vapours, left the room.

She saw the doctors still continuing their discussions. But Bianchon's opinion won the day and they were only arguing about the best way of conducting the experiment.

'In any case, there'll be a splendid post-mortem examination,' said one of his opponents, 'and we'll have two specimens, so that we'll be able to make comparisons.'

Lisbeth went back with Bianchon, who approached the sick-bed without appearing to notice the foul smell emanating from it.

'Madame,' he said, 'we're going to try out on you a powerful drug that might save you.'

'If you save me,' she said, 'shall I be as beautiful as I used to be?'

'Perhaps,' said the wise doctor.

'It's well known what your *perhaps* means,' said Valérie. 'I'd be like those women who've fallen into the fire! Leave me completely to the Church. Now I can be attractive only to God. I'll try to be reconciled with him. That will be my last flirtation. Yes, I must *do God*!'

'That's my poor Valérie's last *bon mot*. I see her old self again in that,' said Lisbeth, weeping.

123. *Crevel's last words*

The Lorraine peasant thought she ought to go into Crevel's room, where she found Victorin and his wife sitting three paces away from the diseased man's bed.

'Lisbeth,' he said, 'they're concealing my wife's condition from me. You've just seen her. How is she?'

'She's better; she says she's saved,' replied Lisbeth, permitting herself this ambiguity in order to set Crevel's mind at rest.

'Oh good,' continued the Mayor, 'for I was afraid I was the cause of her illness. There are risks in being a commercial traveller in perfumery. I've been reproaching myself. If I were to lose her, what would become of me? On my word of honour, children, I adore that woman.'

Crevel sat up in bed and tried to strike his attitude.

'Oh, Papa,' said Célestine, 'if you could be well again, I'd receive my stepmother. I promise you.'

'Poor little Célestine,' said Crevel, 'come and kiss me.'

Victorin restrained his wife, who was springing forward.

'Perhaps you're unaware, Monsieur, that your illness is infectious,' said the lawyer gently.

'That's so,' replied Crevel. 'The doctors are congratulating themselves on having found in me some kind of medieval plague they thought was lost; they're making a big song and dance about it in their Faculties. It's very funny.'

'Papa,' said Célestine, 'be brave and you'll get over this illness.'

'Don't worry, children. Death looks twice before striking a Mayor of Paris!' he said with ludicrous composure. 'And then, if my district is so unfortunate as to lose the man whom it has twice honoured with its votes (there— you see how fluently I express myself!), well, I'll know how to pack my bags. I'm a former commercial traveller; I'm used to departures. You see, children, I'm a freethinker.'

'Papa, promise me to let a priest come to your bedside.'

'Never,' replied Crevel. 'What do you expect? I've sucked the milk of the Revolution. I haven't Baron d'Holbach's* intellect but I have his strength of mind. I'm more than ever a Regency* type, a grey Musketeer,* an Abbé Dubois,* a Maréchal de Richelieu!* Damn it all! My poor wife, who's going out of her mind, has just sent me a fellow in a cassock, to me, an admirer of Béranger,* the friend of Lisette,* the child of Voltaire and Rousseau! The doctor said to me, to try me out, to find out if the disease was getting me down, "Have you seen Monsieur l'Abbé?" Well, I imitated the great Montesquieu.* Yes, I looked at the door, see, like this,' he said, turning three quarters round as in his portrait, and stretching out his hand authoritatively, 'and I said:

> . . . That slave, he came.
> His order showed, but nothing gained.*

His order is a nice pun which proves that in his last moments Monsieur le Président de Montesquieu retained all his charming wit, for they'd sent him a Jesuit! I like that passage . . . one can't say of his life, but of his death. Oh, the passage! Another pun! The Passage Montesquieu.'*

Victorin Hulot gazed sadly at his father-in-law, wondering if folly and vanity did not have a power as strong as that of true greatness of soul. The causes which activate the springs of the soul often bear no relation to the results. Can it be that the strength of character of a great criminal is of the same nature as that with which Champcenetz* proudly went to the guillotine?

At the end of the week, after terrible suffering, Madame Crevel was buried, and two days later Crevel followed his wife. Thus the provisions of the marriage contract were annulled and Crevel inherited from Valérie.

The day after the funeral, the lawyer saw the old monk again and received him in silence. The monk held out his hand without a word, and, also without a word, Maître Victorin Hulot gave him eighty thousand-franc notes, taken from the money found in Crevel's desk.

The younger Madame Hulot inherited the Presles estate and an income of thirty thousand francs a year. Madame Crevel had left three hundred thousand francs to Baron Hulot. On his majority, the scrofulous Stanislas was to have Crevel's house and twenty-four thousand francs a year.

124. *One aspect of speculation*

Among the many admirable organizations founded by Catholic charity in Paris, there is one, founded by Madame de la Chanterie, whose aim is to arrange civil and religious marriages for working-class couples who are living together.

Our legislators, anxious to have the registration fees, and the dominant middle class, eager to have the lawyers' fees, pretend to be unaware that three quarters of the working class cannot afford fifteen francs for their marriage contracts.

In this matter, Paris solicitors are much worse than

barristers. Paris barristers, a much maligned body, undertake lawsuits free of charge for those unable to pay, while solicitors have not yet decided to draw up marriage contracts for the poor, without charge.

As for the Treasury, the whole machinery of government would have to be set in motion to induce it to make concessions in that respect. The Registrar's office is deaf and dumb.

The Church, too, levies dues on marriages. In France, the Church is excessively mercenary. In the house of God, it indulges in a disgraceful traffic in stools and chairs which infuriates visitors, although it cannot have forgotten the Saviour's anger when he drove the money-changers from the Temple. But if the Church is loath to abandon its dues, we must appreciate that its charges, said to be for the upkeep of its buildings, constitute nowadays one of its resources, and so it is the State that is to blame for the situation and not the Church.

At a time when people are far too concerned with negroes and petty offenders in the police courts to bother about the sufferings of decent people, this combination of circumstances means that a large number of respectable couples live together outside marriage, for want of thirty francs, the lowest price at which the legal profession, the registry office, the town hall, and the Church can unite two Parisians in marriage. Madame de la Chanterie's organization, founded for the purpose of bringing poor couples back into line with the laws of Church and State, seeks them out and finds them all the more easily because it relieves their poverty before it ascertains their civil status.

When Baroness Hulot was completely well again, she resumed her former activities. It was then that the worthy Madame de la Chanterie asked her to add the legalizing of informal marriages to the charities for which she already conducted investigations.

One of the Baroness's first inquiries in this field was made in the dubious quarter, formely called *Little Poland*, bounded by the Rue du Rocher, the Rue de la Pépinière, and the Rue de Miromesnil. It survives there like a subsidiary of the Faubourg Saint-Marceau. To describe this quarter, it will be enough to say that the owners of certain houses, inhabited by manual workers without work, by unscrupulous scrap-merchants, and by down-and-outs engaged in risky occupations, dare not collect their rents and cannot find bailiffs who are willing to evict the insolvent tenants.

At the present time, the activities of speculators, who aspire to change the face of this corner of Paris and to build up the waste ground which separates the Rue d'Amsterdam from the Rue du Faubourg-du-Roule, will no doubt alter the character of the population, for in Paris the trowel is more of a civilizing instrument than is generally realized. By building handsome, attractive houses with porters' lodges, laying pavements in front, and making shops there, speculative building, because of the high rents charged, drives away vagrants, families with no furniture, and bad tenants. And so these districts get rid of their dubious inhabitants and foul slums, where the police set foot only when the law requires.

In June 1844, the appearance of the Place Delaborde and its neighbourhood was still far from reassuring. The fashionable pedestrian who happened to walk up these frightful streets from the Rue de la Pépinière, would have been amazed to see aristocrats rubbing shoulders there with the dregs of the underworld.

In these districts, where ignorant poverty and acute distress proliferate, the last public letter-writers in Paris survive. Wherever you see the two words *Public Letter-writer* in a large running hand on white paper stuck on the window of some entresol or filthy ground-floor premises, you can safely assume that the quarter is a haven for a large illiterate population and consequently for misfortune, vice, and crime. Ignorance is the mother of all crimes. Crime is, above all, a consequence of inadequate reasoning.

125. *In which we are not told why all the stove-fitters of Paris are Italians*

It so happened that during the Baroness's illness this quarter, for which she was a second Providence, had acquired a public letter-writer who had set up business in the Passage du Soleil, its name being one of those antitheses familiar to Parisians, for it is particularly dark. This letter-writer, thought to be German, was called Vyder and was living with a girl of whom he was so jealous that he would never let her go out except to respectable stove-fitters in the Rue Saint-Lazare; they were Italians, like all stove-fitters, and had been settled in Paris for many years.

Baroness Hulot, acting on behalf of Madame de la Chanterie, had saved this family from an inevitable bankruptcy, which would have made them destitute. In a few months prosperity took over from poverty and religion entered hearts that formerly had cursed Providence with the energy peculiar to Italian stove-fitters.

One of the Baroness's first visits, therefore, was to this family. She was happy at the sight that met her eyes inside the house where these good people lived, in the Rue Saint-Lazare, near the Rue du Rocher. Above the shops and the workshop, now well equipped and swarming with apprentices and workmen, all Italians from the valley of Domo d'Ossola, the family lived in a little flat, to which work had brought plenty. The Baroness was received as if she had been the Blessed Virgin in person. After looking round the premises for a quarter of an hour and being obliged to wait for the husband to find out how the business was faring, Adeline fulfilled her duty as a saintly spy by enquiring about any unfortunate people that the stove-fitter's family might know.

'Oh, dear lady, you are so kind, you would save the damned from hell,' said the Italian woman. 'Near here, there's a girl to be saved from perdition.'

'Do you know her well?' the Baroness asked.

'She's the grand-daughter of one of my husband's former employers, called Judici, who came to France at the time of the Revolution, in 1798. In Emperor Napoleon's day, old Judici was one of the leading stove-fitters in Paris. He died in 1819, leaving his son a handsome fortune. But the son squandered it all on loose women and he finally married one who was smarter than the rest; she's the mother of this poor little girl, who's just turned 15.'

'What happened to him?' asked the Baroness, very struck by the similarity between this Judici's character and her husband's.

'Well, Madame, the little girl, called Atala, left her parents and come to live near here, with an old German, at least 80 years old, called Vyder, who does all their business for people who can't read or write. If only this old libertine, who, they say, bought the girl from her mother for fifteen hundred francs, would at least marry the youngster—for he can't have long to live and they say he may have an income of several thousand francs a year. Well then, the poor child, who's a little angel, would be out of harm's way, and above all freed from poverty which will corrupt her.'

'Thank you for telling me of a good deed to be done,' said Adeline. 'But one must go carefully. What's this old man like?'

'Oh, he's a decent fellow, Madame. He makes the child happy and he doesn't lack common sense; for, you see, he left the district where the Judicis live, I think, to save the child from her mother's clutches. The mother was jealous of her daughter and she may have had an idea of profiting from her beauty, of turning the child into a *young lady*. Atala remembered us and she advised *her gentleman* to settle near our house. And since the old chap saw what we're like, he lets her come here. But get her married, Madame, and you'll be doing a deed worthy of you. Once she's married, the child will be free. In this way she'll escape from her mother, who keeps a wary eye on her and who, to make money out of her, would like to see her in the theatre or getting on in the horrible career she's started her on.'

'Why hasn't the old man married her?'

'He didn't have to,' said the Italian woman, 'and although old Vyder isn't really an unkind man, I think he's cunning enough to want to keep control of the child. But once he's married, well, he's afraid, poor old fellow, of what comes to all old men.'

'Can you send for the girl?' said the Baroness. 'If I were to see her here, I'd find out if anything can be done.'

126. *A second Atala, quite as much of a savage as the first one,* but not as good a Catholic*

The stove-fitter's wife made a sign to her eldest daughter, who went out immediately. Ten minutes later she returned, holding by the hand a 15-and-a-half-year-old girl, a beauty of the specially Italian kind.

From her father, Mademoiselle Judici inherited the kind of skin which is sallow by daylight but, in the evening, by artificial light, becomes dazzlingly white, eyes of oriental size, shape, and brilliance, thick, curling eyelashes like little black feathers, jet-black hair, and the regal bearing of Lombardy which makes a foreigner, taking a Sunday walk in Milan, think that every porter's daughter is a queen.

Told by the stove-fitter's daughter about the visit of the great lady of whom she had heard, Atala had hurriedly put on a pretty silk dress, ankle-boots, and a smart little cape. A bonnet with cherry-coloured ribbons added to the impression made by her lovely head. The child stood in an attitude of naïve curiosity, watching the Baroness out of the corner of her eye, quite amazed at her nervous trembling.

The Baroness sighed deeply at the sight of this masterpiece of feminine beauty, sunk in the mud of prostitution, and she vowed to bring her back to the path of virtue.

'What's your name, my child?'

'Atala, Madame.'

'Can you read and write?'

'No, Madame, but that doesn't matter, since Monsieur can.'

'Have your parents ever taken you to church? Have you made your first communion? Do you know your catechism?'

'Papa wanted to have me do things like what you're talking about, but Mama was against it.'

'Your mother!' exclaimed the Baroness. 'Your mother's very unkind, then, is she?'

'She always used to beat me. I don't know why, but my father and mother were always quarrelling about me.'

'Has no one ever spoken to you about God?' asked the Baroness.

The child opened her eyes wide.

'Mama and Papa often used to say "for God's sake", "God blast", and "my God",' she replied with a taking naïveté.

'Have you never seen a church? Have you never thought of going into one?'

'Churches? Oh, Notre-Dame, the Panthéon, I've seen them from a distance, when Papa took me into Paris, but that didn't happen often. There are no churches like that in the faubourg.'

'In which faubourg used you to live?'

'In the faubourg.'

'But in which faubourg?'

'Why, in the Rue de Charonne, Madame.'

The inhabitants of the Faubourg Saint-Antoine never call that well-known district anything but the *faubourg*. For them it is the faubourg *par excellence*, the most important of all faubourgs, and even the factory-owners understand by that word the Faubourg Saint-Antoine.

'Has no one ever told you what's right and what's wrong?'

'Mama used to beat me when I didn't do things the way she wanted.'

'But didn't you know you were doing wrong when you left your parents to go and live with an old man?'

Atala Judici looked haughtily at the Baroness and did not reply.

'The girl's quite uncivilized,' Adeline murmured.

'Oh, Madame, there's plenty like her in the faubourg,' said the stove-fitter's wife.

'But, good heavens, she knows nothing, not even what wrong is! Why don't you answer me?' asked the Baroness, trying to take Atala's hand.

But Atala was annoyed and drew back.

'You're a crazy old woman,' she said. 'My father and mother had had nothing to eat for a week. My mother wanted to make me something very bad, for my father beat her and called her a thief. But then Monsieur Vyder paid all my father's and mother's debts and gave them money— oh, a whole bagful! Then he took me away and my poor Papa cried. But we had to separate. Well, is that wrong?' she asked.

127. *The preceding chapter continued*

'And are you very fond of this Monsieur Vyder?'

'Am I fond of him? I should think I am,' she said. 'He tells me nice stories every evening. And he's given me pretty dresses and underwear and a shawl. Why, I'm rigged out like a princess and I don't wear sabots any more. And for two months now I haven't known what it is to be hungry. I don't eat potatoes any more. He brings me sweets and sugared almonds. Oh, chocolate almonds are delicious. I do anything he wants for a bag of chocolates. And then my old Père Vyder is so kind; he looks after me so well, so nicely, that it makes me see what my mother ought to have been like. He's going to get an old servant to look after me, for he doesn't want me to get my hands dirty doing the cooking. He's been earning quite a bit of money this last month and every evening he brings me three francs, which I put in my money-box. Only he doesn't want me to go out, except to come here. He's a love of a man, so he does whatever he likes with me. He calls me his little puss, but my mother only called me little bitch, or dirty hussy, or thief, or vermin, and I don't know what else.'

'Well then, why don't you get married to Père Vyder, my child?'

'But I have, Madame!' said the girl, full of pride, looking at the Baroness without a blush, her brow serene, her eyes untroubled. 'He told me I was his little wife, but it's very tiresome being a man's wife. In fact, if it wasn't for the sugared almonds!'

'Good heavens,' said the Baroness under her breath, 'what kind of a monster can it be who could take advantage of such complete, pure innocence? To set this child back on to the path of virtue would atone for many sins. *I* knew what I was doing,' she said to herself, thinking of her scene with Crevel. 'But *she* is totally ignorant.'

'Do you know Monsieur Samanon?' Atala asked coaxingly.

'No, my dear. But why do you ask me?'

'Really and truly?' said the innocent creature.

'Don't be afraid of Madame, Atala. She's an angel,' said the stove-fitter's wife.

'It's because my old dear's afraid of being found by this Samanon and he's in hiding. But I'd very much like him to be free.'

'And why?'

'Well, then he'd take me to Bobino* and perhaps to the Ambigu.'*

'What a charming creature,' said the Baroness, kissing the little girl.

'Are you rich?' asked Atala, fingering the Baroness's cuffs.

'Yes and no,' replied the Baroness. 'I'm rich for good little girls like you, when they're willing to be taught Christian duties by a priest and walk in the right path.'

'In what path?' asked Atala. 'My legs are good for walking.'

'The path of virtue.'

Atala gave the baroness a sly, amused look.

'Look at Madame. She's been happy since she returned to the bosom of the church,' said the Baroness, pointing to the stove-fitter's wife. 'You've got married in the way animals mate.'

'Me!' replied Atala. 'But if you're ready to give me what Père Vyder gives me, I'd be very glad not to be married. It's a bore! Do you know what it's like?'

'Once you're united with a man, as you are,' continued the Baroness, 'virtue requires you to remain faithful to him.'

'Till he dies?' asked Atala, with a knowing look. 'I won't have long to wait. If you knew how Père Vyder coughs and snorts! Peuh! Peuh!' she wheezed, imitating the old man.

'Virtue and morality require that the Church, which represents God, and the town hall, which represents the State, should consecrate your marriage. You see Madame. She got married legally.'

'Will that be more fun?' asked the child.

'You will be happier,' said the baroness, 'for no one will be able to blame you for your marriage. You will please God. Ask Madame if she got married without receiving the sacrament of marriage?'

Atala looked at the stove-fitter's wife.

'What's she got that I haven't?' she asked. 'I'm prettier than she is.'

'Yes, but I'm an honest woman and *you* can be given a nasty name.'

'How can you expect God to protect you if you trample divine and human laws underfoot?' said the Baroness. 'Do you know that God holds a paradise in store for those who obey the commands of his Church?'

'What is there in paradise? Are there theatres?' asked Atala.

'Oh, paradise!' said the Baroness. 'It has all the delights you can imagine. It's full of angels with white wings. We can see God there in his glory, we'll share his power and be happy there every moment for all eternity.'

Atala Judici listened to the Baroness as she might have listened to music, and seeing that the girl was incapable of understanding, Adeline thought she should adopt a different approach and speak to the old man.

'Go home, dear, and I'll go and talk to Monsieur Vyder. Is he French?'

'He's Alsatian, Madame. But he'll be rich all right. If you'd pay what he owes that nasty Samanon, he'll pay back your money. For he says that in a few months he'll have six thousand francs a year and then we'll go and live in the country, far away, in the Vosges.'

The words *the Vosges* plunged the Baroness into a profound reverie. In her mind's eye she saw her native village again.

128. *Recognition*

The Baroness was roused from these painful thoughts by the greeting of the stove-fitter, who came to show her evidence of his prosperity.

'In a year, I'll be able to pay back the money you lent us, Madame, for it's God's money; it belongs to the poor and unfortunate. If I do well, you'll be able to dip into our purse one day. Through you, I'll repay the help you gave us.'

'At the moment I don't want money from you,' said the Baroness. 'I want co-operation in a good deed. I've just seen the little Judici girl who is living with an old man, and I want to have them married in church, legally.'

'Oh, Père Vyder! He's a very decent, nice fellow, who gives good advice. In the two months he's been here the poor old man has already made friends in the neighbourhood. He keeps my accounts in order. He's a brave colonel, I believe, who's done good service under the Emperor. Oh, how he loves Napoleon! He has a decoration but he never wears it. He's waiting till he's re-established his affairs, for he has debts, poor dear man. I think he may even be in hiding, with the bailiffs after him.'

'Tell him that I'll pay his debts, if he's willing to marry the child.'

'Oh, that's soon done. Why not go there now, Madame? It's only two steps away, in the Passage du Soleil.'

The Baroness and the stove-fitter set out for the Passage du Soleil.

'This way, madame,' said the stove-fitter, pointing down the Rue de la Pépinière.

The Passage du Soleil runs, in fact, from the beginning of the Rue de la Pépinière through to the Rue du Rocher.

Half-way down this recently constructed passage, with shops let at a very modest rent, the Baroness noticed, above a shop-window screened by green taffeta curtains high enough to prevent the inquisitive glances of passers-by, a sign with the words PUBLIC LETTER-WRITER, and on the door:

BUSINESS AGENCY
Petitions drawn up,
Accounts put in order, etc.
Work carried out confidentially and promptly

Inside it was like the waiting-rooms where Paris omnibus passengers wait for their connections. An inside staircase presumably led to the entresol flat, lit from the gallery, which went with the shop. The Baroness noticed a blackened whitewood desk, cardboard boxes, and a shabby, second-hand armchair. A cap and a green taffeta eye-shade, attached with filthy copper wire, indicated either precautions taken for disguise or a weakness of the eyes to be expected in an old man.

'He's upstairs,' said the stove-fitter. 'I'll go up and tell him and get him to come down.'

The Baroness lowered her veil and sat down. A heavy step shook the little wooden staircase, and Adeline could not restrain a piercing cry when she saw her husband, Baron Hulot, wearing a grey knitted jacket, old grey flannel trousers, and slippers.

'What can I do for you, Madame?' said Hulot gallantly.

Adeline got up, grasped Hulot's arm, and, in a voice broken with emotion, said:

'At last I've found you!'

'Adeline!' cried the Baron in amazement, and he closed the shop door. 'Joseph, go out by the side-entrance,' he called out to the stove-fitter.

'My dear,' she said, forgetting everything in her over-flowing joy, 'you can return to the bosom of your family. We're rich. Your son has an income of a hundred and sixty thousand francs a year. Your pension is unencumbered; you have arrears of fifteen thousand francs that can be cashed simply on presentation of a certificate that you're alive. Valérie is dead and has left you three hundred thousand francs. People have quite forgotten about you. Come, you can return to society, and you'll find a fortune waiting for you in your son's house. Come, and our happiness will be complete. I've been looking for you for nearly three years and I had such high hopes of finding you that I have a flat ready waiting for you. Oh, leave this place. Leave the appalling situation I see you in.'

'I'm quite happy to go,' said the Baron in a daze, *but can I bring the little girl with me?*

'Hector, give her up. Do this for your Adeline, who has never asked you for the least sacrifice. I promise to give the child a dowry, to arrange a good marriage for her, and to have her educated. Let it be said that one of those who made you happy is happy herself and will never again lapse into vice, into the gutter.'

'So it's you', said the Baron with a smile, 'who wanted to make me get married? Stay here for a moment,' he went on. 'I'll go and get dressed upstairs; I've some decent clothes there in a trunk.'

When Adeline was left alone, she looked round the horrible shop and burst into tears.

'He was living here,' she said to herself, 'while we live in luxury! Poor man! How he has been punished, he who was the most well-dressed of men!'

129. *Atala's last word*

The stove-fitter came to say goodbye to his benefactress, who told him to fetch a cab. When he returned, the Baroness asked him to take little Atala Judici home with him and to do so there and then.

'You can tell her', she added, 'that if she's willing to be put under the guidance of Monsieur le Curé at the Madeleine, on the day she makes her first communion I'll give her a dowry of thirty thousand francs and a good husband, some fine young man.'

'My oldest son, Madame! He's 22 and he adores the child.'

Just then, the Baron came downstairs. His eyes were wet with tears.

'You're making me leave the only creature whose love for me has been anything like yours. The child's in tears, and I can't leave her like this.'

'Don't worry, Hector. She's going to be with a respectable family and I can answer for her behaviour.'

'Oh, in that case I can go with you,' said the Baron, escorting his wife to the carriage.

Hector, once more Baron d'Ervy, had put on a blue cloth frock-coat and trousers, a white waistcoat, a black cravat, and gloves.

When the Baroness had taken her seat inside the cab, Atala slipped in, gliding like an adder.

'Oh, Madame, let me come with you and go wherever you're going,' she said. 'Look, I'll be very good and very obedient. I'll do everything you tell me. But don't take Père Vyder away from me. He's my benefactor; he gives me such lovely things. I'll be beaten!'

'Come, Atala,' said the Baron, 'this is my wife and we must leave each other.'

'That lady! As old as that!' replied the naïve girl. 'And she trembles like a leaf. Oh, look at her head.'

And she mockingly imitated the Baroness's trembling.

The stove-fitter, hurrying after the little Judici girl, came to the carriage door.

'Take her away,' said the Baroness

The stove-fitter took Atala in his arms and forcibly carried her off to his house.

'Thank you for this sacrifice, my dear,' said Adeline, taking the Baron's hand and pressing it with ecstatic joy. 'How you're changed! How you must have suffered! What a surprise for your daughter and your son!'

Adeline talked as lovers talk when they see each other again after a long separation, pouring out a thousand things at once.

130. *Return of the prodigal father*

Ten minutes later, the Baron and his wife arrived at the Rue Louis-le-Grand, where Adeline found the following letter waiting for her.

'Madame la Baronne—Monsieur le Baron d'Ervy stayed for a month in the Rue de Charonne, under the name of Thorec, an anagram of Hector. He is now at the Passage du Soleil, under the name of Vyder. He calls himself an Alsatian, is a public letter-writer, and lives with a girl called Atala Judici. Take great care, Madame, for an active search is being made for the Baron, on whose behalf I don't know.

The actress has kept her word and remains, as always, Madame, your humble servant,

J.M.'

The Baron's return aroused transports of joy, which reconciled him to family life. He forgot little Atala Judici, for excessive indulgence in his passion had made his emotions as fickle as a child's. The family's happiness was clouded by the change in the Baron. When he left his chidren he was still fit and well, but he returned looking almost like a centenarian, broken, bowed, his appearance coarsened.

A splendid impromptu dinner, arranged by Célestine,

reminded the old man of the opera-singer's dinner-parties and he was quite dazzled by his family's splendours.

'You're celebrating the return of the prodigal father,' he whispered to Adeline

'Hush! That's all forgotten,' she replied.

'But where's Lisbeth?' the Baron asked, noticing the old maid was not there.

'She's in bed, I'm sorry to say,' Hortense replied. 'She doesn't get up at all now and soon we'll have the sorrow of losing her. She hopes to see you after dinner.'

At dawn the next morning Victorin Hulot was informed by his porter that his house was surrounded by men of the Municipal Guard. Officers of the law were looking for Baron Hulot. The bailiff, who was following the porter, presented a properly drawn-up summons to the lawyer, and asked him if he was willing to pay on his father's behalf. It was a matter of ten thousand francs of bills made out to a money-lender called Samanon, who had probably lent two or three thousand francs to Baron d'Ervy. Victorin asked the bailiff to dismiss the guard and he paid up.

'Will that be the end of it?' he wondered anxiously.

131. *In praise of forgetting*

Lisbeth, already quite wretched at the good fortune that was shining on the family, could not withstand this happy event. She became so much worse that Bianchon gave her no more than a week to live; she was conquered at the end of that long struggle that was marked for her by so many victories. All through the terrible death throes of pulmonary tuberculosis, she kept the secret of her hatred. What is more, she had the supreme satisfaction of seeing Adeline, Hortense, Hulot, Victorin, Steinbock, Célestine, and their children all in tears, around her bed, mourning her as the good angel of the family.

Baron Hulot, on a nourishing diet that he had not known for nearly three years, regained his strength and was almost himself again. His recovery made Adeline so happy that her nervous trembling abated considerably.

'She'll be happy in the end,' Lisbeth said to herself, the day before she died, as she saw the kind of veneration with which the Baron treated his wife, whose sufferings had been described to him by Hortense and Victorin.

This thought hastened the end of Cousin Bette, whose funeral was attended by a whole family in tears.

Baron and Baroness Hulot, realizing they had reached the age when complete rest is desirable, gave Count and Countess Steinbock the magnificent first-floor flat and went to live on the second floor.

Through his son's efforts, at the beginning of 1845, the Baron obtained a post in a railway company, with a salary of six thousand francs; that, together with his six thousand francs' retirement pension and the money left to him by Madame Crevel, gave him an income of twenty-four thousand francs a year.

As Hortense's financial affairs had been separated from her husband's during the three years of their estrangement, Victorin no longer hesitated to invest in his sister's name the two hundred thousand francs left in trust, and he gave Hortense an allowance of twelve thousand francs. Wenceslas, now the husband of a rich woman, was in no way unfaithful to her. But he idled his time away, unable to make up his mind to start any piece of work, however small. Once more an artist *in partibus*,* he was a great drawing-room success; he was consulted by many art-lovers. In short, he became a critic, like all ineffectual men who do not fulfil their early promise.

Each household, then, enjoyed its own income, although they all lived together as one family.

Having learned from her many misfortunes, the Baroness left the management of financial affairs to her son and so limited the Baron to his salary and pension. She hoped that the smallness of his income would prevent him from relapsing into his old bad ways. But, by a strange good fortune that neither mother nor son expected, the Baron seemed to have given up the fair sex. His calm way of life, ascribed to natural causes, at last so reassured his family that they enjoyed to the full Paron d'Ervy's restored amiability and charming qualities. He was invariably attentive to his wife and children; he went with them to the theatre and into society, where he reappeared, and he did the honours of his son's drawing-room with infinite charm. In short, the reformed prodigal father gave his family the liveliest satisfaction. He was a pleasant old man, completely finished, no doubt, but witty and retaining only those elements of his old vice that could be turned into a social virtue. Naturally, everyone at last felt completely reassured. His wife and children praised the father of the family to the skies, forgetting the deaths of the two uncles! Life cannot go on without a great deal of forgetting.

132. *An appalling ending, but true to reality*

Madame Victorin, who managed this large establishment with great housekeeping skill, due no doubt to Lisbeth's teaching, had been obliged to employ a cook. The cook had to have a kitchen-maid. Kitchen-maids are ambitious creatures nowadays, intent on finding out the cook's secrets, and they become cooks themselves as soon as they know how to blend a sauce. Kitchen-maids, therefore, are changed very frequently.

At the beginning of December 1845, Célestine engaged as kitchen-maid a plump Norman girl from Isigny, short, with solid red arms and a very ordinary face, as stupid as a play written to order; it was only reluctantly that she agreed to abandon the typical cotton bonnet worn by the girls of lower Normandy. This girl, as well-padded with fat as a wet-nurse, looked as if she would burst at any moment out of the cotton material which she draped round her bodice. One would have said that her ruddy face had been carved out of stone, so solid were its tanned contours. Naturally, no one in the house paid any attention to the arrival of this girl, called Agatha, the really cheeky kind of girl that comes up every day from the provinces to Paris.

Agatha did not appeal much to the cook as, having served carters in a suburban inn where she had worked, she spoke very coarsely. Thus, instead of making a conquest of the chef and getting him to show her the great art of cookery, she was the object of his contempt. The cook was courting Louise, Countess Steinbock's maid. And so the Norman girl, thinking she was ill-used, complained of her lot.

She was always sent out on some pretext or other when the chef was finishing off a dish or putting the last touches to a sauce.

'I'm certainly out of luck,' she said, 'I'll go somewhere else.'

Nevertheless she stayed on, though she had already asked twice to go.

One night, Adeline, woken by a strange sound, found that Hector was not in his bed beside hers, since, as is appropriate for old people, they slept in twin beds. She waited for an hour but the Baron did not return. Filled with alarm, dreading some tragic disaster, perhaps a stroke, she first went upstairs to the floor above, to the attics where the servants slept. She was attracted to Agatha's room as much by the bright light streaming out of the half-open door as by the murmur of two voices.

She stopped, appalled at recognizing the Baron's voice. Seduced by Agatha's charms and by the calculated resistance of that frightful slut, he had been brought to the point of uttering these hateful words:

'My wife hasn't long to live, and if you like you can be a baroness.'

Adeline uttered a cry, dropped her candlestick, and fled.

Three days later, having received the last rites the previous evening, the Baroness was on her death-bed, surrounded by her weeping family.

Just before she died, she took her husband's hand, pressed it, and whispered to him:

'My dear, I had nothing but my life left to give you. In a moment you'll be free and you'll be able to make a Baroness Hulot.'

And they saw tears falling from the dead woman's eyes, a sight that must be rare.

The fierce persistence of vice had conquered the patience of the angel who, on the brink of eternity, let slip the only words of reproach she had uttered in her whole life.

Baron Hulot left Paris three days after his wife's funeral.

Eleven months later, Victorin learned indirectly of his father's marriage to Mademoiselle Agatha Piquetard, which had taken place at Isigny on 1 February 1846.

'Parents can oppose their children's marriages, but children cannot prevent the follies of parents in their second childhood,' said Maître Hulot to Maître Popinot, the second son of the former Minister of Commerce, who mentioned the marriage to him.

APPENDIX

THE MONEY PLOT OF *COUSIN BETTE*

The financial transactions between the characters of the novel are central elements of Balzac's plot, but they are not easy to follow. The following gives a rough guide to allow the modern non-specialist reader to grasp what is actually going on.

The novel opens in 1838. Hulot has no capital left and lives on his official salary of 25,000 francs per annum. He is in urgent need of a large capital sum (*a*) to repay IOUs (bills of exchange) signed on his behalf by Adeline's uncle, Johann Fischer; (*b*) to satisfy the demands of Valérie Marneffe; and (*c*) to provide a dowry and a marriage trousseau for his daughter Hortense, which ought to cost about 200,000 francs given the family's social standing. To meet these commitments he takes out an insurance policy on his own life, with a term of three years and a benefit of 150,000 francs, which he uses as security for a loan of 70,000 francs from the banker Nucingen (see *Père Goriot* for another episode in Nucingen's crooked career). The loan will be repaid either by 80,000 francs from the proceeds of the insurance policy should Hulot die, or by Hulot's entire annual salary over the three-year period (3 x 25,000 = 75,000, representing 2.4 per cent interest, a reasonable rate in a period of negative inflation), covenanted to one of Nucingen's 'front men', Vauvinet. In addition, Hulot sells Johann Fischer's grain business and assorted official favours (on the limit of legality) for 40,000 francs, making 110,000 francs immediately available. Of this, 40,000 francs are destined for Valérie Marneffe, 60,000 francs for Hortense's dowry and 5,000 francs for her trousseau, leaving Hulot a mere 5,000 francs to live on for three years. The IOUs are paid off at the last minute by a further cash advance from Vauvinet, against another set of signed IOUs.

Hulot then sends Fischer to Algeria to extort grain from the Arabs and to resell it to the French Army at inflated prices: Hulot's administrative position in the War Ministry allows him to approve the deals. The racket is expected to produce 200,000 francs in two years. It seems therefore that Hulot managed to spend 192,000 francs on Valérie Marneffe between 1838 and 1841. Does this vast sum include the 40,000 francs raised in 1838? Are these sums actually received by Hulot? Perhaps not, since the baron raises a further 300,000 francs by mortgaging his son Victorin's house on the Boulevard des Capucines. In early 1841, Hulot asks Fischer to let him have another 100,000 francs, but the racketeer is unable to oblige and requests instead the urgent dispatch to Algeria of 200,000 francs to stave off disaster: for his racket is on the verge of being blown open. At the same time, Vauvinet begins to close in on Hulot, demanding the settlement of the IOUs now swollen by interest charges from 30,000 to 60,000 francs. At this point Hulot is absolutely insolvent.

Adeline then attempts to raise the 200,000 francs to save her uncle from disgrace by offering herself to Crevel, but she fails. Fischer is saved in the end by Hulot's brother, the Maréchal, who surrenders his entire fortune of 152,000 francs to the Minister for War, and complements it with 48,000 francs' worth of securities held in Hortense's name, of which Cousin Bette was the beneficiary. (There is a discrepancy in this turn of the tale, for at an earlier stage of the novel those same securities had been reckoned to be worth only 15 or 16,000 francs. They gave Bette a very modest regular income of 1,200 francs per annum.)

Hector Hulot disappears in disgrace in 1841, and the family fortunes suddenly begin to prosper. Victorin's property increases in value as the area between the Boulevard des Capucines and the Rue de la Paix becomes the centre of the new luxury trades in the Paris of the 1840s. The rent-roll rises to 100,000 francs per annum. The Minister for War returns to Victorin the 200,000 francs surrendered by his uncle the Maréchal (on what authority, and for what reason, it is hard to imagine). He also appoints the younger Hulot to government posts worth 18,000 francs per annum. With a degree of financial magic, Balzac has Victorin's mortgage debt reduced dramatically in the early 1840s, allowing him to invest a large part of the 200,000 francs to produce an income of 10,000 francs per annum for his mother Adeline and his sister Hortense.

The Crevel money-mountain is easier to track. At the start, in 1838, it stands at about 2 million francs, producing an annual income of 80,000 francs: a truly princely level of wealth. Crevel also possesses 300,000 francs' worth of speculative stocks and shares. By 1843, when Crevel marries Valérie, his fortune has risen sharply, since he pays 3 million francs for the property at Presles, and keeps enough in government securities (about 750,000 francs, at prevailing interest rates) to give him a regular income of 30,000 francs per annum. At that point, Valérie herself has about 1 million francs in securities, and a corresponding income of 40,000 francs per annum. Most of that fortune must have come from Crevel, and from lucky or clever investments: she had bled Hulot dry, for sure, but he never had anything approaching such large sums to give to his diabolical mistress. Crevel himself admits at one point to having spent 400,000 francs on Valérie; some part of this was doubled by speculating in Orléans railway company shares.

The combined fortunes of Crevel and Valérie thus come to roughly 4.75 million francs at the time of their deaths. Balzac gives a scrupulous account of its disposal. Victorin takes 80,000 francs in banknotes from Crevel's study desk to pay off Vautrin. Valérie leaves Hector Hulot 300,000 francs. Célestine, Crevel's daughter and Victorin's wife, inherits the property at Presles, worth 3 million; thus the major part of the Crevel fortune is destined to pass on to Hector Hulot's grandchildren. Célestine also inherits an income of 30,000 francs per annum, that is to say a capital of about 750,000 francs; Stanislas, Valérie's son by Marneffe, gets Crevel's own house and an income of 24,000 francs per annum, about 600,000 francs' worth of securities: and it all adds up to approximately 4.73 million francs.

'Respectability . . . begins at 50,000 francs of annual unearned income', Valérie declares. The bare minimum for survival as a student in Paris in that period was reckoned by Balzac to be 1,200 francs per annum. A modest provincial landowner might have an earned income of about 3,000 francs, much the same as a junior magistrate or a university professor. A top lawyer in Paris might make 20–30,000 francs; a dandy would get through 25,000 francs a year not counting gambling debts. Day-wages for labourers varied between 1 and 1.5 francs. The disparity between rich and poor in Balzac's world—which is in this respect the best source of information that there is on the real world of July Monarchy France—is more reminiscent of the situation in the poorest third-world countries nowadays than in any part of Europe; but almost equally striking is the huge gap between the professional middle classes (teachers, lawyers, even government servants of high rank, such as Hulot) and the vast fortunes of the 'new rich' like Crevel, Nucingen, and Valérie. There is no sign in Balzac's last novels that any more equitable distribution of capital and income would emerge from the system he described: on the contrary, the grandchildren of the new rich are set fair to be even richer, and the grandchildren of the poor seem condemned to continuing poverty.

EXPLANATORY NOTES

3 *Don Michele Angelo Cajetani, Prince of Téano*: (1804–82), Roman man of letters married to a relative of Madame Hanska.

three Schlegels: Johann Schlegel (1719–49), German playwright and critic, had two more celebrated nephews, August Wilhelm (1767–1845), scholar, critic, translator of Shakespeare, Orientalist, and poet, and Friedrich (1772–1829), writer, critic, originator of many of the ideas of the early German Romantic movement and of comparative philology.

Porcia, San Severino, Pareto, di Negro, and Belgiojoso: Italians to whom Balzac had dedicated others of his works.

4 *Homo duplex*: Latin for 'man is twofold'.

Buffon: (1707–88), French naturalist.

res duplex: Latin for 'everything is twofold'.

Diderot: (1713–84), French thinker and writer. *This is not fiction* is one of his short stories.

Louis XVIII's ordinance: Louis XVIII's charter of 1814 provided for two-chamber government in France.

Poor Relations: this dedication was intended for the two novels, *Cousin Bette* and *Cousin Pons*, both dealing with poor relations.

5 *milord*: four-wheeled, two-seater carriages.

National Guard: a form of citizen militia first established in 1789. In 1831 it was reorganized as a force for the defence of the constitutional monarchy, with a greater proportion of prosperous upper middle-class members.

Legion of Honour: a non-hereditary order, instituted by Napoleon as a reward for military and civilian services.

6 *1809 campaign*: the campaign by the Napoleonic army against Austria which ended in the defeat of the Austrians at Wagram.

Intendant-General of the armies in Spain: Spain having become virtually a French satellite, a joint Franco-Spanish army invaded Portugal in 1807 in order to extend control over the whole peninsula.

7 *Restoration*: the period from the defeat of Napoleon in 1814, comprising the reigns of Louis XVIII and Charles X, who had to abdicate after the 1830 Revolution, is known as the Restoration. The short period in 1815 known as the 'Hundred Days', during which Napoleon returned to France before his defeat at Waterloo, is of course excluded.

Tartuffe: the main character in Molière's play *Tartuffe*, a religious hypocrite who worms his way into the home of Orgon and there tries to seduce Orgon's wife Elmire.

Poitiers or Coutances: French provincial towns, one in the centre west of the country, the other in the Cherbourg peninsula.

8 *Empire clock*: a clock dating from the days of the Napoleonic Empire, which ended in 1815.

10 *Chamber*: the Chamber of Deputies, the French equivalent of the British House of Commons. A deputy is the equivalent of a British MP.

11 *Paris prefecture*: the Paris administration.

Regency: Louis XV succeeded to the French throne in 1715, when he was a child of 5. The period from 1715 to 1723, when Philip of Orleans was Regent, had a reputation for dissolute living and lax moral standards.

César Birotteau: the main character in Balzac's novel of that name.

14 *Duprez*: (1806–96), a famous tenor of the period.

15 *Mademoiselle de Romans*: it was said that Louis XV had young girls abducted and brought up especially to provide for his pleasures. Mademoiselle Romans (the 'de' is an invention of Balzac's) was one of these girls.

16 *Saint-Simonism*: a system of social philosophy inaugurated by the Comte de Saint-Simon (1760–1825) and continued after his death by his disciples. Female emancipation and community of property were amongst their ideas, but there was confusion between their theories on these two matters.

Madame Schontz, Malaga, and Carabine: courtesans who appear in many Balzac novels.

17 *Golden Calf*: the story of the Golden Calf is told in Exodus 32.

Kellers: rich bankers in Balzac's novels.

Marquis d'Esgrignon: the main character in Balzac's novel *Le Cabinet des antiques*, he also appears elsewhere in Balzac's works as a young society aristocrat.

Duc d'Hérouville: a wealthy aristocrat, of dwarf-like stature, who appears in several of Balzac's novels.

the thirteenth district: at that time Paris had only twelve districts. To say that a couple is in the thirteenth district is a way of saying that they are living together without being legally married.

19 *our King*: Louis-Philippe, who succeeded to the French throne after the 1830 Revolution, when Charles X was forced to abdicate, was of a younger branch of the Bourbons and liked to be called King of the French rather than King of France. The 'our' has satirical overtones, for it suggests that Louis-Philippe, who had a 'bourgeois' rather than aristocratic life-style, was very much the king of the 'nouveaux riches', vulgar upstarts like Crevel.

21 *La Reine des Roses*: the name of César Birotteau's shop in Balzac's novel of that name.

26 *Republic*: the French monarchy was abolished in 1792, when a Republic was declared. The Republic continued and extended the war which had already broken out between France and Austria; in January 1793 it staked a claim to a frontier on the Rhine, and by March 1793 the French Republic was at war with all Europe except Switzerland and Scandinvia.

27 *Madame du Barry*: (1746–93), mistress of Louis XV, natural daughter of a poor woman of Vaucouleurs. Thanks to her wit, charm, and beauty, she became the King's official mistress and her influence over him was absolute until his death.

Madame Tallien: (1773–1835), leader of the social life of Paris after her marriage to the revolutionary Tallien in 1794.

Bronzino: name given to the Florentine painter Angelo Allori (1502–72). His portrait of Bianca Capello is in the Uffizi gallery in Florence.

Jean Goujon: (1520–66), distinguished French sculptor.

Diane de Poitiers: (1499–1566), mistress of Henry II of France. Goujon's sculpture, *Venus coming out of her bath*, is in the Louvre.

Signora Olympia: Olympia Pamphili, whose portrait is in the Doria-Pamphili gallery in Rome.

Ninon: Ninon de Lenclos (1615–1705), French courtesan, who became a leader of fashion in Paris and the friend of many distinguished men.

Mademoiselle George: stage-name of Marguerite-Joséphine Weimer (1787–1867), famous for her acting, beauty, and temper.

Madame Récamier: (1777–1849), a woman of great beauty, charm and tact, who inspired many passions. During the Napoleonic period and the Restoration, the most eminent figures in politics and literature met in her salon.

28 *d'Orsay, Forbin, and Ouvrard*: Comte Alfred d'Orsay (1801–52), was famous in London as well as in Paris, gifted with exceptional good looks, a charming manner, brilliant wit, and artistic ability. Comte de Forbin (1777–1841), a painter and archaeologist as well as a handsome man, was director of the Royal museums and galleries during the Restoration. Gabriel-Julien Ouvrard (1770–1846) was better known for his banking skills than for his good looks.

Directory: from 1795–1799 France was ruled by a 'Directorate' of five. It was a period of reaction against the austerity of the Reign of Terror.

29 *the Feltre ministry*: the Duc de Feltre was Minister of War during the Restoration till 1817.

Spanish war: in 1823 a French army was sent to Spain to assist the Spanish king in the civil war which had begun there in 1820. French intervention re-established the Spanish king on his throne.

1830: cf. note to *our King* on p. 19.

younger branch: i.e. Louis-Philippe.

30 *prima donna assoluta*: absolute first lady.

31 *exploits in 1799 and 1800*: these are recounted in Balzac's novel *Les Chouans*.

31 *Pactolus*: a river in Lydia whose golden sands became proverbial. Lydia was the gold country of the ancient world of the Greeks.

33 *Ninon*: cf. note to p. 27.

36 *Fontainebleau*: Napoleon abdicated at Fontainebleau in 1814.

   1815: Napoleon returned to France from Elba in 1815 and for a 'Hundred Days' was again master of the country till his final defeat at Waterloo.

38 *Ninon*: cf. note to p. 27.

   Richelieu: Armand du Plessis, Cardinal de Richelieu (1585–1642), chief minister of Louis XIII.

41 *Calabrian-like*: Calabria is a district of S. Italy.

   Giotto: (1266–1337), the most important Italian painter of his time.

43 *Grand-Duke Constantine*: at the Congress of Vienna in 1815, Poland was divided between Prussia, Austria, and Russia. The Russian Emperor, Alexander, granted the Poles a constitution which declared the kingdom of Poland, to be united to Russia in the person of the Tsar, as a separate political entity. The head of the kingdom was to be a lieutenant of the Emperor and had to be a member of the Imperial house or a Pole. In 1826 the Grand-Duke Constantine, the Emperor's brother, became the Imperial lieutenant.

   the defeat: in 1830–1 a military revolt took place in Warsaw, the Poles being defeated by the Russians. The kingdom was then reduced to the position of a Russian province.

44 *Ô Matilda*: an aria from Rossini's opera *William Tell*.

   Livonia: a Baltic province ceded by Poland to Sweden in 1660 and then by Sweden to Russia in 1721. There seems to be some confusion here for both Steinbock and Bette (and for Balzac too) between a Pole and a Livonian. But for the Grand-Duke Constantine a Livonian was a Russian, and that could explain the favour shown to Steinbock by the Grand-Duke.

   Charles XII: (1682–1718), King of Sweden, celebrated for his military victories, particularly over the Russians at Narva (1700), though he was defeated by the Russians at Poltava (1709).

45 *1812 campaign*: Napoleon's campaign against Russia.

placed him in a school: cf. note to *Livonia* on p. 44.

Benvenuto Cellini: (1500–71), Italian metal-worker and sculptor.

Mademoiselle de Fauveau: (1803–60), French sculptress of some renown in her day.

Wagner: either Martin Wagner (1777–1858), painter, engraver, and sculptor, who lived in Paris in 1803, or Friedrich Wagner (1803–76), a less well-known engraver but one who spent his whole working life in Paris.

Jeanest: either Louis-François, sculptor, who worked mainly in industry, or his son Émile (1813–57), who did his best work in England, where he settled in 1845 or 1846.

Froment: François-Désiré Froment (1802–55), celebrated goldsmith.

Meurice: goldsmith, stepfather of F.-D. Froment.

Liénard: Michel-Joseph-Napoléon or Paul, wood-carver, who did some work for Balzac's house in the Rue Fortunée.

46 *Donatello*: (1408–66), Italian sculptor. His equestrian statue of Gattamelata in Padua included the first horse to be cast in bronze.

Brunelleschi: (1377–1446), Italian goldsmith, sculptor, and architect. His great work was the building of the dome of the cathedral at Florence.

Ghiberti: (1378–1455), Italian sculptor, creator of the bronze gates of the baptistry at Florence.

Jean de Bologne: Giovanni da Bologna (1529–1608), an important sculptor whose work was more generally admired for three centuries than that of any sculptor except Michelangelo.

50 *Brillat-Savarin*: (1755–1826), French lawyer, politician, and writer, author of a celebrated work on gastronomy.

51 *Robert le Diable*: opera by Meyerbeer, first performed in 1831.

54 *1830 Revolution*: the Revolution which deposed Charles X and brought Louis-Philippe to the French throne; cf. note to p. 19.

55 *Forzheim* (or Pforzheim): W. German town where Marshal Hulot's military achievement won him his title.

57 *Henri III and his favourites*: Henri III (1551–89), King of France from 1574, bestowed favours on a small group of handsome young men, known as his *mignons*.

Marguerite's lovers: Marguerite de Valois (1553–1615), sister of Henri III and queen consort of the King of Navarre who became Henri IV of France; well-known for her licentiousness as well as for her *Mémoires*. Her role in conspiracies during the French wars of religion cost the life of her lover, the Seigneur de la Môle, in 1574.

58 *the legitimist newspaper*: *La Gazette de France* had its office at 12 Rue du Doyenné. Its circulation declined from an average of 11,000 in 1831 to 3,300 in 1845.

Cambacérès: (1753–1824), one of the three consuls who ruled France after the *coup d'état* of 18 brumaire (9 Nov. 1799, which overthrew the Revolutionary government. In 1804 he was made arch-chancellor of the Napoleonic empire and exercised extended powers during Napoleon's absences.

59 *Medusa's head*: in Greek mythology, one of the three gorgons, monsters whose heads were covered with crawling serpents instead of hair, and who could turn into stone anyone who looked at them. Medusa, the only mortal among them, was killed by Perseus, who cut off her head while looking at her reflection in a mirror.

63 *Algiers*: the French conquered Algeria in 1830. But in 1839 Algerian armed resistance under the Arab chief Abd-el-Kader led to war with the French which lasted till his defeat and capture in 1847.

64 *Pilastre du Rosier*: (1756–85), French physicist and aeronaut.

Beaujon: (1708–86), French financier, whose name was given to a district of Paris.

Marcel: dancing-master of Louis XV.

Molé: (1734–1802), eighteenth-century actor.

Sophie Arnould: (1744–1803), celebrated opera-singer.

Franklin: Benjamin Franklin (1706–90), American statesman and scientist, who negotiated the alliance between America and France in 1766 and was then appointed plenipotentiary in Paris.

69 *Kosciusko*: (1746–1817), Polish patriot, who led the Polish rising against Russia in 1794. He is reputed to have said *Finis*

Poloniae ('It's the end of Poland') when defending Warsaw against the Russian advance in October 1794.

Charles XII: cf. note to p. 44.

71 *the Emperor*: the Tsar of Russia, Nicholas I 1796–1855), who succeeded Alexander I in 1825.

73 *Clichy*: debtors' prison in the Rue de Clichy.

75 *Chaumière*: public dance-hall in the Boulevard du Montparnasse.

Notre-Dame-de-Lorette quarter: district inhabited by girls of easy virtue, called 'lorettes' after the name of the local church.

80 *patchouli*: a penetrating perfume.

81 *Pompadour*: Madame de Pompadour (1721–64), mistress of Louis XV for many years, was a great patron of literature and art.

Greuze: (1725–1805), celebrated genre and portrait painter, whose works have a charming sentimentality.

Watteau: (1684–1721), famous genre painter, especially of shepherds and shepherdesses in the fashionable costumes of the period (*fêtes galantes*).

Van Dyck: (1599–1641), celebrated Flemish artist, who painted many portraits of European aristocracy as well as religious and mythological subjects.

Ruysdaël: (1602–70), Dutch painter best known for his landscapes.

Guaspre: name given to the landscape painter of Italian origin, Gaspard Dughet (1613–75).

Rembrandt: (1606–69), the most influential and creative Dutch artist of the 17th century.

Holbein: (1497–1543), German painter renowned for the realism of his portraits, particularly those recording the court of Henry VIII of England.

Murillo: (1618–82), popular Spanish religious artist.

Titian: (1489–1576), painter of the Venetian school regarded as one of the greatest Renaissance artists.

Teniers: (1610–90), Flemish painter known for his genre scenes of peasant life.

81 *Metzus*: (1466–1530), Flemish painter known as the *Antwerp-Blacksmith*.

Van Huysum: (1682–1749), leading Dutch painter of still-life arrangements of flowers or fruits.

Abraham Mignon: (1640–79), German painter remembered primarily for his still lifes.

82 *d'Esgrignon, Rastignac, Maxime, Lenoncourt, Verneuil, Laginski, Rochefide, La Palférine*: aristocratic members of high society who appear in other Balzac stories.

Nucingen and du Tillet: two successful bankers who appear in other Balzac stories.

Antonia, Malaga, Carabine, and Madame Schontz: courtesans who appear in other Balzac stories.

They call you Hulot! I know you no more!: parody of a well-known line from Corneille's tragedy *Horace*, 'Alba has appointed you, I know you no more!' (II. iii. 502).

84 *Monsieur Sauce*: one of those responsible for stopping Louis XVI at Varennes when he tried to escape from Paris in 1791. Louis XVI was executed in 1793. In 1795 Napoleon, then a successful young general, used firearms to suppress a rising in Paris, leaving two to three hundred killed or wounded.

87 *Chevaliers Bayard*: Pierre du Terrail, Chevalier de Bayard (1473–1524), a famous French captain who distinguished himself by his bravery in the Italian wars of Charles VIII, Louis XII, and François I.

89 *Prince Eugène*: Eugene of Savoy (1663–1736), Austrian general, considered to be the greatest military strategist of his time.

92 *there's more behind this than you think*: quotation from Racine's tragedy *Phèdre* (I. iii. 269).

the Princes: the sons of Louis-Philippe.

97 *Prince Royal*: the eldest son of Louis-Philippe.

98 *Canova*: (1757–1822), Italian sculptor. His works were extremely lifelike and recalled the spirit and style of ancient Greece.

101 *Terborch*: (1617–81), Dutch painter, particularly skilful in his rendering of texture in draperies.

103 *Rocher de Cancale*: fashionable Parisian restaurant where many dinner parties take place in Balzac novels.

106 *Saint Teresa*: (1515–82), Spanish nun and saint, whose intense piety led her to plan a reform of the Carmelite order to which she belonged and to secure the foundation of many reformed Carmelite convents.

in a shower of gold: in Greek mythology, Danaë, daughter of Acrisius, King of Argos, was shut up in a tower by her father, since an oracle had foretold that he would meet his death at the hands of a son born of Danaë. Jupiter visited her in a shower of gold, and a son Perseus was born. He accidentally killed Acrisius with a quoit.

107 *all along the river*: quotation from a popular nursery song.

Monsieur de Turenne: (1611–75), celebrated military commander of Louis XIV. His successes were largely due to his thoughtfulness and calculation.

108 *Sèvres*: French town near Paris, celebrated for its porcelain ware.

Wagram: Austrian village near Vienna, where Napoleon won a famous victory in 1809.

Sain and Augustin: Sain (1778–1847) was a pupil of Augustin (1759–1832), a leading miniature painter at the time of the Restoration. Sain painted miniatures of Napoleon and Josephine as well as of Charles X.

109 *picador*: a man whose task it was to arouse the bull to anger before a bullfight.

Pythoness: in ancient Greece the oracle at Delphi spoke through the mouth of a priestess, called a pythoness. After a three-day fast, the pythoness chewed laurel leaves, and in a state of exaltation, sat on a tripod above an opening giving forth noxious vapours. Her whole body then shuddered, her hair stood on end, and foaming at the mouth she answered the questions she had been asked.

111 *Charenton*: lunatic asylum near Paris.

112 *the earthenware pot against the iron pot*: reference to a fable by La Fontaine (1621–95), whose moral is that one should associate only with one's equals.

115 *1830*: cf. note to p. 19.

115 *1793*: date of the execution of Louis XVI and the abolition of the monarchy.

116 *an Iago and a Richard III*: that is to say, a character as jealous and scheming as Iago in Shakespeare's *Othello* and as Richard III in his play of that name.

117 *magna parens rerum*: these Latin words mean the 'great mother of things', not the 'mother of great things'.

Mohican: Fenimore Cooper's novel about N. American Indians, *The Last of the Mohicans* (1826), had become very popular in Paris.

118 *Saint-Denis quarter*: commercial quarter of Paris.

121 *César Birotteau's fortunate successor*: a reference to Balzac's novel *César Birotteau*. From being an employee in César Birotteau's perfumery shop, Crevel rose to being its proprietor. Cf. note to p. 11.

122 *Exhibition of manufactured goods*: Balzac may be referring here either to an exhibition of 1825 or to one of 1834.

Pierre Grassou: the story of Pierre Grassou is told in Balzac's short story of that name.

Canova: cf. note to p. 98.

123 *Boule*: Parisian cabinet-maker and wood-carver (1642–1732), whose works were highly valued.

unfortunate predecessor: i.e. César Birotteau, whose career ended in bankruptcy. Cf. notes to pp. 11 and 121.

124 *Chevet*: fashionable Parisian caterer.

Zaïre ... Orosmane: in Voltaire's tragedy *Zaïre*, Zaïre, a Christian princess, a prisoner of the Turks, is loved by Orosmane, a Muslim prince who wants to marry her, and is thus typical of an enslaved beloved.

Regency: cf. note to p. 11.

Pompadour: cf. note to p. 81.

Maréchal de Richelieu: (1696–1788), great nephew of the cardinal (cf. note to p. 38), distinguished French nobleman and courtier, renowned for his wit and immorality.

126 *Déjazet*: (1797–1875), well-known actress of the time, famous for her liveliness, wit, and private life as well as for her acting talent.

Hagar: Egyptian slave who, in the Bible, becomes the concubine of Abraham (Genesis 16).

127 *deer-park*: the house at Versailles where Louis XV kept girls in a kind of harem; so called because it stood in a district, long since built over, used by Louis XIII as a sort of deer-farm.

130 *Dulcinea*: the 'ideal-lady' worshipped by Don Quixote in Cervantes' famous tale of that name. She was in reality an ordinary peasant girl, but Don Quixote saw her as a model of physical and moral perfection. The name is used, slightly ironically, to mean the girl of a young man's dreams.

one of the cleverest wits of the last century: the Prince de Ligne (1735–1814).

Bellegarde: Gabrielle d'Estrées, Henri IV's mistress, had the Duc de Bellegarde as her lover.

137 *Agnès*: in Molière's play, *L'École des femmes*, Agnès is a young girl brought up in total ignorance, who yet manages to outwit her middle-aged guardian and would-be husband.

147 *a line of French verse*: Nucingen is here misquoting a line from Racine's tragedy *Bérénice* (III. iv. 945).

Danaë: cf. note to p. 106.

152 *let us be friends, Cinna!*: quotation from Corneille's play *Cinna* (v. iii. 1701).

156 *Fabert*: (1599–1662), a distinguished soldier who became a marshal of France, but, unlike Napoleon, did not become an emperor.

Correggio: (1494–1534) famous Italian painter, rival of Raphael.

Laïs: celebrated Greek courtesan of the 4th century BC.

Sophie Arnould: (1744–1803), celebrated opera-singer, also renowned for her witty remarks of which a collection was published in 1813.

Madame de la Baudraye the main character of Balzac's novel *La Muse du Département*.

158 *Louis XV's first surgeon*: Louis XV having remarked to his first surgeon, La Martinière, 'I see I'm no longer young, I must slow down', the doctor is said to have replied, 'Sire,

your Majesty would do better to remove his harness', i.e. give up his licentious ways altogether.

160 *Holy Alliance*: alliance formed in 1815, after the fall of Napoleon, between Russia, Austria, and Prussia. The rulers of these countries ostensibly bound themselves to let their conduct towards their own peoples, and their relations with others, be animated solely by a spirit of mutual helpfulness and Christian fraternity, according to the precepts of Holy Scripture. The alliance had dissolved by 1825.

161 *Tantalus*: in classical mythology, a king condemned by Jupiter to perpetual hunger and thirst. He is often represented as standing in the middle of a river whose waters retreat from his lips whenever he wants to drink, and under trees whose branches escape his grasp whenever he wants to pick their fruit.

164 *Louis XII*: (1462–1515), 52 when he married Henry VIII's sister, aged 16. Louis was by then in poor health and died three months later.

166 *bandoline*: a viscous, scented hair lotion, used to make the hair look glossy.

167 *this bloodstained Nun*: a reference to a terrifying, debauched nun in the English horror novel *The Monk* by M. G. Lewis (1775–1818).

Cranach: (1472–1553), eminent German painter.

Van Eyck: either Hubert (1365–1426) or his brother Jan (c. 1380–1440), the most distinguished Flemish painters of their period.

Isis: goddess of ancient Egypt.

Montyon prize: prize founded by the Baron de Montyon (1733–1820) in 1782 for works of moral value and for acts of virtue, to be awarded by the French Academy.

168 *the shopping-basket handle*: reference to a proverbial French phrase, *to make the shopping-basket handle dance*, meaning to make a bit on the side, referring to servants.

174 *Jacob Desmalters*: Roman-style furniture and Egyptian-style ornaments (following Napoleon's Egyptian campaign) were popularized by Jacob Desmalters (1770–1840) to form the Empire style.

175 *Robert Lefebvre*: (1756–1830), the most sought-after por-

trait painter of the Napoleonic period. Amongst many portraits of eminent people, he painted those of Napoleon, his two wives, and his mother and sister. A portrait by Lefebvre was a sign of success under the Empire and so, in Madame Hulot's drawing-room, is an indication of past glory.

186 *Junot's campaign in Portugal*: Napoleon appointed General Junot commander of the campaign against Portugal in 1807. He conquered the country in less than two months but was beaten by the Duke of Wellington's forces and had to leave the country in 1808.

conquerors of Brazil: the Portuguese conquest of Brazil was completed in 1594. If Montès is the great-grandson of one of the conquerors, his forebears must have been exceptionally long-lived!

the siege of Mantua: in 1796 Bonaparte had to subdue the garrison of Mantua, to which he was laying siege, and to deal at the same time with the Austrian army which had taken refuge there. The capture of the town marked the end of his Italian campaign.

187 *Murat*: (1767–1815), distinguished Napoleonic general, renowned for his courage, husband of Napoleon's sister Caroline, King of Naples from 1808 to 1814.

Mirabeau: (1749–91), the most distinguished orator of the French Revolution.

198 *Saint-Preux*: a main character in Rousseau's novel *La Nouvelle Héloïse* (1761). He falls deeply in love with his pupil, Julie d'Étanges, and she reciprocates his passion.

199 *the silver drug*: the two metals to be won by cultivating the god of commerce are presumably gold and silver. The god of commerce is Mercury and mercury is another name for quicksilver, which was used as a drug in the treatment of venereal disease. Crevel's elaborate pun is thus a way of saying that Marneffe has a venereal disease.

205 *Regency*: cf. note to p. 11

Pompadour: cf. note to p. 81.

Maréchal de Richelieu: cf. note to p. 124.

Les Liaisons dangereuses: celebrated novel (1782) by Choderlos de Laclos, whose hero is a cynical and unscrupulous seducer of women.

209 *nothing imaginary in your title*: a reference to Molière's play *Sganarelle ou le Cocu imaginaire*.

Canillac: the Marquis de Canillac (1674–1765) was the close friend and companion of the Regent in his licentious pleasures.

211 *Silenus*: in Greek mythology, the companion of Dionysus, god of wine; often represented as an oldish man with shaggy hair and beard.

Gubetta: spy and accomplice of Lucretia Borgia in Victor Hugo's play *Lucrèce Borgia*.

212 *Arnal*: (1794–1872), popular comic actor of the day.

213 *a cousin from America . . .* : expression often used to describe a relative who returns from abroad with a fortune and rescues his family from poverty.

219 *Curtius*: in 362 BC the earth in the forum at Rome gave way. Soothsayers predicted that the resultant chasm could only be filled up by throwing into it Rome's greatest treasure. Marcus Curtius, a patrician youth, mounted his horse in full armour and leaped into the abyss, which then closed over him.

220 *Murat*: cf. note to p. 187.

221 *Leo X*: Pope from 1513 to 1521, was a great patron of the arts.

Phidias: (c.490–432 BC), great sculptor of ancient Greece.

223 *Prometheus' sin*: in classical mythology, Prometheus formed a man out of mud and, to give him life, stole fire from heaven.

Figaro: character in Beaumarchais's plays, *The Barber of Seville* (1775) and *The Marriage of Figaro* (1784).

Lovelace: character in Richardson's novel *Clarissa* (1749).

Manon Lescaut: character in the Abbé Prévost's novel *Manon Lescaut* (1731).

Polymnia: Greek statue of the Muse of lyric poetry, in the Louvre.

Julia: Roman statue representing the goddess Juno, but with the form and features of Julia, daughter of the Roman emperor Augustus.

224 *Paganini*: (1784–1840), celebrated Italian violinist, remarkable for his technical brilliance.

228 *Telemachus*: in Fénélon's didactic romance *Télémaque* (1699), Telemachus, son of Ulysses, sets out in search of his father. He is shipwrecked on the island where his father had been detained by Calypso, who exerts her charms on Telemachus to console herself for Ulysses' departure.

231 *Austerlitzes*: Napoleon won one of his greatest victories over the Russians and Austrians at Austerlitz (1805).

234 *Madame de Maintenon*: (1635–1719), from 1674 the mistress of Louis XIV and secretly married to him after the death of his queen, Marie-Thérèse. She was a modest, discreet, intelligent woman, capable of great self-control and inclined to piety.

Ninon: cf. note to p. 27.

236 *Carabossa*: the bad fairy of fairy tales who turns up at christenings with an evil gift.

Louis XI: (1423–83), crafty and unscrupulous French King, who succeeded in dominating the feudal lords and increasing the power of the monarchy.

237 *Iris and Chloë*: minor Greek goddesses, whose names are often used for shepherdesses in pastoral poetry.

Manon: the fickle heroine of the Abbé Prévost's novel *Manon Lescaut*; cf. note to p. 223.

Célimène: the society coquette in Molière's play *Le Misanthrope* (1666).

240 *Samson . . . Delilah*: the story of Samson and Delilah is told in Judges 14.

Omphale: in Greek mythology, Hercules fell in love with Omphale, ruler of Lydia. To please her, he is said to have spun wool and put on a woman's clothes, while Omphale wore his lion's skin.

Spinoza: (1632–77), Dutch philosopher of Portuguese Jewish parentage, excommunicated for his unorthodox views.

241 *Marius*: (157–85 BC), Roman general. After many victories and great popularity, he clashed with his rival Sulla, was obliged to flee along the coast of Latium and was taken prisoner near Minturnae, whose inhabitants put him on a

ship which landed him at Carthage in N. Africa. The Roman governor, however, sent an officer to bid him leave the country. Marius' only reply was, 'Tell the praetor that you have seen C. Marius a fugitive, sitting among the ruins of Carthage'.

241 *Judith*: heroine in *Judith*, a book of the Apocrypha. She cut off the head of Holofernes in order to save her people.

242 *Camille Maupin*: a character in Balzac's novel *Béatrix* and in other stories of the *Comédie humaine*. She is an exceptional woman, being a successful writer as well as a leader of society.

243 *Phèdre's declaration to Hippolyte*: In Racine's play *Phèdre* (1677), Phèdre makes an impassioned declaration of love to her stepson Hippolyte.

246 *Pythoness*: cf. note to p. 109.

Rocher de Cancale: cf. note to p. 103.

247 *Benvenuto Cellini*: cf. note to p. 45.

257 *fructus belli*: Latin expression meaning 'the fruits of war'.

258 *augurs*: in ancient Rome the augurs were priests who foretold the future from the flight or song of birds, the appetite of sacred chickens, and the like. But faith in these superstitious predictions did not last and Cicero thought that two augurs could not look each other in the face without laughing.

271 *Madame de Merteuil*: the partner in corruption of the cynical and unscrupulous hero in Choderlos de Laclos's novel *Les Liaisons dangereuses* (1782); cf. note to p. 205.

284 *La Nouvelle Héloïse*: celebrated romance (1761) by Rousseau, told in the form of letters; cf. note to p. 198.

291 *Jan*: the painter and writer Laurent Jan (1809–77) was a good friend of Balzac's.

293 *July celebrations*: festivities to commemorate the three days of the 1830 revolution, 27, 28, and 29 July.

302 *July festivities*: cf. note to p. 293.

306 *Charter of 1830*: when Louis XVIII was restored to the French throne in 1814, he granted a charter which, amongst other things, provided for freedom of the press. Ordinances issued by Charles X in 1830 violated the 1814 Charter by

abolishing that freedom. This led to the revolution of July 1830, which forced Charles X to abdicate and established Louis-Philippe as a constitutional monarch. A charter voted by the Chamber of Deputies and accepted by the King replaced the Charter of 1814.

309 *Gros-René*: Gros-René is a servant in Molière's play *Le Dépit amoureux*, but the phrase is in fact used by the servant Alain in L'École des femmes (ii, iii).

Carême: (1784–1833), celebrated French chef, who worked for many distinguished and royal personalities.

Marchesa de Pescara: Vittoria Colonna (1490–1547), daughter of the High Constable of the Kingdom of Naples, married the Marquis de Pescara, who contributed greatly to the victory at the battle of Pavia but died as a result of his wounds in 1535. Though gifted, beautiful, and much courted, she devoted the rest of her life to her husband's memory.

Diane de Poitiers: cf. note to p. 27.

310 *Maecenases*: Maecenas was a celebrated patron of the arts in Rome at the time of the Emperor Augustus. His name has come to mean a wealthy supporter of literature and the arts.

311 *Danaïdes*: in classical mythology, the fifty daughters of Danaüs. On their wedding nights all but one killed their husbands. As punishment they were condemned to fill a bottomless cask with water.

312 *Saint Lawrence*: (d.258), one of the most venerated Christian martyrs, celebrated for his Christian valour. It is reported that he was roasted to death on a gridiron.

313 *Dubois when he kicked the Regent three times*: it is said that the Regent (Philippe, Duc d'Orléans, Regent during the minority of Louis XV, 1715–23) disguised himself one day as the servant of the Abbé Dubois (his former tutor, who rose to be an archbishop, cardinal, and minister), who took advantage of the situation to kick his master three times.

316 *Charter*: cf. note to p. 306.

'*God of the Jews, you prevail!*': from Racine's play *Athalie* (v. vi. 1768).

Golden Calf: cf. note to p. 17.

317 *Maréchal de Richelieu*: cf. note to p. 124.

319 *Egeria*: the nymph Egeria, legendary advisor to Numa Pompilius, second King of Rome.

our present distinguished minister: Guizot, an important minister in the reign of Louis-Philippe, was closely linked to the Princesse de Lieven, widow of the Russian ambassador to London; she was his constant adviser in political matters.

Cumaean Sibyl: most famous of the Sibyls (prophetesses), she was consulted by Aeneas before he descended into the underworld.

323 *Another guitar*: this title is taken from one of Victor Hugo's poems.

328 *Lovelace*: cf. note to p. 223.

329 *Edmé Champion*: (1764–1852), an orphan supported by charity, who became a rich jeweller and vowed to devote himself to the relief of poverty in Paris. Dressed in a blue cloak, he distributed soup and clothing to the poor.

Montyon: cf. note to p. 167.

330 *in fiocchi*: Italian phrase meaning 'in full dress'.

331 *Marshal Masséna*: (1756–1817), one of Napoleon's outstanding military commanders.

Arcola: the taking of the bridge at Arcola was one of Bonaparte's achievements in his victory against the Austrians in 1796.

Kaiserlichs: name given by Napoleon's soldiers to the Austrian soldiers.

333 *go to Neuilly*: i.e. to see the King, who had a favourite residence at Neuilly.

334 *rival of Bernadotte's*: Charles Bernadotte (1764–1844), Marshal of France with a distinguished career in the Revolutionary and Napoleonic wars. He was adopted by the King of Sweden in 1810 and became King of Sweden in 1818.

335 *a piece of Crown property*: the Chamber of Deputies had raised objections to the 18 million francs proposed for the King's civil list, reducing it to 12 million. The Chamber also refused to give the château and estate of Rambouillet (bought by Louis XV, who joined it to the property of the Crown) to Louis-Philippe's son, the Duc de Nemours.

Treasury official: there had been a considerable scandal when a Treasury official named Mathéo absconded with 1,800,000 francs. In another notorious case an official of the Bank of France, Kessner, embezzled 4,500,000 francs.

337 *Béresina*: in 1812 Napoleon's army, in retreat after the failure of his campaign against Russia, suffered tragic losses in the crossing of this river.

339 *Sganarelle*: a name frequently given to stupid or malicious lower-class characters in French comedy, particularly in Molière's plays, e.g. in *Le Médecin malgré lui*.

342 '*The Paris news item ... thinks*': a parody of a line from Voltaire's play *Oedipe* (IV. i): 'Nos prêtres ne sont pas ce qu'un vain peuple pense: / Notre crédulité fait toute leur science' (Our priests are not what a foolish people thinks: / It is our credulity which constitutes all their learning).

343 *Les Chouans*: the first novel Balzac published under his own name (1829). In it Hulot plays an important part as a leader of the Republican armies which suppressed a Royalist rising in Brittany.

Vandamme: General Vandamme had been captured by the Russians in 1813 and imprisoned at Wintka on the Siberian border. He returned to France in September 1814.

344 *Condé*: the Prince de Condé (1621–86) was a distinguished military commander in the reign of Louis XIV and responsible for many of the great French victories of that period.

347 *Neuilly*: cf. note to p. 333.

348 *Chouan uprising*: the uprising in Brittany which is the theme of Balzac's novel *Les Chouans*; cf. note to p. 343.

Madame: the eldest son of the King of France was known as 'Monsieur', his wife as 'Madame'. In 1832 'Madame' was the Duchesse de Berry, who made an abortive attempt to recapture the French monarchy for the family of Charles X, who had been deposed by the revolution of 1830.

353 *Gourville*: (1625–1703), condemned for having embezzled state funds when a tax official in Guienne (one of the old provinces of France of which Bordeaux was the capital). He had been a lover of Ninon de Lenclos (cf. note to p. 27) and was saved by her.

354 *Sardanapalus*: a legendary debauched king of Assyria, sup-

posed to have reigned from 836 to 817 BC. He was the theme of a play by Byron (1821).

354 *C'est Vénus tout entière à sa proie attachée*: a celebrated line from Racine's tragedy *Phèdre* (i. iii). (It is Venus with all her might gripping her prey.)

356 *Schontz*: in Balzac's novel *Béatrix*, madame Schontz is a courtesan whose lover is the Marquis de Rochefide.

Fénélon: cf. note to p. 228.

Ourcq water: the Ourcq is a French river linked to the Seine by a canal. Its waters were used to increase the supply of water to the public fountains in Paris. Water from the Seine was carried by water-carriers to individual houses and was much more expensive.

357 *Ambigu-Comique*: a Paris theatre.

thirteenth district: cf. note to p. 17.

358 *Mabille*: a popular public dance-hall founded by a dancing-master called Mabille.

d'Aiglemont: in Balzac's story *La Maison Nucingen*, the Marquis d'Aiglemont is one of the victims of Baron Nucingen's shady financial dealings.

360 *Bartholo*: the jealous guardian of the heroine in Beaumarchais's play *The Barber of Seville*, which formed the basis of Rossini's opera of that name.

the Augustes, the Hippolytes, the Nestors, the Victors: these four men's names are representative of the different types of men who might tempt Olympe away from Hulot. Augustus was a powerful Roman Emperor; Hippolytus a handsome young man whose stepmother Phaedra fell in love with him (the theme of Racine's tragedy *Phèdre*); Nestor the oldest prince at the siege of Troy, renowned for his wisdom; and Victor means conqueror.

ors: the word *or* in French means gold, and Josépha is making a pun linked to the final syllable of the last two names mentioned.

368 *happy*: in view of the word 'unhappy' in the following line, it sems likely that this is an oversight on Balzac's part or a misprint, and that the correct reading should be 'unhappy'.

Marlborough: a reference to the well-known French popular song which starts 'Malbrouk s'en va-t-en guerre / Ne sais quand reviendra' (Malbrouk is off to the war, I don't know when he'll come back).

375 *Misfortune's noble victim*: this comes from Sacchini's opera *Oedipus at Colonna* (1787), performed at the first public appearance of King Louis XVIII and his family after the Restoration; this line addressed to the King aroused great public enthusiasm.

377 *Boule*: cf. note to p. 123.

Joseph Bridau: an artist who appears in many Balzac novels and is a main character in *La Rabouilleuse*.

Malibran: (1808–36), the most famous singer of her day.

Allori: (1577–1621). His painting *Judith and Holofernes* is in the Pitti Palace in Florence.

Bronzino's nephew: Allori was in fact the great-nephew of the Florentine painter Bronzino (1502–72).

379 *Matilda*: a character in Rossini's opera *William Tell* (1829). Cf. note to p. 44).

382 *La Chaumière*: cf. note to p. 75.

383 *Funambules*: Parisian theatre presenting popular entertainment programmes.

cock: this is a pun on the French word *poule*, which means (1) hen; (2) prostitute; (3) pool at billiards.

Melun: the central prison at Melun.

386 *Marat*: (1743–93), Revolutionary leader, responsible for some of the worst excesses of the French Revolution, assassinated in his bath by Charlotte Corday.

388 *Faubourg Saint-Germain*: district of Paris where the old aristocracy lived.

390 *Fouché*: Joseph Fouché (1759–1820), four times Minister of Police between 1799 and 1815.

Lenoir: Jean Lenoir (1732–1807), twice Lieutenant-General of Police.

Sartines: Antoine Sartinez (1729–1801), immediate predecessor of Lenoir as Lieutenant-General of Police.

399 *the Moor of Rio de Janeiro*: the full title of Shakespeare's play is Othello, the Moor of Venice.

400 *Aspasia*: celebrated for her beauty and wit, she was the mistress and virtual wife of the Athenian leader Pericles.

Lucretia: wife of Tarquinius Collatinus who was raped by her husband's cousin Sextus, son of the King of Rome, Tarquinius Superbus. After telling her husband, she committed suicide. This incident led to the overthrow of the ruling Tarquin family and the establishment of the Roman Republic.

Boule: cf. note to p. 123.

404 *Vautrin*: an important recurring character in *La Comédie humaine*. He is an escaped convict of consummate ability who finally becomes chief of police.

406 *Countess Pimbèche*: a character in Racine's comedy *Les Plaideurs*, a typical inveterate litigant.

407 *Combabus, the voluntary Abélard*: Combabus, favourite of Antiochus I, King of Syria, castrated himself for fear that he would not be able to resist the attractions of the King's wife, Stratonice. The medieval French scholar Abélard was forcibly castrated by the uncle of Héloise, whom he had secretly married.

Bocage ... d'Anville: the geographer Jean-Baptiste Bouguignon d'Anville (1697–1782) had drawn the maps for the *Ancient History* published from 1730 to 1738 in 13 volumes by Charles Rollin (1661–1741). Jean-Denis Barbié du Bocage (1760–1825) was d'Anville's only pupil.

Montyon prize: cf. note to p. 167.

Catoxantha: a rare kind of beetle.

408 *Amphitryon*: in Greek mythology, a Theban prince whose wife, having been visited by Zeus in the form of her husband, gave birth to Hercules. Molière wrote a play based on this theme and by reference to his play the name has come to mean a host.

409 *Longchamps*: race-course and review ground in the Bois de Boulogne to the west of Paris.

Valognes: a small town in Normandy which produces butter, poultry, cattle, and lace.

Cydalise: a fashionable name in French literary circles in the 1830s. It was the name of a young woman who died prematurely and whose beautiful white skin was praised in a sonnet by the poet Théophile Gautier.

411 *shibboleth*: a word used as a password by the Gileadites under Jephthah during their war with the Ephraimites, as recounted in Judges 12.6. It comes to be used as a sign of recognition between members of a particular group or party.

the horrible dessert of the month of April: this could refer to the fact that no fresh fruits were available in April and that the dessert consisted of dried fruits and nuts.

412 *Clichy*: Parisian debtors' prison.

414 *Madame de la Baudraye*: principal character in Balzac's novel *La Muse du Département*. After she had given up everything for Lousteau, she left him because of his dissolute behaviour.

François I: King of France from 1515 to 1547.

415 *Médor*: a character in Ariosto's poem *Orlando Furioso* (1516), whose name became typical of faithful love and devotion. It thus became a very common name for dogs, hence the 'growl'.

416 *King of Holland*: William of Nassau, whose obstinacy resulted in the loss of Belgium in 1830.

418 *Maison d'Or*: a restaurant, new in 1840, which became very fashionable.

421 *Longjumeau postilion*: a reference to a light opera of 1836 by A. Adam which contained the lines: 'Oh! oh! oh! oh! Qu'il était beau, / Le postillon de Longjumeau!' (How handsome he was, the Longjumeau postilion!)

422 *Roland in a fury*: a reference to Ariosto's poem *Orlando Furioso* (1516).

423 *Mignard*: (1606–68), French painter.

Girodet: (1767–1824), French painter celebrated for his bright colouring.

426 *urbi et orbi*: a Latin expression meaning 'to the city and to the world', normally used with reference to Papal proclamations.

Vulcan's nets: in classical mythology, Vulcan, the husband of Venus, surprised her with Mars and trapped them both in nets before summoning the other gods.

427 *Gavarni*: (1804–66), lithographer and caricaturist, celebrated for his sketches of Parisian life and witty captions.

442 *Baron d'Holbach*: (1723–89), distinguished French atheistic philosopher.

Regency: cf. note to p. 11.

grey Musketeer: nobleman from one of the two companies of the king's household cavalry. They were distinguished by the colour of their horses, grey and black.

Abbé Dubois: (1656–1723), minister during the Regency.

Maréchal de Richelieu: cf. note to p. 124.

Béranger: (1789–1857), celebrated writer of popular poems and songs.

Lisette: typical working-girl featured in Béranger's poems.

Montesquieu: (1689–1755), distinguished French thinker and writer. According to Voltaire, Montesquieu on his deathbed dismissed a Jesuit priest who wanted him to give up all his papers so that irreligious passages could be deleted.

That slave, he came / His order showed, but nothing gained: a quotation from Racine's play Bajazet (I. I).

443 *The Passage Montesquieu*: this alley-way no longer exists, it led into the Rue Montesquieu.

Champcenetz: (1760–94), Royalist guards officer, wit, and journalist, guillotined in 1794.

448 *Atala . . . the first one*: the first one was the heroine of the well-known novel of that name by Chateaubriand (1768–1848). She was a N. American Indian convert to Christianity who refused to marry the man she loved because she had promised her mother to become a nun. Too weak to fulfil the vow, and unable to resist her love, she took poison and died.

451 *Bobino*: Parisian theatre frequented by students and working-girls.

Ambigu: seats at the Ambigu theatre cost from 40 centimes to 5 francs, those at Bobino cost from 30 centimes to 1.25 francs. Hence Atala's 'perhaps'.

459 *in partibus*: the phrase was used of a bishop who had the title but no diocese. Here it describes a man who is called an artist but never really practises as such.

THE WORLD'S CLASSICS

A Select List

SERGEI AKSAKOV: A Russian Gentleman
Translated by J. D. Duff
Edited by Edward Crankshaw

A Russian Schoolboy
Translated by J. D. Duff
Introduction by John Bayley

HANS ANDERSEN: Fairy Tales
Translated by L. W. Kingsland
Introduction by Naomi Lewis
Illustrated by Vilhelm Pedersen and Lorenz Frølich

LUDOVICO ARIOSTO: Orlando Furioso
Translated by Guido Waldman

ARISTOTLE: The Nicomachean Ethics
Translated by David Ross

JANE AUSTEN: Emma
Edited by James Kinsley and David Lodge

ROBERT BAGE: Hermsprong
Edited by Peter Faulkner

R. D. BLACKMORE: Lorna Doone
Edited by Sally Shuttleworth

MARY ELIZABETH BRADDON: Lady Audley's Secret
Edited by David Skilton

CHARLOTTE BRONTË: Jane Eyre
Edited by Margaret Smith

EMILY BRONTË: Wuthering Heights
Edited by Ian Jack

GEORGE BÜCHNER:
Danton's Death, Leonce and Lena, Woyzeck
Translated by Victor Price

JOHN BUNYAN: The Pilgrim's Progress
Edited by N. H. Keeble

FRANCES HODGSON BURNETT: The Secret Garden
Edited by Dennis Butts

LEWIS CARROLL: Alice's Adventures in Wonderland
and Through the Looking Glass
Edited by Roger Lancelyn Green
Illustrated by John Tenniel

GEOFFREY CHAUCER: The Canterbury Tales
Translated by David Wright

ANTON CHEKHOV: The Russian Master and Other Stories
Translated by Ronald Hingley

Ward Number Six and Other Stories
Translated by Ronald Hingley

WILKIE COLLINS: Armadale
Edited by Catherine Peters

No Name
Edited by Virginia Blain

JOSEPH CONRAD: Chance
Edited by Martin Ray

Lord Jim
Edited by John Batchelor

Youth, Heart of Darkness, The End of the Tether
Edited by Robert Kimbrough

DANIEL DEFOE: Colonel Jack
Edited by Samuel Holt Monk and David Roberts

THOMAS DE QUINCEY:
The Confessions of an English Opium-Eater
Edited by Grevel Lindop

CHARLES DICKENS: Christmas Books
Edited by Ruth Glancy

Oliver Twist
Edited by Kathleen Tillotson

BENJAMIN DISRAELI: Coningsby
Edited by Sheila M. Smith

FÉDOR DOSTOEVSKY: Crime and Punishment
Translated by Jessie Coulson
Introduction by John Jones

ARTHUR CONAN DOYLE:
Sherlock Holmes: Selected Stories
Introduction by S. C. Roberts

ALEXANDRE DUMAS *fils*:
La Dame aux Camélias
Translated by David Coward

MARIA EDGEWORTH: Castle Rackrent
Edited by George Watson

GEORGE ELIOT: Daniel Deronda
Edited by Graham Handley

Felix Holt, The Radical
Edited by Fred C. Thompson

JOHN MEADE FALKNER: The Nebuly Coat
Edited by Christopher Hawtree

SUSAN FERRIER: Marriage
Edited by Herbert Foltinek

GUSTAVE FLAUBERT: Madame Bovary
Translated by Gerard Hopkins
Introduction by Terence Cave

A Sentimental Education
Translated by Douglas Parmée

ELIZABETH GASKELL: Cousin Phillis and Other Tales
Edited by Angus Easson

My Lady Ludlow and Other Stories
Edited by Edgar Wright

WILLIAM GODWIN: Caleb Williams
Edited by David McCracken

J. W. VON GOETHE: Faust, Part One
Translated by David Luke

H. RIDER HAGGARD: King Solomon's Mines
Edited by Dennis Butts

THOMAS HARDY: A Pair of Blue Eyes
Edited by Alan Manford

Tess of the D'Urbervilles
Edited by Juliet Grindle and Simon Gatrell

NATHANIEL HAWTHORNE:
Young Goodman Brown and Other Tales
Edited by Brian Harding

HESIOD: Theogony *and* Works and Days
Translated by M. L. West

JAMES HOGG: The Private Memoirs and
Confessions of a Justified Sinner
Edited by John Carey

HOMER: The Iliad
Translated by Robert Fitzgerald
Introduction by G. S. Kirk

THOMAS HUGHES: Tom Brown's Schooldays
Edited by Andrew Sanders

HENRIK IBSEN: An Enemy of the People, The Wild Duck,
Rosmersholm
Edited and Translated by James McFarlane

Four Major Plays
Translated by James McFarlane and Jens Arup
Introduction by James McFarlane

ELIZABETH INCHBALD: A Simple Story
Edited by J. M. S. Tompkins

HENRY JAMES: The Ambassadors
Edited by Christopher Butler

The Bostonians
Edited by R. D. Gooder

The Spoils of Poynton
Edited by Bernard Richards

M. R. JAMES: Casting the Runes and Other Ghost Stories
Edited by Michael Cox

JOCELIN OF BRAKELOND:
Chronicle of the Abbey of Bury St. Edmunds
Translated by Diana Greenway and Jane Sayers

GWYN JONES (Transl.):
Eirik the Red and Other Icelandic Sagas

BEN JONSON: Five Plays
Edited by G. A. Wilkes

CHARLES KINGSLEY: Alton Locke
Edited by Elizabeth Cripps

RUDYARD KIPLING: The Day's Work
Edited by Thomas Pinney

Stalky & Co.
Edited by Isobel Quigly

J. SHERIDAN LE FANU: Uncle Silas
Edited by W. J. McCormack

CHARLOTTE LENNOX: The Female Quixote
Edited by Margaret Dalziel
Introduction by Margaret Anne Doody

LEONARDO DA VINCI: Notebooks
Edited by Irma A. Richter

MATTHEW LEWIS: The Monk
Edited by Howard Anderson

KATHERINE MANSFIELD: Selected Stories
Edited by D. M. Davin

CHARLES MATURIN: Melmoth the Wanderer
Edited by Douglas Grant
Introduction by Chris Baldick

HERMAN MELVILLE: The Confidence-Man
Edited by Tony Tanner

PROSPER MÉRIMÉE: Carmen and Other Stories
Translated by Nicholas Jotcham

MICHELANGELO: Life, Letters, and Poetry
Translated by George Bull with Peter Porter

MOLIÈRE: Don Juan and Other Plays
Translated by George Graveley and Ian Maclean

GEORGE MOORE: Esther Waters
Edited by David Skilton

JOHN HENRY NEWMAN: Loss and Gain
Edited by Alan G. Hill

MARGARET OLIPHANT:
A Beleaguered City and Other Stories
Edited by Merryn Williams

OVID: Metamorphoses
Translated by A. D. Melville
Introduction and Notes by E. J. Kenney

THOMAS LOVE PEACOCK: Headlong Hall and Gryll Grange
Edited by Michael Baron and Michael Slater

EDGAR ALLAN POE: Selected Tales
Edited by Julian Symons

JEAN RACINE: Britannicus, Phaedra, Athaliah
Translated by C. H. Sisson

ANN RADCLIFFE: The Italian
Edited by Frederick Garber

PAUL SALZMAN (Ed.):
An Anthology of Elizabethan Prose Fiction

SIR WALTER SCOTT: The Heart of Midlothian
Edited by Claire Lamont

MARY SHELLEY: Frankenstein
Edited by M. K. Joseph

PERCY BYSSHE SHELLEY:
Zastrozzi *and* St. Irvyne
Edited by Stephen Behrendt

SIR PHILIP SIDNEY:
The Countess of Pembroke's Arcadia (The Old Arcadia)
Edited by Katherine Duncan-Jones

CHARLOTTE SMITH: The Old Manor House
Edited by Anne Henry Ehrenpreis

TOBIAS SMOLLETT: The Expedition of Humphry Clinker
Edited by Lewis M. Knapp
Revised by Paul-Gabriel Boucé

Peregrine Pickle
Edited by James L. Clifford
Revised by Paul-Gabriel Boucé

ROBERT LOUIS STEVENSON: Kidnapped and Catriona
Edited by Emma Letley

Treasure Island
Edited by Emma Letley

BRAM STOKER: Dracula
Edited by A. N. Wilson

R. S. SURTEES: Mr. Facey Romford's Hounds
Edited by Jeremy Lewis

Mr. Sponge's Sporting Tour
Introduction by Joyce Cary

JONATHAN SWIFT: Gulliver's Travels
Edited by Paul Turner

WILLIAM MAKEPEACE THACKERAY: Barry Lyndon
Edited by Andrew Sanders

LEO TOLSTOY: Anna Karenina
Translated by Louise and Aylmer Maude
Introduction by John Bayley

War and Peace (in two volumes)
Translated by Louise and Aylmer Maude
Edited by Henry Gifford

ANTHONY TROLLOPE: The American Senator
Edited by John Halperin

Dr. Thorne
Edited by David Skilton

Dr. Wortle's School
Edited by John Halperin

Orley Farm
Edited by David Skilton

IVAN TURGENEV: First Love and Other Stories
Translated by Richard Freeborn

VILLIERS DE L'ISLE-ADAM: Cruel Tales
Translated by Robert Baldick
Edited by A. W. Raitt

VIRGIL: The Aeneid
Translated by C. Day Lewis
Edited by Jasper Griffin

The Eclogues and The Georgics
Translated by C. Day Lewis
Edited by R. O. A. M. Lyne

HORACE WALPOLE: The Castle of Otranto
Edited by W. S. Lewis

IZAAK WALTON and CHARLES COTTON:
The Compleat Angler
Edited by John Buxton
Introduction by John Buchan

MRS HUMPHREY WARD: Robert Elsmere
Edited by Rosemary Ashton

OSCAR WILDE: Complete Shorter Fiction
Edited by Isobel Murray

The Picture of Dorian Gray
Edited by Isobel Murray

MARY WOLLSTONECRAFT:
Mary *and* The Wrongs of Woman
Edited by Gary Kelly

ÉMILE ZOLA:
The Attack on the Mill and other stories
Translated by Douglas Parmeé

A complete list of Oxford Paperbacks, including The World's Classics, OPUS, Past Masters, Oxford Authors, Oxford Shakespeare, and Oxford Paperback Reference, is available in the UK from the Arts and Reference Publicity Department (RS), Oxford University Press, Walton Street, Oxford OX2 6DP.

In the USA, complete lists are available from the Paperbacks Marketing Manager, Oxford University Press, 200 Madison Avenue, New York, NY 10016.

Oxford Paperbacks are available from all good bookshops. In case of difficulty, customers in the UK can order direct from Oxford University Press Bookshop, Freepost, 116 High Street, Oxford, OX1 4BR, enclosing full payment. Please add 10 per cent of published price for postage and packing.